WITHDRAWN
NDSU

EMIN PASHA

AND THE

REBELLION AT THE EQUATOR

A STORY OF NINE MONTHS' EXPERIENCES IN THE
LAST OF THE SOUDAN PROVINCES

BY

A. J. MOUNTENEY-JEPHSON

(One of Stanley's Officers)

WITH THE REVISION AND CO-OPERATION OF

HENRY M. STANLEY, D.C.L., &c., &c.

WITH MAP AND NUMEROUS ILLUSTRATIONS

THIRD EDITION.

NEGRO UNIVERSITIES PRESS
NEW YORK

Originally published in 1890
by Sampson Low, Marston, Searle & Rivington, London

Reprinted 1969 by
Negro Universities Press
A DIVISION OF GREENWOOD PUBLISHING CORP.
NEW YORK

SBN 8371-1949-9

PRINTED IN UNITED STATES OF AMERICA

This Book is Dedicated to

HELENA

COUNTESS DE NOAILLES

WHO HAS EVER BEEN MY KIND FRIEND,

AND

BY WHOSE WISH I JOINED THE EXPEDITION FOR THE RELIEF OF

EMIN PASHA.

PREFATORY LETTER

BY

HENRY M. STANLEY.

LONDON, *August*, 1890.

MY DEAR JEPHSON,—
My marriage and my illness are two causes, either one of which had they occurred separately would have sufficiently explained the delay which has rendered me unable until now to make any kind of effort to comply with the wishes of yourself and of my English and American publishers, that I should introduce your book to your readers on both sides of the Atlantic. But, really, your book needs no introduction from me : those who have read "*In Darkest Africa*" know well the estimation in which I hold you.

From my own personal point of view, I can say with all sincerity that I am well pleased to know that you have actually written this book. I was of course well aware that you lost no opportunity during our wanderings through the Dark Continent of making notes of all you saw and all you did; but to convert these rough notes into an intelligent and consecutive narrative required much thought and much labour.

I confess I had pictured you, on your return to civilized society from the pangs of starvation, the troubles of camps, and the weary wanderings in that dismal forest, as plunging into luxury and revelling in the delight of being able for awhile to do absolutely nothing. On the contrary I find that you have scorned inglorious ease, and burnt the midnight oil in writing this narrative; you have done well. It was your bounden duty to write it, and you could not, if you would, have rid yourself of the responsibility. Of course you might have begun your narrative at the beginning of our expedition, but I think you have done wisely in not treading out again already threshed corn. You have commenced your story where a great gap occurred in my own narrative, a gap which you alone could fill up. You have told your story with so much modesty, and such absolute truthfulness and loyalty to myself, that I cannot but feel pleased and grateful to you. There is within the covers of your volume much matter that is quite new to me, much that is extremely thrilling and exciting, and the whole is related with very enviable literary tact and skill.

When I despatched you, full of pluck and resolution, on the first expedition, to convey my letter to Emin, and messages to his people, I knew that I was entrusting a most important mission to your care, but I little dreamt that it would result in committing you to nine months' residence in an unknown and hostile country—that you would be subjected to a long imprisonment and to imminent risk of death at the hands of those misguided people you sought to save.

On April 20th, 1888, I sent you up Lake Albert with a letter to Emin, and on the 29th of the same month he accompanied you back to Kavalli. Finally, on May 22nd, I left you at N'sabé with Emin Pasha, and you returned with him up the Lake, conveying my address, which you were to read to his soldiers, and so prepare them all for prompt and immediate evacuation of Equatoria, whilst I returned in search of the rear column.

Then followed long months of suspense, and it was not till January, 1889, that I again heard from you. Your very interesting letter to me, bearing the date February 7th, 1889, from Kavalli, being in fact your report, briefly and distinctly told, conveyed to me all, or nearly all, the information I have hitherto had of those months of suspense on our part and anxiety and suffering on yours. It will therefore be readily understood that a consecutive and extended narrative, giving in full detail an account of all your adventures, must necessarily be to me, of all men, most interesting.

I am aware that all your fellow-officers have been engaged in making valuable notes of the expedition, and probably some of them will print their narratives. Certainly they all have my best wishes : the special and peculiar interest, however, of your narrative is that it does not in the least traverse my ground, as theirs necessarily must, though from their own standpoint. Mr. Troup has written, and Mr. Bonny has written—each no doubt describing what he has seen and done from his own point of view, and I hope that my most valued friend Dr. Parke will soon find time to give us an account of his own experiences. Mr. Ward too, I believe, has a book in hand. Then the time is coming when we may hope to see what Dr. Emin has to tell the world. You will remember that I have sometimes playfully accused you of being an Eminist. I am not now altogether disposed to withdraw that soft impeachment. The impression which your book will convey to an impartial reader is that of much admiration, and even affection for Emin in certain aspects of his character, whilst you have not been blind to his manifest shortcomings as a governor. It is not necessary that I should here express at any length the opinion which I have formed of Emin. This may be best epitomized by a short extract from a letter addressed by me to my German publishers, and which has appeared only in the German edition of my book. The Germans are just as excitable and emotional as the French.

"In the matter of Emin, for instance, what were they to Emin or he to them before he was brought out of Negroland by us? Emin was English in sentiment though the nature of him was essentially German. It was English service he aspired after, whatever he may be now. His letters to the British Foreign Office prove it. But what business was it of mine one way or the other? I did not proceed to assist a German or an Englishman, but an ideal governor who had fixed himself in my imagination as a man eminently worthy of assistance. He was a lieutenant of Gordon's, had been sent far into Equatoria—was besieged, as I thought, by the Mahdists, and I hoped that a supply of ammunition would enable him to hold out until the effect of further light upon his position would be a more general desire to assist him. . . . Starting as I did with a preconceived liking, and favourably prejudiced, why should I not do the same for Emin as I did for Livingstone? Simply because Emin would not let me. He contrived in the most extraordinary way to give an obliquity to my regard for him. There are some things about him which are as much a mystery to me as ever. . . . If I could find any part in me that vexed him in any way, shape, or form, I would punish it severely, but until some one finds it out I must even be content to be lost in perplexity. I was with him twenty-six days on my first visit, and my diary is full of pleasantness, pleasant chats by the Lake shore, and of pleasing restfulness. A good deal of letter-writing passed between us, and every epistle marks mutual pleasure. . . . How he came away will best be told by the book, which reveals each day's doings. The truth must be told, however, that from my point of view he remains as incomprehensible now as then in the camp of Kavalli. Everybody will make up his own mind about him—some kindly, and some with severity. I only affect to be the reflecting medium. . . . It is probably his morbid sensitiveness and pride that have been his greatest obstacle, in this, as at other times. His fall at Bagamoyo has certainly upset every theory I ever had of him. When he went into the hospital, a shadow came between him and me of so thick a nature that quite obscured the happy relation that I thought was ever to be between us. All our officers, even Casati, are dumb-founded, and none of us dare venture an opinion as to the cause."

Yet we must none of us forget, that, whatever

divergences may arise between individuals, or between national sentiments in the course of the progressive rise of Africa from primeval obscurity, our task should be above the controversies of the moment as it aspires to be nothing less than our contribution to the civilization of a continent which I believe in the future will yield to no other in serviceableness to humanity.

The want of an International Copyright Law was never more apparent than in your case. A thousand pounds sterling was paid on your behalf for the privilege of assisting in the relief or rescue of Emin Pasha. And you gave three years and three months of your life towards effecting whatever was needed to place a worthy man out of danger. And yet the narrative of your experiences, which might return you perhaps some part of your outlay in pecuniary value over and above the cost of publication, cannot be published in America with any profit to yourself unless you become an American citizen, or an American citizen joins with you in writing it.

But what a commentary on the copyright laws! when an English author cannot get simple justice unless he collaborates with an American;—there must surely be something in the existing law, or want of law, against which common sense and common honesty should protest with all their power.

As for the cloud of advertising impostors who I doubt not, will buzz around your book as they have buzzed around mine on both sides of the Atlantic with unauthorized imitations, and long extracts with which they had no right to meddle, these may be left with one word of warning to the contempt with which the public will inevitably visit them. The reader of your book will plainly perceive why I have been induced to assist you by writing some portion, though it is needless to specify it.

May all your career, my dear Jephson, alike as author and man of action, be worthy of this fair beginning! With all my heart I commend to American and English readers this true tale of work manfully and nobly done and so modestly told.

Yours always sincerely,

HENRY M. STANLEY.

PREFACE.

SINCE my return from Africa I have been asked by many people to write about my experiences with Emin Pasha in the Equatorial Province, which extended over a period of time from April 22nd, 1888, when I first reached M'swa, to January 31st, 1889, when I left Emin's province to rejoin my leader, Mr. Stanley.

My friends have urged that I alone can fill in this gap in the story of the expedition, and I have therefore consented to write.

Enough is now known of Emin Pasha for people to readily understand that he was not the man all Europe supposed him to be; or "a second Gordon," as some of his admirers termed him.

Proud of his Province, and trusting in the loyalty of his people, he asked Mr. Stanley to leave one of his officers to help him in preparing his people to start for the coast if they wished to do so, and to make a report upon the Province.

Mr. Stanley nominated me, and left me with Emin on his return to Yambuya, to bring up the rear column.

I had not been in the Province long, before I began to see things which surprised me greatly, and which I could not but deplore. Discipline, as I understood discipline, was not enforced, for Emin's orders were openly discussed and questioned by his people.

So firmly, however, was the idea fixed in my mind that Emin was all we supposed him to be, that for a time I only saw with a passing feeling of wonder certain things which then I could not understand.

I knew that Emin had held his province for many years, for which he had gained the admiration of Europe. I had read his letters to England, in which he described the heroic stand his people made against the encroachments of the Mahdi. I had also read his appeals to the people of England to be true to their philanthropic and humanitarian traditions, and I knew how the English people had risen as one man to answer those pathetic appeals.

In addition to these letters, Dr. Felkin had further excited the popular sympathy on Emin's behalf by a highly coloured description of Emin's Province, of his work, and of the wonderful way in which he had been able to instil some of his own enthusiasm into the hearts of his devoted followers. This account appeared in the *Graphic* of January, 1887, on the eve of the departure of the Expedition, and was eagerly read by every one.

It may be readily understood, therefore, that for a time I was unable to divest my mind of the belief in Emin's wisdom and capabilities as a governor.

It was not until I had witnessed many deplorable examples of his weakness and vacillation that I began to lose faith in his judgment, and it was not until afterwards, when I had conversed frequently with his people and himself about things in his province, and the repulse of the Mahdi's forces four years before, that I found out that Emin had only told part of the story; only that part which was creditable to his people.

It was perhaps natural that a man who professed to love his people should prefer to dwell rather on their good qualities than on their bad ones. Still his story, as related in his letters, completely misled the people of Europe.

Instead, therefore, of our being received with open arms by Emin's people, as he himself had given us to expect, we were distrusted by them, and from the very first they conspired to rob us and turn us adrift.

It was difficult, even after nine months in the Province, to understand what Emin's people really wanted, and what his own ideas really were.

To-day no words were strong enough for Emin to describe the baseness and fickleness of his people; to-morrow, a word of distrust from me about these very people was a signal for grave displeasure at my opinion. He, like his people, made a resolve one day only to break it on the next, or in true Oriental fashion to make some compromise.

It may be that owing to his long residence in hot countries and his consequent ill-health, his natural incapacity to act promptly was greatly exaggerated.

I have therefore endeavoured to relate my story as simply as possible, and must leave my readers to draw their own conclusions.

I have no wish to bear hardly on Emin, and have said no more about his want of firmness than I think is absolutely necessary in order to make the story intelligible. To me he was always kind, he was generous, and, in minor details, ready and thoughtful.

In an ordinary individual his weakness might have been of little consequence, but what is only a small failing in a private person becomes a grave fault in the governor of a country, and leads assuredly to ruin and disaster.

Emin was *par excellence* a scientist, and I have it from himself that he originally took service as a doctor under the Egyptian Government in order to extend the scientific researches in the Equatorial

Province, which he had already been following for years in the East. Chance only had made him Mudir. It was this work which absorbed his deepest sympathies, leading him sometimes to neglect the duties of his position.

Before concluding this preface, I take the opportunity of briefly expressing my thanks to Mr. Stanley for the assistance he has so readily given me in preparing my book for publication; assistance which has in many ways been of great value to me.

A. J. MOUNTENEY-JEPHSON.

LONDON, *August*, 1890.

CONTENTS.

CHAPTER I.

START TO FIND EMIN.

Receipt of letter from Emin Pasha—Nyanza Plain—Launch of *Advance* on the Nyanza—Zanzibari crews—Their song—Arrival at Kanama—Friendly reception by natives—Uledi's warning—Dialect and gestures of natives—Striking scenery of Lake shore—Lake villages—Unpleasant taste of Lake water—Baboons—Chief Mogo—Kajalf speaks of Emin—Soliloquy—Emin's first station reached—Reception at M'swa—Shukri Aga—I tell our story—Our tattered condition—My luggage—Emin's unaccountable inaction—More news of Casati—Zanzibaris happy!—Emin's letter—Suliman Effendi—Cultivation round M'swa—Cloth-making—Meeting with Emin—Suggestions about return route—Emin's kindness—Emin learns the origin of the Expedition—Our letters stopped in Uganda . . . 1

CHAPTER II.

MEETING OF STANLEY AND EMIN—PLANS DISCUSSED.

Steamer *Khedive*—Her condition—Emin arrives in our camp—Reception by the Zanzibaris—Our camp at N'sabe—Emin wishes Stanley to leave one of his officers—Plan made for relieving Fort Bodo—Stanley and Parke start on return journey—Death of Mabruki—Emin's love of entomology—Attack on Kibero—Kabba-regga's punishment—Chief Ouma—Chief Ouma's visit—Lur dance—Smells peculiar to different tribes—We arrive at Tunguru—Rapid falling of Lake Albert—Intriguing of Egyptian clerks—Punishment of intriguers—Story of the mutiny of 1st Battalion—Character of Emin's officers—Khedive's letter—Nubar Pasha's letter—Stanley's address to Emin's soldiers—Letters read to the people—" We will follow our

xvi   *Contents.*

                                                              PAGE
Governor!"—The people's natural desire to remain in
Province—From Tunguru to Wadelai—Boki's village—
Boki's imprisonment—Description of country—Lowness of
Nile—Chief Okello—Native ornaments—Chief Wadelai .   28

CHAPTER III.

FROM WADELAI TO DUFILÉ.

Arrival at Wadelai—Emin's compound and house—Signor
Marco—Farida—Emin's scientific proclivities—Wadelai
Station—The Wahuma—Reminiscences of Sir Samuel
Baker—Nyadué, or the Morning Star—Deputation from
1st Battalion—Endeavour to relieve Fort Bodo—Faratch
Aga—State of affairs at Rejaf—Hamad Aga's estimate of
Emin—Doubts as to Emin's wisdom—Faratch Aga's
shame—Emin acts a farce—Ferocity of crocodiles—Bari
crocodile-hunters—Answer of soldiers of Wadelai—Emin's
ivory—Start for Dufilé—Blocks on the Nile—We reach
Dufilé—Curious custom—Description of Dufilé Station
—Government buildings—Hawashi Effendi—Hawashi
Effendi's estimate of Egyptian guile—An Arab feast—
Hawashi Effendi's warning—More doubts   .   .   .   60

CHAPTER IV.

TROUBLE IMPENDING.

We start for Rejaf—A herd of elephants—Country near Dufilé
cataracts—Chor Ayu—Laboré station—Selim Aga—
Donkeys of the country—Bari women—Arrival at Muggi
—Abdullah Aga Manzal—Thievish propensities of Emin's
soldiers—Arrival at Kirri—Bachit Aga—Gordon's favourite
amusements—Bari ornaments and dress—State of the
country occupied by 1st Battalion—The soldiers of Kirri
distrust us—Speaking to the people of Kirri—Makraka
music and dance—Letter from Hamad Aga—Confirmation
of my worst fears—Insubordination of the soldiers of Kirri
—Our return to Muggi—Alarming news from Kirri—
Emin's sad story—Soldiers of Rejaf come to see Emin—
Emin's confidence in his soldiers—News from Hawashi
Effendi—Story of Taha Mahomet—Strangers in Latooka—
Bari chief's generosity—My servant Binza prays—Possible
return of the Mahdists—Evacuation of Muggi begun—
Satisfactory condition of country round Muggi—Good in-
fluence of Abdullah Aga Manzal   89

Contents.

CHAPTER V.

THE BARI TRIBE.

PAGE

Physique of the Baris—Dress—Iron ornaments—Powers of chiefs—Fines for different offences—Modes of making war—Weapons—Hunting—Huts and villages—Storing food—Polygamy—Dogs—Cattle—Method of tending cattle—Milking—Domestic animals—Alimentation—Tobacco—Bari cookery—Relations between married people—Ceremonies connected with child-birth—Ceremonies connected with marriage—Position of women—Funeral ceremonies—Religious superstitions—Office of rain-maker—Their customs and position 125

CHAPTER VI.

BEGINNING OF THE REBELLION.

Arrival at Laboré—Reading of the letters—Mutiny of the soldiers—Speaking to the mutineers—Soldiers' distrust of their Mudir—Demeanour of Emin's followers—The mutineers send for me—Departure for Chor Ayu—The Mahdists at Boa—Khedive's letter sent to Rejaf—Emin's opinion of the Khedive's letter—Desertion of Emin's orderly—Letter announcing rebellion of 2nd Battalion—Emin's distress at the news—Short-sightedness of Emin's people—Our departure for Dufilé—Rain and sunshine—Dreary appearance of country—We prepare to enter Dufilé 145

CHAPTER VII.

OUR IMPRISONMENT AT DUFILÉ.

We approach Dufilé—Attitude of the people—Entry into the station—Surrounded by sentries—Insults of the soldiers—Greeting of the Circassian tinker—We are imprisoned—The contrast to our entry a month before—Selim Aga consults the mutineers—Fadl el Mulla's reason for rebelling—The mutineers of Rejaf are sent for—Our life in prison—Our servants insulted—Hawashi Effendi's position—The rebels form a plan to entrap Stanley—News from M'swa—Stanley's supposed arrival at Kavallis—Arrival of rebels from Rejaf—My orderlies are examined—I go before the rebel council—Questioned by the rebels—Letters read before the council—"You and your master are impostors!"—My tirade against the rebels—"Chivalry in a negro"—Fadl el Mulla asserts himself—Emin signs the papers—Steamer to be sent to M'swa—I prepare to start in steamer—Start from Dufilé—Unpleasant experiences on board—Arrival at Wadelai—Little Farida—Five children at a birth—Consultation with the Wadelai soldiers—General discontent in Wadelai—Atmosphere of treachery 160

CHAPTER VIII.

STEAMER JOURNEY WITH REBELS.

Kodi Aga's defection—Sand bar—Arrival at Tunguru—Stanley's arrival contradicted—Casati's grievances—Abdullah Vaab Effendi—Casati's life in the Province—Reason of his coming to Africa—His treatment by Kaba-regga—Suliman Aga beaten by his soldiers—Vita's house looted—Emin's Irregulars—Departure of steamer for M'swa—Moslem protestations of friendliness—Influence of Egyptians on the Soudanese—Message from Shukri Aga—Shukri Aga's ruse—Seizure of ammunition by rebels—From Tunguru to Wadelai—Drunken officers set fire to huts—Breakfast of African dainties—Farida and the necklace—Steamer journey to Dufilé—Emin's judges—Arrival at Dufilé—Sad fate of the Kirri clerk 191

CHAPTER IX.

THE REBEL COUNCIL.

Fadl el Mulla opens proceedings—Accusations brought against Emin—The first day's proceedings close—Indictment against the Governor—Signing of Emin's deposition—What is to be done with the Mudir?—Emin longs for a glimpse of trees—The case of Hawashi Effendi—Fury of the people against him—Accusations proved—Spoliation of Hawashi's property—Osman Latif—Khedive's letter credited—Emin to be sent to Rejaf—Suspense—Books—Quarrels among the rebels—Binza's wife's head is too hard—Flogging of women—Visit to Osman Latif—General desertion to the rebels—Emin's disappointment—General discontent of the soldiers—Emin makes his will—Letter from Osman Latif—Plans made by the rebels—Trial of Vita Hassan—Vita Hassan questions me—Inability of the people to help themselves—A pretentious people—Emin's house looted—Spirit of "*laisser faire*" in the Province   201

CHAPTER X.

ARRIVAL OF THE MAHDI'S FORCES.

The Mahdists are upon us—General consternation—Intelligence department—Council called in haste—Soldiers are despatched to Rejaf—Defenceless state of the Province—Arrival of the Peacock dervishes—The Bible and the sword—Letter from the Mahdist general—Emin commanded to surrender—Rebels ask Emin's advice—Abderrahim, son of Osman Latif—His courageous behaviour—The rebels' plans—The dervishes are examined—The Khartoum steamers—Royle's book on Egypt—Stores in the arsenal of Khartoum—Fugitives arrive in Dufilé—Robbery and violence among the soldiers—Emin's unselfishness—Letter from Osman Latif—The blow falls—Rejaf taken—General rising of the natives—Torturing of the dervishes—Brave fanatics—More news of the fall of Rejaf—A dangerous step to take—Superstition of the soldiers—Dufilé put into a defensive state—My advice to the rebels—Bravery of the dervishes—Their cruel death—Martyrdom 241

CHAPTER XI.

PRISONERS ON PAROLE.

Letter from Hassan Lutvi—Rumours of Stanley's arrival—Rising of the natives—Emin's house searched—Position of affairs at Muggi—Letter of warning written to Stanley—Osman Latif is sent to Wadelai—Mustapha flogs his wife to death—Children drowned in the river—Extraordinary weather—Epidemic among the cattle—Insubordination of soldiers at Wadelai—Shuli sorcerer—Abdullah is the thief—Arrogance of Emin's soldiers—Negro troops—Emin's treatment of his soldiers—Second disaster at Rejaf—Officers killed in the flight—Stories told of the soldiers—Rebels decide to send us to Wadelai—Emin's farewell at Dufilé—Our arrival at Wadelai—Enthusiastic reception to Emin—Cowed attitude of people at the outbreak of the rebellion—Emin free from all responsibility—Joy of people at Emin's return—Our position at Wadelai—Europeanizing the negro—Possible improvement of negroes—Ropes of sand—Spread of Mahdism—Reported outbreak of Irregulars—Rumour of approach of Mahdists—Inactivity of the people—Egyptian effrontery—The soldiers make a demonstration—Emin unable to speak out—Emin declares he knows his people—A contemptible Egyptian 272

CHAPTER XII.

FLIGHT FROM WADELAI.

News of the fall of the northern stations—Council of war held—Soldiers implore Emin to take charge of them—Flight decided on—We prepare for the flight—We throw away our treasures—I disable the *Advance*—Binza, a regular character—Our flight from Wadelai—Desertion of the soldiers—Strange baggage of the fugitives—Heart-rending scene at the river—Curious ideas about evacuation—We camp—Arrival of the steamer—Letter from Selim Aga Matara—Description of the siege of Dufilé—Emin decides to go on—Further particulars of the siege of Dufilé—Cowardice shown by the soldiers—Our narrow escape—Conduct of soldiers in former Mahdi war—Rumours accounted for—We reach Okello's—Arrival at Tunguru . 315

CHAPTER XIII.

SUSPENSE AT TUNGURU.

Rumoured meeting of Irregulars untrue—Emin decides to stay where he is—More letters from Dufilé—Wrong impressions given by Dr. Felkin—Strange silence as to the real position of affairs—Letters of rebel officers to Selim Aga—Accusations brought against Emin—Mischief made by the chief clerk—Soudanese tricked by the Egyptians—Suliman Aga arrives wounded at Tunguru—Indifference of Soudanese to pain—Beating the dervishes to death—Walks near Tunguru—Visit from Mogo—Christmas Day—Death of Suliman Aga—An Arab funeral—The last chronicles of Lupton Bey—The taking of Bahr el Ghazal—Negroes cut off the refugees—Dufilé is abandoned and burnt—Birds of the Equatorial Province—A day's shooting—Sketch of the dwarfish tribes of Central Africa 338

CHAPTER XIV.

NEWS OF STANLEY AT LAST.

The Council sits at Wadelai—Emin will not move—Saleh Aga

surrounded by natives—Method of declaring war—The grain tax—Natives on the verge of rebellion—Death of Boki—Quarrels among the officers—Drunkenness and debauchery at Wadelai—Grass fires—Their effect on trees—Biblical scenes—Stanley at last!—His letters to me—Official letter to Emin—A tale of death and disaster—Wreck of the rear column—Deaths of Barttelot and Jameson—Saleh Aga's perverseness—Saleh Aga cowed—Emin writes to Stanley—Preparations for a start—Arrival of the steamer—Rumours of Stanley's strength—Proceedings of the Council confirmed—Emin a man of compromises . 376

CHAPTER XV.

START TO JOIN STANLEY.

I leave Tunguru for M'swa—Hot sulphur springs—Arrival at M'swa — Shukri Aga's helpfulness — Arrangements for refugees—Woman's gratitude—Left in the lurch—Consultation with Lur chiefs—Letter to Emin—Choosing a body-guard—Friendly tribes sacrificed—Final start in canoes—" Taking fire from a stone "—Native salutations—Magunga—Magala's complaint—Melindwa's country—Thievish Lurs—Dignified bearing of Wahuma—Contrast between soldiers and Wahuma—I reach Katonza's village—Enforced delay—My looking-glass creates a sensation—Fatiguing palaver with Katonza—We ascend the mountains—Met by Stanley's couriers—Boisterous welcome by Zanzibaris—I rejoin my leader—Letters from home . . 410

CHAPTER XVI.

EMIN'S RELIEF.

Our camp at Kavallis—A difficult story to tell—Plans discussed—Stanley sends for Stairs—Letter despatched to Emin—Among friends again—Letter from Emin—Emin's arrival at Wéré—Zanzibaris welcome Emin—Pasha's story—Unlooked-for turn of Fortune's wheel—Refugees require carriers—Start with Emin for Kavallis—Patient Zanzibaris—Emin's and Stanley's second meeting—Stairs and his party arrive—The Expedition re-united—" Dead! Master! Dead! "—Reflections 442

CONCLUSION.

Emin's unreasoning acerbity—Treatment of women on the march—Major Wissmann's letter—Emin's curious forgetfulness—Emin's attack upon Stanley—Accident to Emin—Treatment of refugees at Zanzibar—Farewell to Emin—A curious combination 461

INDEX 481

LIST OF ILLUSTRATIONS.

FULL-PAGE ILLUSTRATIONS.

Description.	Name of Artist.	Name of Engraver.	To face page
Portrait of Mr. Jephson	From a photograph by permission of M. Walery	Annan & Swan.	Title
Start to find Emin	Speed	Krakow	4
Portrait of Emin Pasha	From a photograph	Cooper	24
Addressing soldiers at Tunguru	Charlton	,,	42
Interior of Emin's house	Speed	Krakow	60
Emin arranging his Specimens	Charlton	Cooper	112
A Bari Village	,,	,,	130
The Mutiny at Laboré	...	Krakow	146
Types of Emin's people	...	,,	152
Entry into Dufilé	...	,,	162
Reading Khedive's Letter before the Rebel Council	...	,,	176
Sitting of the Rebel Council	Speed	,,	210
Our Prison in Dufilé	...	...	224
Torturing the Peacock Dervishes	...	...	262
Peacock Dervishes passing through Guard-House	Speed	Krakow	270
Upsetting of a Canoe in the Nile	,,	,,	278
The Flight from Wadelai	Charlton	Werdmuller	324
Evening on Lake Albert at Tunguru	Speed	Cooper	366
News of Stanley at last	S. Berkeley	,,	388
Good-bye to Emin	,,	,,	410
Escape from Tunguru to join Stanley	Charlton	Werdmuller	422
I rejoin my Leader	Berkeley	Cooper	442

OTHER ILLUSTRATIONS.

Description.	Name of Artist.	Name of Engraver.	Page
African Ragamuffins	Mrs. H. M. Stanley	Cooper	Title-page.
Chief Mogo	Charlton	,,	12
M'swa Station	,,	,,	35

List of Illustrations.

Description.	Name of Artist.	Name of Engraver.	Page
Lur Dance	Charlton	Cooper	38
Boki's Wife intercedes for her Husband	,,	,,	56
View from Wadelai	,,	,,	64
Landing at Dufilé		Werdmuller	80
Plan of Dufilé Station	Jephson	Cooper	82
Herd of Elephants	Charlton	Werdmuller	91
Selim Aga Matara	,,	Cooper	94
Bari Man	,,	,,	126
Bari Woman	,,	,,	127
Bari Cattle and Goat	,,	,,	133
Bari Cooking Pots and Gourd	,,	,,	137
Bari Hoe for Men	,,	.,	141
Bari Spud for Women	,,	,,	141
On the Road from Laboré to Dufilé	,,	,,	157
Portrait of Captain Casati	From a photograph	Werdmuller	193
Farida and the Necklace	Charlton	Cooper	205
Osman Latif teaching his Children	,,	,,	228
Hadji Fatma's Joy	Speed	Krakow	291
Breaking up of the *Advance*	,,	,,	319
Dwarf with Bow and Arrow	Mrs. H. M. Stanley	Cooper	370
A Woman's Gratitude	S. Berkeley	,,	414
Sighting Stanley's Zanzibaris	Speed	,,	439

MISCELLANEOUS ILLUSTRATIONS.

Map of the Equatorial Province	To face	1
Facsimile of the Mahdi's Letter	,,	480

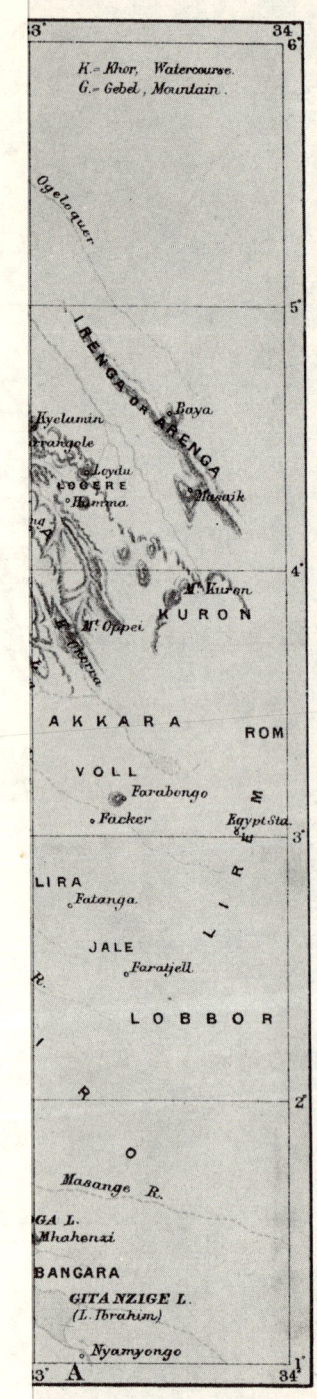

EMIN PASHA

CHAPTER I.

START TO FIND EMIN.

Receipt of letter from Emin Pasha—Nyanza Plain—Launch of *Advance* on the Nyanza—Zanzibari crews—Their song—Arrival at Kanama—Friendly reception by natives—Uledi's warning—Dialect and gestures of natives—Striking scenery of Lake shore—Lake villages—Unpleasant taste of Lake water—Baboons—Chief Mogo—Kajalf speaks of Emin—Soliloquy—Emin's first station reached—Reception at M'swa—Shukri Aga—I tell our story—Our tattered condition—My luggage—Emin's unaccountable inaction—More news of Casati—Zanzibaris happy!—Emin's letter—Suliman Effendi—Cultivation round M'swa—Cloth-making—Meeting with Emin—Suggestions about return route—Emin's kindness—Emin learns the origin of the Expedition—Our letters stopped in Uganda.

READERS of "In Darkest Africa," and of Mr. Stanley's letters to the Emin Relief Committee, which have appeared in the English journals, will remember that on our first arrival at the Albert Nyanza in the middle of December, 1887, we were soon compelled to retrace our steps, and march back to the forest. They will also remember that our sudden return from the Lake was due to the fact that Emin—though informed of the advance of an expedition to his relief, which would make for the south-west corner of the Lake—had taken no steps to communicate with the natives, or to warn them of our expected appearance in their neighbourhood. Consequently we could gain no intelligence of him, nor were there any means of conveying a message to him. The natives possessed no canoes of sufficient size to navigate the Lake, and the steel boat *Advance*, with which we had purposed to sail to Wadelai, we had been obliged to leave far behind in the forest at the Ituri River near Ipoto, as our men, distressed by sickness, and weakened by months of hunger, were utterly unable to carry her.

On the 8th January, 1888, we selected a site for a halting-place at Ibwiri, about 130 miles west from Lake Albert, and began the construction of Fort Bodo, in which while waiting for the rear column, and the coming up of our convalescents, our surplus stores, and weakly men could be housed. Meantime Lieutenant Stairs, with 100 men, was sent to the Ituri, 90 miles westward, to bring up the boat. This being done, the Fort completed, fields sown and planted for the subsistence of the garrison, we set out on April 2nd for the Albert Nyanza, to again try and find Emin ; but this time we possessed the steel boat *Advance* in which we might search for him.

On the 18th of April the advanced column of the Emin Pasha Relief Expedition had reached the neighbourhood of Lake Albert for the second time, and formed camp at the village of a chief called Kavalli,—who was a fine specimen of the shepherd tribe Wahuma. The chief soon after our arrival produced a letter which was addressed to Mr. H. M. Stanley, commanding the Relief Expedition. It proved to be the first communication from Emin Pasha, Governor of Equatoria, the man whom we had come so far to relieve. It was dated Tunguru, March 25th, 1888, which was said to be at the north end of Lake Albert.

A day or two after, Mr. Stanley ordered me to take the steel boat down to the Lake, and with a chosen crew to proceed to inform Emin that we had arrived, and that the first instalment of relief was ready. Surgeon Parke, our good doctor, and a body of men were detailed to escort us down to the Lake shore. We reached the Lake with the boat in good order, and I immediately began to screw the sections together.

It had been hard work getting the boat down the steep mountain to the plain below, on the other side of which lay the Lake. The men were, however, in good condition, and worked cheerily, and we were able to camp at a large village in good time, having marched eleven miles. The natives were very friendly, and brought presents of goats and corn. This large plain, which lies on the south-west shore of the Lake, surrounded by an amphitheatre of high rugged mountains, is most beautiful. It is like a great park, picturesquely studded with thickets and beautiful trees. On the short sweet grass herds of antelope and buffalo may be seen peacefully grazing. It is a perfect hunter's paradise. On April 21st we reached the Lake shore, and at once began to get the boat put together.

Parke and I were to part here, he to return to Kavalli's with the rest of the men, and I, with my boat's crew, was to start off in search of Emin.

My crew of fifteen consisted of some of the best men in the expedition, as Stanley had allowed me to choose my own boat's crew. I had chosen those who from time to time had rowed the boat up the Congo and Aruwimi, who were all tried men, and thoroughly at home in the boat. The faithful Uledi was coxswain, and Murabo and Sudi, who had both been with Stanley on former expeditions, were pulling the stroke oars. The rest were fine active men, and all young. It is a most important thing to take young men for any particular mission, as the negro, after arriving at the age of twenty-five, loses as a rule the power of acting quickly and promptly, which is not the case with a European. By the time I had got the boat put together and our five days' provisions on board, it was one o'clock. I gave the order to shove off, and the forty-five men who were returning to Stanley's camp with Parke dashed into the water, and pushed us far out into the lake, with loud cheers. Parke swung his cap over his head, and he and his men wished us good luck, and gave us three cheers, to which we responded from the boat. " Now, boys ! " I said, turning to the crew, " pull as you never pulled before, and Inshallah we shall see the Pasha, whom we have already toiled so long to reach, in two or three days." They responded with a shout of " Inshallah, Master ! " and, bending their backs to the oars, sent the boat flying gaily through the water. Murabo struck up one of the crooning but not inharmonious songs which the Zanzibar boatmen usually sing when rowing, and to which they keep time with their oars. He sang of the forest and the troubles we had gone through, of praise of our great chief, Bula Matari, of the miles we had marched to help the Pasha, of our nearness to him now, and of our troubles ended. The crew joined in a chorus in which the names of Bula Matari and the Pasha were mingled.

There was a fresh breeze which ruffled the face of the lake into tiny waves, the sun was shining bright,

START TO FIND EMIN.

to the west was the beautiful park-like plain through which we had passed that morning; in the distance to the east, the noble mountains of Unyoro rose almost perpendicularly from the lake. Everything seemed fresh and bright and beautiful, and one's spirits rose to the occasion; the men seemed to feel it too, and, putting their whole strength into the oars, sent the boat bounding through the water.

We passed Nyamsassie Island, where the natives came and looked at us timidly from behind the bushes; we swept through a narrow channel between the mainland and the island, and entered a big bay some eight miles broad from point to point. Here were great herds of hippopotami rolling and plunging in the water, and we had to steer out into the lake to avoid them, as they often attack and destroy boats or canoes in passing.

Some twelve miles ahead, the plain ended and the mountains turning sharply to the east came sheer down into the lake, in one great headland. At the foot of the mountains we could see in the distance the blue smoke rising from a large village, and I pointed this out to my men as the place where I intended to camp that night.

Emin had written to Stanley from a place called Tunguru, but Katto, one of Kavalli's brothers, whom I had in the boat with me, and who was to act as interpreter for me with the natives along the lake shore, said that there was another Egyptian station called M'swa, some distance nearer to us, and that we should take from three and a half to four days to reach it in the boat.

As we neared the mountains we could see that the village was a very large one, and was surrounded by groves of bananas. There were a good many canoes drawn up on the beach, and numbers of fishing nets were spread out to dry; the population evidently lived principally by fishing. We could see the natives hiding in the grass and behind the huts, and just peering out to look at us. Katto stood up in the bow of the boat, and making signs of friendship, and shouting out friendly words, told the natives we were the people of Bula Matari, the great white chief (Inkama), who had just reached the lake, and who was going to visit his brother Mlidju at the north end of the lake. He told them Bula Matari's son was in the boat, and wished to sleep at their village. After consulting some minutes together, during which time Katto kept up a running fire of friendly greetings, the natives came down in a large body to the water's edge and told us they would be glad to make friends with Bula Matari's son, and would allow him to sleep at their village and would give his people food.

After some little further talk we ran the boat ashore at about 5.30.

I landed and was introduced to the chief, who told me his name was Vaju, and that the name of his village was Kanama; he asked me my name, and I told him it was Bubarika, and that I was a son of Bula Matari. Vaju was a villainous-looking old fellow with a face deeply marked with small-pox, he had only one eye, but Yankumbu, his son, some twenty-five years old, had the pleasantest face and manners, and one felt instinctively he could be trusted. I then ordered the boat to be hauled up, as the lake was getting rough, and a tolerably large sea was tumbling in on the strand. Uledi, on hearing the order, said to me "Master remember Bumbireh, and the Bwana Mkubwa's story of it; don't let them haul the boat up too far." However, we were obliged to haul her clear of the water, or she would have been broken by the sea, but I had her in a position so that at a moment's warning we could run her into the lake.

I ordered the men to light their camp fires on the beach, and sleep all round the boat with their guns beside them. I slept in sight of the boat in front of Yankumbu's hut, and he introduced me to his wife and little baby, of which he seemed very fond.

Vaju and some of his chiefs brought me some fish, and came and sat all round me, whilst I was eating my dinner, watching me use my knife and fork with the greatest interest.

We had a long talk, and he told me how he had heard of Bula Matari's arrival at the lake four months before, and of the great number of guns we had with us. He told me he had heard that on our return a second time to the lake, all the tribes except the Waregga, who were a bad people, had made friends with us, and he wanted also to be friends with Bula Matari. I asked him if he knew Mlidju (Emin), and he said that Mlidju, who had come down the lake two months before in his big fire-boat, had stopped at his village for a couple of hours, and had given him a large brass bangle, which he showed me, as a present.

I sat up till late, talking with the natives, who seemed to have made great friends with my Zanzibaris; and they were laughing and talking together half the night.

The Zanzibaris travel with caravans through so many different countries that most of them know sufficient of the dialects of a great number of the tribes of Eastern Central Africa, and they eke out what few words they know with a great many expressive gestures, so that they are quite able to make themselves understood by the natives.

I was up at 4.30, and had my breakfast of dried fish, and porridge made of Indian corn flour. At 5.15 I ordered the boat to be launched, the natives coming down in great numbers to help us to put her into the water. They brought me a present of some chickens, bananas, and several jars of *pombê*, or native beer, obtained from a kind of malt made with M'tama corn. They parted from us with reiterated expressions of friendship, and hoped that I should have a happy meeting with my white brother. One was struck afresh by the childlike simplicity, good nature and hospitality of these negroes who had never seen us before, and who had absolutely nothing to gain by our friendship.

We now passed along most beautiful scenery. The mountains rose abruptly from the lake to a height of nearly three thousand feet. Great rocks stand out like huge fortifications into the lake, which dashes against these giant walls with a noise like thunder, and sends up showers of spray. Fine trees are growing in all the slopes and crevices in the rocks, and all the gullies are full of trees, amongst which huge baboons and chimpanzees, vervet and colobus monkeys abound. The latter are black with a fringe of long white hair all round them, and look particularly graceful as they climb the rocks or leap from tree to tree.

Here and there a fish eagle perches upon the trees overhanging the water, and from time to time utters its mournful cry. Brilliant kingfishers, red, white, and blue, dart about in the sunshine, looking like great butterflies. The whole of the wooded shore is teeming with life, and it was perfect paradise to let one's eyes roam idly over this lovely scenery as we glided along in the setting sun.

Here and there were cascades of clear cold water leaping out from the bushes and dashing some hundreds of feet into the lake below. Most of the larger cascades had formed flat deltas of land, sometimes as much as five acres in extent. These extended into the lake, and were covered with short grass and small mimosa bushes. On all these small plains natives had built their villages, and lived chiefly by fishing or making salt. These little settlements were very pretty and peaceful-looking, each had its flock of goats grazing on the smooth lawn, and was surrounded by its grove of bright green plantains. Some of the natives were lying idly about among their goats and chickens, smoking their pipes; whilst others paddled about in their tiny one-man canoes, and looked after and set their fishing nets. Women were to be seen on the lake shore, laughing and talking as they cleaned and prepared the fish for curing in the sun. Everything looked peaceful and calm, and the people happy and contented; they were real little arcadias where one might peacefully dream away one's life.

As we neared each of these settlements, I landed Katto on the beach, and he ran in front of us and told the villagers we were friends, and were merely passing along the lake to visit Mlidju. The natives therefore remained in their villages, and hailed us good-naturedly as we passed, but they were very much astonished at the iron boat with the Egyptian flag flying astern.

The sun was intensely hot on the water, and it was almost intolerable sitting in the boat, every steel plate of which was burning hot. I had unfortunately nothing on my head but a cloth deer-stalker hat. I got my water-bottle constantly replenished from these cool cascades, for though the water of the lake is as clear as crystal, it is lukewarm, and has an unpleasant, soft, soda-like taste, and a draught of it seems neither to refresh nor to satisfy one. The men declared it was salt, and would not drink it, and always drank from the cascades, the water of which was cold, aërated, and beautifully refreshing.

We passed numbers of huge baboons sitting and walking about unconcernedly on the beach, with their tails aloft in the shape of a crook, and their sterns of a brilliant sky-blue colour. The way they hold their tails gives them a most comical appearance. They took not the smallest notice of us, but just sat and blinked at us as if we were an every-day sight. The natives, I was told, hold them in great fear.

We were all very much amused by a little incident which happened. Kibyia, one of my men, was walking along the beach, keeping pace with the boat, when suddenly a huge baboon stalked out from behind a rock, and confronted him about five yards off. He stopped short, and exclaimed, "Hallo, what's your name?" and the baboon put his head on one side and looked at him as if to ask him the same question. After gazing at each other for a few seconds, they determined not to make the acquaintance any closer, and each turned his back and walked away from the other.

I shot an enormous fellow who was sitting on a rock about eighty yards off; he had a splendid skin, and I should have liked to have got it, but as the lake was rough and the shore rocky, I dared not land, for the slightest touch on a rock sends a hole through the bottom of these thin steel boats.

In a village belonging to a chief called Boganza we picked up Mogo. He was one of Emin's Lur chiefs, and had brought down his letter to Stanley to Nampigua at Nyamsassie, who had given it over to Kavalli, who handed it to Stanley on our arrival at his village five days before. He was on his way back to Emin, so we took him on with us in the boat. He was a queer-looking, ragged fellow, with a very good-natured face, huge ears, thick lips and flattened nose. A bright red handkerchief was round his head, a big necklace of opal-coloured beads encircled his neck, and an enormous brass bracelet was on his wrist, these ornaments being presents, he told me, which Emin had given him. A girdle of large iron beads of native make held together his dirty, ragged clothes of goat-skins, and his long matted hair was fantastically plaited up and drenched with oil. A bow, basket-work quiver of arrows, pipe and crooked walking-stick, all huge of their kind, completed his get up. He was eminently " a thing of shreds and patches." He brought with him sundry packets of salt and tobacco, and several large jars of pombé, which my men very soon finished for him.

We camped that evening at 5.30 at Magunga, one of the villages such as I have described, and from it we could see Emin's station some twelve miles off, with smoke rising in clouds from the fields about the station where natives were burning weeds.

CHIEF MOGO.

The chief's son, Kajalf, came down to receive us on the beach, he was a particularly nice-looking young fellow, and was followed by several natives bringing me, as presents, large bunches of bananas and strings of dried fish; he also brought two goats which I handed over to my Zanzibaris. He was anxious that I should go up and sleep in his village, but I preferred to camp out in the open in order to be near the boat; moreover, the huts were horribly stuffy and were swarming with vermin. From him I learned that he was very good friends with Emin, and often made trips to the station, the name of which he told me was M'swa. Emin had often, he said, protected him against

Melindwa, a powerful chief whose country adjoined his, and he believed Emin himself was now at M'swa. On one side of the village was a large sandy flat, through which the water from a cascade in the mountain-side ran and found its way to the lake, in a stream large enough to turn a water mill. By the side of this stream we camped, and the Zanzibaris killed the two goats and made ready for a big feast.

After dinner I had my chair brought down to the beach, where a narrow strip of sand ran out into the lake. Here I sat down with the waves lapping up the shore, and the Nyanza lying in the bright moonlight like a silver carpet at my feet. I sat there smoking my pipe with the cool breeze of the Nyanza playing round me, and the voices and laughter of my men reaching me faintly across the water. What would to-morrow bring forth? Here I was within sight of the goal which we had been struggling and fighting to reach for the last fifteen months. To-morrow I should probably see the man of whom all the civilized world had been talking, and to whom I, the humble emissary of our great leader, was bearing tidings of encouragement and relief at last. But the feelings of triumph which rose in one's mind were saddened as one thought of the trials our people had gone through, and of the hard deaths of so many of our faithful men.

We started off at 6.30 with the Egyptian flag flying at the masthead, and I improvised a sail out of one of my blankets as there was a fair wind. The men pulled like madmen, and we flew along before the wind and reached M'swa at a little before nine o'clock. A guard of honour was drawn up on the beach to receive me, and a grand salute of guns was fired, and then with flags flying and trumpets playing the Khedevial Hymn, I was escorted up to the station which stood on the top of a low flat hill about a quarter of a mile from the lake.

Here I learnt, to my great disappointment, that Emin was at Tunguru, a day's journey distant. I would have gone on in the boat there, but Shukri Aga, the chief of the station, told me he had heard from the natives last night, that a white man was on his way up the lake in a boat, and he had sent messengers early in the morning to Emin to tell him the news. He said Emin would come down at once in his steamer, and would be here by midday the next day, in which case I considered it best to stay where I was, as I might miss him on the way if I went on in the boat.

The station was made entirely of bamboo and grass, and was exquisitely clean and neat, and all the huts were airy and cool. The chief of the station, Shukri Aga, was dressed in a long blue uniform tunic with enormous gold naval epaulettes, cherry-coloured trousers, high-heeled French boots, large sword, and fez. The soldiers had a sort of loose uniform of the cotton cloth which is made in the Province, and like that which is made in the Northern Soudan, cartridge belts of leopard skin or half-tanned leather, white knitted tabooshes, and country-made slippers, and nearly all were armed with Remingtons.

The whole people turned out *en masse* to welcome me and kiss my hands—a horrible custom, and one from which I suffered much during my stay in the Pasha's Province.

Arrival at M'swa.

I was taken into a large barazan, or receiving-room, built of bamboo. There was a couch with a Turkish carpet on it, and pillows for me to recline on, and chairs were placed near it for the officers and chief people of the station, all the rest of the people stood in the background or crowded in the doorways. My Zanzibaris, who had been well embraced by all the people and hailed as deliverers and brothers, were accommodated with a mat and sat behind me.

A gourd full of snowy curds was brought in for me, and large jars of M'tama beer were given to my men. We then had a long talk, for the people all wanted to know about us, and as I sat and recounted, as simply as I could, the story of our wanderings in the forest, loud exclamations of wonder and pity were heard all round, and the greatest excitement prevailed. They told me Emin was well and in no difficulties, he had been expecting us for a long time, and had built this station when he heard that he should look for us at the south-west corner of the lake, in order to have a station near us.

I then wrote a hasty note in pencil, and despatched it by two friendly natives, who promised to start off at once in a canoe and hand it to Emin.

The people all looked so smart and clean in their costumes of snowy white or brown cotton cloth, such a contrast to us, the relief party, who had arrived in rags and dirt, and who looked in far greater need of relief than they. My Zanzibaris had only pieces of skin and scraps of native bark cloth, and in such very scanty quantities as hardly to render them decent.

I was dressed in a torn and patched suit, which I had made out of an old checked flannel set of pyjamas, an old flannel shirt—the only one I possessed—and my feet were shod in a pair of shoes, also manufactured by myself, out of the raw skin of a black-and-white-spotted cow with the hair left on.

When I had finished talking I was shown into a large hut, made of bamboo, about twenty-eight feet square, beautifully lofty and cool.

They brought me an enormous omelette, some delicious bread, and a great bowl of milk for my mid-day meal.

How delightful it was to sit and eat this good food after being without a decent meal for so long! I ate quantities of bread and drank great draughts of milk, and felt quite sorry when I could eat no more.

Not having slept much for the last three or four nights, owing to the anxiety I had felt, I lay down on an angarep (bed) and slept for four hours.

I was awakened by a servant bringing in a large round iron sponge bath full of warm water, a round piece of soap, which was manufactured by Emin's people in the Province, and an Egyptian loofa. I had not ordered the bath, but they evidently saw how dirty I was, and so, I suppose, thought it would be acceptable.

It may be imagined how delightful it was to have a good scrub after having been for five months without soap, and now for the first time since I had left Yambuya I felt really clean.

With what loathing and disgust one put on one's dirty old clothes again! They had been patched, and washed, and worn till they were quite threadbare.

Reception at M'swa.

A servant, dressed in clean white cotton cloth, brought in my "luggage," and placed it respectfully on a stool. It consisted of an old tent bag, in which there were some boots manufactured by myself, my journal, a couple of pairs of very holey stockings, and two blankets; also an old basket containing a leg of goat wrapped in green leaves, a kettle, two plates, a knife and fork, and some very black and disreputable-looking cooking pots. When my very dirty-looking worldly possessions were brought in by this clean well-dressed person, I felt that I visibly blushed.

In the evening a big deputation of people came to see me in my house, mats were placed on the ground outside, and they all squatted down and talked. Shukri Aga told me that five months before Emin had received a letter from Mr. Holmwood, the acting Consul-General at Zanzibar, telling him that Stanley was coming to bring him relief, and that he must expect him about the end of September at the south-west corner of the lake, as Stanley was going to open a route viâ the Congo. Since then he had been most anxious about our non-arrival. One fellow said, "The Pasha won't sleep much to-night when he hears you are here."

If Emin heard we were coming so long ago as that, and that we should probably arrive at the south-west corner of the lake, I cannot understand how it was that he took no steps to smooth the way for us. It would have been such a simple thing for him to go down in one of his steamers to the south end of the lake and make friends with the natives, tell them we were coming, and leave a letter for Stanley in the hands of some friendly chief, telling him of his whereabouts and how we could best reach him. Or he might have told the natives to tell Stanley to stop where he was on his arrival, and get the chief to send some of his people to M'swa with the news.

This would have saved us over four months of hard work and disappointment, for we had to carry all the ammunition we were bringing for him back into the forest and place it in a fort which we were obliged to build.

Nelson and Parke might have moved up to his Province, and this constant going backwards and forwards with our tired and worn-out men might have been avoided, to say nothing of the lives we lost on these journeys.

As events turned out, poor Barttelot's assassination and Jameson's sad death might have been avoided had Emin acted with simple common sense.

It was not apparently till after he had heard from the natives that we had actually arrived at the lake and turned back, that he took any steps to help us. Moreover, it had been Stanley's intention on our arrival at the lake the first time, had he been able to get a canoe, to send me round the lake to Kibero, to ask Captain Casati, who was living there, to accompany me to Wadelai. Had this been done, the crew of the canoe and I would have probably fallen into Kaba-regga's hands, all for the want of a word of warning from Emin.

Shukri Aga told me of many atrocities Kaba-regga, king of Unyoro, had committed, and how he had expelled Captain Casati.

It appears Casati did not get on well with Kaba-regga, and the Arabs had doubtless helped to widen the breach between them, until it culminated in an outrage which might have cost Casati his life. One morning Kaba-regga's people came into Casati's house, seized him and tied him up to a tree. After having completely looted his house, they loosed him and turned him adrift almost naked. Orders were given to the natives to give him no food, and to have nothing whatever to do with him. This news had been brought to Emin by a native, and he had gone over immediately in his steamer to the Unyoro side of the lake. On cruising down the shore, he had seen a white garment being waved as a signal at the end of a pole, and went off in the steamer's boat to see what it was. Here he found Casati, who had been hiding in the grass for three days with hardly a crust to eat. He was in a most deplorable state, and had on only a shirt and tattered pair of trousers. I was told Casati was now with Emin at Tunguru.

After breakfast next morning a good many people came in to see me, and a large number of native chiefs from the countries round came in to greet me, and stare at the new white man who had just come into the country. They were all very anxious to hear where we had come from, and to learn something about the great dark forest into which none of their people had ever penetrated, but about which they had ever heard rumours of perpetual twilight, and of savage and treacherous people. In the afternoon I went to see my men, and found them comfortably lodged in a boma with five or six huts in it, which they had all to themselves. They welcomed me clamorously, and told me how well they had been treated. Each man had had a new cow-hide given him to sleep upon, a bullock had been killed for them, and numerous dainties in the shape of butter, milk and flour had been supplied. But what seemed to strike them most was the fact that once more they had their food cooked for them by women, which to them, after the hardships they had gone through, seemed to be the height of luxury. Uledi said to me, "Master, we have only to eat, drink, sleep, and smoke, and you know that is paradise to a Zanzibari."

I wrote a letter to Stanley, telling him I had reached Emin's station, but as he was away there would be a delay, so he must not be anxious about us. This I sent by some friendly natives who promised to take it down the lake in a canoe, and deliver it into Stanley's hands in four days.

Next morning an Egyptian officer called Suliman Effendi arrived, and handed me a letter from Emin, which was as follows :—

"Tunguru, 24th April, 1888.

"DEAR SIR,—Your letter of yesterday reached here this night. Be heartily welcome amongst us; we have waited for you many a long day. I proposed to start at once to rejoin you at M'swa; the steamer having gone, however, to fetch some corn, and the people being busy with their fields, I must necessarily delay until the steamer returns. I have sent for and expect her to-morrow. It goes without saying that at her arrival I start.

"I have given orders to my men to provide for all your needs, and those of your men; please therefore to acquaint Shukri Aga, the officer in charge of the station, with your wants. Suliman Effendi, the bearer of this, has to stay with you until my arrival.

"Hoping to see you very soon,

"I am, yours very faithfully,

"Dr. Emin."

Suliman Effendi, a nice-looking Egyptian, was dressed in a spotless white uniform, he spoke a little French, but only of the feeblest kind. He sat and talked with me some time, and told me of the state of excitement into which the Pasha and all the station had been thrown on receipt of the news that the long-looked-for help had at last arrived. He paid me a great many compliments, saying he put his neck beneath my feet, and I only had to command him, and so on, the usual Oriental style of compliments. In the evening I walked round the place with him and Shukri Aga, who showed me all there was to be seen.

The station was beautifully situated, and, if held by determined men, would be perfectly impregnable to the attacks of natives, armed only with bows and spears, but an enemy armed with guns would command it from the hills above.

The mountains here, which are some 2500 feet high, form a kind of amphitheatre, in the bend of which is a large fertile plain some 5000 or 6000 acres in extent and nearly on a level with the lake. From the middle of this plain rises a large mound about 300 feet high, on the flattened summit of which the station was built. This plain, which is watered by a fine large stream falling from the mountains in a large cascade, is very densely populated, and comprises one of the largest settlements of the Lur tribe. Large villages, with immense flocks of sheep and goats, were to be seen from the station dotted all over the plain, every acre almost of which was under cultivation. Large fields of m'tama, Indian corn, sweet potatoes, and ground nuts, mingled with groves of bananas, surrounded the villages. Immediately below the station were the cultivations of the soldiers and Government officials, which consisted chiefly of patches of cotton, Indian corn, m'tama, millet, sessam, balmias, Kolokasias and vegetables of different kinds.

The station was built in two separate blocks, one containing Emin's compound, divan, and strangers' houses, the other consisting of the soldiers' and officials' quarters. Each family had a small compound to itself, in which there were three, four, or more huts, according to the size of the household. Between the two blocks was a large parade ground, in the middle of which were the Government store houses, and a high staff from which flew the Egyptian flag. The entire station, bomas and huts, was built of bright yellow bamboo, in some cases plastered over with a mixture of mud and cow dung, and the houses were thatched with grass.

On the grass land between the station and the mountains was a large kraal containing some hundreds of cattle, sheep and goats. There was evidence of abundance of food of all sorts.

I saw numbers of women, boys, and even soldiers walking or standing about the station carrying large bunches of raw cotton under their left arms, from

Description of M'swa Station.

which they spun thread by rapidly twisting a little crooked distaff. When a number of bobbins of cotton thread were finished they were stretched in lengths along posts like miniature rope-walks, and were then ready for weaving.

They took me into a large open hut, at one side of which a trench had been dug, and an exceedingly primitive spindle was fitted into it, which was worked by an intelligent looking negro lad. Several qualities of cotton cloth were made here, some remarkably fine for the women's clothes, and some of a coarser description for the men's tunics and loose Turkish trousers. The men's clothes were usually dyed a warm reddish brown colour, from a solution made by soaking the bruised bark of a wild fig-tree in water. These fig-trees grow in great numbers all through the entire country. The cloth had a slightly fluffy appearance, it was almost as warm as flannel and was wonderfully strong and serviceable.

On April 26th, at about five o'clock in the evening, Emin's steamer came in sight. She was just rounding a rocky headland about five miles off when I first saw her.

The soldiers all turned out, and the officers put on their best uniforms to receive their governor; the little cannon belonging to the station being got ready to give him a salute. I walked down from the station to the beach, followed by my boat's crew, carrying our big Egyptian flag, there to await Emin's landing. It was almost dark before the steamer dropped anchor, my men firing a salute as the boat neared the shore. As soon as the boat touched the strand, Emin leaped ashore and welcomed me with both hands. Again and again he repeated words of welcome and cordial greeting as he held both my hands in his. I should not have recognized him from the picture and description Dr. Felkin had given of him. Instead of the "tall man, of a military appearance," I saw a small, wiry, neat, but most unmilitary-looking man, with unmistakable German politeness of manner.

He spoke English with much ease and fluency, and expressed himself with great sympathy and kindness. He was followed by Captain Casati, a short, middle-aged man, burnt almost black from exposure to the sun. He did not understand English, but could talk a little French.

When the greetings were over, Emin put his hand on my shoulder in a fatherly manner, and we walked up to the station together, followed by all the officials. We sat outside talking in the bright moonlight, and it was late before Emin retired to read the letter I had brought him from Stanley. He told me we could not start for the south end of the lake for two days, as it would take the whole day to collect wood for the steamer.

Early in the morning some delicious strong coffee, sweetened with honey, was brought me in a little dainty Turkish cup. Before I had finished dressing, Emin came into my hut, and sat on my bed talking to me as I dressed. We then went out and sat in the cool divan, and I brought out my maps and showed him our route up the river. He was much struck by the position of the Nepoko River, and the point where it falls into the Aruwimi. He had heard a good deal about it from Dr. Junker, who I believe

PORTRAIT OF EMIN PASHA.

Page 24.

had not quite decided to which watershed it belonged.

He knew the Monbuttu country very well, and the place where Dr. Junker had crossed the Nepoko, some 120 geographical miles distant from the point where it fell into the Aruwimi. He seemed to think that this would be an excellent route by which to transport his people, and ivory down to the Congo in canoes. I pointed out to him the immense difficulties of such a route, the numberless rapids and cataracts in the river, and the starvation he would experience on the road. But of course, I said, Stanley would be able to tell him the pros and cons of such a route better than I.

I handed over to him a sheet of the *Graphic* newspaper containing an account of him and his work by Dr. Felkin, and numerous illustrations of people and scenes in his Province.

All my men came up to pay their respects to him. He thanked them for all they had done for him and his people, and promised to give them some cloth to cover their nakedness. I pointed out Uledi and Murabo to him, both of whom he knew by name, having read about them in Stanley's book " Through the Dark Continent." Of course they were delighted at the idea of getting cloth—poor fellows, they did indeed look shabby. He handed them over to Vita Hassan, a Tunisian Jew, who had been sent up to the Equatorial Province eight years previously as apothecary and assistant to Emin, he now acted also as storekeeper and general helper, and was most useful. Emin spoke very highly of him. After breakfast, the Pasha produced a cigar, which Dr. Junker had given him three years before. This will convey some idea of the careful way in which Emin preserved everything. He told me he had kept it all this time in case of a festival. It was a great treat to me after being accustomed only to native tobacco for so many months.

Seeing my tattered state, clothes were brought to me by Emin's orders, two coats and a pair of trousers made of cotton cloth. The native tailor—an Egyptian who had been transported to Emin's Province for highway robbery—took my measure for knickerbockers, and the shoemaker was called in to measure me for shoes. A quantity of red Manchester cloth was also given to my servant to put in my hut.

Emin then took out his note-book, which, like everything he had, was a pattern of neatness, and insisted on my telling him of my wants. With a good deal of hesitation and some shyness at begging in this wholesale manner, I told him some salt, soap, a note-book, and a little oil would be most acceptable, all of which things he wrote down, grumbling all the time at the smallness of my demands. He enumerated several things he could give me, and seemed to take the greatest pleasure in being able to give them. His kindness was overwhelming, and evidently thoroughly genuine. It was such a pleasure to me to get some one quite new to talk to, especially such a clever, intelligent man, whose conversation must at all times be deeply interesting.

Emin asked me to tell him the origin of the Expedition, who were its promoters, how it was got up, and all about the officers.

I told him about it, and the widespread feeling

of interest which existed, not only in England but all over Europe, concerning his welfare and safety. The tears started to his eyes, and grasping my hand, he said, "How can you thank me for the few things I can give you, and be shy about taking them? If I lived for a hundred years I could not thank the English people enough for their disinterested kindness in sending me help, when I have been abandoned by my own Government for so many years."

Emin told me he had received a short letter from Mr. Holmwood, the acting Consul-General at Zanzibar. It was dated February 7th, 1887, and told him that an Expedition under Stanley, for his relief, was starting by the Congo route some time in March, and that he was expecting Stanley to arrive in Zanzibar on his way to the Congo in a fortnight's time. He should look for him some time in September, at the south-west corner of the lake. The two letters written by Stanley and Holmwood at the end of February, which had been despatched by special couriers, *viâ* Uganda, to Emin, had not reached him.

They were probably still in Uganda, for Emin told me there were several loads of letters, etc., waiting for us there. Mwanga, the King of Uganda, forwarded them, but they were stopped on the frontier of Unyoro by Kaba-regga's orders, and were returned to Uganda.

CHAPTER II.

MEETING OF STANLEY AND EMIN—PLANS DISCUSSED.

Steamer *Khedive*—Her condition—Emin arrives in our camp—Reception by the Zanzibaris—Our camp at N'sabe—Emin wishes Stanley to leave one of his officers—Plan made for relieving Fort Bodo—Stanley and Parke start on return journey—Death of Mabruki—Emin's love of entomology—Attack on Kibero—Kaba-regga's punishment—Chief Ouma—Chief Ouma's visit—Lur dance—Smells peculiar to different tribes—We arrive at Tunguru—Rapid falling of Lake Albert—Intriguing of Egyptian clerks—Punishment of Intriguers—Story of the mutiny of 1st Battalion—Character of Emin's officers—Khedive's letter—Nubar Pasha's letter—Stanley's address to Emin's soldiers—Letters read to the people—"We will follow our Governor!"—The people's natural desire to remain in Province—From Tunguru to Wadelai-Boki's village—Boki's imprisonment—Description of country—Lowness of Nile—Chief Okello—Native ornaments—Chief Wadelai.

On April 26th, at eight o'clock, we started off in the steamer *Khedive* which was like a small farm-yard, for there were on board numbers of cattle, milch cows, goats, sheep, and chickens, whilst the hold was filled with grain for our people. These were the stores which Stanley had asked Emin to bring him to enable him to camp on the lake shore where food was scarce.

The *Khedive* was one of the steamers brought up by Sir Samuel Baker when he was annexing the Province in 1870, for the Khedive, Ismail Pasha. She was built by Samuda and was still a fine strong boat, some eighty-five feet long, with a beam of eighteen feet. It was wonderful that she should be in such good order, it spoke well for Emin's carefulness in keeping her in such repair. Her boilers were, however, getting somewhat weak, though her engines were still good, and Emin dared not press her to go more than five knots an hour. He had besides this another small steamer, the *Nyanza*, and two large iron whale boats, all of which were brought up by Sir Samuel Baker. He told me that these steamers and boats had been of the greatest use to him and had helped him materially to hold out in his Province so long.

We reached our anchorage near Nyamsassie Island, opposite the place where I had put the boat together, at about seven o'clock. We found Stanley had marched down to the lake that day from Kavalli's, and was encamped about three miles down the shore, a little way inland. Late as it was, Emin decided to go and see Stanley that night. Numbers of our Zanzibaris came rushing down to the shore, carrying torches made of dry grass, firing their guns into the air, and shouting in the maddest manner. As we landed from the boat, we were met by Dr. Parke, who came down to the shore to meet Emin, and conduct him and Casati to the camp. The Zanzibaris were wild with excitement, and in their anxiety to help him across the broken ground near the shore fairly lifted him off his legs. He was conducted into our camp amid the triumphant shouts of all our people. Stanley received him with great warmth and courtesy, and we were soon all seated in front of his tent discussing the contents of five bottles of champagne, which Stanley produced out of an old pair of stockings, having carefully saved them for this great occasion.

The scene in camp was picturesque and impressive then in the extreme. Huge fires had been made, which lit up the branches of the overhanging trees with a lurid glare, beneath which the Zanzibaris were madly dancing, and singing one of their forest songs relating to the story of our wanderings and privations and of the meeting of Stanley and Emin.

Late that night Emin returned to the steamer, carrying with him the packets of letters we had brought him.

Next day, Stanley ordered me to march the column along the lake shore, and choose a good place for a camp, as he had promised Emin to stay with him there some days, before returning to bring up the rear column.

After marching about five miles, I chose a splendid place, called N'sabe, where the plain suddenly rose to a height of fifty feet above the lake. The grass was short, and there were a number of fine acacia and tamarind trees scattered about. Here we pitched our camp, Emin and his people establishing themselves below us, some 200 yards distant.

Stanley has written of our stay on the lake shore from April 28th to May 24th, and of his frequent conversations with Emin on the subject of his leaving the country with us. He has written all about it, so I will therefore merely pass on to that time which concerned my stay with Emin.

I will here quote an extract from my journal, which I wrote at the time.

"*May* 18*th*.—Stanley came over to my tent this

morning, and told me that Emin had asked him to leave one of his officers with him when he returned to bring up Barttelot and the rear column, and that he had consented and nominated me. It appears Emin had told Stanley that his officers were exceedingly sceptical about us, and did not believe we came from Egypt. He has therefore asked Stanley to leave one of his officers with him until Stanley's return here with the rear column. He would wish this officer to be his guest, to go round with him to all his stations throughout the Province, and address the people, explaining to them who we were and the reason we had arrived here. He would wish this officer to read the Khedive's and Nubar Pasha's letters to the people of each station; also a proclamation from Stanley to the soldiers. The people would be drawn up to hear what was said, and could ask Stanley's representative any question they pleased about the road, &c., and he could answer them. Emin thinks that this alone would satisfy them, and convince them that we came from Egypt. It could then be seen if the people were willing or not to come out with us; and, in the event of his people refusing to leave and he himself coming out with us, it could never be said of him that he had deserted his people. After giving me this explanation, Stanley asked me if I accepted the post. I said I would think about it. Though I should be doing the work of the Expedition, I did not like leaving Stanley for so long a time (it would probably be for seven or eight months), especially as there is such a lot of hard work yet to be done, and I don't want to get out of it. He told me I should help him very much by getting things ready, so that he could start for Zanzibar with as little delay as possible on his return. He told me to go and see the Pasha first, if I liked, and have a talk with him before giving him my answer. In the afternoon I went over to Emin, and had a long talk with him. He repeated to me more or less what he had said to Stanley, and begged me most earnestly to remain with him. He said he believed I should be doing a most important work for the Expedition by going round his country with him, and speaking to his people. I therefore said I would stay with him, and in the evening I told Stanley of my decision; I am, however, strongly drawn towards the return journey, and would elect to remain with Stanley if it rested entirely with myself. Stanley, however, wishes me to stay, and Emin urges me to remain—so I must remain,—and so it is decided.

"If by going round and addressing the people, I can induce them to come out with us, I shall do good work. At the same time it seems so strange to us who have come out to help these people, that it is necessary first to explain who we are. I think there must be a screw loose somewhere.

"At my suggestion it has been decided that after I have been round to all the stations, and have seen the people, that I, and if possible Emin as well, will go with a party of soldiers and carriers to Fort Bodo, and bring the officers and loads left in charge up to the lake.

"We shall build a station here at N'sabe, and Emin has promised to give us thirty or forty soldiers to help us to garrison it, and to send us down supplies in the way of cattle, goats, and corn, for officers and men. Emin said it will probably take us from two to three months to do our work in the Province, but it may of course take more than that; it is always impossible in Africa to say " I will do such and such a thing on a certain day," so many unforeseen circumstances may arise to prevent it. We very much doubt if Emin will be able to go, as there will probably be a good deal for him to do in arranging for the start to the coast. But that does not signify, if he gives me sufficent carriers and soldiers I can do it just as well by myself. The work of building and fortifying a station, and leading my little expedition to Fort Bodo, is a work I shall enjoy thoroughly. I am writing to Nelson, to tell him I hope to be at Fort Bodo with lots of supplies in a little more than two months. Poor old chap! I expect he wants cheering up a bit, for he has been so ill and low-spirited for a good many months now."

On May 24th, Stanley and Parke started off on the return journey, leaving me with Emin. Stanley left three Soudanese soldiers with me as orderlies, and Binza as a servant. He was a Niam Niam boy, who had attached himself to Dr. Junker, and after being with him about four years followed him to Zanzibar. He spoke Arabic and Ki'swahili, and was to act as my interpreter.

One of our men, Mabruki, had been fearfully wounded by a buffalo, and he also was left with me, but died a few hours after Stanley had left. We remained a couple of days at N'sabe after Stanley's departure, for the steamers were short of hands and a large amount of wood had to be collected to enable us to do the twelve hours' steaming to N'sabe. The camp looked very dreary when the Expedition had left, and I felt rather lonely and deserted.

Emin had his collectors out shooting birds for his collections, and I went out and got some good butterflies and beetles. It is wonderful what an interest he took in it, his face quite lit up if any one brought him in some beetle or bug of an uncommon species. None of the letters we had brought him gave him such pleasure as those relating to his scientific researches.

There was one from the British Museum, announcing the safe arrival of a consignment of several boxes of skulls, skins, birds, and bugs, which he had sent off some months before. He talked delightedly of the letter for days.

Several of the chief scientific societies had written telling him that his name was enrolled among their members.

All these letters gave him the keenest pleasure and satisfaction.

On May 28th we started off for M'swa, but there was something wrong with the engines, and we only reached Magunga that night, a place twenty miles from M'swa, and at which I had slept about a month ago, when I went in the boat to meet Emin.

We left the hot, stuffy steamer, and had our angareps put on the strand where I had formerly slept. A large camp fire was made, by the light of which we had our dinner, and turned into bed early. At 12 o'clock, however, rain began to descend heavily, and soon our blankets were wet through and through.

Without shelter we sat in a dripping state, and were glad when morning came.

We reached M'swa station at 10.30, and here began my stay in Emin's Province.

M'SWA STATION.

On arriving at M'swa, Emin told me he intended organizing an attack on Kibero, the place in Unyoro whose people had looted Casati's house, tied him up, and expelled him from the country by Kaba-regga's orders. Emin thought that if this was allowed to pass without punishment it would prove only the commencement of a long series of attacks on his people by Kaba-regga.

Kibero is a district containing several large villages, and chiefly derives its importance from its being the only place in that part of the country where salt in any quantity is made. It supplies almost the whole of Unyoro, Uganda, and the surrounding countries with salt.

The steamers, containing 100 men, started off in the middle of the night and reached Kibero, which is situated on the other side of the lake opposite M'swa, before daybreak next morning. During the day we could see clouds of smoke rising from the other side of the lake in the direction in which Kibero lay. The steamers returned in the evening, bringing several hundred large packets of salt, over 600 goats and sheep, innumerable chickens, and quantities of other things of all sorts. Emin's soldiers had met with great resistance from the people, a good many of whom had guns; they had killed a number of the Kinyoro, and had captured an old Tower musket of which Kaba-regga's people have numbers. The officers reported that there had been such an immense quantity of salt that they could not load up the steamer with it, and had been obliged to make great fires and burn it.

This was a great blow to Kaba-regga, for the salt being there in such large quantities showed that the supply for the rainy season had not yet been broached. The rainy season had just begun and no more salt could be made for several months, so that the entire trade had received a check and the punishment would be widely felt. Some of the soldiers brought me in some rather pretty iron and brass necklets and bracelets, and a large basket-work shield with a spike in the middle, shaped like those of the old Crusaders.

One of the first people to come to pay me a visit was a Lur chief called Ouma. He was an exceedingly powerful chief and had a large number of warriors. Formerly he was a firm ally of Unyoro, but some time before Kaba-regga had for some reason tried to have him assassinated, upon which he had made friends with Emin. Even this friendship had been clouded by an absurd incident.—

Some months before when Ouma was visiting the station, he asked the Pasha for an iron chair such as he was sitting upon. He said, " We are both great chiefs, and you sit on an iron chair, therefore it is only right on great occasions that I should sit on an iron chair also." Emin told him he only had one, but sent him a very nice cane chair instead. This present was indignantly refused, and from that day till he visited me, Ouma had not been near the station. Hearing there was a white stranger in the place he now came to see me, and brought me a present of a beautiful leopard skin. He seemed very much surprised that a white man could reach here, and asked Emin how I had come. The Pasha explained to him that as the Khartoum and Unyoro roads were closed, his friends had opened up another road through the forest, and told him that there were many of us on the way. He immediately exclaimed, " Ah, he's a big man, I can see, and will give me a good present." Emin told him that all our goods were behind, but that he would give him a present for me, with which arrangement he was perfectly satisfied. These people were the most inveterate beggars. Ouma was a fine strong fellow, he must have been at least 6 ft. 4 in. in height, and was broad and large in proportion. He had a laughing, rollicky manner which was most taking. He gesticulated a great deal and clinched each argument he brought forward with a huge expectoration, which he sent

LUR DANCE.

to a distance of several yards with a precision of aim which was truly astonishing. He was always accompanied by his prime minister and chief counsellor, a little, nervous, laughing fellow, who tried to smooth over his chief's somewhat brusque remarks. Ouma had brought all his people to dance before us, and after talking some time we went out to see the dance which had already begun in the station square.

There were some hundreds of natives dancing in a large circle, within which was a band of about fifty people beating drums of all shapes and sizes, and blowing long ivory or wooden horns, which last were covered with hide and gave out very deep notes. There were also many kinds of pipes, made out of the stems of gourds, which sounded like penny whistles. The noise made by the drums, horns, pipes and cries of the dancers was almost deafening as we approached. The men danced round with their backs turned outwards in a sort of slow, swaying motion, while some sixty women danced outside the circle to the tune (?) of the pipes, and emphasized the time by jingling the bangles which reached from their ankles to their knees.

They were entirely without clothes, with the exception of a long tail of red string, which hung down behind from a string round their waists. The great feature in the dance seemed to be to wag their tails as much as possible. They came and danced immediately in front of us, and the effect of sixty red tails wagging at us to the time of the pipes and jingling bangles was most ludicrous. Natives seem to delight in dancing, they will dance on for hours until the perspiration pours down them in streams without showing any signs of fatigue. At about five o'clock the dancing, which had been going on without intermission since mid-day, ceased. These Lurs were as a rule an ugly people; they moreover made themselves more ugly by plaiting sheep's or goats' wool in their hair so that it hung down all round their heads in a long fringe. Many of them daubed their heads with fat, mixed with a kind of red ochreous clay.

Some of them are exceedingly fine men, but as a rule they are small, and have a particularly unpleasant smell. Emin told me that each tribe has its own peculiar smell, and that when you got to know the different people, you could almost distinguish, blindfolded, to what tribe they belonged, merely by the smell. I am quite sure I should know *these* people blindfolded! I remember our Zanzibaris in the forest telling us that all the cannibals had such a bad smell.

Near this station there was a large tract of virgin forest, in which there were numbers of chimpanzees. This is an interesting fact to naturalists, for I believe it was never known before how far east the habitat of chimpanzees extended.

Almost every day I had a touch of fever which rendered me perfectly useless.

As there were so many officials away on different duties, I did not address the people before leaving M'swa.

On June 6th, we arrived at Tunguru, which was about nine miles from the north end of the lake. There had formerly been a station near here called Mahagi; it was built by Gordon, but had been abandoned when the stations of M'ruli and M'gungu had been given up some years before. Rather more than two years previously, Emin, wishing to establish stations to the south, on hearing of the fall of Khartoum, had built this station on what was then an island. Owing to the rapid fall of the lake it had now become a peninsula, and stood on a long spit of sand running about a mile and a half into the lake. This spit is constantly increasing, owing to the fall of the lake

Arrival at Tunguru.

and the constant silting up of the sand. The mountains, which to the south of the station come right up to the lake, gradually deflect towards the southwest, thus forming a broad flat plain between them and the shore. This plain extends almost to Wadelai, which was some thirty miles distant.

The station was built in a long narrow line, and was without defences of any sort. There are large numbers of crocodiles and turtles here, which may be seen swimming about or sleeping on the sandbanks. The natives collect quantities of their eggs, which they dig out of the sand.

Since arriving at Tunguru I had bad fever, day after day, and was able to do but little.

The chief of the station, Suliman Aga, was away when we arrived, having gone up to the mountains to collect the grain-tax from the natives. During his absence considerable mischief had been done by two Egyptians named Achmet Effendi Mahmoud, a clerk, and Abdul Wahab Effendi, a lieutenant who had been transported here from Egypt for having been mixed up in Arabi's rebellion. These two men, it appeared, had been brought down to our camp at M'sabe by Emin. During the time they were there they had gone to Stanley and had complained of the Pasha, against whom they brought all sorts of charges. Stanley merely told them that he could take no notice of their complaints, it was no business of his, if they had anything to say against their Governor they must wait till they got to Egypt. He dismissed them, but did not think it worth while to say anything about it to Emin. On the steamer's returning, to bring up fresh supplies of grain to our camp, Emin had sent these two men, amongst others, back to their duty at Tunguru. Finding on their return to Tunguru that the chief of the station was away, they immediately began to make mischief. They spoke to the people in the station and declared that Stanley was an impostor and adventurer, and had not come from Egypt, but that he was in league with the Pasha, who had formed a design with him to take the people out of the country and hand them over as slaves to the English. They also sent letters to the different stations containing words to this effect.

On our arrival all the station officials came, as the custom was, to kiss our hands and to assure the Pasha of their loyalty and devotion. These two Egyptians came with unblushing faces, and made the usual compliments also. Next day, however, the Soudanese officials all came before the Pasha, and told him what had been going on in the station since the return of these two officers.

Emin instantly mustered his people, and the clerk, lieutenant, and two other Egyptian officers were arrested. The clerk, Achmet Effendi, being sent as a prisoner to Dufilé, the three other officers being made prisoners in their houses. This, however, was not effected without a good deal of talking, which breach of discipline surprised me greatly.

Emin then addressed the soldiers and told them of the punishments he had awarded to the conspirators, and enjoined them not to be led away by such people. He further told them that on the return of Suliman Aga and the rest of the soldiers, I, as the representative of Stanley, intended to address them and explain fully to them all about

ADDRESSING SOLDIERS AT TUNGURU.

Intriguing of Egyptians.

our Expedition. The soldiers answered him enthusiastically, and assured him of their loyalty and devotion.

On my expressing great surprise at the whole affair, Emin told me more fully of the trouble he was in about his soldiers of the 1st Battalion at Rejaf. The story was as follows:—

Nearly four years before, after the repulse of the Mahdi's people by Emin's soldiers, he wished to abandon all the northern stations of Makraka, Lado, and Rejaf, and concentrate his people to the south, in order to open a road to Zanzibar. He built a station at Wadelai as his headquarters, and established Tunguru on the lake. The soldiers of the 1st Battalion, however, refused to move, and were further instigated to rebel by an Egyptian officer, another of those concerned in Arabi's rebellion, who said he did not believe that the Government at Khartoum had fallen, and that their Governor was deceiving them. He added, "Why should we be afraid to oppose Emin Pasha, when we in Egypt were not afraid to rebel against the Khedive himself?"

The result was that the soldiers declared they would no longer obey their Governor's orders, and openly rebelled against him. An insulting letter was sent to Emin, signed by all the officers and clerks belonging to the 1st Battalion. Shortly after this, two attempts were made by a certain Ali Aga Djabor, a Soudanese captain of the 1st Battalion, to capture Emin, and carry him off in chains to Rejaf. Since that time the 1st Battalion had defied their Governor, and had from time to time sent him insulting letters. Some of the Egyptian and Soudanese officers established themselves in Makraka and the countries round, where they led the lives of bandit chiefs, and treated the natives with great cruelty.

The 2nd Battalion declared themselves loyal and faithful to their Governor, and Emin told me he trusted the soldiers implicitly, and was sure of their obedience to his orders. At the same time he said there were certain officers of the 2nd Battalion, chiefly Egyptians, whom he knew were unfriendly to him.

He spoke very strongly about the Egyptian officers and clerks, of whom there were some fifty-six in the Province, and complained bitterly of the policy of the Egyptian Government, which had turned his Province into a sort of Botany Bay, to which all the scum of Egypt had been banished. By his showing, there was scarcely an Egyptian in the Province who was not at that moment undergoing a sentence of banishment from Egypt for such crimes as murder, rebellion, or highway robbery.

This was a very great revelation to me, for though we all knew, from what he had told us at N'sabe, that things were somewhat difficult in his Province, we had no idea that rebellion had taken such a hold on his people. I was further surprised that Dr. Junker, who was in the country when the rebellion of the 1st Battalion broke out, should have said nothing about it in Europe. From Captain Casati I got a further insight into things, and felt convinced there would be trouble. He told me that Emin could not, or would not, see how serious the position of affairs in the country had become.

When Suliman Aga returned to the station, I sent for him, and spoke to him about leaving the country. He said, " Where the Pasha goes, my soldiers and I follow " ; he put his two hands together so as to form a circle, and said, " These are my soldiers, and the Pasha goes in the middle, that is the way we will travel, by whatever road the Pasha wishes."

He spoke of what had happened in the station during his absence, and said what an endless source of trouble the Egyptians, and particularly the clerks, had ever been to the Governor, but he said their ideas by no means represented the ideas of the Soudanese, who were dead against them.

The next day Emin ordered all the people to be mustered, in order that I might address them, and read them the Khedive's and Nubar Pasha's letters, and also Stanley's proclamation to the soldiers, which were as follows :—

" *To His Excellency Mehmed Emin,*
"*Mudir of Hatalastiva.*

" Some time ago I commended you for your bravery and for the stand you and your officers and soldiers made, and for your victory over the adversities which beset you, I have rewarded you by conferring upon you the exalted rank of a general, and I have confirmed every promotion you have conferred on your officers, and have informed you of all this by my sovereign letter of November 29th, 1886, No. 31. And most certainly this letter reached you, together with the post forwarded by

our Prime Minister, His Excellency Nubar Pasha.
I am very pleased with your good behaviour and
with whatever you have done, you, your officers and
soldiers, and therefore my Government has busied
itself with the means to extricate you, and save you
if possible from the straits in which you find yourself.
And now there has been constituted a force, under the
direction of Mr. Stanley, the famous savant, who is
known in all parts of the world for his great qualities
and pre-eminence as a traveller. This Expedition is
now ready to start for you, and with it whatever
you are in need of in the way of provisions of every
description, to bring you, your officers and soldiers, to
Egypt, by the road Mr. Stanley considers is most
preferable and easiest to march on. Therefore I
command you, by this my order, sent by the hands of
Mr. Stanley, to make known to you all these things,
that after the arrival of this you will communicate
them to your officers and soldiers, and read before
them my Sovereign greetings with the intention to
inform them of this. At the same time I give to
you, to your officers and soldiers, full liberty to rest
where you are, or to do your best to come out with
the Expedition which is now sent to you. Our
Government has decided to pay you and all the
employés, officers and soldiers, all the appointments
and allowances due to you. If, however, any one,
officer or soldier, wishes to rest in the country, he is
free to do so, but he does so on his own responsibility,
and must not in future expect any assistance from
this Government. And now make them understand
all this distinctly, and communicate it word for word
to all your officers and soldiers, in order that every

one may make up his mind. This is our Sovereign Order.

"MOHAMMED TEWFIK."

"*Eight Jumad Owel*, 1304.

"*To His Excellency Mehmed Emin Pasha, Governor of the Equatorial Province.*

"I have sent you by means of the English Consulate at Zanzibar, a letter from our August Sovereign, by which he thanks you for the bravery and courage shown by you, your officers and soldiers, by which he commends you for your gallantry, perseverance and victory over the adversities which beset you, and by which he expressed his appreciation of you, and conferred on you the exalted rank of a general, and confirmed the promotions and rewards you have conferred on your officers. At the same time I informed you that an Expedition would be sent out; and now this Expedition has been constituted under the direction of Mr. Stanley, who will hand you this letter, and this Expedition is now ready to start to you . . . for Egypt by the road which seems best to Mr. Stanley. . . . Our August Sovereign gives you, your officers and soldiers who are with you, full liberty . . . to be able to come back with the Expedition which is now sent to you. But you must understand and make it understood at the same time by all your officers, soldiers and others, that if any one wishes to stay in the country where he is now, he is free to do so, but he will do it on his own responsibility, and need not expect the slightest assistance from this Government in future. And this is what our August Sovereign wishes you to make distinctly understood to any one wishing to stay there. There is no need to inform you that we will pay you, your officers, soldiers and civil servants, the wages and allowances due to you, in consequence of our August Master's having confirmed all your ranks. This is all, and I hope Mr. Stanley will find you in good health and safe. This is my sincere wish and what I wish you all. Written 9th Jumah Owel, 1304, corresponding to Feb. 2nd, 1887. No. 2.

" NUBAR,
" *Reis Medglis en Nuzar* "
(*i.e.* President of the Council of Ministers).

The blanks in Nubar's letters were owing to some parts of the letter being erased by damp.

It will be seen from these letters that no direct order was given to Emin or his people to leave the Province, nor was any promise of employment given to them when they reached Egypt. The letter of Nov. 29th, 1886, which the Khedive speaks of in his letter, never reached Emin.

The following is Stanley's address to the soldiers :—

" *Soldiers of Emin Pasha.*

" After a long journey from Zanzibar, I have at last reached your Nyanza, and seen your Pasha. I have come expressly at the command of the Khedive Tewfik, to lead you out of this country and show you the way to Egypt. For you must know that the river el Abiad is closed, that Khartoum is in the hands of the followers of Mohammed Achmet, that the great Pasha Gordon and all his people were killed over three years ago, and that the country and river between Wady Halfa and the Bahr Ghazal is occupied by your enemies and by the rebels.

"Four times have the Khedive and your friends made attempts to help you. First Gordon Pasha was sent to Khartoum to bring you all home, but before he could safely leave Khartoum, that city was taken and he himself killed.

"Next, the English soldiers came near to Khartoum to try and help Gordon Pasha, but they were four days too late, for Gordon was dead and Khartoum was lost.

"Next came Dr. Fischer, by way of the Nyanza of Uganda, but he found too many enemies in the path, and returnèd home and died.

"Next came Dr. Lenz, by way of the Congo, but he could not find men enough to carry his goods, and he also went home.

"I tell you these things to prove to you that you have not been forgotten in Egypt. No, the Khedive and his vizier Nubar Pasha have always kept you in mind though they could not reach you. They have heard from your Pasha, by way of Uganda, how bravely you have held to your posts, and how staunch you have been to your duties as soldiers.

"Therefore they sent me to tell you this, and to say to you that you are well remembered and that your reward is awaiting you. At the same time, the Khedive says that if you think the road is too long, or are afraid of the journey, that you may stay here, but if you do so you are no longer his soldiers, and that your pay stops at once, and that if any trouble befall you hereafter you are not to expect any help from him. Should you decide to obey him and follow me to Egypt, I am to show you the way to Zanzibar, and there put you on board a steamer, and take you to Suez, and thence to Cairo, and that your pay continues until you arrive in Egypt, and that all promotions made here will be secured to you, and all rewards promised you here will be paid in full.

"I send one of my officers, Mr. Jephson, to read to you this message, and that you may know that he comes from me I lend him my sword. I now go back a little way to collect all my people and goods, and bring them here. After a few months—Inshallah—I shall return to hear what you have to say. If you say, 'Let us go to Egypt,' I will then show you a safe road, and will accompany you and not leave you until you stand before the Khedive. If you say, 'We shall not leave this country,' then I will bid you farewell and return to Egypt with my own people, and give the Khedive your answer.

"May God have you in his safe keeping.

"This is from your good friend,

"STANLEY."

The soldiers, clerks, and employés were all drawn up in line, and were dressed in their smartest uniforms and clothes. They really looked extremely well, with five Turkish flags flying, and the trumpeters in their bright red suits drawn up at the head of the line. As Emin and I approached, the flags were dipped while the trumpeters played the Khedivial Hymn. I then spoke to them, through Binza, and made them a short address, telling them the origin of the Expedition and a few of our experiences on the road, and the reason why Stanley had sent me to speak to them. I then called upon the clerk of the station to read the Khedive's and Nubar Pasha's letters, which were in Arabic, and after these were finished I read them Stanley's address.

When I had ended several men made short speeches all expressive of their loyalty and devotion to their Governor. After telling them I would send for them to-morrow to receive their decision, as to whether they elected to stay in the country or leave with us, they gave three cheers for the Khedive, and were dismissed.

Accordingly the next day I had all the people in to hear their decision.

First came Suliman Aga, the head of the Regular soldiers at Tunguru, and chief of the Station, he brought with him his lieutenant and six non-commissioned officers. I further explained to them that the evacuation of this country would not be an easy thing, and that they would have to work hard on the road if they came out with us. I then asked them if they wished to go to Egypt; to which they replied, they had talked it all over amongst themselves, and had decided if the Pasha stayed, they stayed; if the Pasha went, they went. Ibrahim Aga, the chief of the Irregulars, next came in with his non-commissioned officers, and to my question as to whether they wished to go to Egypt or not, they returned the same answer as the Regulars had given me. These people came from the country round about Dongola, and were the most useful of Emin's people. Then followed the clerks and civil employés, who gave me precisely the same answer as their predecessors.

It was plain to me, therefore, that the feeling of these people was not for going to Egypt.

They all spoke most respectfully of Effendina (the Khedive), but he was to them only a person in the clouds. They were all told he was their Sultan, and that the flag they were so fond of flying on every occasion was his flag, but all they knew of him was that he sent them fine words, but through all these years had neither helped them nor sent them their pay. They wanted a real man, whom they could look up to as their Governor, who would look after them and clothe them. The Khedive's letter only promised to give them their pay up to the time they arrived in Egypt, and said nothing whatever about future employment. Moreover, most of these so-called Soudanese had been recruited from the Dinka, Madi, Boru, Shefalu, Niam-Niam, Bongo, Makraka, Monbuttu, or Moru tribes, and the country was more or less like their own homes, where they could keep up large households and live on the fat of the land. Even if they had been promised employment in Egypt, they could never have supported their people on their pay, and they would never be willing to get rid of their women and children. Egypt offered no attractions for them whatever, so it was hardly surprising when they answered that they wished to follow their Governor, who had looked after them and clothed them all these years.

With the Egyptians it was of course different, and Emin thought they would go out under any circumstances.

Suliman Aga afterwards suggested that it would be a good thing, if this country was no longer considered tenable, that the people with their Governor should be conducted to a country within reach of the sea, and left to settle there. It was peculiar that he should have thought of this plan, for Emin had made it himself in one of his letters to Nubar Pasha some months before.

Stanley, when he reached the lake, had made three propositions to the Pasha, one of which was a suggestion that Emin should take his people and settle them in Kavirondo, on the Victoria Nyanza, if they did not wish to go to Egypt. This plan, therefore, of Suliman Aga's agreed with both, but I did not say anything about it, as I had been strictly enjoined to understand that our first duty was to the Khedive.

Owing to Emin's having a good deal to do after being away so long, and my constant attacks of fever, we were unable to get away from Tunguru till June 25th. It was decided that we should go to Wadelai by land, as Emin wished to settle some difficulty which had arisen between his people and a native chief, whose country we should pass through on our way to Wadelai. The soldiers were all drawn up as usual, to salute the Governor, and at 6.30 we started from the station.

Emin rode a donkey and I an Abyssinian mule, which was lent me by the apothecary, Vita Hassan; it was a handsome little animal, like a black Shetland pony, and carried me very well. Emin, whilst riding, took observations every few minutes with a prismatic compass; he was anxious to lay down the road between Tunguru and Wadelai, and so complete a survey of all the roads connecting his stations.

The country through which we passed was a fine open plain, lying between the mountains and the lake, dotted here and there with trees and flowering shrubs. After a couple of hours we came upon a fine patch of acacia jungle, very dark and abounding with game. This we skirted and reached a part of the plain more thickly covered with trees and shrubs, among which there were flocks of springbok and kudu feeding, and guinea fowl in plenty. All along the road were footprints of elephants, leopards, and hyenas, showing clearly in the soft mud.

At about ten o'clock we got out again into the open plain, where there were a good many villages in little clusters, and large herds of goats might be seen feeding in different parts of the plain, each herd being tended by two or three natives fully armed with bows and spears. Round each village, or more correctly speaking, round each circular group of huts, was a boma or fence of dry mimosa bushes, the branches of which were covered so completely by a network of cobwebs that each village seemed encircled by a curtain of the finest white gauze. The huts were of the usual beehive shape, very untidily made of grass. The natives plaster the inside to a height of three feet with a mixture of mud and cow dung, forming a sort of dado all round the hut. Each hut had a peculiar porch which looked like a huge poke bonnet. With the exception of a few patches of ground planted with pot-herbs, there were no signs of cultivation near the villages. The natives fear the raids of Kaba-regga's people, and have their fields of millet, Indian corn and potatoes in the distant hills, keeping only a small quantity for present use in the little granaries which stand in the middle of the villages. We stopped half an hour and rested under the shade of a large fig-tree close to the principal village belonging to Boki, the chief of this district. The natives brought quantities of cold clear water in large earthen crocks for the men, and for me a good sized bowl of curdled milk, which was very refreshing after the long ride in the sun. From here we got a good view of the end of the lake, which gradually narrowed to where the Nile made its exit, and flowed away, a good-sized river, in an almost due northerly direction. We could see it in the distance winding like a silver ribbon through the plain. To the east we got a distant view of some splendid mountains in Unyoro, rising in three sharply-defined peaks, which must have been 7000 feet high. On the opposite side of the river was the site of the station of Magungu, which had been abandoned three years before on account of Kaba-regga's hostility. A pleasant breeze came up from the lake and stirred all the leaves of our tree, which gave us a delightful feeling of coolness and repose.

Just before we started, Boki's favourite wife came and prostrated herself before the Pasha, and begged him to release her husband who was in prison at Tunguru. It appeared that Emin five months before had intrusted a letter for Kaba-regga to Boki, who promised to deliver it. He paid him handsomely in ivory for his trouble, but a month before the letter was found in Boki's hut by one of the soldiers, who brought it to the Pasha, so Boki was consigned to prison. In answer to her request Emin promised that her husband should be released, he was much too soft-hearted to be able to withstand the prayers of a weeping woman.

After resting an hour we started on again, for we

BOKI'S WIFE INTERCEDES FOR HER HUSBAND.

had a long way to go before we reached our camping-place. The plain through which we passed was thickly covered with acacias and jasmine. These acacias are covered with long sharp prickles, growing out of a sort of round hollow ball, in which numbers of small black ants make their nests. What with the prickles and the ants an acacia thicket is an unpleasant place to ride through. This kind of acacia never grows into a large tree, but only reaches a height varying from fifteen to twenty feet; they have feathery, white blossoms, which have a very good smell, and with it and the scent of the jasmine the whole air was heavy with perfume.

There were numberless butterflies flitting about among the blossoms, but we could not stop to catch any, much to my regret, for there were several kinds which I had not seen before. Late in the afternoon we passed over two broad, flat, low-lying plains, scarcely two feet above the level of the river. At high Nile these are generally several feet under water, but though this was just the time for high Nile, there had been so little rain that year that the river was scarcely higher than at low Nile. Emin remarked that he had never seen such a low Nile since he had been in the Province, and we talked about the probabilities of its being a very low Nile in Egypt. Since then I heard in Cairo that the Nile of 1888 was the lowest Nile known in Egypt for fifteen years. From this it may be seen, even at that distance from its mouth, what a great influence the White Nile has upon the main river. At 4.30 we reached a district belonging to a chief called Okello, who knew of our coming, and had prepared a cluster of huts for us. He was a fat, jolly old man, but was very dirty and smelt badly. He was formerly a persistent enemy of Emin, but he had completely come round, and he now counted him as one of his best friends. We dined off kabobs, which are little lumps of meat and fat, skewered alternately on a stick and roasted in front of the fire,—a very favourite dish among the Turks. We turned into bed early, for I was tired, having come sixteen miles in the blazing sun, half of which distance I had done on foot.

Next morning we started off at four o'clock. The sun had not yet risen and it was beautifully fresh and cool. The country we passed through was very pretty and slightly hilly, but there were absolutely no streams on the way. At eight o'clock we stopped in a village, the chief of which was Amadji, a fine high-bred looking young fellow, and nicely dressed in well-cured skins. I noticed here that most of the women had a peculiar ornament of clear white quartz stuck in their lips. These ornaments, clear as crystal and beautifully polished, were some three inches long and moved up and down in the most comical manner when the wearer was speaking.

Amadji sent ten of his men with us, each carrying a large earthen lota of water to give our people to drink on the way. The road led through a beautiful park-like country, and along the ridge of some low wooded hills, from which we occasionally got lovely views of the river. We reached our camping place early, which was in a fine grove of tamarind trees, and Emin's men made us large grass huts in an incredibly short time. Below us lay the river, with its banks fringed with papyrus swamps, from which, towards evening, clouds of mosquitos and insects of all sorts rose and drove us at an early hour to take refuge under our mosquito curtains.

All night long leopards and hyænas were prowling about the camp, and several times during the night there was a stir to drive them away. The next day, after going about a couple of hours, we came to a large group of villages, governed by a chief whose name was Wadelai. The district round and Emin's station were called after him. We found him waiting for us in front of one of the villages with some of his chiefs. He was an enormously fat old man, with a good-natured face, dressed in a long dirty robe like a nightgown ; I have never before seen a native so fat, ordinarily in their own countries they are thin.

We waited here for some time, as Emin had several matters to arrange with him. When the " Shauri " was finished we started on, and soon got a distant view of Wadelai station, the place from which Emin last wrote, and upon which the attention of the civilized world was fixed when we left England. It was situated at the top of an isolated hill, 300 feet high, which rose abruptly from the river. We passed through a beautiful little acacia forest, the acacias were not of the prickly sort, but grew into large forest trees. There was no undergrowth, but only grass, upon which the sunlight fell through the trees in little chequered patches. A delightfully cool breeze blew through it, and tumbled showers of white blossoms about us.

CHAPTER III.

FROM WADELAI TO DUFILÉ.

Arrival at Wadelai—Emin's compound and house—Signor Marco—Farida—Emin's scientific proclivities—Wadelai Station—The Wa-huma—Reminiscences of Sir Samuel Baker—Nyadué, or the Morning Star—Deputation from 1st Battalion—Endeavour to relieve Fort Bodo—Faratch Aga—State of affairs at Rejaf—Hamad Aga's estimate of Emin—Doubts as to Emin's wisdom—Faratch Aga's shame—Emin acts a farce—Ferocity of Crocodiles—Bari crocodile-hunters—Answer of soldiers of Wadelai—Emin's ivory—Start for Dufilé—Blocks on the Nile—We reach Dufilé—Curious custom—Description of Dufilé Station—Government buildings—Hawashi Effendi—Hawashi Effendi's estimate of Egyptian guile—An Arab feast—Hawashi Effendi's warning—More doubts.

At 11.30 we reached Wadelai. The soldiers were all drawn up and saluted their Governor in the usual way. This being Emin's head-quarters and the seat of government, the soldiers were all picked men and were much better dressed than those in the other stations, and there was a perfect regiment of clerks and officials of all sorts dressed in flowing white cotton cloth robes. A guard of honour, playing a lively tune, escorted us through the station to Emin's divan, which was a large round hut made of bamboo; it was nicely furnished and had a homelike air about it. Two large bookcases full of books greatly added to the look of comfort. Here all the officials, military and civil, came in to greet

INTERIOR OF EMIN'S HOUSE.

Emin and me, and the usual disagreeable kissing of hands had to be gone through. A long line of them entered at one door and after greeting us passed out through the other. This ceremony being over, Signor Marco, a Greek merchant, who had formerly come into the Province to trade, but was now an enforced resident, as all the roads to the coast were closed, came to see us. He looked after the Pasha's house and transacted his private business for him when he was away. He now came in to make his report, and brought Emin's little girl, Farida, with him. Some years before, the Pasha had married an Abyssinian lady, and by this marriage there were two children, a boy and a girl. The boy died soon after he was born, and his mother died shortly after Farida's birth, of some internal complaint.

Emin, who seemed to be very devoted to the child, brought her in his arms to see me, and told me of his wife's death, which even after a lapse of three years he seemed to feel very deeply. He said, "The little Farida is all that is left to me in the world now." She was a pretty little girl, not darker in complexion than her father, and greatly resembling him. She was dressed picturesquely, like a little Arab girl, but looked exceedingly delicate.

A nice hut had by the Governor's orders been built ready for me, and was in the same courtyard as the divan, round which was a pretty shady garden, full of lime, orange, pomegranate and custard-apple trees, all in full bearing. Some fine flamboyant and acacia trees, of a species which grows in Uganda, were also planted near the divan, and gave a pleasant shade. In the middle of the courtyard was a rain gauge, and a little building like a summer-house, in which were Emin's aneroids, wet and dry thermometers and other instruments. He always took meteorological observations three times a day, and had observations for the last seven or eight years; these notes should be extremely interesting and valuable to scientists.

Opening from this outer court was an inner courtyard enclosing from ten to fifteen huts, most of which were occupied by Emin's servants and retainers; there were also numbers of granaries which contained corn and sesame for the household. Chickens, ducks, goats, guinea-fowls, cats and dogs, grey parrots and a tame eagle wandered about this inner court-yard. It was a perfect little village in itself.

My hut was cool and nicely furnished in a rough way, there was an angarep, and native-made chairs and tables, in the drawers of which was a great collection of dried frogs and beetles, and all round the walls I hung some magnificent leopard skins which had been brought me as presents by the soldiers. There was, however, an unpleasant smell, and going to the back of my hut to see what it was, I was further reminded of Emin's scientific proclivities. There lay a large basket full of imperfectly cured skulls, which were some of the Pasha's anthropological specimens of the different tribes in his Province. Their destination was the British Museum, where they were to be sent for comparison with the skulls of other tribes. I felt strongly tempted to throw them over the wall; but remembering Emin's tenderness for such things, and the probable labour with which he had collected them, I sent for a servant and they were removed by several black women with much talking and laughter.

Wadelai itself was a large station, and must have contained nearly 2000 inhabitants; it had fine broad streets, and the whole was surrounded by a ditch and earthworks. At each corner of the station, the planning of which showed great care, were small forts flanking the ditch, each being armed with a mountain gun. It was built in exactly the same style as M'swa station, which I have already described, and was situated on a hill rising abruptly from the river, which was divided here into two channels by an island some mile and a half long.

The country opposite was exceedingly beautiful, all grass, but well wooded; it sloped gently up from the river till it formed a long ridge of low hills, beyond which is the country of the Shulis, one of the finest and most peaceful tribes about here. The country round Wadelai is occupied by the Lur tribe, which also possesses a small tract of land on the other side of the river between it and the hills. Here also were a good many of the Wa-huma tribe, or Wa-tusi as they are called in this country, of whom Stanley has written. They are a nomadic tribe, whose only occupation is to tend their flocks and herds; they are supposed to be of royal blood, Stanley calls them Shepherd Kings.

Years ago, Speke started a theory that these Wa-huma have sprung from the Galla tribes, but Emin inclines to the belief that the Gallas are descendants of the Wa-huma.

They are a tall, high-bred looking people, with comparatively sharp noses and thin lips, a great contrast to the Lurs, who are as a rule, a short thick-set race, not much given to war, but intelligent and fairly industrious.

All round the station were extensive fields of corn and sesame belonging to Emin's people. Sesame is

VIEW FROM WADELAI.

a plant like a balsam, from the seeds of which a fine oil is expressed, and is much used by the people for cooking.

All along the side of the river, for a distance of two miles, lay the station gardens, in which were grown a variety of native herbs and vegetables, such as onions, tomatoes, balmias, kolokasias, peas, and several sorts of beans.

This being the seat of government, Emin had a

great deal to do, and immense numbers of letters to answer which had accumulated during his long absence. Nearly every day I had an attack of fever, it seemed to have regularly got into my system. Emin, who is a doctor of the old-fashioned school, gave me a strong emetic which did wonders, and for a time drove away the fever.

Even during the few weeks I had been in the Province, I could not help being struck with the fact that nearly all the good and lasting things had been brought into the Province by Sir Samuel Baker. I constantly heard about him and Lady Baker, and in speaking to the soldiers many of them said, with an air of pride, "We are not Gordon's or Emin's, but Baker's soldiers." Soldiers coming from Latooka and Unyoro have often spoken to me about the Bakers, he as Mlidju, or the Bearded One, and Lady Baker as Nyadué, or the Morning Star, by which name she was called in admiration of her fair-haired beauty. Many of the old soldiers were glad enough to gossip about them. One old fellow told me that Baker Pasha was a real man, and always led his own men in a fight; he told me he was very good to his people, but awfully severe, and then added, with a smile, "Baker Pasha was the head, but Nyadué was the hat." There was a story which was told about Lady Baker. A certain Faratch Aga, a Soudanese sergeant belonging to Baker Pasha's body guard, having twice deserted was condemned by Baker to be shot. The man was bound to a tree, and a squad of soldiers told off to shoot him. Lady Baker, hearing of this, ran out of her hut into the square, her hair flying in the wind, and with uplifted hand stayed the execution of Faratch until she had pleaded for his pardon from Sir Samuel Baker. The man was pardoned and released, and from that time there was no more devoted servant to the Bakers than he.

I cannot vouch for the truth of these stories. I merely repeat them as I heard them whilst gossiping with Emin's people. But though the work which Baker so gallantly begun twenty years ago was about to fall to the ground, his name, and that of Lady Baker, still lived fresh in the memories of the people.

Among the letters Emin found awaiting him here on his arrival was one from Hamad Aga, the Major of the rebellious 1st Battalion of soldiers in Rejaf. This man had always been loyal to Emin, but he was quite unable to stem the tide of rebellion which had been stirred up by the Egyptian officers, and had simply been swept along, against his will, with the flood. He wrote to say that the officers of the 1st Battalion, hearing that an expedition had arrived at the south end of the lake, with ammunition from Egypt, to the people, were now convinced that their Governor had been right, and wished to apologize for what they had done, and make their submission to him. They had therefore decided to send him (Hamad Aga), Faratch Aga, a captain, Sheik Moorajan, the chief priest, and a lieutenant as their envoys to the Governor, to ask his pardon, and to beg him to come down to Rejaf, bringing with him Mr. Stanley's representative, whom they were all desirous of seeing. Their Governor might dictate his own terms to them, and they would obey all that he commanded. Emin therefore decided to await the coming of the envoys, who were to arrive in ten days' time. He was at that time exceedingly ill. There was something wrong with his heart, and he experienced, on making the least exertion, great difficulty in breathing, so that he was glad to remain quiet for a few days. He was very low about himself, and said that unless he could get rest and quiet in a cool climate, he felt he had only a year or two more to live. He told me that the thirteen years of hard work and anxiety which he had spent in Africa, especially the last five years since he had been abandoned and left to his own resources, had completely worn him out.

Mindful, however, that time was slipping on—it was then July 7th—and there were only a few weeks to the time when by my promise to Nelson I should be nearing Fort Bodo, I spoke to the people about building a station at N'sabe, and going on with me to the fort to bring up the officers and goods. To their Governor and to me they answered that before taking any steps in that direction, they would wish to hear what their "brethren" in the northern stations had to say; moreover, it was harvest-time, and they could not leave before reaping their crops. I thought this a somewhat peculiar answer to give to an order from their Governor, but my eyes were being gradually opened to the fact that Emin could no longer command in his own Province. I could see that the 2nd Battalion, in whom he trusted, were not obedient in important matters, though they were ready enough to bow before their Governor, and do his bidding in all minor details. My promise had been given to Stanley that should Emin give me sufficient soldiers and carriers, I would relieve Fort Bodo, and build a station at N'sabe. Without soldiers, without carriers, I could do nothing towards fulfilling my promise.

I could only therefore go on to the northern stations, speak to the people there, and then return to Wadelai, to again urge the soldiers to help me.

Emin seemed very hopeful about the embassy which was coming from Rejaf. We heard that the officers of the 1st Battalion were tired of the long reign of disorder there, that all the natives in the country round had retired, owing to their being badly treated by the rebels, and that there were now no cattle to be got. The soldiers' grain crops had moreover failed, owing to the want of rain, and things there were in a generally uncomfortable state.

It appeared that this Faratch Aga, who was coming to see Emin, was the very man whom Lady Baker saved. Knowing of his devotion to the Bakers, I determined to use it as a sort of moral lever to move him to act loyally to his Mudir. Emin told me that when the envoys came, he did not wish to see them, but desired me to see them, and to try and show them the enormity of their crime in rebelling. He intended to forgive them in the end, if he felt sure of the sincerity of their expressions of regret for what they had done, but he did not wish to appear to forgive them too easily. After speaking to them, he wished me to tell them that their Governor was very incensed against them, but that I would intercede with him for them. It was a farce, but as he wished it, I agreed to carry it out. Soon after the officers arrived, Hamad Aga came in to see me. He was a tall, thin Soudanese, with a nice expression and grey hair. He gave me a short account of all that had happened at Rejaf, and told me things were in a very bad state there, and that there was little or no food in the country round, owing to the ill-treatment of the natives by the rebels. He said that the soldiers robbed right and left, and no one was able to check them, that they were ready enough to obey their officers in anything that was bad, but if any order was given with a view to checking the wholesale robbery of the natives it was totally disregarded. He deplored the influence the Egyptian officers and clerks had always exercised in the country, and said that the whole of the mutiny against the Governor in Rejaf had been stirred up by an Egyptian officer, a certain Mustapha Effendi, who had been sent up to the Province for being concerned in Arabi's rebellion. He spoke very highly of Emin, and said he had always been most self-sacrificing to his people, but that he was not firm enough with them. These people, he said, required the rod, and that the Governor never gave them. According to Hamad Aga the people were tired of the long reign of confusion, and were sincere in their protestations of amendment, and were most anxious to see me at Rejaf and hear from my own lips our story. He wound up by saying, " All will come right, now that you have arrived." This I very much doubted, for I was getting terribly sceptical about these people. On the one side I had the Pasha, with his vast experience, assuring me that his people were good and faithful, and to back up what he said there was the fact that they had repulsed the attack of the Mahdi's General Keremallah, and had held the country ever since, though cut off from all supplies. Again, too, all Europe was ringing with praises of the Pasha's wisdom and firmness, and we had left home and people with the strongest enthusiasm for the man who for so many years had held out against all difficulties, and whom we believed to be one of the most sagacious men in Africa. On the other side, a still small voice within me whispered, "Beware." And yet, I thought, who am I, with my small experience, to set up my opinion against that of this man, of world-wide fame, with his long years of experience and practical administration? Was it wonderful, therefore, that I distrusted my own judgment and for the time being turned a deaf ear to the prompting of that still small voice?

After Hamad Aga had left my hut, Faratch Aga came in to see me, bringing me a present of some finely carved wooden bowls and several large and handsome Monbuttu knives. After the usual compliments had been exchanged, my health tenderly inquired after, and I had admired the workmanship of the presents, he asked me about the Expedition. My story was hardly finished when he inquired eagerly for news of Sir Samuel and Lady Baker, if I knew them, and if they were well. Now, I thought, is the time to apply the moral lever.

I told him that the eyes of all Europe were upon this Expedition, and doubtless Sir Samuel Baker was following all its movements with the deepest interest and would be one of the first, when we returned home, to ask eagerly for news of his former Province and of the people who had fought so bravely for him.

I added, "What will Baker Pasha say, what will Nyadué think, when I tell them you have joined the mutineers in the rebellion against your Governor?"

The tears started to his eyes, and he wrung his hands with a gesture of shame and regret. This was evidently his vulnerable point, for he seemed quite overcome at the thought of the Bakers hearing that he had joined the rebellion.

He told me he had joined the mutiny and put his signature to the insulting letters which had been sent to the Governor, not because he had felt any enmity against the Pasha, but because he had weakly allowed himself to be led on by the others, and had not sufficient moral courage to refuse to join them.

He made profuse promises of amendment for the future, and implored me not to tell Baker Pasha what he had done, but to suspend my judgment until I had seen that he really meant to be loyal after this to the Governor, and cut himself off from his former confederates.

Next morning Hamad Aga, Faratch Aga, the priest, and the other officer came in to see me, and I further explained to them all about the Expedition. Emin had refused to see them when they arrived, and they now asked me to go over with them and intercede with him on their behalf.

Emin received them coldly, and talked with them a long time, upbraiding them with their treachery and insubordination. He told them that for more than three years they had disobeyed his orders and had refused to help him, and now that relief had come and he no longer needed their help, they came to beg his pardon. He ended by saying he would have nothing whatever to do with them, which considerably surprised them, and made them more humble than ever. With tears in their eyes they begged him to forgive them, and made all sorts of promises for the future; however he still refused to listen to them, and left the divan. I then told them I could quite understand the Pasha's not being able to forgive them, for rebellion and ingratitude were the hardest things to forgive. I told them to go back to their quarters, and I would try and lessen the Pasha's feeling of resentment against them. They thanked me and went away dejected but hopeful. It was Emin's idea that if they were forgiven too cheaply they would not afterwards value their pardon sufficiently.

In the evening I heard that Hamad Aga had been preaching to the soldiers and telling them that they must not get drunk while I was in the station, for it would be terrible for the Christian to see them in a drunken state. Poor simple fellow! If he only knew how many so-called Christians get rich in ivory and merchandise by importing gin and making the pagan negroes drunk!

The number of crocodiles in the river here was wonderful. In the daytime the sandbanks in the river were covered with them, and at evening they might be seen swimming about in the river with their noses and heads just above the water. They were very fierce here, and large numbers of women and children were carried off by them every year. They waited till the women had waded into the river up to their knees, to draw water in their earthen jars, and then made a dash at them under water and carried them away. Emin had a stockade, such as one sees in a horse pond, run out into the river into which the crocodiles were unable to enter, and had ordered them to draw water in this enclosure, but the women, for some reason or other, preferred to draw water from the open river, the result was that numbers of them were carried away. I was told they would even laugh and joke about it, and on entering the water call out, " Are you not hungry ? wouldn't you like some meat to-day?" With such people it was useless to take precautions.

There was at that time in the station a family of negroes, belonging to the Bari tribe, who lived entirely by hunting crocodiles. The meat of young crocodiles they ate, the skin they sold for leather, and the teeth for making necklaces; but the part which they most prized was a small gland which contained a strong secretion of musk; this was dried and hung round the neck, and was greatly valued as a charm.

They had a small boy with them, whom they used to send into the water as a decoy, while they themselves hid in the grass. As soon as a crocodile made a dash at the boy, they rushed into the water, and buried a big iron hook to which a rope was attached in the folds of skin under its neck, and having hauled it out of the water, beat it to death with clubs. A crocodile was caught by them, and they brought it up to my hut to show me. It was alive, but had its jaws tied round with rope so that it could not bite. After I had examined it, I undid the rope and let it loose, and it retired into a corner of the compound where it made little dashes, and snapped at every one who approached it. It was afterwards taken away, killed, and stuffed, and put up over the gate of the station. Stuffed crocodiles, put up over the entrance of a courtyard or house, were supposed by these people to bring good luck. I noticed that the crocodiles here and in the lake were of a light greenish colour, with broad bands of black round them.

Whilst at Wadelai I saw a curious wedding custom, which prevails among the Soudanese. Two Soudanese were to be married, when, on the evening before the wedding, a number of young Soudanese gathered in front of the bride's hut, and forming a circle, began to sing and whip each other with hippopotamus hide whips until the blood came. This, it appears, was to show the bride what a plucky race her husband was sprung from.

After a few days Emin sent for Hamad Aga and the other officers from Rejaf, and said he had decided to forgive them if he found they were sincere in their protestations; and he would accompany them to Rejaf, where I would speak to the people. They all professed to be exceedingly grateful and glad that we were to go to Rejaf.

Hamad Aga every day came in to see me, and from the many conversations I had with him, I learned he was one of those who did not like Egypt, and had no wish to go there. He said it would be far better for the people that we should take them to some good country within reach of the sea, and settle them there. This was the second time one of Emin's officers had made this proposition.

As it was decided that we were to go on to Dufilé on our way to Rejaf, I addressed the soldiers and employés before leaving the station. There were over 200 soldiers here and a regiment of clerks and employés, and it was quite a business speaking to them and getting their decision on the subject of leaving or remaining.

I addressed them much in the same way as I had done at Tunguru, and asked them to come in the day following to give me their views about the evacuation of the Province.

They all said, as the people at Tunguru had said, "We will follow our Governor; if he goes, we go; if he stays, we stay."

Kodi Aga, who was the chief of the station, a man in whom Emin placed great reliance, came to me afterwards and said he thought it would be well for the people to follow us to some country nearer civilization, where they could settle down. He said that the people could never support their women and children in Egypt, and they would not be willing to give them up. He added, that of course the Egyptians and such people as had relations there would prefer to go to Egypt. This was the third time this proposition had been made to me, so I could only infer that the feeling, at any rate, of the people in this part of the Province was against going to Egypt.

I again, therefore, had the Soudanese officers and non-commissioned officers up before me, and, speaking to them said, "From what I have heard from certain officers, I understand that it is not your wish and that of the soldiers to go to Egypt, but to follow us with your Governor to a country somewhat nearer the sea, and there to settle down. Is this your wish?" I was answered by a deafening "Aywah" from all.

This answer was conclusive. The feeling was evidently against going to Egypt.

The Egyptians, Circassians, and Khartoum people, however, naturally wished to return to Egypt, where most of them had relations and friends.

Before leaving the station, Kodi Aga took me round the storehouses and showed me the government ivory, of which there were vast quantities, all arranged in different heaps, according to the size of the tusks. There was one tusk shown me which weighed 140 lbs., and was the largest tusk I have ever seen in Africa. Emin told me there were large stores of ivory also in Dufilé, and he had somewhere about 1000 tusks in Monbuttu, which he had left in charge of one of the friendly chiefs of that country. The value of the ivory in government storehouses, he said, was 75,000*l*., but this was estimating it at the rate of 8*s*. a pound, but as the price of ivory is now 12*s*. a lb. at the coast, it would make the real value of the ivory in the Province 112,250*l*.

All this ivory would have to be abandoned, as we could never carry it down to the coast. It was grievous that so much money should have to be thrown away.

The Pasha told me he had for three years given up collecting ivory, as he knew it would never be of any use to him; and had he continued to collect it, he would have had double the amount.

Early on the morning of July 16th we started in

the steamer for Dufilé, which was sixty geographical miles distant from Wadelai. The navigation of the upper river ends there, for a few miles below Dufilé there are large cataracts, and the river flows between two long ranges of mountains in a series of falls and cataracts as far as Rejaf, where it again widens out, and is open for navigation right down to Khartoum. We therefore had to make considerable preparations for a march of seventy-five geographical miles overland to Rejaf.

The river between Wadelai and Dufilé is extremely difficult for navigation, as it divides into innumerable channels, forming islands overgrown with reeds and papyrus, among which a steamer has to thread her way most carefully.

Here and there the river broadens out, forming large lagoons, in which are to be seen numerous herds of hippopotami, plunging and diving, and sending up large jets of spray from their noses.

Heavy rains must have been falling in the countries drained by the higher waters of the river, for in a couple of days it had risen nearly two feet, and had become a deep chocolate colour. The current also was considerably more rapid, and the whole face of the river was covered with floating vegetation, which in some places formed small floating islands, on which I saw herons and different kinds of waterfowl seated. It is this floating vegetation which forms huge blocks in the Nile; these in times gone by, when steamers were running between the upper Provinces and Khartoum, used to stop navigation sometimes for months. The last block which occurred took Lupton Bey two years and a half to clear away with two steamers. Large iron hooks fastened at the end of strong ropes were used in this work. These were hooked into the compressed vegetation, which was dragged away by the steamers and allowed to drift down the river. So compact were these blocks, that dead crocodiles and hippopotami were frequently found when clearing away the vegetation, into which they had been carried by the current and were unable to extricate themselves.

On the way to Dufilé we were obliged to stop at a place called Bora, to take in a fresh supply of wood, which was brought down to the steamer by natives of the Shuli tribe. They were fine, strong, well-developed men, with pleasant, good-natured faces; but had not a vestige of clothing on them, except a few necklaces made of crocodile teeth.

The surrounding country was rather fine, great rolling grass savannas dotted about with Palmyra palms. These bear a large orange fruit, which grows in clusters like cocoa-nuts, and are about the same size. They have a strong smell, very like a melon. They contain a large white kernel, round which grows a sort of orange, stringy flesh, which Emin's people make into a kind of sherbet. It has a sweet, bitter taste, which is very sickly. The natives grind the kernel into flour which they mix with millet flour and make into cakes.

All day we steamed down the river, the banks of which were fringed with vast papyrus swamps, and camped at 8 p.m. on the first solid ground we reached.

Here mosquitoes abounded in such numbers, and were so fierce that we were glad to retire behind our mosquito curtains as soon as dinner was finished.

Arrival at Dufilé.

Next morning, early, we steamed away, and the river again formed into one channel and was very broad and fine. Great numbers of water-birds, herons, pelicans, storks, cranes, and divers perched upon the rocks, of which there were a good many, rising from the bed of the river. Ducks, geese, and moor-hens abounded along the banks, which are here covered with small forests of Ambatch. The wood of this tree is lighter than cork, and is used by the natives for making floats for their fishing lines and baskets.

At midday, on July 14th, we steamed into Dufilé, which was the largest, and one of the oldest established of Emin's stations. The original station was built by Gordon; but Emin, finding it unhealthy, moved it a few hundred yards up river, where the banks were higher. Two wharves built of piles ran out into the river, and against these the two steamers were able to lie.

The soldiers were all drawn up in two lines, and gave us the usual salute when we landed, the Khedivial Hymn being played by the trumpeters. As I landed from the steamer the soldiers cut the throat of a bullock, and I was made to step over the blood, which flowed from it in streams. This, they told me, was the custom among the people when they wished to welcome with honour, a stranger coming into the country for the first time.

We were escorted by the usual guard of honour, into a large square, in the middle of which there were some large trees of the fig tribe, and under these was a raised platform made of earth and enclosed by brick walls about a foot high, looking like a band stand. Here chairs were placed ready for us. We sat down, and sherbet being served, the station officials came to greet us. We then went to our houses, which were situated in a compound some hundred feet square, and surrounded by a boma of bamboos eight feet high. The houses set apart for the Pasha and me were exceedingly well built, and were lofty and cool. The walls were three feet six

LANDING AT DUFILÉ.

thick, and built of sun-dried bricks; there were proper doors and windows with folding shutters, and the floor was strewn with clean white sand; they were the best houses I had seen in the Province. The other huts in the compound were for the kitchen, orderlies and servants. Growing immediately behind the huts were two tall palmyra palms upon which numbers of herons roosted at night, and disturbed us by their angry croaking.

In the cool of the afternoon Hawashi Effendi came over to show me round the station. It was a large square, well-planned station, surrounded on three sides by a ditch twelve feet deep, and fifteen feet broad; the soil which was dug out of the ditch being thrown up inside, forming earthworks some eight feet high; the fourth side was bounded by the river. At each corner of the station was a raised bastion on which was a mountain gun, these bastions flanked the earthworks and commanded the ditch. Two main roads ran crossways through the station, that running up from the river terminating in a large postern-gate, which also served for a guard-room. This was the chief entrance of the station. The other road ran at right angles to this, both ends terminating in small postern-gates, and being side entrances to the station. These gateways were guarded by heavy wooden gates studded with iron. The station, if defended by a determined garrison, would be impregnable, for there were no hills near from which it could be commanded.

At the intersection of these cross-roads was a large square, in the centre of which were three enormous fig-trees. Under these was the raised platform I before mentioned. So dense was the shade, that on the hottest day it was always cool and dark under these trees. This was the general meeting-place of the officers, where they met in the evening to smoke and gossip.

Under these trees, Baker, Gordon, Gessi, Prout, Mason Bey, and all the celebrities of the Equatorial Province, have sat and talked, as they had their coffee and cigarettes and settled the affairs of the

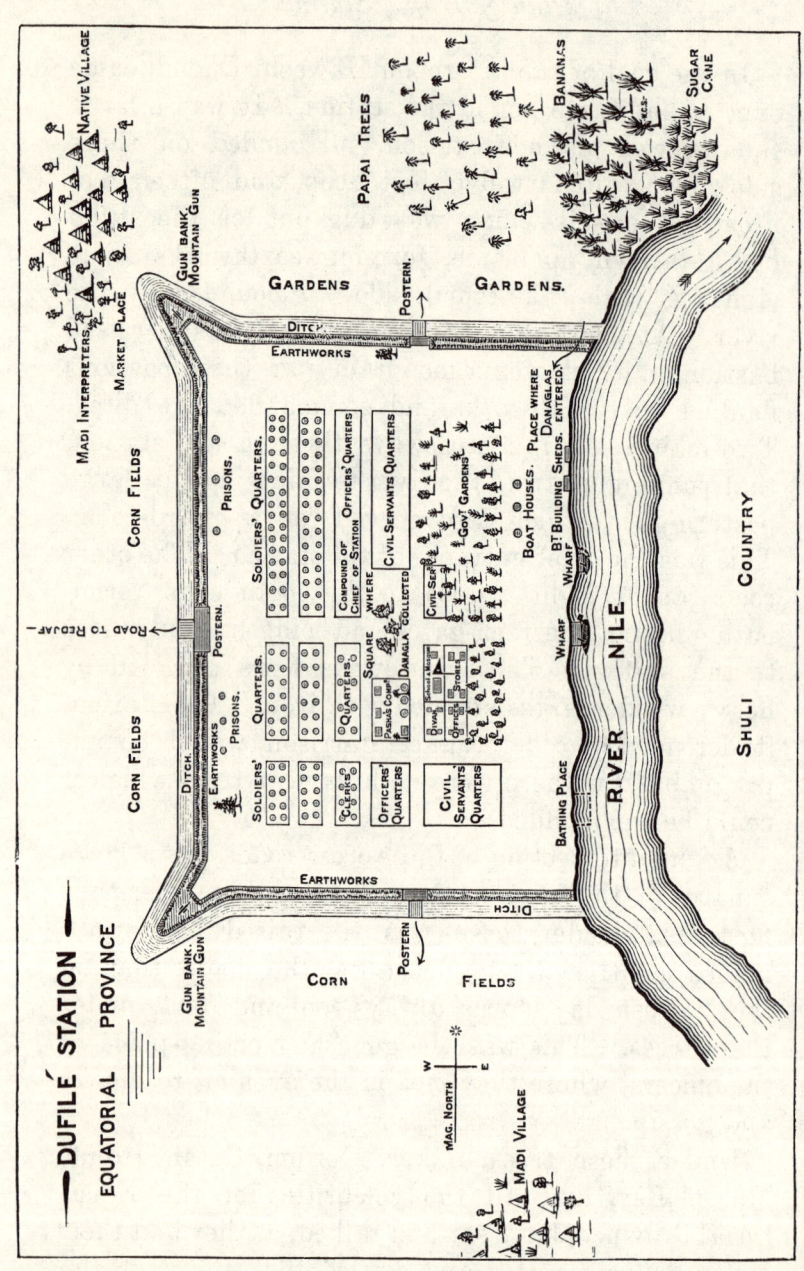

PLAN OF DUFILÉ STATION.

Province. Here too, poor Lucas sat with Emin, and talked sadly of the disappointment of his hopes and the ruin of his Expedition. Emin had a hundred stories of the conversations which had passed beneath these trees; of the times when Gordon sat there with his map and compasses, and unfolded to him plans, sometimes romantic and high-flown, but always bearing the stamp of genius upon them. Scenes were soon to be enacted beneath these trees which would throw all others into the shade.

On one side of the square was situated Emin's compound, and on the opposite side was a large compound containing numbers of huts, which had been built for Stanley and his people under the supposition that they would visit the station. Looking south was the compound of Hawashi Effendi, the chief of the station; in this compound was a beautiful shady grove of large orange and lime trees all in full bearing, and loaded with fruit.

On the side of the square nearest the river, the road broadened out towards the mosque, schools and Government gardens, and a lovely view of the river might be obtained down the road, which was arched over by magnificent trees. The mosque and schools were fine buildings in brick. Both school and mosque were presided over by a priest, who Emin told me had been banished here for being concerned in a murder case in Egypt. He now taught the children of the officials to read and write from the Koran, he had prayers as prescribed five times a day, and was the spiritual adviser and lawyer of the station.

The Government buildings were all built in brick, in

a firm, solid style, and the mosque was really a triumph of architecture for this out-of-the-way country. It was a large square building, neatly finished and whitewashed, and carpeted all over with a very nice kind of matting which was made in the country. It was further decorated with numbers of ostrich eggs, which were suspended in mid-air from the roof, the apex of the roof outside was also decorated with ostrich eggs. These eggs were, I believe, the recognized decoration for mosques, but I do not know what they are supposed to represent. Facing the river were the Government Gardens, which were full of fine fruit trees and vegetables, they were extremely shady and pretty, and were very well kept.

Between the gardens and the river ran a kind of broad esplanade, on which were situated the boat-building sheds and stores for spare machinery, bolts, iron bars, and tools of all sorts, remains of the vast stores which were brought up by Sir Samuel Baker. There was a boat on the slip almost ready for launching, she was of the pattern of the ordinary Nile nuggar, with no ribs, but built of thick rough planks held together by heavy iron bolts. Emin had built a good many of these, and had found them very useful, as the two whale-boats brought up by Sir Samuel Baker were somewhat worn out and unsafe.

There were large gardens belonging to the officials, all round the outside of the station, containing big patches of peas, beans, onions, garlic, balmias, endive, and spinach, and amongst these gardens were great numbers of orange, lime, pomegranate, custard, apple, guava, and papai trees, all bearing freely. In the swampy ground along the river's edge were large plantations of bananas and sugar-cane. For a radius of two miles round the station were vast fields, in which the station people grew ground-nuts, millet, red and white dhurra, tullaboon, sesame, and Indian corn.

All these products did remarkably well here, and wheat and rice fairly so, but these latter were not grown in any quantities.

Near the station was a market-place, where meat, salt, vegetables, mats, etc., were sold. Here also were bootmakers' and carpenters' shops, and sheds where mats and cotton cloth were made. Small villages belonging to the Madi tribe were built near the station; these people lived under the immediate protection of the station, and acted as porters or interpreters when required. The place was thoroughly well kept up, and the station neat and clean, being swept twice a day. In fact the whole station was as complete as it was possible to make it in this country, where people had been left to depend on their own resources for so long a time. There were abundance of cattle and goats, corn and vegetables, and the people lived in a luxury, which they could never afford in Egypt. The Pasha had every reason to be proud of this station, which he had taken so much trouble to develop.

As evening drew on we sat under the trees in the square, and, when coffee and cigarettes had been served, Hawashi Effendi came up to gossip.

This man was an Egyptian, a bimbashi or Major, and was the senior officer of Emin's troops. He was banished here for selling government stores to the enemy, in the war against Abyssinia. Like most Egyptians, he was a great scoundrel; but, unlike the usual type, he worked himself, and made others under him work too. He was greatly disliked by his people, for he was exceedingly high-handed and grasping; but he was most useful to Emin, for he obeyed orders, and if the Pasha told him to do a thing, Emin knew it would be done.

There was something very cynical about Hawashi Effendi's scoundrelism, he was not the least ashamed of it. He was telling me what blackguards the Egyptians were, upon which Emin looked at him and asked, "And you?" "Oh," said Hawashi Effendi, "you know, your Excellency, I am just as bad as the rest." Turning to me, he went on to say, "You are quite a stranger in this country, so bear in mind what I am going to tell you, and be warned by what I say. In this country there are only Soudanese and Egyptians. If a Soudanese comes at you with scowls on his face and a loaded gun, whilst on the other hand an Egyptian comes to you with a carpet and a friendly salutation, turn to the Soudanese, he with his loaded gun will do you less harm than the Egyptian with his smiles and carpet."

Hawashi Effendi gave a very smart dinner that night in my honour. Chairs were placed in his divan round a small low table upon which was a large brass tray. Round this Emin and myself, Hawashi Effendi, Hamad Aga, and Vita Hassan, the apothecary, sat and dipped our fingers into the dishes of food which were brought.

The great dish, the *pièce de résistance*, was a goat roasted whole and stuffed with onions, groundnuts and beans. Hawashi Effendi seized it in his hands and wrenched off the legs and shoulders; he then broke its back, pouring out all the stuffing from the stomach into the dish. It was a highly unappetizing-looking operation, for the grease oozed through his fingers as he tore it to pieces. This dish, however, I found very good eating, particularly the stuffing of ground-nuts. There were a great number and variety of dishes, some of which were rather liquid and sloppy, and I, being unused to this style of eating, found some difficulty in getting the food to my mouth. The great fault in the cooking was that everything was swimming with butter or oil, and as it is considered the height of bad manners not to eat freely of every dish your host provides, I rose from dinner with the feeling of being perfectly stuffed. After dinner basins were brought round, and a sort of bean powder, which forms a lather like soap, was provided to wash our hands with. When coffee had been served I took my pipe and went outside, where I had a long conversation with Hawashi Effendi about affairs in the Province. He had a bad word to say for most people, but spoke well of the Pasha, though he said he was not sufficiently firm with the people, who imposed on him by their politeness and protestations of loyalty, while all the time they were working and intriguing against him. He said that though he did not like Hamad Aga, the Major of the 1st Battalion, he thought he was to be trusted, though, he added, " He has no influence with his officers or soldiers."

In the soldiers and officers he had no confidence, and warned me to be careful how the Governor and I ventured amongst them. He wondered, he said, why we should go down there. I explained to him that the soldiers in the southern stations had refused to help me to build a station at N'sabe and relieve Fort

Bodo until they had heard what their brethren in the northern stations of Rejaf and Kirri had said. And I told him that the Pasha considered there was nothing for us to do but to go down and see them. He concluded by saying that now I had come, he trusted all would be well, but warned me to be careful how the Governor and I trusted ourselves among the soldiers of the 1st Battalion.

This conversation had a great effect on me, for it strengthened the doubt, which was daily growing stronger in my mind, that Emin had not grasped the situation, and did not really know his people. Stray words which had been let drop by different people,—words which at the time had not conveyed much meaning to my mind, kept rising before me, as I lay awake all night, thinking, thinking, thinking. Ah! for five minutes only, now, with Stanley, to listen to his clear shrewd advice. In five minutes he would have grasped the situation, and told me promptly how to act. And yet he had told me to be guided, more or less, by Emin. The question in my mind was, should I be guided more, or should I allow myself to be guided less, by what he said. I had too little faith in my own judgment and experience, and could not decide the question. Looking back on it all now, and knowing what I do of Emin's people, my wonder is that I should have hesitated a moment. Yet had I gone against Emin's advice and judgment, I should have had to reverse all our preconceived ideas of him, and the opinion of all Europe. It may be understood that that was a difficult leap to take, and I required further confirmation of my doubts before taking the plunge.

CHAPTER IV.

TROUBLE IMPENDING.

We start for Rejaf—A herd of elephants—Country near Dufilé cataracts—Chor Ayu—Laboré station—Selim Aga—Donkeys of the country—Bari women—Arrival at Muggi—Abdullah Aga Manzal—Thievish propensities of Emin's soldiers—Arrival at Kirri—Bachit Aga—Gordon's favourite amusement—Bari ornaments and dress—State of the country occupied by 1st Battalion—The soldiers of Kirri distrust us—Speaking to the people of Kirri—Makraka music and dance—Letter from Hamad Aga—Confirmation of my worst fears—Insubordination of the soldiers of Kirri—Our return to Muggi—Alarming news from Kirri—Emin's sad story—Soldiers of Rejaf come to see Emin—Emin's confidence in his soldiers—News from Hawashi Effendi—Story of Taha Mahomet—Strangers in Latooka—Bari chief's generosity—My servant Binza prays—Possible return of the Mahdists—Evacuation of Muggi begun—Satisfactory condition of country round Muggi—Good influence of Abdullah Aga Manzal.

I ROSE on the morning of July 17th, dejected and depressed, and while we drank our coffee before starting on the march, I ventured to tell Emin of my conversation with Hawashi Effendi the evening before. He affected to make light of it, but told me he had decided not to go straight down to Rejaf, but to remain at Kirri, a station two days' march this side of Rejaf, and send on Hamad Aga and the other officers to tell the officers of the 1st Battalion of their meeting with us. After doing this, Hamad Aga was to send us a letter to Kirri, telling us what he thought about the position.

Somewhat reassured by this plan, we started off on our march to Chor Ayu, a small station seventeen miles from Dufilé, situated at the junction of the river Ayu with the Nile.

Our caravan was quite an imposing one, there were over 200 porters, so that with the clerks, officers, soldiers, and servants, there must have been 400 people. We marched out of the station between two lines of soldiers, flags were flying and trumpets sounding, and my feeling of depression soon vanished as we rode along through the cool morning air. For nearly an hour we passed through the fields of corn, etc., belonging to the station. I was surprised at the extent of the cultivation here; this station would, I think, have been self-supporting even without the native grain tax. We got a fine view of the station with its fields of corn lying below us in peace and plenty as we reached the summit of a low hill, before descending by a steep and broken path into the valley beyond. The road lay through a plain between the river and a high chain of mountains which ran parallel to it. It was well clothed with trees, chiefly of the acacia tribe, and intersected here and there by small mountain streams which cut deep beds in the rocky soil.

On passing through a grassy gorge we came upon numberless signs of elephants in the shape of broken trees, soil torn up, and a broad track made by the passage of many feet. In a few minutes we saw a sight such as I had never seen before. Close to our left, and moving parallel to us, was an immense herd of nearly 200 elephants. People who have never seen a large herd of elephants gathered together in their wild state, can form no idea how impressive such a sight is. This great number of huge black bodies moving slowly along, with their long white tusks gleaming in the sun, was perfectly overpowering. Wherever you looked, for the space of half a mile, nothing was to be seen but elephants marching

HERD OF ELEPHANTS.

sedately along at the foot of the mountains. The very face of the plain seemed moving. Here and there the ranks were broken by the rather clumsy gambols of little elephants who broke from the herd and performed a series of awkward-looking plunges in the open. I noticed that a very large elephant, a perfect mountain of flesh, marched some fifty yards ahead of the herd by itself. I mentioned this to Emin, who told me that when a herd of elephants was travelling, the largest female always goes in front. It is curious that in a herd of elephants a female should always lead, while in the case of buffaloes we always noticed the biggest bull acted as pilot of the herd. Emin further told me that with geese or cranes he had noticed that, either swimming or flying, the female was always ahead. Emin's men, seeing the elephants, a few of which were not more than 200 yards distant, began to whistle and imitate cocks crowing; they did this in the belief that it would prevent the elephants from charging; for they have a superstition that the sound of whistling or the crowing of cocks is particularly offensive to them, and when elephants hear it, they invariably make off.

At mid-day we reached a part of the plain where the mountains gradually closed in from the east and west, and ran parallel to the river; not more than a quarter of a mile distant from it, the path descended from the high plain, and ran close along its left bank. On the opposite side of the valley the mountains rose abruptly from the river, which being closed in by them is very narrow here, and thunders over the rocks in one long series of rapids. The country is perfectly beautiful and of a wild, park-like description. Small valleys, full of fine trees, ran up into the mountains, while the little plain between the river and the hills was covered with short-cropped grass, and dotted about with large, finely-shaped trees. There was an inexpressible air of quiet and peacefulness about it. Shut in on all sides by the mountains, one experienced a feeling of security and retirement. We lunched under the

Chor Ayu Station.

shade of a spreading tree close to the river's edge, and rested for an hour on the short sweet grass.

At 4.30 we reached Chor Ayu, a small station close to the river, surrounded by fields of corn and ground-nuts. Owing to the post having miscarried in some way, our huts were not made ready for us; but I had fever, and was very glad to lie down in any sort of hut. Khamis Aga, the chief of the station, came in to pay his respects, but was coldly received by the Pasha, who was not at all pleased with the state the station was in.

This was the smallest of Emin's stations, the garrison consisting of only twenty-five soldiers and two officers. Emin had formerly built it in order to defend the ford of the Ayu, the crossing of which was constantly disputed by a tribe of unfriendly natives, who lived in the mountains above. It is a good sized river, and in the rainy season must bring down a large body of water. It was crossed by a large strong nuggar which had been built at Dufilé. It was curious, seeing how long the Egyptian Government had been established here, that so many of the small tribes round about should be still unfriendly. I suspected that when the governor's back was turned a good deal of license was allowed the soldiers by the officers, most of whom had something against them in Egypt. The tribes on the opposite side of the river here had never been subdued, and it was not far from here, when Gordon was governor of the country, that poor Linant de Bellefonds, whom Stanley met in Uganda in 1875, was killed by the natives.

The next day, somewhat late, we began our march for Laboré, which was two and a half hours distant. The character of the country was much the same as that through which we passed the day before, but the narrow plain between the two stations was entirely under cultivation, groundnuts seeming to be the chief thing cultivated here. At ten o'clock we reached Laboré, a good-sized station on the top of a high, rocky hill, overlooking the river. The soldiers, of whom there were ninety and seven officers, were drawn up, as usual, to salute the governor as he entered. Our compound was below the station on a narrow flat between it and the river. Selim Aga, the chief of the district, Surore Aga, chief of the station, and the rest of the officers came in to see us in our compound, bringing with them the inevitable offering of coffee and sherbet. The huts were very nice and cool,

SELIM BEY.

the sides being formed of basket-work of split bamboo.

In the cool of the afternoon we went up to the station, and paid Selim Aga a visit in his house and drank coffee. He was the biggest Soudanese I had yet seen. He must have been at least six feet four inches in height, and was enormously fat and broad. He was a great easy-going fellow, with a good-natured, cherubic face, and had a little shrew of a wife who kept him in splendid order. He was one of those officers who came down to see Stanley when the Pasha was staying with us in our camp at N'sabe. He said he hoped all would be well now that I was going to Rejaf to speak to the people. He told me he intended to speak to the soldiers of Laboré, and prepare them for our return; but he seemed, from what he said, to distrust Surore Aga, his second in command. After talking with him some time, we went over the station. It was not nearly so nicely kept or clean as the stations to the south of Dufilé, which were more immediately under the Pasha's eye. The ground was rocky and uneven, and the station was enclosed by a thick, strong, drystone wall, which was further supplemented by thick bushes of mimosa thorns fixed on the top. This used, so Emin told me, to be a good place for cotton, but I found it difficult to get much cotton cloth. Selim Aga told me it had been one of the worst years ever known for cotton, owing to the drought.

Leaving Laboré station next day, we started for Muggi, a seven hours' march distant. The mountains here again receded from the river, and the path lay through a fine broad plain some distance from the Nile.

The riding donkeys in this country are strong but very slow, and I usually walked most of the way. There are great herds of them in a country to the east of the Dinka country, but the natives only use them for milking, and not as beasts of burden. We now passed out of the country of the Madi tribe, and entered that of the Baris. The country was pretty, though nothing particular; but there were numbers of birds, and I longed to take a gun and go out after some of them. I was becoming quite imbued with the Pasha's taste for ornithology, and found it a most interesting subject. There were numbers of brilliant scarlet weaver birds, and steel blue Lamprocolii, flitting about in all directions, in the long grass.

As we neared the station of Muggi, there were very extensive Bari cultivations on both sides of the road, and large numbers of guinea-fowl and geese might be seen in the fields, feeding upon the grain. There were a great many women working in the fields perfectly nude, with the exception of a small apron made of bright rings of iron like chain-mail. They also had long tails of string hanging down behind, which were useful to them whilst kneeling, which is their usual posture when working in the fields. I noticed, with surprise, that most of the women and many of the men had enlarged knees of that sort which is known in England as a "housemaid's" knee. It was, I presume, the result of this kneeling posture. The doors in the huts we passed were so low, that it was only possible for the owner to enter on his hands and knees; this would, no doubt, also help to develop the disease, for small particles of sand continually entering the skin would set up an irritation. I was told, that although this disease was very disfiguring, it was not painful. Most of the Bari women we saw working in the fields had their babies perched on their backs. It is queer on entering a Bari field, to see ten or a dozen women at work on their knees each with her little, black, fat piccaniny on her back.

On arriving at Muggi we did not enter the station, but went straight to our compound, which was some distance off, and right on the bank of the river, which falls here in rather a fine cataract. The rush of the water so close to the huts was extremely pleasant, it is a sound I always like. Abdullah Aga Manzal, the chief of the station, and one of Emin's most trusted officers, soon appeared with the coffee. He was very anxious we should stay some days here, but we were in a hurry to get on and finish the Rejaf business in order to enable us to return to the southern stations and start off for Fort Bodo. Abdullah Aga struck me as being more intelligent than most of the Soudanese officers I had seen in this country. They, as a rule, asked me merely to tell them about the Expedition and our experiences on the road, and they always questioned me closely about the difficulty of getting food, and so on. But Abdullah Aga asked questions about the natives we had encountered on the way, and was greatly interested in comparing their modes of warfare, cultivation, physique, etc., with the tribes and people he had seen in the forest countries, such as

Monbuttu, Niam-Niam, and Makraka. I was greatly pleased with the short conversation I had with him.

On July 19th we made an early start for Kirri, distant four and a half hours' march. The country was poor but pretty, all up and down with gullies and streams, and hills covered with short grass. There were in places large circles and squares of stones marking what were once the sites of extensive Bari villages. The Baris had long since abandoned their villages near the road, and had built new settlements behind a low range of hills lying some distance to the west. Emin's soldiers, by their overbearing ways and thieving propensities, made it impossible for the natives any longer to have their villages on the road. As we got further towards the north, where the stations were not immediately under Emin's influence, I could see by the many marks of deserted villages, and the almost entire absence of cattle or goats, that the soldiers evidently robbed the natives to such an extent, that they were forced to leave their villages and cattle and remove their goods away from their thievish influence. I could see that if ever Emin's people did fall into the hands of the natives they would experience short shrift at their hands, for they evidently did not love the rule of the "Turks," as they called them. We passed a long distance through some broken ground where there were many curious geological phenomena. There were natural terraces lying so evenly in one direction that they looked as if they had been built. There were also strange upheavals and subsidences in the rocks, and curious strata, such as would delight the heart of a geologist.

Early in the day we reached Kirri, a small station, rendered smaller by the number of desertions which had taken place amongst the soldiers, who, under the influence of the Rejaf faction, had deserted to a station they had made in the Makraka country.

Bachit Aga, the chief of the station, remained loyal to the Pasha, but was quite unable to check the desertions; he was useful and obedient, but was rather a drunkard. Our compound was away from the station, close to the river, built on a little cliff high above it. This was Gordon's favourite spot where he used to stay whenever he could get away from his work at Lado, and, like Gladstone, to amuse himself by cutting down trees. Bachit Aga had an amusing story of Gordon's disgust when the chief of the station suggested that he should fetch some men to clear away the tree, and so save his Excellency the enormous trouble he seemed to be putting himself to.

We found on our arrival, that the station people, in order to make our huts extra nice, had just plastered the floors with fresh cow-dung; this if left to dry for a couple of days, makes an excellent floor, but as it was, our huts were rendered quite untenable. However, a number of Bari women were called in, and soon gave the huts a completely new flooring of clean white sand. They were then fumigated by burning a peculiar kind of gum, which has a smell like pastiles; it is found extensively in this country. I was greatly pleased by the industry and good nature shown by the women while performing this service for us. Their ornaments were very pretty, most of them had bands of leather round their waists covered with little bright, round discs of iron, these discs were also hung round the belt like a fringe of sequins; depending from the belt in front was an apron made of iron rings, like a coat of mail. Sometimes numbers of iron chains hanging down in front were worn instead, or a large square of leather with cylindrical-shaped pieces of iron, the thickness of a lead pencil, sewn on to it.

Round their necks were solid iron necklets of all shapes and sizes, while the usual bangles round their wrists and ankles were also worn.

Another ornament I noticed was a kind of girdle made of round, flat disks of shell strung closely on strings, and worn round and round the waist several times, from this a long thin tail of strings hung down behind.

Altogether the Bari woman is a highly decorated, but unclothed person,—the men, like those of the Madi tribe, are all perfectly naked.

In the afternoon we went up and had coffee with Bachit Aga, and went over the station. It was small and rather ill-kept, and was surrounded by a high dry built stone wall with thorny bushes placed on top. All the stations north of Dufilé were built in this way, and it would be almost impossible for natives to take them.

The Pasha, according to the plan he had made at Dufilé, decided to stay here; he sent Hamad Aga and the other officers of the 1st Battalion down to Rejaf, and intended to await Hamad Aga's report before moving.

He told Hamad Aga to inform the soldiers at Rejaf that he would remain here for a few days and if they came and made their submission, he would forgive them on condition they handed over to him the officers who first instigated them to rebel. Should they refuse to do this, he would leave them to themselves, and retire the garrisons of Kirri, Muggi, Laboré, and Chor Ayu to his southern station, preparatory to leaving the country on Stanley's return. He told me he thought that if the officers refused to obey him, that numbers of soldiers would desert from the Rejaf faction, and join him. This I very much doubted.

Emin had his collectors out shooting birds, he intended, whilst waiting for an answer from Rejaf, to employ his time by adding to the large collections he had already made.

At night numbers of swallows roosted in our huts; they were of a particularly pretty sort, the head and back being steel blue, the throat brown, and the belly white, they were somewhat smaller than the European species. The people round brought me in wonderful curiosities in the way of bangles, necklets, girdles, knives, and carved wooden utensils. Some of the boatmen brought me in some Bari bows and arrows. The bows were long, and made of split cane of the bamboo species, and were strung with a piece of fine twisted hide. The arrows were over three feet in length, with heavy iron heads, eight inches long, and horribly barbed; they had no feathers, for the iron heads being so heavy they fly straight without them. They were thickly coated with poison made of the juice of the Euphorbia Candelabra tree, they were somewhat clumsily finished and had a niche in the end to fit into the string. Neither the bows nor arrows were so beautifully made as those of the forest natives, who seemed to take a pride in decorating them, and polishing them up.

After waiting a few days, letters came in from Hamad Aga, saying that on arriving at Rejaf he had called all the officers together, and told them that the Mudir was at Kirri, and that he would come down to Rejaf, and speak to the people, if the officers would first go to him and make their submission. The officers answered that they had written for Ali Aga Dgabor and Mahmoud Effendi el Adeini to come from Makraka to consult with them as to what should be done, and that they preferred to await the coming of these two officers before moving.

These two men were the ringleaders of the rebellion, who, contrary to the Pasha's orders, had established themselves in Makraka, taking with them half the garrisons of Bidden, Kirri, and Rejaf, together with a large amount of ammunition from those stations. Here, as I said before, they led the lives of robber-chiefs, and lived by making raids on the natives, seizing large numbers of cattle and women, and hanging, shooting, and mutilating the people. Both these men were among the worst of the many scoundrels in Emin's Province, and the officers were evidently afraid of acting without them. Emin, however, said that if he could only see Ali Aga Dgabor, he was quite sure he could bring him round to his side. He decided therefore to wait for his arrival from Makraka. I thought it was a very dangerous experiment for him to make, and that it was no use waiting and losing time. I had received orders to go round to all the stations in the Province, but not being able to go down to Rejaf, it was no use remaining here. I wished to carry out those orders as quickly as possible and return, for I was getting very uneasy about things, and this uneasiness was further increased by a conversation I had with the clerk of the station. He told me that Achmet Effendi Mahmoud, the clerk of Tunguru, whom Emin had imprisoned on his return from Stanley's camp for preaching sedition in the country, had written to Kirri, to say that I was only a tool put up by Emin and Stanley to deceive them; that we had really only come from Uganda, and the Soudanese orderlies I had with me were only sent as a blind; that the Expedition was merely an Expedition of travellers, and had nothing to do with Egypt; and added, had the Expedition come from the Khedive, he would have sent 300 and not three soldiers only.

"But," I asked the clerk, "what can it matter whether we have come from Egypt or not, so that we are willing to help the people?"

He replied that unless the people believed we came from Egypt they would never move.

I was getting tired and utterly sceptical about these people, and begged Emin to start without delay for the south. It was therefore decided that I should address the people of the station, and that on the following day we should begin our return march to Dufilé.

The next day I spoke to the soldiers and read them the Khedive's letter and Stanley's proclamation. I then addressed them shortly and incisively, for I was disgusted with their stupidity and want of gratitude. I reminded them that for thirteen years their Mudir had toiled for them, and represented to them that it was to their advantage to hold to him now, and not to listen to what the officers in Reja had told them. However, if they preferred listening to other words than ours, they were free to do so, and remain in the country. As for Stanley, when he returned, those people who were ready could follow him, but he would not wait for any who were not prepared to start at once, for we had already spent too long a time in this country. I finished by drawing a picture of what their position would be when left to themselves. I told them that their ammunition would only, with great care, last a certain time, perhaps for a year, and after that the natives, whose hatred they had gained by a hundred acts of violence, would sweep the greater number of them from the face of the earth. Those few who could escape would have to arm themselves with spears and bows, and take to wearing green leaves, or return to nakedness. They would become just like the natives themselves, and revert to the state from which Emin took them years ago,—a state for which they now had the greatest contempt. Moreover, every man's hand would be against them.

They seemed greatly struck by these last remarks, for it was their pride to consider themselves civilized and well clothed, and it was a great blow to that pride to be told that in the course of a year they would have to return to their former savage state.

One of the non-commissioned officers stepped out, and said, " What a pity it is you do not go down to Rejaf, and speak these words to the soldiers, for if they heard the words you have spoken to-day, they would see their position clearly, and there would be no more trouble."

Bachit Aga came in next morning to see me, and brought his officers and non-commissioned officers with him. He had always behaved well during the mutiny, and though he belonged to the 1st Battalion, had refused to put his name to the insulting letters which had been sent to Emin. He was of course for going with the Governor, whether to Egypt or elsewhere.

I was, however, not prepared for the emphatic manner in which the rest of the officers and people declared they wished to go out with us, and were ready to move south whenever their Mudir ordered them. They told me that all the people had been talking of what I had said to them yesterday, and now fully realized what their position would be if they refused our help. They begged to be taken away from the reach of the officers in Rejaf, and asked me to put down what they said in my kitaab (book), for which they seemed to have great respect; for they had heard I wrote down daily everything that happened in the Province. They had heard that I had a wonderful gun which they asked me to show them. I showed them my Winchester with fifteen cartridges in it, with which they were greatly pleased. Later on in the day Emin sent for me, and, on going into his divan, I found that a deputation of soldiers had come down to see him. They said some one in the station had told them that Stanley would not allow them to take their women, children, and slaves with them if they went out with us, and asked if it were true. I told them we had nothing to do with their domestic arrangements, and that as far as we were concerned they might bring with them whom they pleased; on that subject they would have absolute freedom. They professed to be satisfied, and went away. In the cool of the evening, Emin and I went up to the station to see a dance got up by the soldiers in honour of the occasion. Nearly all these soldiers were natives of Makraka. The music was more like music than any I had before heard among the natives. There were long and short horns, made of gourds and cowhide, and different sized drums, while each dancer held a wicker rattle with which he beat time to the step of the dance. The tune consisted of six or seven deep notes from a large horn, these being repeated over and over again, to an accompaniment of drums and rattles. In the distance it sounded well, and rather pathetic. The Makraka dance is not so energetic as some of the tribal dances, and exhibits none of the indecencies of the Lur dances. The dancers give a sort of double shuffle on each foot as they move sedately round the group of musicians. The women move and dance in an exceedingly graceful manner.

On returning to our compound a messenger put a letter into Emin's hand; it was from Rejaf, and written by Hamad Aga.

The following is a literal translation from the Arabic:—

"*To his Excellency the Governor of Hatalastiva.*

"After having kissed your hands with all veneration, I ask God the Highest not to keep me long from your Excellency's presence. I beg to report I am still in Rejaf, and look anxiously for an opportunity to leave here, where I am detained, and rejoin your Excellency. I now report for your favour, that I have heard that the officers here have conspired to retain your Excellency here, should you honour this place with your presence. They do not intend to permit you to return, but propose to start by way of Gondokoro, to rejoin their Government, which they are convinced still exists at Khartoum.

" Your Excellency is not unaware of what these people are capable, and as I consider it my duty through my devotion to you to inform your Excellency of this, I venture to expose this plot. As for myself, since my arrival here, I have not entered in any way into affairs, and whatever has been done, has been done without consulting me. It is my utmost wish now to find a way to escape from here. If our Lord gives me His hands and saves me, praises be to Him; but if not, His will be done. This is all I am able to tell your Excellency.

"(Signed)   HAMAD MAHOMET.
" July 28th, 1888.   Major, 1st Battalion."

Here was the confirmation of all my worst fears. The cloud which had risen in my mind, no bigger than a man's hand, was now growing and darkening and gradually overshadowing my belief in Emin's wisdom.

Hamad Aga's messenger told us he had been despatched secretly at night; that immediately on Hamad Aga's delivery of Emin's message to the soldiers, they formed this plot to entrap him. He said that all the soldiers were greatly incensed against their officers, and would, he was sure, join Emin, if he went to Rejaf, in arresting them. This was too dangerous an experiment to make, though Emin still seemed to believe that the people could be eventually brought round.

Nine months before certain of the officers and soldiers of the 1st Battalion had made an attempt to capture Emin in this very place, and fearing that there might be a repetition of the same thing, it was decided we should at once retire on Muggi.

Before starting Emin, with a view to beginning the evacuation of the station, ordered Bachit Aga to send all the ammunition of the station with us, reserving sufficient for the present needs of the people. After we had gone about a mile, a soldier came running after us with a note from Bachit Aga, saying, that on taking the ammunition from the storehouse to send it after us, the soldiers had closed round and refused to allow it to be taken from the station. Emin merely sent back a message that he insisted on its being sent at once!

Such an open act of insubordination was outrageous, and I begged him to return and see that his order was carried out himself. I knew that had Stanley given an order, and heard that his people had refused to carry it out, he would very soon have been on the spot to see it obeyed in person. But Emin seemed to be incapable of prompt action. This was the further proof I required to confirm all the doubts which had risen in my mind at Dufilé nearly a fortnight before. From that day I lost all faith in Emin's advice and assurances with regard to his people; I felt that a heavy cloud was

Emin's Indecision.

gathering over us, and that serious trouble was impending.

The soldiers had now, so to speak, defied his orders, and he could look no longer for obedience from them. We reached Muggi in the afternoon, and in the evening a messenger came in from Kirri, saying that the soldiers had refused to obey the second order Emin had given them.

As I foretold, mischief was the result, for in the morning Bachit Aga sent word that the soldiers were deeply incensed at the Pasha's ordering the ammunition to be removed without giving them warning of his intention to evacuate the station. He said they evidently thought that their Governor was trying to deceive them in some way, and that they had declared they would not trust him, but would go over to the rebels at Rejaf. With negroes especially it is fatal to give an order, unless you know it will be carried out. Had the Pasha returned just that short distance to the station, a few words would have been sufficient to put the soldiers right, and what proved to be the beginning of the long series of troubles we afterwards experienced, might have been avoided. We heard that messengers from Kirri had been sent down to Rejaf to tell the rebels what had happened. Two days before, the soldiers of Kirri had declared they would obey their Governor, and begged to be taken away from the influence of the 1st Battalion; to-day, they were in rebellion against him, and declared they would join the Rejaf faction. What could be done for such people, and how could any dependence be placed in their promises of loyalty?

In the afternoon I spoke to the soldiers, and read

them the Khedive's and Stanley's letters; there were in all ninety soldiers in Muggi, and it was generally believed that it was the most loyal garrison north of Dufilé.

Emin depended very much on Abdullah Aga for showing the people an example in starting at once to evacuate the station, and transporting his garrison to Dufilé. It was his object to get all the stations north of Dufilé moved up south to the water way, whence he would be able to transport them by means of his steamers to the south end of the Lake. He thought that if the rest of the garrisons once saw Abdullah Aga and his people moving for Dufilé, they would all follow his lead.

In the middle of the night Emin came into my hut and woke me up. He had just received a letter from Bachit Aga, the chief of Kirri, saying that that evening, soldiers had arrived from Rejaf and had seized all the ammunition, and had made him a prisoner in his own house. It was only what I expected after what had happened the day before. He read me the letter, and asked me my advice; he also sent for Abdullah Aga to hear what he had to say about it. I advised him to send off a few soldiers and as many carriers as he could get down to Kirri, with a letter from him to be read out before all the people. He should say in this letter that any one who wished to join the Rejaf faction was perfectly free to do so, for the Khedive's orders were that they might stay where they were if they pleased. But that if there were any people who preferred to cast in their lot with him, there were soldiers and carriers ready to conduct them on to Muggi. That he wished to have only willing people with him, and would compel no man to follow him against his will. He adopted this plan at once, and at 3 a.m., by moonlight, a party of soldiers and carriers left Muggi, commanded by Ismail Aga, a smart young Soudanese officer.

I pitied Emin terribly, he was worn out by years of residence in the Equatorial Province, with all its unceasing anxiety. He had stuck to his people, and had repulsed the Mahdi's attacks unaided by the outside world, and now for the last three years the trouble of rebellion had been added to his other anxieties. He told me he was perfectly worn out by it all, and would gladly lay down his burden, "But," he said, "who will take it up?"

I had a long talk with him that night, and I felt ashamed, as I listened to his story, that I had been so irritated by his want of promptness two days ago. It is difficult for a young man, full of vigorous life, to understand how hard it must sometimes be for an elderly man, worn out in body and mind by long years of hard work and anxiety, to act with energy and promptness.

Emin had been over ten years in the Turkish service as a surgeon, and most of that time, he told me, had been spent in very hot climates, such as Syria, and different parts of Asia Minor, Armenia, Persia, Arabia, and Tripolis. After that he had entered the Egyptian service, and had been in the Equatorial Province for thirteen years, the climate of which is most trying to Europeans, and for the last eight or nine years had had all the responsibility of the government on his shoulders. During the first years of his governorship he had seen, with despair and indignation, all his best efforts for the good of his Province and people, checked and ruined by the shameful policy of the government at Khartoum. For the last five years, since he had been cut off from the outside world, it had been all he could do to hold his own against the troubles which beset him, and to clothe and look after the people under his care, a people who seldom showed any gratitude. He was in such a state of nervous exhaustion, that he seldom got more than two or three hours of sleep at night, and his heart gave him great pain and anxiety.

It was only at times when the troubles of his Province, his sleeplessness and anxiety about his work, combined to make his burden seem almost heavier than he could bear, that he gave way to melancholy, and to a feeling of despair, as to who would take up his work should he be obliged to relinquish it.

But such fits of melancholy never lasted long, and as a rule, he was cheerful and busy. His one recreation was in his ornithological researches, for which he had a great passion. His collectors went out daily and brought him in many rare kinds of birds, and in his leisure time he might be seen measuring and classifying his specimens, with all the fresh interest of an ardent ornithologist. A brave man who bore up against his trials, and unhesitatingly gave up the best years of his life for the good of his people, beset with troubles from within and without,—he must always be, to any one who had seen him in his country and known him, an object of admiration and

EMIN ARRANGING HIS SPECIMENS.

Page 112.

sympathy; whilst his kindness of heart, unselfishness, and generosity, ought to make those who knew him intimately, sincerely attached to him.

I shall never forget that night, when we sat together till morning broke, talking of many things and of the turn affairs in his Province were, I felt, too surely taking. He told me of his life, of his hopes and fears, his struggles and disappointments, and all with a simple earnestness which touched me with remorse when I thought how often I had allowed myself to be irritated by his want of energy and decision.

In the evening the soldiers from Kirri returned, and we were amazed when we were told that they had brought an officer and fifteen of the Rejaf soldiers with them. Abdullah Aga Manzal came in to tell us the story. It appeared that Ismail Aga, the officer who went down to Kirri in charge of the Muggi soldiers, had, on arriving at Kirri, spoken to the Rejaf soldiers, and told them how foolish they were to behave as they were doing, and asked them if they could cite a single case of their Governor's having ill-treated them, whether he had ever taken anything from them, or, knowingly, done a single act of injustice to them. To these questions they all answered, "No." Again he said, "Has your Mudir not clothed you, fed you, given you guns and ammunition, tended you when you were sick, and been a father to you for thirteen years?" To this they answered, "Yes." "Then," continued Ismail Aga, "why not come and see him now and make your submission?" With one accord they said they would start for Muggi and see him.

Half of them therefore came with their lieutenant, and the other half said they would come the next day with their captain.

Late in the afternoon they were brought before Emin, who at first spoke harshly to them, but finally addressed them quietly, and argued away their doubts. They told him that it was the fault of their officers that they had been insubordinate to him, and that they were all now anxious to see him at Rejaf, and asked him why he had not come down to see them. He answered, "Because your officers made a plot to capture me." They appeared to be very angry at this, and said they would tell their companions what their officers had done.

Emin then asked me to speak to them.

I told them we had come here because their Governor had written to England for help for his people, and the English people had agreed to join the Khedive in sending them help. Yet at the time their Governor had been writing to Europe, and telling how bravely they had fought against the Mahdi, and asking help for them, they were plotting to rebel against him. They all shook their heads and said, "Yes, we have done badly, but it was our officers' fault." I read them the Khedive's letter, and explained it to them, and told them that we had come out from England, had seen the Khedive, and had come many thousand miles to help them, and now that we had arrived with ammunition, etc., for them, they asked us who we were, and said they did not believe we came from Egypt, instead of thanking us for what we had done. I went on to say that I blamed their officers most, but that I considered them almost as bad for allowing themselves to be led away by slanders against their Governor when they had his own words to go by. They appeared to be very much ashamed of themselves, and promised all sorts of things, not one of which, I knew, they would carry out. For the time they were probably sincere, and perhaps, if they had had their women and children on the spot, they would have been content to follow us, but when they got down to Rejaf among their fellows who had not seen Emin, I knew their loyalty would quickly evaporate, and things would be just as before. No doubt, on their return to Rejaf their officers would be very angry at hearing what they had done, and would see they were watched in future.

Emin was very hopeful about it all, and thought that these few men would leaven the whole lump at Rejaf. I said I was sceptical, upon which he said, "At any rate the good seed had been sown," and I answered in the words of scripture, I feared it had fallen on a rock, and would quickly wither away.

The soldiers, before returning to Rejaf the next day, came in to see us, and repeated much of what they had said the day before, but were still more emphatic in their expressions of loyalty. The Pasha gave them a calf and some goats, with which they were much pleased, for they had not tasted meat in Rejaf for a very long time. They promised to send the rest of their companions at Kirri down to see the Governor. Emin thought all would yet be well. It was wonderful that he should, after long years of experience among them, place such confidence in people who had already deceived him half a hundred times.

In the afternoon Emin got a letter from Hawashi Effendi at Dufilé, saying that he had sent out a party of soldiers into the Shuli country, on the east side of the river, to collect the grain tax from the natives. One of the chiefs told Hawashi Effendi's officer that a party of Khartoum people, under the leadership of Taha Mahomet, had arrived in Latooka. They were all armed with guns, and had a large number of armed negroes with them. He further said he had sent out a party of soldiers to try and get more news about them, and added, "I trust in God they are people from our Government in Khartoum."

Here was Hawashi Effendi, one of the most intelligent of Emin's people, still half believing that the news of the fall of Khartoum was false! He had seen Stanley at N'Sabe, and had heard from him all about the affairs in Egypt, and yet he could not divest himself of the idea that Egypt still governed at Khartoum. The stupidity of these people was maddening, it was like talking to a brick wall, and it was impossible for a European to understand their way of arguing and thinking. As Mrs. Poyser says, "you must be a bat to know what the bats are flying after," in the same way one must be an Egyptian or Soudanese, to understand the working of their minds.

We were, of course, greatly excited by the news which, coming at this time, might be very unfortunate. Emin told me this Taha Mahomet was very well-known in these countries. He had originally come up from Khartoum, as a horse-boy to Sir Samuel Baker, in his first expedition, when he discovered the Albert Nyanza. Baker had stayed in Latooka some months, and when he left, Taha Mahomet remained in the country, where little by little he gathered people and guns to him, and gradually became a person of considerable consequence. When Gordon came up as Governor of the Equatorial Province, Latooka was included in that Province, and with that singular choice of agents which so frequently characterized Gordon when Governor, he made Taha Mahomet Governor of the Latooka country. In 1879, when there was a block in the Nile for over two years, Emin sent him down to Khartoum by land, with letters to Gordon, who was then Governor-General of the Soudan. Gordon detained him in Khartoum, and would not allow him to return to his country, but finally sent him to Bahr el Ghazal to help Gessi Pasha, who was then fighting against Sebehr. He was present at the taking of Dem Sebehr, Sebehr's stronghold, and Gessi afterwards sent him on to Emin with high recommendations, and the request that he should give him employment. After he had been a month at Lado, Emin received a letter from Gessi requesting him to send down Taha Mahomet to him in chains, for things had transpired concerning his being mixed up in some large stealing case, after the sacking of Dem Sebehr. He was sent down to Gessi, and was heard of no more in the Province. Some time afterwards, when Emin was in Khartoum, he enquired after him, and was told that Taha Mahomet had lost all he had, and had started for Kordofan, and had died on the road. We now heard of him as being in Latooka. Emin said that he must have at least 300 guns with him, for he would never dare to enter that country with less. We had no doubt that he had communication with the Mahdi's people in Khartoum, for it was extremely unlikely that he would have come all that way into the country to establish himself unless he was sure of getting fresh supplies of ammunition. The purpose of his coming would probably be for getting ivory and slaves. As he had settled in Latooka, which was Egyptian territory, without permission, we naturally supposed he had come as an enemy. Such an event happening at this time was unfortunate, and might prove most disastrous, for the Latooka country was only three days' journey from Rejaf, and five from Dufilé, and this settlement of Taha Mahomet's might have turned out to be an asylum for all the disaffected people in the Province.

The Pasha thought that the Rejaf officers were almost certain to go over to him when they heard the news, but he thought that the soldiers would not do so, for in all probability their guns, women, and slaves would be confiscated, and they themselves made slaves. But they were so foolish, there was no knowing what they might do. There were some Latooka people in Laboré station, and Emin sent orders to Selim Aga to send them out towards Latooka to find out who the people actually were, what was their number, and object in settling there. It was of course quite possible that it was not Taha Mahomet, but some of the Mahdi's people from Khartoum, who were coming up a second time against Emin's people. He said he thought it was by no means improbable that there would again be fighting as there was three years before. The poor Pasha's misfortunes seemed ever to be on the increase. Abdullah Aga begged Emin to stay a few days until the work of evacuating the station had been fairly started, for, he said, the Governor's presence was a great incentive to the people to move.

Game and birds of all sorts abounded round Muggi. Emin's collectors had brought in a couple of bustards of a very rare species; he was very pleased at getting them, for only five specimens of them had ever been brought to Europe. These were brought out by the Marquis Antinori from Abyssinia; he praises the flesh of these birds, which he says is far superior to that of any other birds in Africa. I went out several times after guinea fowl, of which there were numbers round the station. I was able to get several, but the shot guns Emin had were of the shakiest description, and the shot being home-made and not perfectly round, spread a good deal and made shooting difficult. One day I was out and got lost and benighted. After wandering about some time, I struck the path, and, as I neared the station, met a party headed by my boy, Binza, with a lantern, who had come out to search for me. I heard that Abdullah Aga, becoming anxious at my non-appearance, had sent out three parties in different directions to try and find me.

The clerk of the station told me that the day before, he had come upon a herd of pigs near the mountains, he had wounded one which came at him, and he had to take to a tree. I told him I would go out with him the next day and see if I could come upon them. We started early and tramped a very long way round the country, but could not find the pigs. There were a few antelope of the striped kind —Tragelaphus Scriptus—but it was impossible to stalk them, as there was no cover and they were so wild. I went into a Bari village on my way back, and stayed there some time talking with the natives through the medium of the clerk of the station, who interpreted for me. The Baris were very friendly, and invited me to come and inspect their huts and household goods, which I was very glad to do, for since I had been amongst them, I had been collecting a variety of facts about them, and I was always pleased at having an opportunity of extending my knowledge of them. I went into several huts and examined all there was to be seen, and bought a bow from the young chief, who told me that the length of a man's bow should be from his chin to the ground. I had to tilt my head backwards to enable my chin to rest on one horn of his bow while the other rested on the ground. It was made of a sort of mountain bamboo, very unlike the ordinary bamboo, and more like a cane. It was ornamented with long strips of iguana skin, which were wound round it; he also presented me with an arrow. I told him to follow me to the station, and I would pay him. He asked me for anything in the shape of clothes, though what he wanted clothes for I could not imagine, for he was perfectly naked, and was always accustomed to being so. On arriving at my hut I gave him one of my old worn-out shirts, and he went away highly pleased. In the evening he returned and told me he was so pleased with the shirt, that he had brought me four more arrows as presents. I mention this, for it is something unusual for a native who is satisfied with a bargain even to admit it, and still more unusual to bring further payment. I was very pleased, for his village was more than two miles from the station, and he had given himself the trouble of walking all the way there and back to bring me the arrows. Several of the natives and a good many of the soldiers had brought me in presents of splendid spears, shields, bows and arrows, and curiosities of all kinds, some coming from countries far to the west. The Monbuttu knives and dwarf's spears they brought me were especially beautiful. Different people had brought me so many things, that I had quite a large collection, but I feared I should only have to throw them away.

We had with us an old soldier who was one of Emin's orderlies, he had at one time been a great drunkard, but was now in the way of being reformed, and had become very religious. He had prayers every night and induced all our boys to join. Emin's servants were excellent pagans, but would have made very bad Mahomedans, so he told them to leave off this practice, which they did without the least demur. I was told, however, that my boy Binza, who was a Niam-Niam, still continued to do what he thought was praying. Someone had written the Arabic alphabet for him, on a piece of paper; in the morning he used to take his mat out, and kneeling upon it, read what was written on the paper two or three times over, and clasping it in his hands bowed himself to the earth at least fifty, instead of the usual five times, which are prescribed by the Mahomedan law. He used then to rise with the virtuous feeling of having done his duty to his God.

I did not forbid him to continue this custom, for I really did not think that the alphabet could do him any harm!

Meanwhile, I had spoken to the soldiers at Muggi, and had told them all about the Expedition. They professed themselves pleased with what I said, and told me they wished to follow their Governor, and would obey him implicitly. Emin had also spoken to them, and told them that he wished at once to evacuate the station, first because he wished to see them started for Dufilé before he went south, and secondly because he had heard that people had arrived in Latooka from Khartoum, and he feared that they must be Mahomet Achmet, the False Prophet's people, or as his people call them the Donagla. These people, he told them, if they were the Donagla, would surely attack the Province, and if they were not concentrated to the south the consequences would be disastrous to them.

They all agreed with what Emin said, and promised to carry out anything he should be pleased to order them to do. He told them first the women and children must be sent to Dufilé, and then the ammunition. To this they answered they were ready to start the evacuation at once. So that during the last days of our stay at Muggi, parties of women, children, cattle, and baggage, had left the station every day. The ammunition was sent straight to Dufilé, and before we left for Laboré nearly half the station had been evacuated. These were the only people in all Emin's Province who obeyed, and went about their work as if they meant something. This, I think, was chiefly owing to their being commanded by a man like Abdullah Aga Manzal, who was intelligent and always ready to obey his Governor.

Muggi was by far the best disciplined of Emin's stations. Abdullah Aga seemed to live in perfect friendship with his soldiers, and was thoroughly respected by them. He alone, too, of all the chiefs of stations to the north of Dufilé was able to prevent his soldiers from robbing the natives round the station. The consequence was that there were numbers of Bari villages near the station the inhabitants of which availed themselves of the protection of the soldiers, and lived in perfect peace and friendship with them, instead of, as was the case in the other stations, moving their villages as far as possible from it.

Near this station large herds of the small cream-coloured cattle of the country might be seen feeding on the savannas, the only place where they were to be seen beween Dufilé and Rejaf; nor was the collecting of the grain tax abused as it was at the other stations. The owner of each hut was supposed to pay a small basket of corn to government, and this tax was collected twice a year. Small parties of soldiers commanded by some scoundrel of an officer would from time to time go out to collect it. It may be imagined how this custom, not in itself bad, was abused. The brutal soldiers would take goats, fowls, and cattle, and even women and children from the natives, who were afraid to oppose them, and they would often demand the payment of the tax three or four times over in the year. This custom existed also in Gordon's time, and has been termed by him brigandage of the worst description.

Of course in the southern stations, which were more immediately under Emin's influence, things were much better, but even there he was unable to entirely check the abuse of this custom.

Abdullah Aga, however, managed to keep his soldiers under control, and the relations between Emin's people and the natives near Muggi seemed to be extremely satisfactory.

CHAPTER V.

THE BARI TRIBE.

Physique of the Baris—Dress—Iron ornaments—Powers of chiefs—Fines for different offences—Modes of making war—Weapons—Hunting—Huts and villages—Storing food—Polygamy—Dogs—Cattle—Method of tending cattle—Milking—Domestic animals—Alimentation—Tobacco—Bari cookery—Relations between married people—Ceremonies connected with child-birth—Ceremonies connected with marriage—Position of women—Funeral ceremonies—Religious superstitions—Office of rain-maker—Their customs and position.

During my stay at Kirri and Muggi, I had collected a good many facts about the habits, customs, etc., of the Baris, a tribe whose people interested me greatly. Their country extended from Laboré to Lado.

Emin also gave me a good many facts about their dress, marriage customs, punishments, etc.

The Baris are a tall, lean race, sometimes measuring over six feet in height, their legs are very long, being quite out of proportion to the length of their bodies, which gives them a peculiar knock-kneed appearance. They are of a dark chocolate colour, the women being somewhat lighter than the men. Their hands and feet are large, the latter being extremely flat, as is the case with most negroes. They have high foreheads, which are very narrow, and give the head a queer pointed appearance. Their eyes are bright, the teeth ordinarily good, but somewhat yellow, the four front teeth in the lower jaw being always extracted. Though the Baris are an ugly race, their faces are not unpleasing and are much more good-natured than the Madis or the Lurs. They do not make good servants and are too cowardly for soldiers. The men are almost always entirely without clothing, and only those who lived near Emin's stations, or were in Government employ, adopted clothing like the soldiers. The girls, until they marry, wear ordinarily a belt made of the cotton of the country, with fringes in front and a very thick tassel behind. This belt is usually decorated with iron ornaments, and is always dyed red with a kind of red ochreous clay which is found in the country. Besides these belts there exist different kinds of girdles of undressed skin or cotton, worked with iron wire, from which are suspended various iron ornaments of different patterns, such as half moons, bells, discs, sequins, or small iron chains. These latter are often woven together so as to form a mail-like apron, which is worn

BARI MAN.

in front. Iron is very valuable in the country, and these iron ornaments are only worn by rich people.

Married women, before having had children, wear in front a fringed belt, and at the back an apron of dressed skin, ornamented with beads or iron, and dyed red. Women, after having had children, abandon the fringed belt, and adopt in addition to the back apron a front apron of the same description.

Both men and women wear iron bracelets and anklets, sometimes five or six, one over another. They have a variety of iron necklaces, worked necklets of the same metal, and wear also round their necks strings of roots, different shaped bits of wood, and wooden whistles. They are very fond of little tortoise shells, but what they prize most are necklaces of dogs' teeth.

BARI WOMAN.

They wear no ear-rings, nor do they perforate their noses like most of the surrounding tribes, and they have no particular tribal marks.

Tattooing is confined to a few incisions only on the upper part of the arms. The heads of both men and women are always shaven and the hairs on the body are always carefully extracted. They are not very particular about washing, but on every occasion love to smear themselves from head to foot with a mixture of oil and red ochre. The oil they mostly use in their country is extracted from the seeds of the stereospermum tree. In spite of this, however, the Baris have no fœtid smell like so many of the surrounding tribes.

There are really no large chiefs among the Baris, but the people are divided into small communities, the chiefs of which are almost despotic, and settle all questions and disputes among their subjects with great fairness. These questions are usually on the subject of cattle-stealing or quarrels about women, and the offenders are punished by fines in cattle, sheep, goats, or iron hoes, in proportion to the magnitude of their offence.

Murderers are fined from ten to twenty cows, and in case of inability to pay, the murderer is handed over to the relations of his victim, who deal with him as they please. Abduction or seduction is punished by a fine of goats, sheep, or iron hoes, not exceeding twenty in number; if the offender is unable to pay he is publicly flogged and expelled from the village. The woman or girl is free from punishment. Stealing is punished by an adequate fine, but if the thief proves incorrigible, his right hand is cut off.

A proportion of every fine belongs to the chief; but he has no right to exact tribute from his subjects, and is allowed only to compel a certain number of them to assist him in tilling his fields. All ivory brought in belongs to the chief.

These small communities are constantly at war with each other, and their mode of warfare is somewhat strange. The chiefs of the opposing parties before a battle, sit down at a certain distance from each other with all the people, and begin to abuse each other, until the people are worked up to the proper pitch for fighting. The chiefs then retire and leave the people to fight it out, whilst they themselves get out of reach of danger. This mode of abusing each other before a battle, reminds one of the old Scandinavians who used to sing "spite songs" at each other. The warriors attack one another, first at a good distance, and gradually, as their blood gets warm, they come to hand-to-hand fighting with spears. The loss of life in these fights is seldom great.

Declarations of war are made by the chief, who sometimes consults his old people, but ordinarily the opinions of old people are not much valued, nor are they treated particularly well.

The weapons used in warfare are bows, arrows, and spears. The bows are large and somewhat stiff, and are made of a sort of mountain bamboo, not unlike cane, the arrows are not feathered, and have very heavy points made of iron or the ebony wood of the country. The latter are always covered with a thick coat of poison, composed of the juice of the Candelabra Euphorbium tree, which, when fresh, produces a strong irritation, but is not always fatal. The Baris in fighting, use no shields, those near the borders of the Dinka country use the heavy clubs of the Dinkas. The same weapons which are used in war are used also in hunting, but the Baris are not great hunters, and if leopards or lions decimate their flocks they do not turn out en masse, like other cattle-breeding tribes, to hunt down the marauders, but prefer to address their medicine men, and obtain from them some charm or spell, for which they pay sometimes very heavily in sheep or goats.

Elephants and antelopes are hunted down by large companies of hunters, the former somewhat rarely, but the latter often. The meat is equally divided among them, but a portion, usually the head and breast, is set aside for the chief. They are very particular about keeping to their own hunting grounds, and if an antelope is wounded and dies in the country of a neighbouring community, the chief is allowed to retain for himself the head and hind leg. The flesh of dogs or carnivorous animals is never eaten. Fishing is largely practised by the Baris, but the canoes that are used by them for fishing or crossing rivers are always small, ill-made, and rickety, owing to there being no large or straight trees in their country. They generally propel them with long poles, and occasionally with long spoon-shaped paddles. Fish are ordinarily caught in baskets or by harpoons, iron hooks are also frequently used. There are professional crocodile hunters, who kill crocodiles with spears or harpoons; these eat the flesh of young crocodiles. The glands, which contain a secretion, smelling very strongly of musk, are greatly prized, they are dried, fastened to strings, and worn as necklaces. In hunting hippopotami, harpoons with lines and floats are used; their meat is highly approved of.

The Bari villages are scattered, and not always

A BARI VILLAGE.

near flowing water. They consist of groups of round huts of different sizes, placed usually in a circular form, but with no enclosure of thorns round them. The walls of the huts are very low and are made of sticks and grass, and are generally plastered over with a mixture of mud and cow-dung.

The grass roof is high and steep, and projects over the walls, so as to form a sort of low verandah all round the hut, this is sometimes closed in so that the huts have an outer and inner wall, the space between the walls being used as a store-room. In the middle of the hut is a fire-place made of long stones driven into the ground at intervals, on which to stand the cooking-pots. There are no fixed sleeping places, but mats made by the women are laid on the ground, while skins are used as coverings; the children sleep promiscuously with the adult people.

The gourds for water, cooking utensils, agricultural instruments, weapons, etc., are suspended from the roof, and become black from the smoke. The huts are very dark, having no windows, and lighted only by small low doorways through which the people have to creep on their hands and knees. Some of the huts, particularly those of the chiefs, have beautifully smooth floors, they are filled with a mixture of mud and cow-dung, and are beaten so hard as to become almost like stone. Some of the floors are neatly paved with little triangular pieces of broken pottery, and resemble black mosaic floors, so beautifully, evenly, and closely, are they fitted together. All the domestic work in fine weather is done out of doors, and each hut has usually a sun shelter where the cooking is done, and the children play.

The doors of the huts are made of split bamboo cane, and cover the doorways very closely, they slide backwards and forwards in a grove, and are fastened on the inside. Before the door of each house is a nicely cleaned floor made of mud and cow-dung, it is always kept in good order, and is used for spreading out corn, vegetables, or flour, to dry.

In the middle of every village there is a large floor of the same description, for dancing. Each hut has its grinding stones, which are worked by women only; it has also one or more granaries made of split bamboo plastered with mud, and standing on high legs of wood or stone,—large ones for corn and smaller ones for sesame or hyptis. These granaries serve also as receptacles for the ornaments or household goods which the owner of the hut has not in every-day use.

Among the Baris, polygamy is limited only by the extent of a man's fortune. Every woman with her children has her own hut and granaries, containing whatever she is able to sow and reap, for the woman has to support herself and her children. She sows, weeds, tends, and reaps her own crops, the husband doing all the heavy work, such as clearing the ground, building her hut, etc. For the purpose of clearing, the men use a large heart-shaped iron hoe fixed to a heavy and cumbersome handle, the women use a neat little spud of the same make for weeding and planting. In every hut there are one or two dogs of the common African pariah species. Though the Baris are fond of their dogs, they do not look after them much, they are therefore great thieves.

The dogs are usually of a yellowish colour, with the toes and tip of the tail white, or of a black colour with tan eyebrows, with the toes and tip of the tail white. This latter is, according to Darwin, the original dog from which all other species have sprung. Domestic animals, besides cattle, goats, sheep, dogs, and fowls do not exist. Occasionally domestic cats are found amongst the Baris, but these have been introduced from Khartoum and are greatly prized by the natives. These cats, however, ordinarily breed

BARI CATTLE AND GOAT.

with the wild cat of the country, and even in the first generation become perfectly wild.

The cattle are of the small humped description, common all over Africa, they are of a whitish cream colour, and rarely have long horns, they are almost always thin and are not good milkers. The Baris love their cattle, and it is the only thing they really look after well; you may take a man's sheep or goats, or even his women, and he will get over it, but take his cattle and he will fight to the death, you may as well take his life, for his life is not worth having without them. Near every village is a high enclosure of Euphorbium trees, with a narrow entrance, closed at night by thorns. This is the cattle kraal. These hedges, by reason of their poisonous thorns, are practically impervious to the attacks of men and wild animals. The ground in the middle of these enclosures is always well swept, the cow-dung is collected in heaps and dried, this is burnt at evening in the midst of the cattle, the smoke protecting them from the bites of the mosquitoes. All round the inside of the kraal there are huts for calves or sick cows and for the watchmen.

In the morning the cows are milked as soon as the village drum is beaten. The milkman, before milking, washes his face and hands, as well as the udder of the cow, and the vessel into which he milks, with cow's urine. Women are never permitted to milk or to meddle in any way with the cows. When milking is finished and the dew is dried, the cattle are driven out by the young men, who are fully armed, and the whole cattle of the village feed together. At about five o'clock the cattle are driven home and again milked. The Baris seldom drink the milk fresh, but prefer it in a curdled state; it is supposed to be more digestible.

Cattle are seldom slaughtered, except on great occasions, such as the death or marriage of a chief, peace after war, and so forth. If cattle die of disease the meat is always eaten. Death is very frequent amongst cattle, from diseases of the lungs and liver. Strong cattle are bled, as is the custom also in Masai land; the blood is mixed with oil and flour and is made into a thick soup, which is much liked and is considered a great delicacy. Raw meat is never eaten.

People will not sell their cattle, and very unwillingly part with those which have to be given as marriage dowries. The sheep and goats are lean and dry like the cows, owing to the poorness of the grass and the numerous parasites which infest the savannas and fasten on to every animal which feeds there.

Each village has a large flock of sheep and goats, and their flesh is eaten comparatively often, their skins are in great request for making belts and girdles. Fowls are frequent, but are small and not very productive.

Every chief has a pet amongst his goats or cattle, and this animal enjoys a kind of veneration. It is considered a great disgrace for a chief to be deprived of it in a raid made by his neighbours.

Red dhurra corn, of a very bitter description, is planted extensively, but is very slow in coming to maturity, the people do not care to supplant it by another kind of dhurra of a sweeter description, for fear of losing their harvest by reason of the millions of weaver birds which infest the country; but they do not attack the red dhurra. The corn is not only used for making bread, but for making a kind of thick muddy drink of an intoxicating description. Sesame is planted extensively for the sake of the oil, which is obtained by roasting and grinding the seed, and boiling the flour in the water. Sesame, likewise after having been made into flour, is made into a kind of porridge and mixed with meat or vegetables.

A small kind of white bean is also grown by the Baris, these, however, do not keep long, and become quickly worm-eaten. Hyptis is a strong-scented plant with a spike full of small blackish or whitish seeds, from which a kind of oil is expressed; the grains are also eaten as porridge. Round hard ground nuts are extensively grown. Eleusine or tullaboon, a small prolific brownish corn, is largely grown, but this species is often destroyed by locusts. Hybiscus sabdariffa is also cultivated, the unripe pods of this plant are slightly acid, and are put into soup, the leaves are eaten like spinach, and the ripe seeds, of a blackish colour, when boiled form a kind of mucilaginous fluid, which is eaten with bread. The seeds of this plant were used by Emin Pasha's people as a substitute for coffee. There are two kinds of tobacco, one with a white and a pink flower, which furnishes a mild tobacco, and one with a yellow flower, which yields a stronger leaf. They are only grown near huts and villages, and never in sufficient quantities to furnish an article of trade. The Baris only put a small amount of tobacco into their huge cup-like pipes, and fill them up to the brim with red hot charcoal, the carbonic gas of which produces a kind of intoxication.

There is no special way of preparing tobacco, it being merely dried in the sun; the Eastern Baris, however, collect the leaves whilst green and pound them in a mortar, they roll the pulp thus made into balls and dry them in the sun. This tobacco has no pleasant smell, the fermentation completely spoiling it.

Besides these plants, pumpkins, gourds, and

climbing potatoes (Helmia) are grown, and from the fields wild plants are gathered and eaten like spinach.

The Baris cooking is somewhat rough, and their cooking pots are not kept very clean. Pottery is always made by the women, from the biggest water jars down to tobacco-pipes. The water and cooking pots are always round at the bottom and are sometimes marked with rows of straight lines, they are of

BARI COOKING POTS AND GOURD.

a dull black and are never coloured in any way. The clay of the country is well adapted for making pottery, which is better and stronger than that of most tribes. Cooking, too, is always done by women, each woman cooks for her own family. On her husband saying he will stay with her that evening she has to prepare a pot of beer for him. The husband eats by himself, and the woman is usually obliged to wait on him, and is not allowed to sit down while he eats. If the man is well disposed, he calls in the children of the wife with whom he is temporarily staying, to eat with him; in an ordinary way, however, the children eat afterwards with the mother. Before meals a small clean mat is spread on the ground. As a rule, Baris are very spare eaters, but they gorge themselves on special occasions. They are, however, able to fast for days together without complaining. Drunkenness is very exceptional among the Baris, although the men daily partake freely of their native beer, made of red dhurra corn.

The relations between married people are as a rule good, and a man rarely beats his wives; a wife with children is hardly ever beaten. The women quarrel a good deal amongst themselves, and are very jealous of each other; their idea of morality is not high, but as the husbands are not very particular, quarrels on that subject seldom arise. Immorality amongst unmarried girls is very uncommon, for a girl of loose character would at once lose her commercial value.

There are no particular ceremonies about childbirth. When a child is born, it is rubbed over with a mixture of oil and red ochre, and this process is repeated every two days. The mother remains in her house for eight days after her confinement, her husband then pays her a visit, accompanied by his own or his wife's mother, and they proceed to name the child. Male children are usually called after animals, female children after flowers, but if the child has some marked physical peculiarity, its name has generally some reference to this. The birth of a female child is as a rule hailed with greater satisfaction than that of a boy, except in cases where an heir is born to a chief; then there is a good deal of drinking and rejoicing. There is a great mortality among Bari children, up to the age of three or four years; this is probably due to their irregular feeding.

At one time the mother will stuff them with food, and at another will leave them for days together with hardly anything to eat. This is evidently the reason why pendant stomachs are so constantly seen in young children. The birth of twins is not unusual, and is always considered lucky. Twins are often called Kenyi and Tomba, and it will be generally found that Baris with these names are twins. As a rule the women are not prolific, a family of four or five children being considered a large one. Girls marry at the age of twelve or thirteen, there is no particular ceremony on this occasion, but a good deal of drinking goes on, and if the intermarrying parties are children of chiefs, some cattle are slaughtered and a big feast is made. The price of a girl has always to be paid before any preparations for marriage can be made, and belong entirely to the girl's father. If, after a certain lapse of time, the newly married woman gives birth to children, her father has to return to her a certain portion of the price paid for her by her husband. These cattle are her own property and go towards the maintenance of her children. If on the other hand she has no children, her husband has the right to send her back to her father, and he may demand the return of a certain number of the cattle he paid for her. Such a woman is permitted to marry again, but her value is somewhat lessened. Women are allowed to visit their relations in distant villages, and it is a recognized rule among Baris that these women should never be molested in any way, even in war time. Thus they are often able to act as ambassadors and peace-makers between contending tribes. Old women are greatly respected, and frequently hold the position of doctors or sorceresses. The mother of a chief is always looked up to, but she has no voice in village councils; old men are not cared for at all.

Baris are generally long-lived for negroes. There are very few deformed people to be seen among them, and fatal diseases are rare; but eye diseases, tumours, and syphilis are common, to guard against this last disease innoculation is sometimes practised, but with no good results, however. Epidemics of small-pox and a low kind of typhoid fever often carry off thousands, and famine arising from drought often adds greatly to the mortality.

When an ordinary person dies there is a good deal of weeping and wailing for a couple of days, and he is buried in a reclining position; but if a person of some standing dies, he is buried in a sitting posture, with a cow hide above and below him, and some corn is put near him. After the grave has been filled in and levelled, an ox is killed and the meat is divided amongst the people. Offerings of flour or corn are laid on the grave, and if any relative of the deceased dreams about him, he hastens to add some new offering to those already given.

There are no traces whatever of a religious belief among the Baris, or a belief in a future life, nor are there any places set apart for worship. The only way in which they show any thought of the deceased is by carving rough images of him and placing them in his house, but there is no particular reverence for these images. If a chief dies, his whole property, wives, cattle, etc., belong to his eldest son, who is free to give to his brothers what he pleases, his sisters do not receive anything. The deceased's wives become the legitimate wives of his son, his own

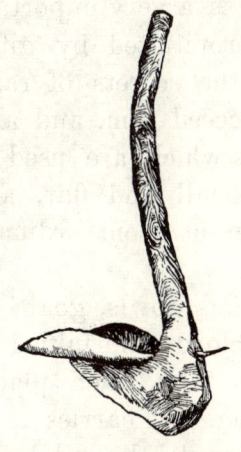
BARI HOE FOR MEN.

BARI SPUD FOR WOMEN.

mother excepted, and she is not allowed to marry again.

As everywhere among negroes, there exist many superstitions, always connected with animals or sorcerers. The howl of a jackal, or the screech of an owl, near a house, forebodes the death of the owner. If anyone sees a hare cross his path, he at once returns home and remains in his house for the rest of the day. The song of a wagtail before the door of a house, foretells the near approach of a guest. The howling of dogs without apparent reason is supposed to foretell the coming of disease. Lions and leopards are believed to be under the control of sorcerers, and never attack men or cattle unless by their order. Hyænas are believed to be forms taken by men who go round to work mischief—this belief also holds among the Arabs.

Rain-makers. The office of rain-maker to a tribe, or to a certain community of a tribe, descends from father to son. The rain-maker is a very important personage, and is constantly propitiated by gifts. The father, on dying, commits the secrets of rain-making to the son who is to succeed him, and also hands over to him certain stones which are used in the charm. These stones are small and flat, and are apparently in no way different from ordinary stones.

When rain is to be made, victims, fowls, goats, or even cows, are killed, and their blood is sprinkled by the rain-maker on these stones. He then places them in a calabash of clean water and carries it to the nearest running water; he puts the calabash, just as it is, in the stream for a quarter of an hour or sometimes longer. He then removes the stones, and buries them, and finally sits on the place where they are buried, continuing the incantations which he has constantly kept up since the beginning of the ceremony. The stones remain buried for some hours or sometimes even for days, and are dug up when the rain comes.

The victims killed at the commencement of the ceremony belong to the rain-maker. Rain-makers constantly incur the wrath of their tribe by their non-success, and are in such cases usually killed and their possessions are confiscated. It is not unusual for the chiefs themselves to be rain-makers. Baker, in his book on the discovery of the Albert Nyanza, gives some very amusing stories of an old Latooka chief, who was the rain-maker of his tribe, and of the shifts to which he resorted to keep up his character before his people. He would constantly come before Baker who had an aneroid, to try and get out of him if there was any chance of rain coming, so that he could announce it to his people, and pose as a prophet, and make capital out of their credulity. He used always to be complaining of the meanness of the presents his people gave him in return for his wonderful gift.

Emin told me that once a chief from the Latooka country fled to him some years before, for protection against his own people, who were enraged against him because he could not bring enough rain. He was obliged to remain for over five months in Emin's station before things could be made sufficiently smooth to admit of his returning to his people.

One of the Bari rain-makers disappeared for some time, either from fear, or perhaps because he was dissatisfied with the value of his presents. The season proved a dry one, and great was the woe of the people at his disappearance. After some time he returned and was received with the greatest rejoicing, presents came in, in numbers, and his character received a fresh lustre from the fact that a dry season had followed his disappearance. These people probably know some simple rules about the weather, and by being carefully observant know pretty well when rain may be expected. Perhaps this fellow, for some reason, foresaw that a dry season was likely to occur, and profited by it accordingly, and instead of waiting and bearing the odium of the people, cleverly turned it to his own advantage.

CHAPTER VI.

BEGINNING OF THE REBELLION.

Arrival at Laboré—Reading of the Letters—Mutiny of the Soldiers—Speaking to the Mutineers—Soldiers' distrust of their Mudir—Demeanour of Emin's followers—The Mutineers send for me—Departure for Chor Ayu—The Mahdists at Boa—Khedive's letter sent to Rejaf—Emin's opinion of the Khedive's letter—Desertion of Emin's orderly—Letter announcing rebellion of 2nd Battalion—Emin's distress at the news—Short-sightedness of Emin's people—Our departure for Dufilé—Rain and Sunshine—Dreary appearance of country—We prepare to enter Dufilé.

We arrived at Laboré on August 12th; it was our intention to stop there for two days, and then to hurry on south to Wadelai, there to again try to get a party started for Fort Bodo. Selim Aga, on our arrival, said that he had spoken to all the soldiers there, and they had declared themselves ready to begin the evacuation of the station. He had sent out a party of Latooka natives with five soldiers, to obtain news of the strangers; but they had not yet returned.

On the day after our arrival I went up to the station with Emin to speak to the people before leaving for the south.

I read the Khedive's and Stanley's letters, and explained as usual everything connected with the Expedition. Whilst I was speaking I noticed that the soldiers were not as attentive as was generally the case, and that there was a good deal of whispering going on amongst them. A large crowd of people too, men, women, and children, had gathered in dense masses on a little bluff, above the place where the soldiers were drawn up in line, and there was an uneasy stir amongst them, as if something unusual was going to happen.

After I had finished speaking, Emin, as was his custom, added a few words to what I had said. Whilst he was speaking, a big bull-headed, sullen-looking Soudanese stepped out of the ranks, and exclaimed, "All you have been telling us is a lie, and the letter you have read out is a forgery, for if it had come from Effendina he would have *commanded* us to come, and not have told us we might do as we pleased. You do not come from Egypt, we know of only one road to Egypt, and that is by Khartoum, we will either go by that road, or will live and die in this country."

Emin instantly sprang forward and seized him, and trying to wrench his gun out of his hand, shouted to his four orderlies to arrest the man, and carry him off to prison. A struggle then ensued, and the mutineer shouted to his companions to help him. Then arose a scene of confusion and uproar which is impossible to describe. The soldiers, breaking from the ranks, dashed at Emin and me with loaded guns, and surrounded us. Shouts of hate and execration were hurled at us as the mutineers hemmed us in with guns pointed at us. Emin drew his sword and dared them to come on. It was a horrible moment as we saw ourselves surrounded by the infuriated soldiery, their fingers

THE MUTINY AT LABORÉ.

moving uneasily on the triggers of their loaded guns, while they cursed us, with their brutal faces distorted with fury, and their eyes gleaming with hatred. For a second it seemed to me that this was to be the ending of all our long struggle to rescue Emin Pasha, and the thought of Stanley and my companions far away, flashed vividly through my mind. At this moment, some one called out that my orderlies were going to seize the powder magazine, and with one of those sudden changes of purpose so characteristic of the negro character, the soldiers wrenched their companion from the grasp of Emin's orderlies, and rushed off to the magazine, bearing their comrade with them with shouts of defiance and contempt. Emin and I were left standing almost alone, for nearly all our followers had run away in terror at the first outbreak. Selim Aga and the other officers had done what they could to quiet the soldiers, but they might as well have tried to still the ocean, for their voices were drowned in the uproar and confusion.

I begged Emin to go down to his house whilst I went up to the magazines, and tried to calm the soldiers, he refused to leave the station, and said he would stop where he was and wait for me.

I took my boy Binza with me, and went up alone to the magazines, round which the soldiers had collected, shouting, and excited. As I approached I was greeted with howls and yells, the soldiers pointed their guns at me, shouting to me to keep off. I said I had merely come to them as a friend, and added, " You see I am alone and unarmed, I have no fear of you, because you are soldiers and not savages."

They lowered their rifles and said, "We will not harm you, you have nothing now to fear from us."

After a minute or two of trying to reassure them, they became sufficiently calmed down to hear me quietly. I told them how wrong they were, and how utterly unnecessary this scene had been, a scene which so nearly ended in the massacre of their Governor, and of me, the representative of Stanley who had brought this Expedition to help them. If they did not want to go, and did not believe we came from Egypt they could have quietly told me so on the following day, for after speaking I had asked them to come and see me and tell me what they thought about leaving the country. They all exclaimed that it was their Governor's fault for seizing their companion. "But," I said, "you surely know enough about the duties of soldiers to understand that if a man steps out of the ranks and defies his Governor he must be put in prison." They said that the soldier might have been wrong, but the Governor, whom they distrusted, had no business to seize him. During the time I was speaking to the soldiers, Emin sent up several messages to entreat me to come away, but I felt now, after the first excitement was over, that I had nothing to fear from the people. The soldiers finally said they would talk it over amongst themselves, and asked me to come up and speak to them alone the next day, but they said they would not allow their Governor to enter the station. I then left them and went back to Emin, and we went down to our compound together.

Had one of those guns which the soldiers were brandishing about, cocked and loaded, gone off, there would have been a general massacre, for if once a gun had been fired, there would have been no stopping the excitement which would have followed, and down we should have gone. The demeanour of some of Emin's followers during the few risky minutes of that first outburst was curious.

Rajab Effendi, Emin's secretary, hid behind a tree, his knees gave way from sheer terror, and he was afterwards found there in a state of utter collapse. Arif Effendi, another clerk, a most peculiar looking little Circassian, ran screaming into Selim Aga's house, where he hid under a bed, shouting out that the Mudir and Mr. Jephson had been murdered by the soldiers, the black women of the house keeping up a chorus of screams. Hassan Aga, the Pasha's hunter, could only sink on his knees and pray, saying, "We have nothing to defend ourselves with, we shall all be murdered! Allah be merciful to us." The orderly, who had prayers with our boys, was drunk, and was trampled underfoot by the furious soldiers, who snatched his gun away from him, and kicked him brutally. Vita Hassan, the apothecary, had, at the first rush, made off to the Pasha's compound, and brought a revolver for him.

Emin was dreadfully excited all the evening, and feared the soldiers would attack us that night, but I felt certain they would not do that. After a while I sent for Selim Aga and the officers of the station, who came down and had a long talk with us. They all expressed themselves horrified at what had happened, and deplored the conduct of the soldiers. However, from what he said, or perhaps more from his manner when he spoke, I felt a great distrust of Surore Aga, the chief of the station. It transpired many days afterwards, that the mutineer who stepped out of the ranks and defied Emin was Surore Aga's orderly, and had been instigated by him to do it. Surore Aga, we eventually heard, had, ever since Stanley's arrival at the lake, been in constant communication with the rebels at Rejaf. I spoke in the evening to Emin's and my orderlies, and commended them for their conduct during the outbreak that afternoon. They had behaved with great courage, and they, together with my servant Binza, had helped me greatly in quieting the soldiers.

Next morning Selim Aga sent down word to me that the soldiers were all drawn up in the station, and would be glad to speak to me. Both Emin's and my orderlies came up and told me they wished to go with me, and Emin begged me to take them, but I refused, knowing that nothing pacifies excited people more than going amongst them alone, with apparently no fear. I say apparently, for I must admit I was not comfortable! Accordingly I went up to the station, followed only by my boy Binza, who was to act as interpreter, but I put my revolver into my pocket in case there should be trouble. I found that all the soldiers and officers were drawn up properly, and saluted me respectfully as I approached. I spoke long with them, and told them the chief fault lay with the soldier who had stepped from the ranks and told us we were liars. They admitted he was wrong, but again blamed their Governor for seizing him, and added that they did not like him and did not trust him. I used the same arguments as those I had used on the day before, and received the same answers. I further asked them why they distrusted their Governor who had been with them for thirteen years. I asked if they had ever known him do an act of injustice or cruelty to them. They replied, on the contrary, he had only done them good.

"Then why," I said, "if you say he has only done you good for thirteen years, do you think he is going to turn against you now?" They answered, they distrusted him because he was going to desert their brethren in Rejaf. I told them it was they who had deserted him and had made a plot to capture him. This they did not believe, and it was no use trying to convince them. However, I told them they were perfectly free to act as they wished, and to profit by or refuse our help as they pleased. We had come many hundred miles to help them, and had fought a great many enemies to reach them, but never in all our fighting against our enemies, had I had so many weapons pointed at me as yesterday, when I, their guest, had come amongst them, wishing only to help the people whom I imagined were friends.

They seemed very much ashamed, and said they regretted what had happened yesterday, so I wished them good morning and left the station.

I found Emin and his people somewhat disturbed by my long absence, for they feared that the soldiers had taken me prisoner.

Soon after, Selim Aga and the officers came down to greet us as we were to start for Chor Ayu that day. They repeated what they had said yesterday, and said the soldiers had been tampered with by some emissary from Rejaf. Selim Aga, the chief of the district, had already had a great many of his goods transported to Dufilé, so it seemed as if he wished to go out with us.

These Soudanese and Egyptians of Emin's Province were an evil lot, they would come up and offer their friendship and protestations of loyalty, when all the time they were plotting in their hearts the darkest treachery against us. My boy Binza once said to me, "Master, these are a rotten people, the good material in them is not sufficient to make a hut, but there is enough evil in them to build a palace."

We reached Chor Ayu in the afternoon, intending to stay three days, for this was a three days' holiday, called Id el Kebir, the most important festival in the Mahomedan year.

A good deal of visiting, drinking, and feasting, goes on during these days, and as neither the Pasha nor myself were well, we preferred stopping for it in the quiet station of Chor Ayu, instead of going on to Dufilé, which would be all noise and confusion. On our arrival, we found a letter from Dufilé. Hawashi Effendi wrote to say, that on getting Emin's order he had sent out another party to try and get further news of the strangers in Latooka. He said that his officer had heard that the people were a party of Irregulars belonging to the Mahdi's people in Bahr el Ghazal. They had landed at Boa, and had made a raid on the people of Latooka, who had turned out *en masse* and given them a serious defeat, upon which the Mahdi's people had retired and recrossed the river in their steamers and boats.

We heard, of course, that the Mahdi's people were in the Bahr el Ghazal Province, but it startled us to

TYPES OF EMIN'S PEOPLE.

hear they had been so close. Things were looking bad. We also got another letter from Hamad Aga in Rejaf, saying that Ali Aga Djabor and Mahommed Effendi el Adémi, the two chief mutineers of the 1st Battalion, had arrived in Rejaf from Makraka. They said they would not come and see their Governor, but that he might come and see them if he liked. This was extremely condescending and kind of them! By the Pasha's advice I wrote to Hamad Aga, saying it had been my intention as Stanley's representative to come down to Rejaf to speak with the people, and read to them the Khedive's letter. Owing, however, to our being informed of their intentions towards us, we deemed it advisable not to come down, but I enclosed a copy of the Khedive's letter, which he could read to the officers and soldiers now that they were all assembled. I further said, that any one in Rejaf who wished to see me now must come to Dufilé.

This copy of the Khedive's letter eventually fell into the hands of the Mahdi's general, who sent it down to Khartoum. It was sent on to Osman Digna, who forwarded it to General Grenfell as a proof that the Equatorial Province had fallen into the Mahdi's hands.

Emin was inclined to think that when the chief rebels in Rejaf heard that the stations to the south were being evacuated, they would march up and carry the garrisons off to Rejaf. From the first Emin had said that the Khedive's letter would have a bad effect on the people, he ought to have *commanded* them to go to Egypt instead of leaving them to decide for themselves. It was a pity, too, when it was decided that the Expedition was to be sent, that some of these people's relations in Egypt should not have been invited to send letters by us to their friends here. This would have at once put an end to their doubts as to our connection with Egypt.

Emin told me that if we had arrived six months later, he would probably have been lost, for his prestige had received a heavy blow in the rebellion at Rejaf. It was unfortunate he had not spoken a word about it in the letters he wrote to Europe, for then things would have been arranged differently.

On the road from Rejaf to Chor Ayu, the pious but drunken orderly ran away, he probably went down to join the rebels at Rejaf. He had been ordered by Emin to proceed to Dufilé to join his company, as he would no longer have him as an orderly. He probably thought that on arriving at Dufilé he would be severely punished by Hawashi Effendi, so he made up his mind to desert to the enemy. There was an end of him and his prayers and drunkenness. None of these people, who appear to be very pious Mahomedans, are ever of much use; it is not a nice thing to say, but it is unfortunately true.

Late on the evening of August 18th, a letter came in from Hawashi Effendi, saying that rebellion had broken out in Dufilé, and he had been made a prisoner. Three officers, Fadl el Mulla Aga, Achmet Aga Dinkaue, and Abdullah Aga el Apt, with 60 soldiers, had that day arrived from Fabbo station and had seized the government store-houses and powder magazine. They then addressed the soldiers and told them that they were fools to listen to what the Pasha,

Stanley, and I had told them, that the road we wished to take them by did not lead to Egypt, the only road to which lay through Khartoum. The letters we had brought with us were forgeries, they were convinced we had not come from Egypt, and had positive proof that we wished only to take the people out of the country and hand them, their wives and children, over as slaves to the English. These words spread like wildfire amongst the ignorant people, and the soldiers readily joined the mutineers. All the officers in Dufilé joined them also, and elected Fadl el Mulla as their chief. They had then liberated all the prisoners.

This was terrible news, for here we were caught in a trap completely. Rejaf, with the rebellious 1st Battalion behind us, and Dufilé with the new rebellion ahead, while to the east and west of us were tribes who had ever been bitter enemies of the Egyptian government. There was no loop-hole for us to escape, and even if we had been able to pass Dufilé, it would have availed us nothing, for the whole people were ripe for rebellion, and would only have captured us and sent us back ignominiously to Dufilé. I pitied poor Emin intensely; personally he was in no fear, for he was plucky from head to foot, but the thing which cut him to the heart was that his people, for whom he had done everything, and given up everything, should so turn against him. He said how deeply sorry he was that he had been the means of bringing me into this nest of unpleasant possibilities. Of course I could only assure him that I was glad I was with him in his trouble.

It was certainly a very terrible position we were in, and there was no seeing where it might end.

Emin sent off messengers by night to Laboré to order Selim Aga to come at once and accompany him to Dufilé, as he was a man of some influence in the Province, and had ever been a good friend to Emin. For the poor Pasha there was no sleep that night, he could only walk up and down, brooding over his troubles. Next day Selim Bey arrived, but there was such heavy rain falling all day that the road would have been impassable for us.

Selim Aga, who was a friend of Fadl el Mulla Aga, the chief mutineer, wrote to tell him not to do anything rash, for the Pasha and he were coming the next day to Dufilé. Another letter came in from Hawashi Effendi saying no violent act had yet been done, that he thought the people were afraid their Governor would compel them to leave the country, and that the mischief had arisen from this misconception. He added, it had long been plain to him that, with the exception of a very few people, no one really wished to leave the country; they were much too comfortable where they were.

I had felt sure for a long time that though Emin's people had most of them answered me enthusiastically, and said they would follow their Governor, that in their heart of hearts hardly one of them wished to move. No representations of the position they would be in if they refused our help ever had the slightest effect on them, everything "to-day" seemed to them to be all right, and they appeared to have no power of thinking of the morrow.

In the evening some soldiers from Dufilé passed, but they skirted round the station and swam across the Ayu higher up. Selim Aga went after them, and

We start for Dufilé.

tried to speak to them, but they ran away. They were evidently taking down letters from the mutineers in Dufilé to the rebels in Rejaf, with whom they would doubtless now make common cause.

On August 20th, we started off for Dufilé, there

ON THE ROAD TO DUFILÉ.

were not sufficient carriers to be got to carry our loads, so we had to leave several of them behind.

There was a tremendous lot of water about, and the Nile had risen more than four feet in the night from the rain of the day before. One could see marks of devastation all round where the water had swept down from the mountains. The torrents and water-courses we passed, which we could see had the day before been deep rushing floods, were to-day only clear trickling streams, so rapidly does the water pass away in this mountainous region.

The distant mountains, which ran parallel to our road, and which in some places developed into solid precipices of rock, with a sheer drop of 600 feet, were all glistening in the bright sunshine from the water which was trickling down their face from the table-lands above. All nature had been drenched.

The day succeeding a long day or night of continued rain is, in Central Africa, generally extremely hot, and that day was no exception to the rule. The sun rose over the hills, which were capped with vapour, while all the valleys and low lands lay wrapped in an impenetrable veil of mist. But after a couple of hours the mists had rolled away, the vapours had lifted, and the sun broke out with a brilliance and fierceness which seemed to pierce to the brain. Towards the middle of the day the heat became almost insupportable as we crossed over the bare and dreary plain. The whole face of the country seemed to quiver in the heat.

I was struck, even more than I had been on our journey down a month before, by the inexpressible loneliness and solitude of this huge rocky waste of uninhabited country. No sort of cultivation, or signs of habitations, were to been seen for miles, nothing but dreary stretches of quartzy plain broken only by huge masses of rocks, torn and upheaved in all sorts of curious forms and shapes, some looking in the distance almost like ruined castles. Over the whole plain were studded dwarfish shrubs and small mimosas. To the west the plain was bounded by a long line of high, rugged, inhospitable-looking mountains, whilst to the east, as far as the eye could reach, the barren plain stretched away into the distant Shuli country. The sight of this plain recalled very forcibly to my mind a passage which I had read somewhere, I think in one of Scott's books, as near as I can remember they were as follows :—

"It is a remarkable effect of such extensive wastes, that they impose an idea of solitude even upon those who travel through them in considerable numbers, so much is the imagination affected by the disproportion between the desert around and the party who are traversing it. Thus the members of a caravan of a thousand souls may feel, in the deserts of Africa or Arabia, a sense of loneliness unknown to the individual traveller, whose solitary course is through a thriving and cultivated country."

On reaching the brow of the hill, from which we could see Dufilé lying below us, about two miles distant, we halted to allow the rear of our caravan to come up.

There were Emin and myself, Vita Hassan, the apothecary, Rajab and Arif Effendis, who were Emin's clerks, Kismullah, Emin's collector and preparer of birds, our servants and orderlies, and some twenty Madi carriers. We stood gazing on the station, wondering what our reception would be like, whether we should be able to make any impression on the mutineers and get them to abandon their plot, or whether we should now take a long farewell to liberty and freedom. We changed our hats and made ourselves tidy, drew the column together in an orderly line, and shaking out all our bravery, in the way of flags and pendants, we set our teeth and prepared to descend into the station.

CHAPTER VII.

OUR IMPRISONMENT AT DUFILÉ.

We approach Dufilé—Attitude of the people—Entry into the station—Surrounded by sentries—Insults of the soldiers—Greeting of the Circassian tinker—We are imprisoned—The contrast to our entry a month before—Selim Aga consults the mutineers—Fadl el Mulla's reason for rebelling—The Mutineers of Rejaf are sent for—Our life in prison—Our servants insulted—Hawashi Effendi's position—The rebels form a plan to entrap Stanley—News from M'Swa—Stanley's supposed arrival at Kavalli's—Arrival of rebels from Rejaf—My orderlies are examined—I go before the rebel council—Questioned by the rebels—Letters read before the council—"You and your master are impostors!"—My tirade against the rebels—"Chivalry in a negro"—Fadl el Mulla asserts himself—Emin signs the papers—Steamer to be sent to M'Swa—I prepare to start in steamer—Start from Dufilé—Unpleasant experiences on board—Arrival at Wadelai—Little Farida—Five children at a birth—consultation with the Wadelai soldiers—General discontent in Wadelai—Atmosphere of treachery.

As we marched down the hill we could see that there were great numbers of people about, all dressed in white, for it was now the feast of Id el Kebir. Large groups of people had congregated outside the station, all talking earnestly together. Amongst these we could see figures moving quickly about, and by their excited gestures it was evident they were exhorting the people to something, we knew not what. On nearing the station these groups broke up, and lined the path along which we were to pass. We could see dense masses of expectant faces appearing above the ramparts of the station, within which a great noise and confusion seemed going on. As we approached there was a deep silence, everyone seemed holding his breath to see what would happen. We rode through the lines of silent people, and entered the station. No salutes had been fired, nor were the soldiers drawn up in line to salute their Governor. Emin at a glance could see that it would have been of no use to speak to the people then, for it was evident that a good deal of drinking had been going on, and everyone was excited. As we passed through the postern gate, an order was given by an Egyptian officer, and sentries took their places in front of and behind us, thus cutting us off from our people. As the sentries took their places, a rush was made at Kismullah, the Pasha's collector, and his gun was torn from his hands, and he and some others were hurried off to prison. At this signal a perfect din of voices arose, the station seemed alive with people, and every one, men, women, and children, pressed forward to witness their Governor's humiliation. The clerks, however, and officers kept in the background, as if ashamed to meet their Mudir's eye. A number of soldiers had collected in the square in front of the prison; they were all more or less excited by drink, and commenced singing and shouting out insulting words about us. These were, I think, the mutineers from Fabbo.

Meanwhile, we were conducted through the station, followed by the shouting rabble, every road and path being choked by the masses of people of all sorts, who eagerly pushed forward to see us as we passed, and to point at us in scorn and derision.

In the square, in front of our compound, an immense concourse of people had gathered to see our final imprisonment, and to show their contempt for us by their insulting gestures. The only man who greeted us that day was a little Circassian tinker. Undismayed by the frowns and threatening looks of the crowd, he started forward and seized the Pasha's and my hands. He could not speak for weeping, but could only raise our hands to his lips, and look at us in speechless misery. We were then conducted into our compound, which was surrounded by a high thick boma or fence, and eight sentries were posted at the entrance, with strict orders to allow no one to have ingress or egress. Thus began our imprisonment.

What a contrast was our entry into the station that day, to our entry little more than a month before! Then, the soldiers had been drawn up to greet their Governor, and pay him all the honour due to his position, while I had been received with acclamations as an honoured guest, the representative of Stanley, the great traveller whom the Khedive had sent to help them. Then, words of cordial greeting fell from their lips, and smiles of welcome were on their faces; now, every face expressed scorn and derision, and their mouths only opened to shout insulting words. The Egyptian incendiaries had indeed done their work thoroughly, and every one was against us!

The jeers and shouts of derision as we entered our compound made my blood boil. The whole square in front of our compound seemed full of half-drunken soldiers, and the shouting and laughing all round

ENTRY INTO DUFILÉ.

made us realize what were the kind of people into whose hands we had fallen.

My servants and orderlies came to me to complain that in getting in our baggage, they had been insulted, jostled, and spit upon by the people in the square outside. I could only tell them that they must bear it as well as they were able, and try to avoid giving any offence to the soldiers.

Neither Fadl el Mulla nor Achmet Aga Dinkaue, the two chief mutineers, had appeared when we arrived. We heard they had taken up their abode in the compound on the opposite side of the square which had been built to receive Stanley and his people.

Our sentries were some of the sixty soldiers they had brought with them from Fabbo, and were completely under their influence.

Emin had brought Selim Aga from Dufilé with him to act as a sort of messenger between him and the rebels if necessary, and he had asked him to go and consult with Fadl el Mulla, and gather what information he could concerning the rebellion.

In the evening, Selim Aga came in to see us, having been with Fadl el Mulla and the chief mutineers for a couple of hours. He told us that the prime mover in the rebellion had been Achmet Effendi, the clerk who had gone and complained to Stanley about Emin, and who had afterwards been imprisoned at Dufilé for spreading sedition in Tunguru. It appeared he had written to Fadl el Mulla, the chief of Fabbo, circulating lies about the Expedition, and when he heard that the ammunition had been moved from Muggi, and the commencement of the evacuation of that station begun, he had at once written to Fadl el Mulla, and asked him to act.

Fadl el Mulla told Selim Aga that one of the chief reasons for the rebellion was that for a long time a strong feeling against Hawashi Effendi, the senior officer of Emin's forces, had been growing among the soldiers and officers. Many complaints had been made to Emin about his grasping and overbearing conduct, but had always been disregarded, and Hawashi Effendi had continued to be the chief of the soldiers.

Another reason was that they thought that there would be an attempt on the part of their Governor and Stanley to compel them to leave the country. They would not be able to carry their women and children and goods with them; moreover, they knew nothing of a road to Egypt *via* Zanzibar, and did not really believe that Khartoum had fallen. A variety of minor accusations were brought against their Governor. Everything, in short, might be summed up in an accusation of treachery on his part to the Khedive and his people, and injustice to his officers. All expressed a strong feeling of dislike against Signor Vita, the apothecary, who, they said, acted as a spy for the Governor and made a great deal of mischief in the Province.

As for me, they said they had personally nothing against me, except that I was an envoy of Stanley, and was helping the Pasha and him to carry out their plans of forcing the people to leave the Province, but they supposed I was only obeying orders. I was free to go about the station, but I should be followed by sentries who would report to them all that I did.

The mutineers had sent for the rebel officers of the 1st Battalion to join them, and also for officers from the stations of Bidden, Kirri, Muggi, and Laboré. When these officers arrived a council was to be held, when it would be decided what steps should be taken with regard to the Governor and Hawashi Effendi for the future safety of the Province. Lists of accusations against Emin and certain officers would be made out, and they would be brought up for trial before the Council, which was to be composed of representatives from every station in the Province. Selim Aga told me afterwards that Fadl el Mulla was much less bad than many of the rebels, but that he was under the influence of Achmet Aga Dinkaue, his second in command, who was one of those violent fanatics who stick at nothing, and the two were entirely in the hands of some scoundrelly clerks and Egyptian officers. From what Selim Aga said, the feeling was strongly against the Governor, for what reason I could not wholly understand, unless it was that he had been a great deal too easy with his people. Selim Aga further told me that the rebel officers had been very reticent and not particularly friendly with him. He gave us more information about Surore Aga at Laboré, and of the part he, in conjunction with his great friend, Achmet Aga Dinkaue, had taken in the getting up of the rebellion.

We had, it appeared, nothing then to do but to wait, with what patience we might, the coming of the rebel officers from Rejaf, for nothing would be settled till they were all assembled. We naturally waited impatiently for their coming, for anything was better than the terrible state of suspense and uncertainty as to our fate.

Meantime, our life, shut up in that small compound, in the middle of a noisy station, was anything but pleasant. People congregated in the square and discussed the turn affairs had taken in a sufficiently loud manner for us to hear what was said. The compound was surrounded by roads, and people passing constantly, took the opportunity of shouting out unpleasant things for our edification. On one side was the school, where the priest taught the children of the station, and the noise they made all day long was unceasing. On another side was the compound of an Egyptian officer, who had a great number of wives and slaves whom he used constantly to be beating, and the cries and shrieks from these unfortunate women were heart-rending.

Selim Aga, after the first day of our imprisonment, had been refused admittance into our compound by the order of the rebel officers; we had therefore to depend on our servants to bring us what information they could gather in the station.

Hawashi Effendi was also a prisoner, but our boys would occasionally be able to smuggle in a note from him, or the few well-affected people in the station, under vegetables or corn, which they had been out to buy for us. Our boys and orderlies complained bitterly of the taunts and insults they had to put up with from the soldiers, who told them that their masters would never be allowed to leave the country, and a variety of other impertinences.

Fadl el Mulla had ordered that soldiers from his own Fabbo Company should always be placed as sentries over us; these were more mutinous and insulting than the Dufilé soldiers, and were more under his control. Fabbo soldiers were also placed as sentries on the store-houses and powder magazines.

Certain portions of the machinery of the engines in the steamers had been taken away, and were kept under Fadl el Mulla's charge, for the sailors were not very friendly to the rebels, and it was feared that they might conspire to help us to escape.

Indirectly we heard various rumours of the intention of the rebel officers towards us, and the soldiers from time to time let drop certain words from which we could understand that our fate was not likely to be a pleasant one. Hawashi Effendi had been very ill when he was made a prisoner, and though he had slightly recovered, we almost expected his imprisonment and troubles would prove too much for him. We were told a plot was to be discussed, on the coming of the rest of the rebel officers, against Stanley and the Expedition, on their return to the lake.

The plan was to go down with the steamers full of soldiers when they heard of his arrival at the lake, to fall upon the camp, seize the guns, ammunition, and all that he had, and then to turn them adrift. I doubted if they would be able to carry out this plan as easily as they imagined, for I had boundless faith in Stanley's caution and wisdom, still, it made me very anxious, and I at once wrote a letter of warning to him, intending to send it on the first opportunity by some faithful messenger to Shukri Aga, chief of M'swa, of whose loyalty I felt convinced.

Meanwhile, day by day, there was an increase in the hundred and one petty annoyances and humiliations to which we were subjected. We heard that the rebel officers of the 1st Battalion, together with the chief priest of the country, were on their way up from Rejaf, and might be expected at Dufilé in a few days.

On the evening of August 26th, we heard, through my boy, that letters had come in from Tunguru and M'swa which were supposed to be of great importance, for Fadl el Mulla, on reading them, appeared to be exceedingly excited, and had at once called a meeting of officers, and had read the letters to them.

The meeting had been held in the rebels' divan, with closed doors, and great secrecy had been kept concerning the contents of the letters, we could not therefore hear what the news actually was.

Emin was greatly troubled by what we had heard, and we sat up late that night talking over it, and making all sorts of conjectures as to what the letters contained.

My boy Binza told me that one letter was from Suliman Aga, at Tunguru, requesting the Mudir to come up as quickly as possible. The stir it made amongst the rebels went to show that something of importance was afloat.

We thought it might be that Kaba-regga's people had attacked one of the stations, or that the Nyanza steamer which was to have attacked one of the Unyoro Lake villages might have been disabled, or that mutiny had also broken out in one of the lake stations. This last would have been a great blow to us as the mutiny had not extended south of Dufilé, and such a thing would cut us off entirely from Stanley. The last and least probable conjecture was that Stanley had arrived. We did not expect him for another four or five months, but it might have been just possible that he had met Barttelot much sooner than he had expected, and had so arrived considerably before his time. But after discussing this last conjecture, we dismissed it as too improbable, and retired to our beds late, having come to no conclusion.

Early next morning I was awakened by Emin coming into my hut. The instant I saw him I knew he had news of importance, for he only had on his pyjamas, and that was a costume he never would have appeared in unless something unusual had surprised him.

The news was that Stanley had arrived at the lake! Oh, glorious and welcome news coming at such a time! I sprang out of bed with an incredulous, "No! Impossible!" Such news was most wonderful and unlooked for.

Selim Aga had that morning early smuggled in a note, saying that there were two letters, one from Kodi Aga at Wadelai, and one from Shukri Aga at M'swa. Kodi Aga's letter said that Stanley and great numbers of men and loads had arrived at the lake, and that he had brought with him three elephants and a large boat. The elephants and boat must, I thought, be mere native exaggerations, probably it was said he had three animals with him (donkeys perhaps), and these excitable people had at once concluded they must be elephants. Suliman Aga had gone down, we were told, in the small steamer to see Stanley.

Shukri Aga's letter was to the Pasha, the mutineers had kept it, though we were told they had not opened it, but were waiting for the arrival of the officers from Rejaf before doing so. Selim Aga told us that on the outside of Shukri Aga's letter was written, "Very important news. Great matter for rejoicing."

We could only wait with the utmost impatience to see what would happen.

Emin said he thought it would be a good thing when the Rejaf officers arrived for me to go to them and try to get them to allow him and me to go down to see Stanley. If they did not allow that, I must try to persuade them to allow me to go down alone, for neither Suliman Aga nor Shukri Aga knew what had happened at Dufilé, and Stanley would be acting quite in the dark. I felt I must warn Stanley somehow, even a short note would do, but if I could get speech with him, things would be so much easier.

However, Emin and I wrote a letter to Stanley, telling him of our position, and full particulars of the country, people, route, &c., with suggestions as to plans, should he think it possible to try and rescue us. I informed him also of the plot which we heard had been made to entrap him, and warned him most earnestly not to trust any one except Shukri Aga.

This letter I intended to confide to the care of the pilot of the steamer *Khedive*, in whom I trusted, to hand it over to Shukri Aga, who would in turn forward it by friendly natives to Stanley. This, of course, I only proposed doing, should the rebels refuse to allow me to join my leader. I felt hopeful of being able to induce them to accede to my request, but poor Emin was sometimes dreadfully desponding, and at such times I did my best to rouse him to a more cheerful frame of mind. I think he was glad to have me with him, but to people who have never been prisoners before, this imprisonment in a small closed-in yard was very depressing, and even I began to feel it terribly, though we had only been prisoners twelve days. The outlook was certainly black enough to depress anyone. It was a terrible thought, that Stanley and my comrades might be walking into the same trap as that into which I had fallen, and I a prisoner, unable to hold out a hand to help, or even to warn them. The idea haunted me night and day, and with strained nerves I awaited my interview with the rebel officers.

Poor Emin, he was utterly beaten down by the weight of his troubles, his bitterest thought was that after all these years of self-sacrifice on his part to his people, they should so turn against him, and that his control over them should be so slight. All Emin's immediate people, his secretaries, clerks, aides, and followers had been put in prison, and we were alone, utterly alone, with absolutely no one in whom we could place the slightest confidence. He was one of those brooding, susceptible natures, and his thoughts at that time must have been torture.

At mid-day on August 31st, the people from Rejaf came in. They marched into the station in triumph, with flags flying and trumpets playing, the soldiers being all drawn up in line to salute them. As if to mock us, the procession marched through the station, and halted opposite our compound, amid the acclamations of the assembled people. After some speeches had been made, the soldiers were dismissed to their quarters, the officers finding huts in the compound occupied by Fadl el Mulla on the opposite side of the square. The arrival of these rebel officers was a great contrast to our lowly entry.

The officers from Rejaf were Ali Aga Djabor, Hamad Aga, Farratch Aga Ajok, Ali Aga Shamruk, Dowel Beyt Aga, two clerks, and Sheik Moorajan, the chief priest of the Province. From Muggi, Bachit Aga Ramadan and two others, from Laboré, Surore Aga, and from each of the other northern stations there were officers whose names I did not know. They brought with them sixty soldiers, drawn from the different stations, and hosts of servants and slaves.

The officers shut themselves up in their compound, and we could hear them across the square in excited consultation. Bugle calls sounded, orders were given, and there seemed to be a general stir and bustle in the station. The soldiers had gathered under the trees in the square, and were laughing and talking together loudly, evidently comparing notes with the rebel soldiers of Rejaf, whom they had not seen for some time.

In the evening great jars of native beer and millet whiskey, which had been prepared by Fadl el Mulla's orders, were carried in to the rebel officers, who, judging from the laughing and shouting and quarrelling we heard, were indulging in a tremendous carousal.

We heard in the evening that a council would be held the next day, and that I was to be examined before all the rebel officers in the divan, and everything about the Expedition was to be closely enquired into. It was also said that Hawashi Effendi would be brought up for trial and witnesses would be called face to face with him, to prove the accusations brought against him.

I was afraid it would go hard with Hawashi Effendi, for every one with whom he had come in contact seemed to have something against him. I hoped the rebels would only strip him, and not hang him, as we had heard was their intention, for he had been faithful to his Government, and had worked well for it, it was chiefly his private character which was so bad.

The next morning Bachit, one of my Soudanese orderlies, came in to tell me that the rebel officers were sitting in council, and had sent over to him, Abdullah and Moorajan, my other two orderlies, ordering them to appear before the divan. I at once ordered them to go, but to be careful what they said, and I told them to answer all questions put to them perfectly truthfully, so that there might be no conflicting evidence in their story. In half an hour they returned, and came to me to make their report. First of all they had been asked who Stanley was, and whether he had come from Egypt. They answered they were soldiers of Effendina, who had sent sixty-four of them with Stanley to bring relief to the Mudir and his people. "Then where are your uniforms, where are your accoutrements?" asked the rebels. My orderlies said their uniforms had been worn out long since in the forest where they had been struggling to carry out Effendina's orders to bring help and ammunition to those very officers who were now questioning them so roughly. The rebels answered, "You are liars, and were only picked up by

Mr. Stanley, who is himself merely an adventurer, you are no real soldiers, and we will put you in chains unless you admit the truth." Upon this Abdullah, a smart young fellow, stepped forward, and holding up his Remington rifle, pointed to the Egyptian brand, the crescent and star, with which the barrel was marked, exclaiming, " This is Effendina's mark, let any officer who chooses put me through my drill, and I will show him whether I am a soldier or not." He was accordingly put through his drill, and I was told he acquitted himself admirably. The rebel officers having asked my orderlies a good many other questions concerning Stanley, the Expedition, and myself dismissed them.

After a short interval they sent for my boy Binza and told him to tell me they wished to see me. I immediately sent him back to tell them I was perfectly willing to come and see them, but that I was not accustomed to receive messages through my servant, if they chose to send an officer over to request my attendance, I should be ready to accompany him to the council. Ali Aga Shamruk, an Egyptian officer, at once came over and politely asked me to accompany him.

At this time the greatest excitement prevailed in the station to hear the result of the first sitting of the Council, and great numbers of people were assembled to see the witnesses as they were conducted by sentries across the square to the rebels' divan. It was the first time since my imprisonment that I had left our compound, and the people looked at me curiously as I crossed the square, but were in no way rude or insulting. I had a nervous feeling that

Before the Rebel Council.

great deal depended on this interview, and on what concessions I could get the rebel officers to make. I took my servant Binza with me to act as interpreter.

On entering the divan the rebel officers, of whom there were some thirty, rose and greeted me quite respectfully. Fadl el Mulla and Ali Aga Djabor, whom I now saw for the first time, came forward, and after telling me they had been elected heads of the Council, introduced me to the different officers, many of whom I did not know. I then told them, as they wished to see me, I was here to listen to what they had to say and answer what questions they wished to ask me. They bowed, and a long silence ensued, during which I had time to glance round and take in the faces of the different officers assembled.

A broad, raised, brick seat ran entirely round the divan, on which were spread a number of clean mats. Here were seated the officers, nearly all of whom were Soudanese. They were a sullen, heavy, bestial-looking lot, with stupid, phlegmatic faces. Here and there was a fawning, treacherous Egyptian. I could see my friend, Surore Aga, of Laboré fame, seated behind me near the door, and as my glance included him his shifty eyes dropped and he looked away. Neither Hamad Aga nor Selim Aga were there. Seated cross-legged on a long mat stretched on the ground were four clerks, with writing materials in their hands, ready to take down my evidence; these were Egyptians and Copts. The three men whose appearance struck me most were the two chiefs of the Council and the chief priest, Sheik Moorajan.

Fadl el Mulla, the promoter of the rebellion, was a tall enormously fat Soudanese of a jet black colour, he had a rather intelligent, and by no means unpleasant face, in fact for a Soudanese he was rather good-looking. Ali Aga Djabor was a Soudanese of the same build and type, and looked his character thoroughly—a bully, robber, and drunkard.

Sheik Moorajan, with his long white robe, big turban and snowy beard, was the most striking figure of all. He was a native of Dongola and had a Jewish Arab face. Whenever I looked up I found his small crafty eyes fixed upon me, eyes which were instantly averted when they met my glance.

After the silence, Fadl el Mulla began to speak in the name of the other officers. He questioned me closely about the Expedition, its origin and aims. I told him how it was got up on account of the interest excited by the Mudir's letters to Europe, and how the Khedive had taken part in it and had given Stanley his final instructions before leaving for Zanzibar. I told him the Mudir's letters had only spoken in the highest praise of the people, and that he had written solely for their good,—he had asked nothing for himself. I then related the story of our wanderings and of our final meeting with Emin as simply as I could. Fadl el Mulla asked if Effendina had really sent the Expedition, why he had not sent some one in his employ, some soldier, or pasha in command, and why, if we came from Egypt, we had not brought letters from their friends and relations there. I answered that Stanley knew Africa better than any living man, and was considered more capable than anyone else to command the Expedition; as to our not having brought letters from their friends, I admitted that was an oversight.

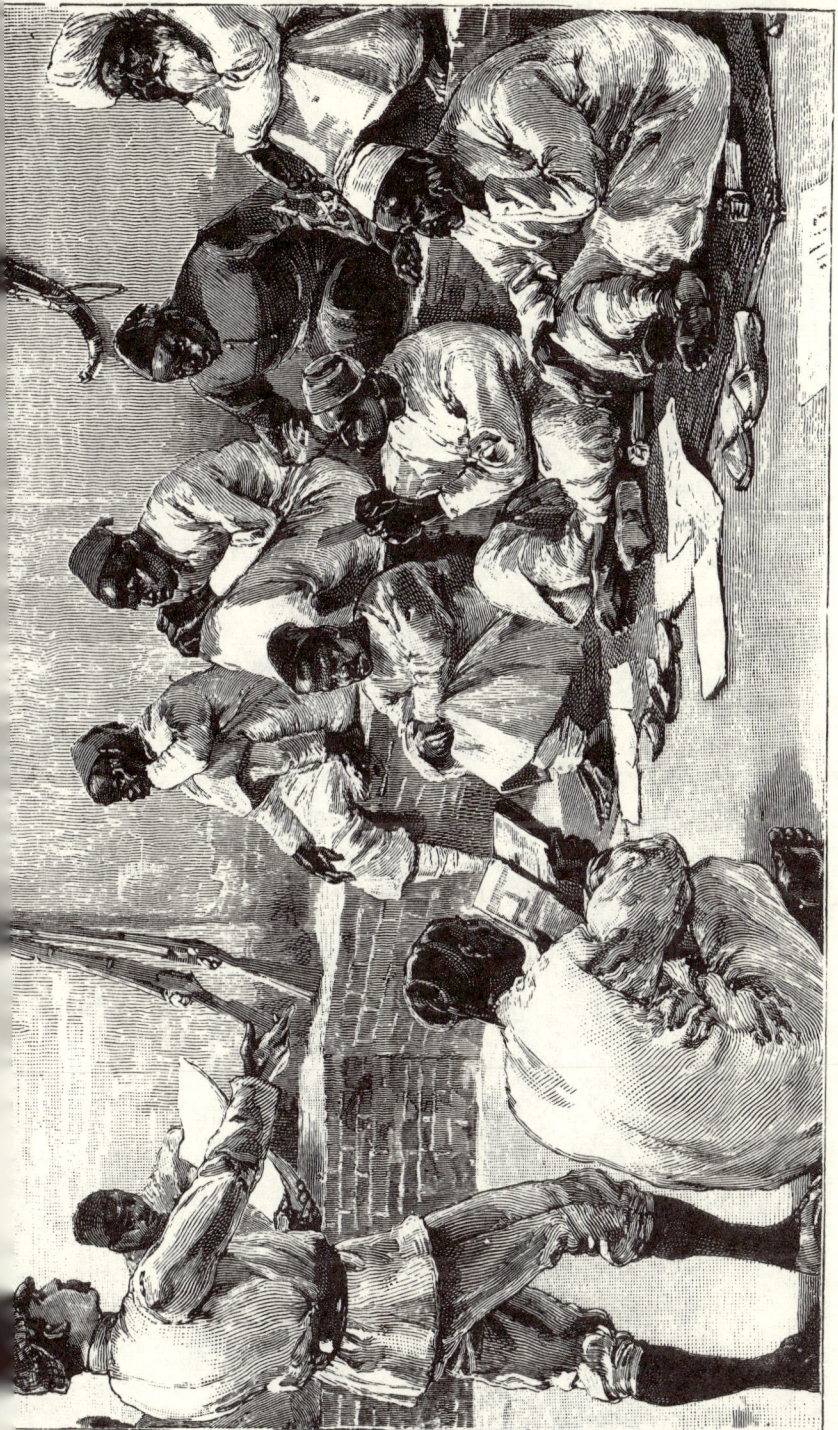

READING KHEDIVE'S LETTER BEFORE THE REBEL COUNCIL.

Page 176.

The rebels here paused and spoke to each other in an undertone, glancing at me from time to time as if I was the subject of their conversation.

Fadl el Mulla then began to question me about the road, and what possibility there would be of getting their children and goods carried in the event of their leaving the country. He also asked me what road we proposed going by, and what chances there would be of finding food, and if there really was a way of getting to Egypt by Zanzibar. I answered all these questions to the best of my ability, and, taking out the Khedive's and Nubar Pasha's letters, I handed them to the chief clerk, and told him to read them aloud so that the people might see that there was no wish on the part of Effendina or their Governor to force them to leave the country if they preferred to remain where they were.

The letters were read out and the signatures carefully examined by the clerks, who said they would like to compare the signatures of the letters with Effendina's signature, which was attached to the brevets confirming their promotion. I told them they were at perfect liberty to do so, and several officers went out to fetch their brevets.

Whilst we were waiting for these to arrive, Fadl el Mulla began to speak of Hawashi Effendi, and told me how he was hated by all the people, how he took their women, seized their cattle, sheep, and corn, and generally abused his position. He said the Mudir had upheld him in all he did, and had intrigued with him against them, for which they were greatly incensed against him. He then asked why the Mudir had not been to Rejaf, why he had given orders for the station of Muggi to be evacuated, and concluded by saying that Emin had arranged with Hawashi Effendi to carry away all the ammunition and leave them stranded and helpless in the country at the mercy of the natives.

I answered all these questions and comments as well as I could, but I saw that I was disbelieved, for the officers constantly interrupted me to ask questions, and made frequent exclamations of incredulity while I was speaking.

Upon the officers returning with their brevets, the signatures of these were most carefully compared with the signature on the Khedive's letter which we had brought with us. Unfortunately, this letter had been injured by damp on our journey through the forest, and the signature was slightly blurred.

The letters were passed from clerk to clerk for comparison; they seemed unable to decide, and there was a good deal of discussion about it. At last, one clerk threw down the letter at my feet, exclaiming, "It is a forgery, and you and your master are imposters." My first impulse was to knock him down, but with a strong effort I restrained myself. Something in my face must have shown the officers how difficult the effort to control my anger was, for they dragged the clerk away and ordered him to be silent.

A great excitement followed, and in the discussion it was decided to send steamers full of people down to Stanley, whom they now told me had arrived in N'sabe at the south end of the Lake.

I told them it was not the slightest use going without taking either the Mudir or myself with them, for Stanley's first question would be, "Where is your Mudir, where is my officer?" and he would at once understand what had happened, and would probably fire on them. I then suggested that they should take the Mudir and me with them, and that we should all go together before Stanley, and hold a consultation in his camp.

This they at once refused to do, and said their Mudir should not move from his prison in Dufilé. Seeing it was useless to press them to adopt this plan, I told them they must take me. This also they refused to do; and said they would tell Stanley that we were busy here, and would ask him to come down with them to see the Mudir and me. I told them they did not know the man with whom they proposed to deal, he would see through the thin covering of their plot like lightning and moreover would act like lightning. Still they refused to let me go. Whereupon I taunted them with treating their guest in this way, and told them they were acting like savages. I had come among them only to help them, and after greeting me on my entry into the country with bows and fine words, they had intrigued against me, my life had been threatened at Laboré, I had been imprisoned and insulted here, and now they had refused to allow me to join my own people. "Do not," I said, "come before me again with your bowings and protestations, and do not offer me your hands, for I know your hearts are full of treachery against me, your guest, who has come to help you. You are savages and not soldiers." At this tirade of mine, a tremendous confusion of tongues arose, some were for punishing me for my rash words, notably

Ali Aga Djabor, and some cried shame. But, at any rate, I had struck the right chord in taunting them with having acted contrary to the strict law of Mahomedan hospitality, I could not possibly have said any bitterer thing to them. There is, too, in these people, these negroes, a certain rough chivalry. Not only have I noticed it here, but I have constantly seen it in our Zanzibaris. "Chivalry in a negro!" I hear some people say in a tone of contempt, and I answer, "Yes, chivalry in a negro, as chivalry in a European." It may not wear quite the same form as ours, but for all that it is chivalry of the truest kind. Touch that string, strike that chord, and you will be answered by as true a strain of melody as ever you could draw from a European.

High above the confusion of tongues rose the voice of Fadl el Mulla. "By Allah! he has spoken truly, and he shall join his people. I am the head of the Council and I swear it!"

With but few exceptions they all agreed, and it was decided that in three days the steamer should start, and I should go with them. This was all I wanted, this was the concession I had been working for, and shaking hands with Fadl el Mulla and bowing to the rest of the officers, I left the divan. I had a horrible fever on me that day, and during the three hours I had been speaking with the rebels in the hot stifling divan my head had gone round, and several times I had nearly fallen. On reaching our compound, I threw myself on my angarep utterly exhausted, and Emin came into my hut to hear the result of my mission.

He had hardly expected that he would be allowed

to leave Dufilé, but was very glad to hear that I had induced the rebels to allow me to go. We discussed what would be the best plan to suggest to Stanley when I reached him, but we doubted if he would consider himself strong enough to seize the steamer, and come down in her to Dufilé to rescue Emin.

A good many rumours were going about the stations concerning the rebels' plan of campaign, some of them so outrageous that it was impossible to believe them. A paper was sent in to Emin, containing a proposition from the rebel officers, that in order to restore confidence among the people, they considered it advisable that Emin should reinstate in their places such officers and clerks as had been degraded and put out of office.

These men had been condemned by court martial, composed of the officers themselves, so that it seemed a most extraordinary thing that they should wish the sentences which they themselves had passed to be reversed. However, Emin giving in to "force majeur," signed the paper.

Many of these men had been condemned for heinous crimes, such as striking their superior officer, stealing, and one case was that of a soldier who had deliberately fired at and wounded his captain, Suliman Aga. One would have thought that the release of these men, whose crimes were nearly all against their officers, would have weakened their influence over the soldiers, but I suppose they thought otherwise. It was a kind of bidding for popularity.

Like the Irishman, they were "agin the Government," whatever had been done under it.

The rebels also requested Emin to sign a paper relating to a change in the administration of the Province; to this he also put his seal. It was decided by the rebels that nothing should be done until they had finished their business with Stanley, or if the news of his arrival was not true, certain officers and clerks from the different southern stations were to be brought down in the steamers, to attend the large council which would then sit at Dufilé. The rebels had told me that the steamer was to start on September 4th, but on the night of the 2nd, I heard from my boy that preparations were being made for a start the next morning. I accordingly sent him down to the steamer to ask the captain what orders he had received. He said he was under an order to start for Wadelai early the next day. Upon this I sent over to Fadl de Mulla to say that I wished to speak to him. He sent two of his orderlies with a polite message to say he would be glad to see me, and accompanied by them I went over to his hut. He offered me cigarettes and coffee, which I accepted, and we sat talking for some time upon impersonal matters, things of travel, African customs, etc. I then asked him how it was that after he had given me his word that I should go in the steamer to join Stanley, that he was sending her off a day sooner than he had said, without telling me a word about it. I told him it was evident to me he was not acting up to his word—his word, upon which I had put a higher value than he himself. After the emphatic way in which he had spoken before the Council, I had gone away, feeling that I could trust him, with the result that I now found he intended to deceive me.

He said it was perfectly true he was deceiving me; that the night before, Ali Aga Djabor, Mustapha Effendi Mahmoud, and some others had come to him, and had urged him to prevent my going; they were angry at my taunting them in the divan. He had unwillingly given in, and had agreed to send the steamer off without letting me know anything about it. He now told me she was to start the next day, and as he had given me his word that I should go, he would see that I went, in spite of the opposition of some of the officers. I thanked him, and left him.

On returning to our compound, I told Emin about my interview, and began at once to get my things ready for the morrow, for I felt I could not trust these people, and if I were not sharp, even now, they might leave me behind. Emin lent me certain things which he thought would be useful to me; indeed, his kindness and generosity in such things was unceasing. He never seemed tired of giving.

He seemed very much down at the idea of being left alone, for I acted as a sort of moral buffer between him and the rebels; he thought that they were less likely to proceed to extremities if I, a stranger, were with him.

However, I knew I was really doing the best for him by going, and would probably be able better to help him out of his difficulties. He gave me a number of commissions to do at Wadelai, and I was to take his collections, and all his journals, and hand them over to Stanley, in case anything should happen to him during my absence. I was also to see and deliver letters to certain people whom he considered were likely to be faithful. He begged me to be most cautious and wary in doing this, for if the rebel officers suspected anything, they and I would probably be at once put into prison. He gave me certain orders to give to his servants in Wadelai, and entreated me to do my utmost to send him news by the hand of some faithful interpreter.

On the morning of September 3rd, I was up early, and had all my things ready, and sent over word to Achmet Aga Dinkaue, who was going in command of the steamer party, to tell him I wanted men to carry my things down to the steamer. He sent my boy away, and had the impertinence to tell him that after the officers' baggage had been put on board, mine should go. Suspecting another effort to leave me behind, I ordered Emin's and my orderlies to take my things at once on to the steamer, lock them into one of the cabins, and to bring me the key.

I then went over to see Fadl el Mulla, to beg him to allow no violence to be done against the Governor during my absence. I told him if violence was once begun, there would be no stopping it, and it would get beyond his control. He assured me that nothing should be done against him, but that everything would wait until the officers had arrived at Dufilé from the southern stations. Ali Aga Djabor came in while I was talking, and again tried to persuade Fadl el Mulla to prevent my going, but he said he had already given his word and would not depart from it.

It was very sad saying farewell to Emin, for there was no knowing what might happen; perhaps I might never see him again. He took my hand, and wished me God speed. I merely wrung his hand in return, for a lump rose in my throat, and prevented my speaking.

On reaching the steamer, I found the rebel officers had not yet come down, but I seated myself on deck to show them I was determined to go whether they liked it or not.

After about half an hour the officers came down, and nearly all the station turned out to see us off. I went up to Fadl el Mulla and told him I wanted to take our boat the *Advance*, which I had with me, down to Stanley. All the officers refused, and said there was no use in taking it as I was coming back to Dufilé, but I insisted, and went myself and stood over the men when they launched her and put in the oars and rowlocks. Fadl el Mulla said he allowed her to go only on condition that I gave him my word that in any case, whether Stanley was at the lake or not, I would return to Dufilé. I readily gave this promise.

It was delightful to be out again, though I had only been in prison a fortnight, the river seemed to me to be so smiling, the grass so green, and the distant mountains so beautiful.

There were eight rebel officers on board and a great number of soldiers. The crowding and confusion on the steamer was horrible.

The officers had their angareps out on deck, and lay down on them all day, so that there was no standing room, and all the soldiers and boys crowded aft to get shelter from the sun. The people were constantly smoking or eating, and spat and eructated all round one. I was, of course, unable to eat anything. No one could imagine how disgusting it was to be herded so closely with these people, moreover, the smell of the cooking with bad butter, and the heat of the engines, and all this under a broiling sun with only a low corrugated iron roof over head, combined to make the place stifling and unbearable. The officers asked me to partake of their food, but I declined with a bland smile.

Most of the people talked to my boy Binza a good deal, and he told me it was chiefly with a view to getting out of him the truth about our coming from Egypt.

Owing to the tremendous heat on the steamer, as a matter of course I got an attack of fever, and in the evening I got the officers to have a place cleared for my angarep. However, at 9 o'clock a violent thunderstorm came on, and soon drenched me through and through, and I lay shivering till the morning. The boys and soldiers had crowded aft when the rain came on to get under the shelter of the iron roof, but the rain drove sheer through the vessel, and several people got under my angarep, and between them managed to pull down my mosquito curtain, which considerably added to my general feeling of discomfort. The result of the wetting was, I got such fearful fever that I could hardly stand up when we reached Wadelai.

Only a few people were at the water's edge to meet the steamer, and they seemed considerably astonished at seeing who was in the steamer, they had heard that there was trouble at Dufilé, but did not know the extent of it.

I at once went to the Pasha's compound, and established myself in my house, where several well

Arrival at Wadelai.

affected people came to greet me and hear the news. Signor Marco and the storekeeper, who was a Christian, were terribly cut up by the news, and the tears rolled down their cheeks as I related the story of our troubles. They told me they had heard no further news concerning Stanley's arrival, and were inclined to think that the report was untrue. This was of course a bitter disappointment to me.

Poor little Farida came in to see me with her nurse, and wanted to know why I had not brought her "Baba" with me, she evidently seemed to think something was wrong, but could not quite understand what it was.

As soon as I had greeted the few people who came to see me I went off to bed, for I was feeling terribly ill and seedy. I woke up next morning feeling very bad, but I had so many things to do for Emin that it was no good giving in to it. I saw several people, to some of whom I delivered Emin's letters. I packed the collections and journals ready to take to Stanley, and interviewed Emin's servants, who all came before me, and assured me of their loyalty to their master. Signor Marco came in, and I transacted a good deal of business with him, and arranged things according to Emin's request. He told me that the rebel officers were closeted with those of Wadelai, but were sitting with closed doors, and he had as yet been unable to hear anything. He told me also the surprising fact, that a week before a native woman had given birth to five children, three boys and two girls. One of the boys had died, but the rest were doing well, as was also the mother. The children were small, but otherwise well formed; the father was a wretched-looking little fellow, who was badly wounded four years before, at Rimo during the Mahdi war. I sent the woman a present of ten dollars.

In the afternoon the rebels and soldiers went over and examined everything in the storehouses and powder magazine. I heard that they proposed to take half of the ammunition down to Dufilé on their return here, and to make that place the head-quarters of the Province.

In the evening I was told that a long council had been held that day, between the Fabbo, Wadelai, and Dufilé officers. The result was that they had halved the ammunition, and had packed it ready for removal. The soldiers did not like this arrangement at all.

The next morning I found that sentries had been posted at my gate, and no one except my servant and orderlies were allowed to enter. Even Marco was forbidden to come and see me! I concluded the rebel officers, seeing the Wadelai people were not particularly friendly to them, were afraid I should plot with them against the faction at Dufilé. So I was again a prisoner.

The next day Marco sent me in a note by one of my orderlies saying, that the rebel officers, finding less percussion caps in the magazine than they expected, threatened to search the Pasha's compound and houses in which they said they were convinced they were hidden. This would mean a wholesale robbery if their threat was carried out. There was great discontent and murmuring among the soldiers at the arbitrary way in which the Dufilé officers were behaving, but I knew it meant nothing, for they were like a lot of sheep, and did whatever their officers told them.

I sent three times for Kodi Aga, the chief of the station, as he had not come in to see me on my arrival; but each time he put my boy off. Emin believed implicitly in his loyalty, and I also had thought him a good fellow; I hardly knew now what to think about him, but I put down his refusal to come and see me to the fact that the rebel officers had forbidden him to enter my hut.

The long delay here was most unfortunate, the people seemed to be idling instead of collecting wood for the steamer, and I was very anxious to ascertain whether the news of Stanley's arrival was actually true. Nor did the rebel officers seem in any hurry to get on, I suppose they did not wish to leave the station, until they had brought round the people to their side. There were constant disturbances in the station and quarrels among the officers and soldiers, which all went to show that the people here were not so strong for the rebellion as the Dufilé people imagined. They were a horrid lot, these people of Emin's, and it was like a nightmare being with them. There is no atmosphere so appalling as the atmosphere of treachery. The hopeless feeling of not being able to put your hand on one person and feel he is to be trusted; to have every word and action twisted and misconstrued by those for whose good alone you are thinking and working! The whole story of the loss of the Soudan is one of treachery. I could understand better now what Gordon must have felt when he gave up his life for the people for whose liberty he had fought and struggled so long, only to find himself distrusted, and every action and endeavour for their good turned against him and misunderstood. What must not Emin have felt, shut up in Dufilé, with those semi-savages around him, thinking only of what fresh insults they could heap upon him, and what fresh concessions they could wring from him? Each night the same drunken scenes going on in the rebels' compound, and not knowing each night whether in their drunken maddened state they might not commit some deed of violence, and plunge the station into wholesale riot and bloodshed. Like Gordon, he too had given up much for his people, and I shuddered when I thought of poor Emin left alone in Dufilé.

Are not such men wasted in such a useless sacrifice? What but utter failure has been the end of all the work done in the Soudan? Everything has been lost by treachery. Ignorance, fierceness, and even cruelty, may be eradicated, but treachery never, it is born in people, and must come out, no civilization will ever do away with it.

CHAPTER VIII.

STEAMER JOURNEY WITH REBELS.

Kodi Aga's defection—Sand bar—Arrival at Tunguru—Stanley's arrival contradicted—Casati's grievances—Abdullah Vaab Effendi—Casati's life in the Province—Reason of his coming to Africa—His treatment by Kaba-regga—Suliman Aga beaten by his soldiers—Vita's house looted—Emin's Irregulars—Departure of steamer for M'swa—Moslem protestations of friendliness—Influence of Egyptians on the Soudanese—Message from Shukri Aga—Shukri Aga's ruse—Seizure of ammunition by rebels—From Tunguru to Wadelai—Drunken officers set fire to huts—Breakfast of African dainties—Farida and the necklace—Steamer journey to Dufilé—Emin's judges—Arrival at Dufilé—Sad fate of the Kirri clerk.

BEFORE leaving Wadelai, I wrote a letter to Emin telling him of all that had happened. This I handed over to Signor Marco, who promised to send it down by a Lur interpreter.

After waiting four days we left Wadelai, and I found that Kodi Aga, the chief of the station, was going with us. I was very sorry, for from this it was evident that he had joined the rebels; I noticed he avoided meeting my eye when I looked his way. It seemed a bad look out for Emin, for he had thoroughly trusted Kodi Aga. Some three or four hours distant from Wadelai, a sand bar runs right across the river, which at low Nile has not much depth of water over it. Here we stuck, and as the steamer was heavily loaded, all the people had to be put ashore, and it was necessary to further lighten her by discharging some of the wood. It was more than five hours before we were able to get across the bar.

All the sandbanks in the river were covered with crocodiles of all sizes, from small babies to huge beasts more than twenty feet long. They are most loathsome looking animals. Owing to the stoppage at the bar, we were unable to reach Tunguru that day, and had to tie up against the bank as soon as darkness came on. These stoppages on the river at night were always unpleasant, for it was the wet season, and it usually rained heavily at night; the mosquitoes too were present in swarms.

The next morning was rainy and bitterly cold, for the river, near its egress from the lake, widens out immensely, and a cold wind swept across the water and chilled one to the bones.

For the first time I here saw wild giraffes, there were great herds of them feeding near the river shore. In the distance they were the queerest looking beasts I had ever seen. They have a peculiar way of straddling out their fore legs when feeding, to enable themselves to reach the grass or anything they want to pick up off the ground, for long as their necks are, they are so high in the withers, that it is impossible for their noses to reach the ground when standing in their natural posture. They all made off as the steamer approached, moving at a slow swinging trot, which made them look most ludicrous.

On arriving at Tunguru we found the small steamer *Nyanza* there, and Suliman Aga to meet us on the beach. He had evidently been drinking, for after shaking hands with me he tried to embrace me, but I managed to avoid this trying ordeal.

The soldiers were all drawn up, and saluted me as

PORTRAIT OF CAPTAIN CASATI.

I passed, and a good many people came to greet me. I walked on to Captain Casati's compound, where he welcomed me with true southern warmth, and asked eagerly for news. Rumours had come down of troubles going on to the north, but he did not yet know what form they had taken. He was terribly depressed when I told him all that had happened, and handed him over a letter from Vita Hassan, the apothecary, which had been entrusted to my care. During Vita's absence Casati managed his house and servants for him. The letter contained a most woe-begone tale of all that had occurred; Vita had evidently written in great depression of spirits.

From Captain Casati I learned that nothing further had been heard of the people, who, according to native report, had reached the neighbourhood of the lake. The natives had only told Shukri Aga's men that a large force of people had arrived at and were crossing "the great river." This I took to be the Ituri.

The news had come from Nampigua, who was one of the strongest of Stanley's native allies.

It was now eighteen days since Shukri Aga had first heard the news, and he had immediately sent Chief Mogo, who had formerly brought us the Pasha's letter, with a letter to leave with Kavalli, another of our native friends. Mogo was to return at once and bring back what news he could of the strangers. He had not yet returned.

The general impression was that it was not Stanley after all, and I myself felt no doubt whatever now that the report was a false one. It is always so difficult to believe native reports; the news gets handed from tribe to tribe with all sorts of additions, until at last the originator of the story would not be able to recognize it.

Casati had a long story of grievances to tell me, against Suliman Aga. How he had given him no corn, and had practically "boycotted" him. Casati was unfortunately situated; he had a boy, Vakeel, to whom he was very devoted, this boy constantly brought him in stories he had heard, and made a good deal of mischief generally in the station. For this he was hated and distrusted by all, and Casati naturally shared in the odium. He was, unfortunately, entirely dependent upon the Government for food and clothes, so that in Emin's absence the chief of the station had it in his power to make things uncomfortable for him.

I established myself in my former hut in Emin's compound, and Vita's servants, by the order of their master, brought me food and everything I wanted, and made me as comfortable as they could.

Abdullah Vaab Effendi, an Egyptian officer whom Emin had imprisoned, but who had since been freed by the rebels, came to see me, and asked me if he could do anything for me; his whole house was at my disposal, etc., etc. He was one of those concerned in Arabi's rebellion, and had spoken strongly against Emin, but now that the rebellion had broken out he seemed frightened at what he had done. He was a good-looking fellow, but had a crafty fox-like look.

Casati came in frequently to see me and to report what was going on in the station, for the rebels would not allow me to leave my compound, and objected to anyone but Casati going to see me. He said he intended returning with me to Dufilé, to try and help the Pasha if possible. Emin and he had had a serious difference soon after my coming into the Province, and had not been on speaking terms for three months, but Casati seemed to forget all about it now that Emin was in trouble.

Casati, during the eight years he had been in Africa, had quite given up European habits, and lived almost like an Oriental. He scarcely ever left his own house till the evening, when he used to go and gossip with the people of the station. He sat in his hut all day and smoked; he had no books, and kept no journal; I never could understand how he managed to pass the time, but he was very helpful to Emin.

Eight years before, Gessi Pasha, who was then governor of Bahr el Ghazal, had sent to the Milan Geographical Society, saying that, if it would send out a geographer to his Province, he would pay his passage up from Khartoum and provide for him entirely while he was there. Thus Gessi would get his Province mapped out, and the Milan Geographical Society would be able to obtain many interesting geographical facts. The proposal was accepted and Casati sent out. Shortly after Casati's arrival in the Bahr el Ghazal, Gessi left for Europe, and died at Suez on his way home. Casati was practically abandoned by Gessi, who left him almost destitute, and he was obliged to retire to Monbuttu, and there lived for nearly three years almost like a native. When he was at last in great straits, Emin rescued him and brought him to live in the Equatorial Province.

For eighteen months Casati had been living near Kibero in Unyoro, where he had been a sort of agent for Emin at Kaba-regga's court, and had been of great use in forwarding letters to Zanzibar by way of Uganda for him. Six months before, Kaba-regga had driven him out of the country, and had destroyed all the valuable geographical observations, which had taken him so many years to collect.

One of the first things the rebels did after holding a short council with their confederates here, was to put Suliman Aga out of office. They went among the soldiers, and told them they were no longer to obey Suliman Aga. The soldiers hated him as he was always beating them, and were ready enough to obey them; I was told Suliman Aga remonstrated and dared the rebels to enter the powder magazine, but he was knocked down and beaten by the soldiers, and a disgraceful scene took place. I could see that the rebel officers were putting a spirit of insubordination into the soldiers, which I felt sure would eventually recoil on themselves, for at this time the people were ripe for rebellion, and were ready enough to do anything against law and order.

The rebel officers had turned everything upside down in the station, and no one, even if he wished it, dared oppose them. They put Saleh Aga, a creature of their own, in Suliman Aga's place as chief of the station.

On the morning of September 11th, all the rebel officers and clerks went over to Vita Hassan's compound and searched the whole place. They felt convinced, they said, that he had concealed Government property there. They found nothing belonging to Government, but helped themselves to a good many things. The women and servants of the household tried to oppose them, but the rebel officers pushed them aside, and a tremendous din ensued.

It was a most unpardonable outrage, and showed how ready the people were to rob and steal and to take advantage of the confusion into which everything had been thrown by the rebellion. There were in the stations of Tunguru and M'swa, a great many people of the country about Dongola. These had come up to Bahr el Ghazal and to Emin's Province for the purpose of trading, years before; they were much disliked by the Regulars on account of their being of the same race as the Mahdi's soldiers. Emin had rescued these people from his soldiers, who after the Mahdi war wished to kill them, and had formed them into a regiment of Irregulars. Nearly all of them were artisans, and knew some trade, such as boot-making or cotton-weaving, some were also saddle-makers, or rough jewellers who made silver ornaments for the women. They were the most useful people in Emin's Province, and had hitherto been protected against the Regulars by Emin.

Now that he was deposed, they were in a great state of fear, and Ibrahim Aga, their chief, came to me saying the soldiers had threatened to kill them. I could only advise him to tell his people to keep in their quarters whilst the excitement lasted in the station, and to avoid giving any offence to the Regulars, who only wanted some excuse now to break out into open violence.

Hamad Aga Dinkaue, the chief rebel of the steamer party, decided to remain in Tunguru, and send the steamer on to M'swa, for it was now certain that the report about Stanley's arrival was false. As I too, felt certain of this, I determined to remain in Tunguru with Casati, it being of no use my going on to M'swa. I communicated my intention to the rebels, who said I might do as I pleased.

After the steamer had gone to M'swa, taking the rebel officers in her, the station became more quiet, and several people ventured to come in and see me. Suliman Aga, who I now heard for the first time was a brother of Fadl el Mulla, came in; he complained bitterly about his treatment at the hands of the rebels, and was loud in his protestations of loyalty to the Mudir, and friendship for me. I listened to it all with impatience, for I was getting so sick of all the Moslem trash these people poured out so volubly, while they were plotting against one the whole time.

Every other man who came to see me assured me that he was my devoted friend and faithful servant, that everything in his house was mine, and I only had to command, that I might put my foot on his neck, and that if necessary he would carry me on his head. They generally ended by asking me to slit their tongues or cut their throats if they were not speaking the truth. The most insulting thing was that they supposed such trash imposed on people.

Abdullah Vaab Effendi also came in to see me, and brought me three wax candles he had made for me by way of showing how devoted he was. He talked a good deal about routes, etc., to be adopted when Stanley returned, and seemed to be very anxious to get out of the country.

This rebellion had been chiefly got up by the Egyptians, and now when they saw that the Soudanese had, so to speak, taken the bit between their teeth, and were likely to plunge the whole Province into confusion and ruin, they were frightened at the storm they had raised and wished to cry off.

They had for a long time been whispering sedition and treason into the ears of the Soudanese, who are a people slow to take in ideas, and slower still to act on them; but when once it has taken hold, and the cumbersome machinery of their brains has impelled them, at length to act, they will go to any extremes in an utterly unreasoning, mad-bull kind of way, and it is useless to attempt to stop them. When once they have got an idea into their heads it is perfectly impossible to eradicate it.

The people who did most mischief in the Province were the Egyptian clerks. They had just a little education, and could read and write, which gave them an immense ascendency over the more ignorant Soudanese. Yet these Egyptians had not sufficient education to use that power properly, but used it only for the vilest ends.

The Soudanese, on the other hand, whilst allowing themselves to be influenced by the Egyptians, nevertheless hated them for it, and despised them for their utter worthlessness and want of courage. The Egyptians then having at length moved the Soudanese to violence, were afraid of what they had done, and wished to avail themselves of our escort to get them out of the trouble which they themselves had brought about. The Soudanese had now turned against them, and they had estranged themselves from the Mudir by their disloyalty; so they had fallen between two stools, and felt by no means comfortable in that position. I had no pity for them, and hoped the Soudanese would take the opportunity of paying off several old scores.

We heard that the steamer was expected back from M'swa three days after her departure from here, but I thought this very unlikely, for that would mean staying only one day at M'swa, and I knew the rebels never left a station till they had finished all the drink, after which they started off for "fresh fields and pastures new." Whilst waiting for the return of the steamer from M'swa, Casati and I were often together. He used to tell me about his experiences in Unyoro, and of the time he spent in Monbuttu. I was able to get many new facts about the dwarfs from him. There are great numbers of these little people in Monbuttu and the surrounding countries, and he had often come in contact with them.

Five days after her departure from here, the steamer returned, bringing in her the rebel officers, further recruited by two officers from M'swa. The clerk of M'swa station came as well, and on arriving paid me a visit. He was returning to M'swa the next day, and had come over ostensibly to buy some cattle, but in reality he had come to report to me how things were going on there, and to give me a message from Shukri Aga.

Shukri Aga, it appeared, on hearing that the rebel officers were coming to M'swa, decided to leave the station under the pretence of going out to collect the grain tax, and told his clerk to let him know when the rebels had gone. He sent a message to say that he thought this was the best way of getting out of the difficulty, for he did not want to offend the rebels, as in such a case they would remove him from his post, and put some rebel in his place, thus cutting off all chance of being able to communicate with Stanley when he should eventually arrive.

This was very sharp of him ; I may add here that he managed to stick to his post during the whole rebellion, remaining unswervingly loyal to the Mudir.

The rebels, not suspecting Shukri Aga's trick, had left him in command of his station, but had brought away with them the thirty-one boxes of Remington ammunition we had brought as a first instalment of relief to Emin, and which had been placed in the magazine at M'swa. The clerk told me they had also taken two boxes of Winchester ammunition, which Stanley had left in Emin's charge, and these belonged to us. Shukri Aga, he said, still believed it was Stanley who had arrived, but it was now thirty days since the news had first reached him, and as there had been no letter or further confirmation of the report, I was convinced it was false.

In the evening I went round to the rebel officers, and told them I had heard they had brought two boxes of Winchester ammunition with them, and requested them to give them up to me as they belonged to the Expedition. At first they refused, but I insisted, and going over myself to the store-house, had them taken out. When it was dark, I sent them over to Casati's house, where they were to remain till I wanted them.

On September the 18th, we left Tunguru with the two steamers, and arrived at Wadelai that same night. We brought down with us a good many officers and clerks from Tunguru, including Suliman Aga. Casati had told Achmet Aga Dinkaue he wished to go down to Dufilé, who gave him permission; he therefore accompanied us also.

On arriving at Wadelai I went to the Governor's compound, Casati going to stay in Marco's house.

I was extremely sorry to find Signor Marco had not sent off my letter to the Pasha. He said that things had been so unsettled in the station, and he had so constantly been threatened by people for being friendly to the Mudir, that he had not dared to send the letter for fear of its being discovered, in which case he would have probably been put in prison.

Emin must have been in a terrible state of anxiety at getting no news from me, for I had been away from him just three weeks, and I had promised emphatically to write to him. I could well imagine his wondering what had become of me and whether Stanley had really arrived or not.

As usual, the rebel officers on arriving had a big carousal. Kodi Aga, on leaving the station, had ordered quantities of beer and whiskey to be made ready, and numbers of large crocks of beer and jars of whiskey were awaiting them on their return.

They were all sitting drinking in a hut in the afternoon, and as they became more drunken, they became also more careless; the consequence was, that in lighting his pipe, one of them set the hut on fire. Being made only of grass and bamboo it quickly flared up, and several adjoining huts were burnt down before the fire could be got under. A year before this, the whole station of Wadelai had been burnt down, and vast stores of ivory were destroyed. The soldiers, remembering this fire, were fortunately quickly on the spot when the alarm was given, and put it out before it had spread much; I heard they had thrown some of Kodi Aga's pots of beer on the flames, which were chiefly instrumental in putting the fire out; this seemed to me a sort of satire.

Several Egyptian, Coptic, and Negro women came in to make their salaams to me, and to beg me to convey their salutations to their Mudir, whom they prayed Allah would soon deliver from the hands of the rebels. They were all beautifully dressed in white robes, and looked very picturesque.

One old negress, Hadji Fatma by name, wrinkled and ugly, came in to see me; she was a regular old character, and made me laugh when she tried to pump up some tears on the Pasha's account.

Emin's servants looked after me very well, and gave me tremendously smart meals; they tried to show their sympathy for our troubles by stuffing me.

At early breakfast, seven o'clock, they brought in an omelet, a dish of honey, hot bread and milk, and a plate full of green Indian corn roasted to perfection. At luncheon and dinner, they brought in all sorts of dishes, with the delightful accompaniment of salad and tomatoes from Emin's garden; the usual cups of Arab coffee being served after every meal. Unfortunately I had not much appetite for all these African dainties, for I dreaded to hear that something had happened to Emin during my absence, and I was full of apprehension when I thought what was likely to be the result of the sitting of the council. I had found Wadelai very unsettled on my return, and I feared things were indeed looking black for Emin, the soldiers seemed quite to have forgotten their resentment against the Dufilé people, and received them quite amicably.

Before leaving, Farida came to say good-bye to me, and taking off a necklace of beads handed it to me, telling me to give it to her Baba. She had heard that the people in Dufilé did not give him much to eat, so I was to take him these beads, and tell him to buy chickens with it. Poor little thing! what European child of four years of age would have thought of such a thing?

FARIDA AND THE NECKLACE.

We left Wadelai very early, intending to reach Dufilé, if possible, the same day, but as usual the wood ran short, and we had to tie up against the bank for the night.

The steamer was fearfully crowded, the general

filth and stuffiness increased to such a degree, that it was almost impossible to breathe. Numbers of people from Wadelai and Tunguru—all the scum of the Province—were coming down to Dufilé with their women, slaves and loads, numbers of sheep and goats, chickens, and even rabbits were huddled together amongst them, and smelt horribly.

A good many of the officers were drunk on starting, and most of them became so before long, for they were drinking throughout the whole day. When anything had to be done on board, everyone started up, and each shouted out a different order at the top of his voice. The result was general chaos and confusion, and a lot of time was wasted. That day's voyage far surpassed all the others, it was like a bad dream. When I looked round me at the different faces, some bestial and sullen, some treacherous, and crafty, and nearly all bad, I thought I had never seen a worse looking lot of ruffianly cut-throats.

And these men were to be Emin's judges, these men had us in their power, and were to pass sentence upon us! What was likely to be our fate in such hands! I could only ejaculate, " Heaven help us !"

We reached Dufilé at about one o'clock the next day, and found that the small steamer—the *Nyanza*—had passed us during the night, and had reached the station by daylight, so that Emin knew of our coming. There was a tremendous crowd down at the wharf to see us arrive, for a great number of people, officers, and clerks, had come in from the northern stations to attend the Council. The station was full of people, and numbers had to be accommodated in the Madi villages outside.

Fadl el Mulla, Ali Aga Djabor, and the chief rebels stood in a group on one side listening to the verbal report which Achmet Aga Dinkaue hastened to make. Casati went up to speak to them, but I merely bowed as I passed. As I hurried along to Emin's compound, several people came forward to greet me, among them one of Emin's orderlies. Eagerly I asked him "How is the Mudir?" and on being assured he was well and unharmed, I passed on with a sigh of relief.

As I reached Emin's compound, one of the sentries placed himself in front of the entrance, and told me that by the rebels' orders I was no longer to occupy the same compound as the Mudir. In a fit of indignation I seized the sentry by the collar, and flung him on the ground. Curiously enough, the other seven sentries merely stood staring at me in utter astonishment, and made no effort to move, and I passed in without further opposition.

I found the Pasha looking fairly well, and he seemed glad to see me back again. He told me when I was away the time had gone terribly slowly, he had no one to speak to, except Vita Hassan, no books to read, and had been able to get hardly any news from the outside. During my absence, the rebels—except that they had always been drinking and fighting—had been fairly well behaved, and had not committed any violence. He said as time went on he had felt certain that the news of Stanley's arrival was false, and he was much touched when I told him that Casati, on hearing he was a prisoner, had at once decided that he would go down to Dufilé to be with him, and help him if possible.

He was very indignant when I told him about the rebels having searched Vita's house, and taken some of his things; he seemed to think that this was probably only the beginning of a long series of such outrages on the part of the rebel chiefs.

He had heard that Achmet Aga Dinkaue had written down from Wadelai, to request permission to search his house also, but Fadl el Mulla had refused to allow it. I further learnt that the reason why they had received the order to search Vita's house, was because the store-keeper at Wadelai had told the rebels he was sure that Vita and the Mudir had secreted Government property in their houses.

This was the man who had wept when I told him and Marco the story of the Pasha's imprisonment! Truly it is impossible to trust Orientals, especially if they are Egyptians! I was sorry to hear that the Kirri clerk, who was a very good little fellow, had been carried off by a crocodile while bathing in the river. A large crocodile had been noticed for many weeks lurking about near the bathing-place, and had already carried off three or four children. The Bari crocodile hunters had therefore been sent for, and they had captured it. It was so large and strong, that they were unable to drag it out of the water alive, but the soldiers had put several bullets into it, and eventually they landed it. It measured over twenty feet six inches, and was the largest crocodile on record in the Province. It was dragged through the station in triumph to the Kirri clerk's house, where its stomach was cut open, and found to contain one of his legs. This was wrapped in cotton, and laid before the widow, which, was I thought rather a doubtful consolation! The leg was finally carried in solemn procession, and buried outside the station.

Casati came in after a while and took up his abode in a hut that was used as a store-house in Emin's compound, so, at any rate, we now had another companion.

CHAPTER IX.

THE REBEL COUNCIL.

Fadl el Mulla opens proceedings—Accusations brought against Emin—The first day's proceedings close—Indictment against the Governor—Signing of Emin's deposition—What is to be done with the Mudir?—Emin longs for a glimpse of trees—The case of Hawashi Effendi—Fury of the people against him—Accusations proved—Spoliation of Hawashi's property—Osman Latif—Khedive's letter credited—Emin to be sent to Rejaf—Suspense—Books—Quarrels among the rebels—Binza's wife's head is too hard—Flogging of women—Visit to Osman Latif—General desertion to the rebels—Emin's disappointment—General discontent of the soldiers—Emin makes his will—Letter from Osman Latif—Plans made by the rebels—Trial of Vita Hassan—Vita Hassan questions me—Inability of the people to help themselves—A pretentious people—Emin's house looted—Spirit of "*laisser faire*" in the Province.

On September 24th, the Council began to sit. It was composed of between sixty and seventy officers, clerks, and employés from every station in the Province. Most of the officers were Soudanese, but the clerks were chiefly Egyptians, Copts, and Khartoum people or half-breeds.

The Council met under the trees in the middle of the square, and a sort of divan was formed by seats being placed upon the raised platform of which I have before spoken. On these were seated the principal members of the Council, while the lesser members found places on a large semi-circle of seats below the platform. Beyond these were drawn up

SITTING OF THE REBEL COUNCIL. Page 210.

the non-commissioned officers, who were not considered members of the Council, but who were occasionally appealed to by their officers.

The whole of the large square was crowded with people, who pressed round the outer circle to hear the proceedings. A non-commissioned officer and a large number of sentries were always on duty to bring up the witnesses and to keep order.

The first meeting lasted from eight in the morning till four in the afternoon, but afterwards these sittings generally lasted from eight till one.

On opening proceedings, Fadl el Mulla stood up and addressed the meeting. He said the Council had been called to consider certain things concerning the Government which had long given great dissatisfaction to the Khedive's subjects in the Province of Hatalastiva. It was the intention of the Council to thoroughly investigate everything concerning the Government since 1885, and to go through all the Government books and papers, which had been brought down from Wadelai, the seat of Government. Mr. Stanley had arrived some months before, and had remained some time with the Mudir, he had gone away intending to return, and had left one of his officers with the Mudir. Events had since then transpired which had proved that the suspicions they had for some time entertained concerning their Mudir were true. He had been asked by certain officers to act on the behalf of the Khedive's subjects, and he had come to Dufilé, and had placed the Mudir and Mr. Stanley's envoy in confinement, there to await the result of the investigation now about to be held.

Accusations on various subjects would be brought against His Excellency Mehmed Emin Pasha, the Mudir of Hatalastiva, against Hawashi Effendi, the senior Bimbashi, Vita Hassan Effendi, the Apothecary, and certain other persons who were suspected of being in league with the Mudir. After these accusations were thoroughly investigated it would be for the Council to pass sentence upon the offenders and to then concert measures for the future peace and prosperity of the Province. He, Fadl el Mulla, had been requested to act as president of the Council, and he had consented, his only wish being for the good of the Province as befitted a faithful and loyal servant of Effendina.

Exclamations of approval greeted this speech and business was then begun.

First, all the Government books containing copies of the Mudir's letters to the Government in Egypt, were gone through, the most important of these being read out by the chief clerk. Much to the astonishment of the Council, Emin had only spoken in the highest terms of his people. Some of the Wadelai clerks, about the worst lot in the Province, exclaimed that they did not believe these letters were true copies of the letters sent to Egypt. Many of the Mudir's letters relating to the management and administration of the Province were next examined and discussed, but nothing wrong could be found in them. Then the accounts were carefully looked into, and Emin's private account with the Government; no irregularities were however to be found there. Everything seemed business-like, regular, and correct.

Baffled on these points, the officers began to discuss certain affairs concerning the Mudir. There was, at this time, at an early stage of the rebellion, a party for the Mudir, and these to a certain extent stood up for him; the result was a war of words between the two parties, the altercation lasting till late in the afternoon.

The proceedings ended at four o'clock without any particularly bad effect, or without much having been decided on, the Council then broke up, and its sitting adjourned till eight o'clock the following day.

We could hear in our compound all that had been going on under the trees outside; it must have been very trying to Emin.

In the next day's sitting the party against the Mudir had it all their own way. It opened by an excited and impassioned address from the clerks, who inveighed against their Governor in the strongest terms, and accused him of all sorts of crimes. They then requested to be allowed to read the indictment they had written against the Mudir, in which all his offences were set down, thirty-seven accusations in all. Permission was granted, and it was read out.

First. The brevet which he said he had received from the Khedive, conferring upon him the rank of Pasha was a forgery; he was no Pasha, but only a Bey made by Gordon. Second. The letters which were written in the Government book in which the Mudir had spoken in praise of his people, and of their behaviour in the Mahdi war, which were supposed to be copies of letters sent to Egypt, were only a blind; no such letters had ever been sent to Egypt. Third. The letters Stanley had brought, as coming from the Khedive and Nubar Pasha, were forgeries. Fourth. That Stanley had not come from Egypt, as the Mudir pretended, but that he was only an imposter and adventurer. Fifth. That the Mudir had conspired with Stanley to take the people out of the country against their will, and hand them over as slaves to the English. Sixth. That the Mudir had made a plot with Keremallah, the Mahdi's general, five years before, to deliver the people, with their wives and children, over to the Mahdi. Seventh. That the Mudir had upheld Hawashi Effendi in all he did, and benefited by his robberies. Eight. That Emin, with Vita Hassan, had four years before poisoned the Major of the 1st Battalion, etc. etc.

The rest of the accusations referred chiefly to neglect of, and injustice to, his people, of favouritism, and the taking of presents. All of these accusations were equally outrageous and absurd.

After the reading of this indictment was finished the clerks again addressed the assembly, and assured the people that they would prove every one of those accusations. They then demanded the instant deposition of the Mudir, and produced the document, in which it was stated the Mudir was deposed on account of disloyalty to the Khedive, and treachery to the people, and peremptorily told the officers assembled to sign it.

They were so staggered by the accusations against the Mudir, and by the vehemence of the clerks in declaring they could prove every accusation they brought forward, that Fadl el Mulla meekly signed it, and his example was followed by all the rest of the rebel officers. There were a few who did not wish to put their seals to it, but they were so threatened and stormed at by the rest, that after making a very feeble resistance they gave in. As I have said before, if the Soudanese are only stormed at with sufficient energy and obstinacy, they nearly always give in eventually.

In the evening a letter was sent in to the Pasha, informing him that by the wish of his people he was deposed, and no longer held any appointment in the Province. He was ordered to put his signature to this. I entreated him not to sign it, for by doing so he would be giving himself away entirely. However, he said he thought he must, and that anything signed under such circumstances could never be considered binding. Casati was also asked what he thought, and he said the Mudir must give in to "*force majeur.*" So Emin put his signature to the document.

It then became the question among the rebels to decide what was to be done with the Mudir. Should he be kept a prisoner here in Dufilé, should he be sent down to Rejaf; to Kirri; or where? I heard that it was even whispered among the worst rebels that he had better be executed. It was a subject upon which the rebels could come to no conclusion, though they were for ever talking about it, and discussing it from every side and every point.

The subject of what to do with the Mudir was constantly put aside, and other subjects brought up for discussion, but as constantly the rebels returned to the same question, and were never able to decide it.

Casati and I were both called several times before the Council, and questioned upon different subjects, and when anything very outrageous was decided on, Casati often spoke against it, and sometimes with good effect. I, of course, in my character of prisoner and envoy of Stanley, had no voice in the Council.

It was curious, that while these people were proposing the most diabolical plots of cruelty, robbery, and disorder, they still clung to a semblance of decency and order, and tried to justify each other in what they were doing. People may not be able to understand this strange combination. I can only say it was so.

During those days of our imprisonment, cooped up in a small yard, closed in by a high thick boma, and surrounded by a noisy station, Emin longed for a glimpse of trees and green grass once more. I discovered that by standing on a chair, we could just see a small patch of green grass with five or six Borassus palms growing on it, some mile and a half from the station. We used, therefore, frequently to mount on our chairs, and stand gazing at this small picture.

After a few days the case of Hawashi Effendi came on, and he was brought before the Council and tried. This case created great interest, for Hawashi Effendi was so hated by all, that everyone was eager to see his downfall and humiliation. He was, moreover, known to be very rich, that is, rich for Hatalastiva, and everyone was eager to get a share in the general spoliation of his property. The downfall of their enemy, and the plucking of such a pigeon, had for everyone the greatest possible attraction.

I had that morning been called on to attend the Council, for there were some questions the rebels required me to answer, and they told me also that they wished me to be present when Hawashi Effendi was called.

In the course of the morning, Hawashi Effendi was brought before them. As he crossed the square guarded by sentries, shouts and execrations arose among the people, and the face of every man, woman, and child, expressed hatred and contempt.

It reminded me of Macaulay's lines,—

> " But when the face of Sextus
> Was seen among the foes;
> A yell that rent the firmament
> From all the town arose.
>
> On the housetop was no woman
> But spat towards him and hissed,
> No child but screamed out curses
> And shook his little fist."
>
> *Lays of Ancient Rome.*

He looked fearfully ill and worn, and had a broken-spirited look, which, though worthless as I knew him to be, went to my heart. It was painful to see a man who had been a power in the Province, and had filled a high place, so beaten down, and in such a position. He was always thin, but now he looked a perfect skeleton. He was nearly seventy years old, and his downfall and imprisonment had told on him.

The chief clerk read the indictment against him, which contained a great number of accusations for having acquired goods, money, women, slaves, cattle, etc., by unlawful means. Whilst listening to the reading of this indictment loud murmurs were heard from all sides, and when it was finished a storm of abuse was hurled at Hawashi Effendi, every one seemed to have something against him, and some insulting epithet to throw at him. He was comparatively unmoved by the outburst, and merely shrugged his shoulders, and turned the palms of his hands, in true Egyptian manner, towards the people. Numbers of witnesses came up to bring accusations, most of which were proved against him;—a long line of them, which seemed as if it was never going to end.

Fadl el Mulla then told him that the accusations had been mostly proved against him, and it was clear that he had not only robbed the living, but the dead. The Council decided that all his goods, money, cattle, goats, etc., should be confiscated, and that such women and slaves as he had taken unlawfully from the people should be returned to their rightful owners.

He gave an order to an officer to take a party of soldiers, and bring all Hawashi Effendi's money and goods before the Council.

This order was obeyed with alacrity; for anything approaching looting suited the Soudanese soldiers exactly.

Soon they returned from his compound bearing numbers of boxes, containing clothes, etc. Tables, chairs, beds, cooking-pots, great jars of oil, honey, and butter, and an indescribable mass of things were brought out and deposited before the Council. He was known to have a great deal of money, but only 400 dollars had been found in his house. On being asked where the rest was, he said that was all he had.

With a look of contempt at him, Fadl el Mulla ordered the soldiers to again search Hawashi Effendi's compound, and to dig up the floors of all his huts. After a close search 400 more were found. The rebels knew there was yet more to come, and ordered a search to be made in the villages of the Madi Interpreters.

After some time, 800 more dollars were found in earthen crocks, hidden under the mud floor of the Madi chief's hut. This was all that could be found for the present.

Fadl el Mulla then turned to me and told me he had heard that on my arrival in Dufilé, Hawashi Effendi had asked me to take charge of certain receipts for money lent by him to different people in the Province. He asked me whether this was true. I answered it was perfectly true. My answer caused a good deal of excitement, and the rebels demanded these papers from me. I told them I would give them up only if Hawashi Effendi wished me to do so. He shrugged his shoulders, and said, "Yes, give them up; what can I do?" I therefore sent for my dressing-case, and handed the bundle of receipts over to Fadl el Mulla. There was a receipt from Dr. Juncker for 700 dollars, and others from different people in the Province to the amount of 600 more. The contents of the boxes were then turned out in the square—such a medley as there was! and inventories were taken of everything. Two changes of clothes and a few cooking-pots were returned to Hawashi Effendi for present use, all the rest being deposited in the Government store-houses. Hawashi Effendi was then conducted back to his hut, and the Council broke up.

Fadl el Mulla told me I was free to go about the station as I pleased, and Hamad Aga and Selim Aga asked me to pay them a visit the next day, and in the morning I went round to their compound.

Here I met for the first time Osman Effendi Latif, the Vakeel, or second in command of the Province. He was an Egyptian, formerly head of the detective force in Khartoum. He had at one time given Emin great trouble, but since the rebellion had been behaving well.

He poured a profusion of compliments upon me, and tried to talk French, but he was quite unintelligible in that language; for instance, he wished to say, " I have seen it," which he rendered in French, " Je suis les yeux." I took a dislike to him, he was so cringing, and servile, a true Egyptian,—though I must say he was very useful to us in sending us information during the rebellion. He promised to do all he could in the way of keeping us *au courant* with what was going on in the Province. I talked long with Hamad and Selim Aga, about things in general, connected with the rebellion, and begged them to try and get the Mudir's place of residence fixed for Wadelai or Dufilé, anything was better than being sent down to Rejaf.

It appeared some days afterwards that the rebel officers were not satisfied with the opinion of certain of the clerks who had given their opinion that the Khedive's and Nubar Pasha's letters were forgeries. Abdul Vaab Effendi, who was considered the best scholar in the Province, and had been in Egypt up to the time of Arabi's rebellion, and knew the Khedive's and Nubar's signatures well, had said he should like to see the letters. Fadl el Mulla therefore sent for them, and Abdul Vaab Effendi, having examined them before the Council, said that there was not the least doubt about it, the letters were genuine, for he had seen these signatures many times in Egypt. They were again examined by the clerks, who pronounced them genuine, and said that after all, Stanley must have come from Egypt. The Khedive's letter was then handed round, and each officer kissed the signature, as was the custom in the country; three cheers being given for the Khedive. Still, however, this, from their point of view, was to make no difference in the accusations brought against the Mudir.

Hawashi Effendi's case was meantime progressing. Three hundred more dollars had been found hidden away in the roof of one of his huts, making in all 3200 dollars accounted for. Soldiers had been out to take inventories of his live stock, and it was found he had 700 cattle and 1100 goats and sheep! These had all been obtained in raids made on the natives, and were to be divided among the people, each getting a share according to his rank.

After a great deal of discussion, Fadl el Mulla announced that at last the Council had made up its mind to send the Mudir to Rejaf and give him over into the charge of Ali Aga Djabor; he was one of the worst of the many scoundrels in the Province, and it would have gone badly with Emin had this decision been carried into execution. It was evident as time went on, that though the Khedive's letter had apparently been accepted as being genuine, three-quarters of the people still doubted it. During the whole rebellion it was impossible ever to find out what they did or what they did not believe, or even what they wanted. They made a plan one day only to contradict it the next. In this I consider lay our chief safety; they were ready enough to make all sorts of plans against Emin, but were never able to agree amongst themselves how those plans should be carried out. It was decided to leave Vita Hassan at Dufilé, but to deprive him of his position under Government. Hawashi Effendi was to be sent in chains to Makraka, but his life was to be spared. On hearing the news, Emin was much down-cast, and though I argued that this decision would probably be reversed the next day, or a few days after, he believed it was final. At this time he gave way entirely. It was not, of course, to be wondered at after all those years of strain; still I wished he could have managed to keep up appearances a little more before his people, on whom this giving way had a very bad effect.

I told him the people would go on talking and talking for weeks to come and would settle nothing; but it was of no use, the slightest rumour against him was sufficient to plunge him into the deepest dejection. The suspense and uncertainty were indeed terrible, and though I tried to shut my eyes to the graveness of the situation, in order to cheer him up, there were times when even I, with all my natural hopefulness, could not have been a very cheerful companion.

Fear he had none; such a thing was not in his composition. But it was the nervousness from want of appetite and sleep, which caused his hand to shake and made him start at every sound.

We had with us Royle's book on Egypt, Cameron's Travels, in French; half a dozen of the Waverley novels, and Mrs. Brown on Cleopatra's Needle.

Where on earth Emin got the latter book from I never knew! These books, even including Mrs. Brown, we read again and again with the greatest interest. With the exception of some medical books and a few old *Graphics*, these were all we had. Those *Graphics* too! How often we looked over them, and with what extreme interest we read all the advertisements, Pears' soap, Bird's custard powder, and all the rest of them!

At this time Casati and I were constantly out in the station, doing all we could to induce those officers who were friendly to Emin, to use their influence on his behalf; they all promised to do what they could, but did not dare to do much openly, for fear of being imprisoned.

Osman Latif behaved very well, and had spoken to all the officers in terms of the strongest disapprobation, of all they were doing, for which he often got into serious difficulty with the rebels. He finally refused to put his name to a paper containing accusations against the Mudir, and on the rebels attempting to make him sign it, he threw himself into the river. The rebels cried out, "Let him perish, do not save such carrion," but some one fished him out in a boat, and he was ordered to remain in his house. This was a great pity, for formerly he had gone about the station constantly, and had smuggled in notes to us.

Fadl el Mulla, in his position of President of the Council, raised the ranks of several of the rebel officers, and he and Hamad Aga were by general consent given the rank of Bey. All officers holding positions in outlying stations, known to be friendly to Emin, were called to Dufilé and degraded; officers friendly to the rebels being put in their places.

Letters from the rebel officers were constantly sent in for Emin's signature, to all of which, by Casati's advice, he put his name. Certainly the saying "L'appétit vient en mangeant" was true in this case, for these letters were more and more frequent, and became more outrageous in their demands.

The Council still continued sitting day after day, deciding different things about the future government of the Province. The rebel officers were now quarrelling a good deal among themselves, for there was to be a general change in the administration, and each officer wanted to secure a good place for himself. One man didn't like his position; another objected to the station to which he was sent; one officer refused to work under some other who was put over him; another refused to work with such and such a man under him. The altercations and quarrels were loud and long, and many violent scenes took place. Fadl el Mulla tried to please all, and succeeded in pleasing none. His position was by no means a comfortable one, for he was besieged by people putting forward all sorts of claims for a good place in the new Government.

The rebels had, during the first sittings of the Council, behaved with some appearance of decency, but after some time this was thrown to the winds, and disgraceful scenes were of frequent occurrence.

The afternoons and evenings were given over to drunkenness and debauchery. In these excited moments the decisions to be agreed upon at the following day's Council were discussed, so that from

OUR PRISON IN DUFILÉ.

day to day our fate hung in the balance. We, in our compound, could hear them shouting, cursing, and quarrelling among themselves, and we felt that any moment they might make up their minds to do some violent deed. It will ever be a mystery to me how we passed through that time unhurt. The Providence which watched over us in the forest, must have been watching over us still.

The soldiers, seeing what was going on, were, from what we heard, exceedingly mutinous and discontented, and I was assured by Selim Aga that the feeling among them was rising strongly in favour of the Mudir.

It was therefore Casati's and my endeavour to do all we could to foster and increase this feeling. We went to such people as were friendly, and got them to speak whenever they could to the soldiers, but we of course had to do this with the greatest care and caution, for all our movements, particularly mine, were closely watched.

At this time, when things were going very badly with us, I was astonished by my servant Binza's coming to me to say he wished to exchange his present wife for another, as he said her head was too hard.

"Good heavens, boy!" I exclaimed, "is this a time to be thinking of marrying and changing wives, when at any hour now the blow may fall and the end come? moreover, you have only bought your wife a fortnight ago."

"Yes, master," he replied, "I know it is no time now to be thinking of such things, but—but her head is *so hard!*"

The stress he laid upon the hardness of his wife's head, and the pathetic tone of his voice as he told me about it, sent me into a fit of laughter, and I gave him permission to change her for a wife with a softer head.

My boy Binza was very useful to me, for he was well liked by all the people, and I used constantly to send him out on gossiping expeditions in the station, and he was able to tell me how the feeling in the Mudir's favour was increasing. He told me the soldiers constantly met in each other's houses, and nearly all agreed how much better things were when Emin was Mudir; they laughed a great deal at the idea of Fadl el Mulla raising the officers' ranks, and styling Hamad Aga, "Bey." Binza frequently brought me in little notes from such few friends as we had outside, these he concealed in his Taboosh, or clothes. Emin's orderlies were taken away from him by the rebels, and were sent back to Wadelai to join their company. This did not much matter, for I had my own three orderlies, and Emin had several servants,—it was only another of the petty humiliations which they delighted to heap upon him.

Things were getting worse and worse, the rebels, not satisfied with the amount of the money they had discovered belonging to Hawashi Effendi, seized all his servants and women, and, tying them up, threatened to flog them unless they confessed where the rest of the money was hidden.

On their saying they did not know, a most cruel scene took place which lasted from early morning till mid-day. The boys were alternately flogged and questioned, but nothing could be got out of them as to where the money was hidden.

Then the women were all flogged, and as the courbach curled round their naked backs their cries and shrieks were heartbreaking. We, from our compound, could hear it all going on in the square; it made our blood boil.

The women confessed that there was a number of molotes or iron hoes hidden underground in the compound; these were unearthed, and put in the Government store-house. Molotes are the current coin among the natives in this part of Africa.

The women were then imprisoned in two huts, Hawashi Effendi being shut up in a small hut by himself. Casati went to expostulate with him, and to tell him it would be better for him to say at once where he had hidden the rest of his money. But he refused. He was in a great state of excitement, he cursed the Mudir, he cursed the country, his fate, the Khedive, the Prophet, and everything he could think of.

The spirit of robbery had evidently taken hold strongly of the rebel officers, for they sent a letter to the Pasha, asking him what money, ivory, cloth, ammunition, and papers he had in his house at Wadelai. It went on to say that unless he did not at once hand over everything to them, they would send down soldiers to enter his house. He answered he had nothing belonging to Government in his house.

The officers apparently not being satisfied with this answer, decided to send off a steamer with two officers and two clerks holding an order to search the Mudir's house. Such officers and clerks as the new Government had taken from the Northern stations, were also sent in the steamer to replace those in the Southern stations, whom the rebels had removed on account of their being friendly to the Mudir. They took with them their families and all their goods, and chattels. Casati was to go down to Wadelai with the rebels to be present while Emin's house was searched. I went to see him off in the morning, there was a great crowd of people on the steamer,

OSMAN LATIF TEACHING HIS CHILDREN.

and four of the most rascally of the clerks and officers were sent to search the Pasha's house. I went afterwards and paid Osman Latif a visit for the first time in his house. I found him seated on a mat teaching his four little boys to read and write. His text-book was the Koran from which all Mahomedan children are taught.

He was very much honoured—so he said—by my coming to pay him a visit, and apologized most profusely for not being dressed to receive me. Had he known I was coming, etc., etc.—the usual Egyptian rubbish.

He was very loud in his professions of regret and anger about all that was happening, and said he was constantly telling the people that if they committed outrages now they would suffer for it hereafter. He was anxious to know, if the worst came to the worst, whether I thought England or Egypt would send an Expedition to avenge these outrages? I answered possibly they might, which seemed to give him great satisfaction. He said, "You are an Englishman, the Mudir is a German, Casati is an Italian, Dr. Juncker, who knows this country, is a Russian. Now, as all the nations of Europe are friendly together, why do they not combine to take the Soudan?" I told him they did not want it. He only answered he knew the English had destroyed Abyssinia, because the king had imprisoned three or four Englishmen, and he did not see why it should not be done again. He begged me to be careful to put down everything which happened in the Province in the book in which he heard I wrote every day. Before going he brought his old mother to see me, a wrinkled old woman, who rather took me aback by imprinting a damp kiss upon each of my cheeks. She called me her son, and asked Allah to bless the Mudir and me.

The long imprisonment and ill-treatment proved too much for Hawashi Effendi's loyalty, for we heard shortly after the general flogging of his people, he had sent a paper to Fadl el Mulla, purporting to be a true account of all the presents he had given the Mudir. The list was an immensely long one, there were great numbers of cows, goats, sheep, money, women, and all sorts of things in it. He had in reality only given the Mudir such small presents as all the people did in a friendly way; now and then some vegetables, or fruit, and sometimes a jar of honey; or if Emin stayed a day or two in passing through the station, a goat or two.

Emin, unlike most of the governors in Egyptian employ, made it a rule, during the whole time he was in the country, never to take a valuable present from any one. Every person I spoke to in the Province bore witness to that fact. But the rebels, being unable to prove any of the accusations they had brought against their Mudir, were only too ready to try and get any handle against him which would impose on the people.

Kismullah, too, his collector and prime favourite, turned against him in the most ungrateful way. Emin had been kindness itself to him, and had done everything for him. From all sides we heard that officers whom Emin had most trusted were going over to the rebels.

I used to feel a disgust and contempt for these people who had no pluck or endurance in them, and groaned over each fresh example of their faithlessness and ingratitude. But, after all, was it quite just? They were at best an ignorant lot of half-civilized people; they saw the Mudir's chances of ever getting his head above water again gradually growing less day by day. Meanwhile their ill-treatment by the rebel officers was daily becoming more unbearable, they were threatened, insulted, and robbed. So to save their wives and children, or rather the means of supporting them, they declared for the rebels, and threw over their Mudir. They admitted he had been good to them, but they all shrugged their shoulders, and said with a deprecatory gesture, "What are we to do?"

Whenever any outrageous piece of ingratitude, on the part of some person whom Emin had invariably befriended, came to light, I always felt furious, and said these people had not one redeeming quality; but are civilized people much better in proportion? Is it not self-interest which governs savages and Europeans alike?

It was not therefore, perhaps, to be wondered at that every day we heard of fresh instances of desertion, of ingratitude and deceit. But it was very sad to see the disappointed, down-look on Emin's face, when fresh instances of the defection, one by one, of his most trusted adherents, came to his ears. He shook his head sadly, and his eyes seemed to say, "*Et tu, Brute!*"

The soldiers were disgusted, more because they were uncomfortable under the new regime than because they liked their Governor. We heard all sorts of rumours of their feeling against the rebels increasing, but we could not put much faith in their help, a few words from the rebel officers being always sufficient to evaporate their loyalty, and all their talking and grumbling only ended in smoke. There certainly was one movement which we hoped might turn out well, but it, like the rest, ended in nothing.

Fadl el Mulla and the other officers had heard that the soldiers had for a long time been discontented, and grumbled a good deal at what was going on. Accordingly one morning Fadl el Mulla had the soldiers mustered, and asked them what was the matter. Five non-commissioned officers stepped out of the ranks, and told him they did not like the new government, and wished for the re-establishment of the Mudir. They were at once seized and put in prison, and Fadl el Mulla, turning to the soldiers, said, "You are fools! When I came here I asked you whether you wished to stay in the country or be taken away to Zanzibar, and have your wives and children taken from you? You said you wished to stay in the country; yet now you tell me you want the Pasha, who intends to do all this against you, for your Mudir. What do you mean by it?"

The soldiers at once answered, "We wish to stay here." So Fadl el Mulla told them to let him hear no more discontent, and dismissed them. After a few hours, however, the soldiers went in a body to the rebel officers, and demanded the release of their companions, saying that if they were not released at once, they would go and break the prison down and release them by force. Their order was instantly complied with, for the rebels felt they could no longer keep the soldiers in check. They however divided a good many of Hawashi Effendi's cattle and sheep among the people, and the soldiers were once more put in a good temper. There were many scenes of this kind, but they ended in the same way, and nothing was done. Emin had been counting greatly upon a rising of the soldiers, and was very depressed at this termination of what he thought was going to be a successful revolt in his favour.

He made up his mind for the worst, and, sending for two officers and a priest, made his will, and asked me, if anything happened to him, to take care of the little Farida. He told the officers and priest that he would sooner blow his brains out than go to Rejaf, and that was what he intended to do if the rebels used violence to him. He further refused to sign any more papers that they might send in for signature. Even though they had deposed him, he was appointed Mudir by the Khedive, and no one had power to judge him.

Less and less food had been sent in to us, and at last the meat supply stopped entirely, and only a little corn, not nearly sufficient for the household, was allowed us.

The following is a translation of a letter to Emin, from Osman Latif; it is an example of the many notes we got, telling us what happened in the station day by day. From it, it will be seen that the soldiers, in spite of the officers' attempts to set them against their Governor, were not altogether against him :—

"My Benefactor,

"I have the honour to tell you what your servant has heard. The soldiers, when the officers read them their decision to put you aside, declared unanimously they did not wish for your deposition. They wished only for the removal of Hawashi Effendi, Ibrahim Effendi, and Abdul Wahad Effendi, and wished you to remain here to look after them, for that you were their father and mother. The soldiers are all united in this opinion. When you were addressed in a letter, and were questioned about ivory and other things, and answered the rebels, 'I am your Pasha and Mudir, and no one can put me under examination, except the Minister of the Interior in Egypt,' you have done well, for what you said is perfectly true, and from this moment they have refrained from troubling you with any questions. The chief clerk, Achmet Effendi Raif, Mustapha Effendi, and others, who have made themselves chiefs amongst the rebels, are very much discomposed, and the council has now become a mere farce. They are moreover getting to be afraid of the soldiers, and fear Mr. Stanley's return. Tell Mr. Jephson to go to Fadl el Mulla, and ask him to let him buy some of the fat-tailed sheep from those which were taken from Hawashi Effendi, before they were all gone. I am sure Fadl el Mulla will give Mr. Jephson whatever he asks. I have heard the rebels have decided to leave you here in Dufilé, as they fear the soldiers, and I am to be sent a prisoner to Laboré, for not having submitted to their Government. But I do not know if this rumour is true.

"Without offence I beg you to make my best compliments to Mr. Jephson. He should be tranquil about what happens; for we are all in the hands of God. I beg you will send me some few words, for a letter is half equal to a personal interview.

"With every respect, I kiss your hands.

"Osman Effendi Latif,
"Vakeel of Hatalastiva."

As our allowance was getting less and less, I had to go out and buy meat from the rebels, or beg for it from such people as were friendly. Emin was very much pained at my having to do so, but it could not be helped. There were the Pasha, myself, and Vita Hassan, my four servants, and Emin's and Vita's as well to feed, so that the food went very quickly.

Hamad Aga, and Selim Aga, were trying to persuade the rest of the rebels to evacuate the stations in Makraka, and all those north of Dufilé, and to establish stations to the south, on the site of those stations in Unyoro which had been abandoned by Gordon. This was the measure Emin had been trying to carry out for over three years, and was one of the principal causes of the rebellion of the 1st Battalion, who did not wish to give up Lado and the Northern stations, never quite believing Khartoum had fallen.

The people at that time in the Northern stations would not hear of it; but now that they had nearly ruined the country about Rejaf by their constant depredations on the natives, many of them saw the necessity of it, for food had become scarce in that part of the country.

The greater part of the rebel officers decided on adopting this plan, but there were some amongst them, particularly Ali Aga Djabor, who would not entertain the idea for a moment. The President of the Council said it was decided that stations should be erected to the south and east at Magungu, Fatiko, M'ruli and most of the other places where stations had formerly existed in Baker's and Gordon's time. Ali Aga Djabor was ordered to go to Rejaf and evacuate the station, bringing all the people up to the east, and to commence building stations there. This he refused flatly to do, and, after a stormy discussion, retired to his house in disgust, where he remained several days drinking and carousing with such of the officers as were against the Council's plan.

The people had become completely demoralized, each had an idea of his own, and wanted to carry it out; nobody, not even the soldiers, could be depended upon to obey orders, and all was anarchy and confusion. The steamers had been plying in a desultory way, drafting clerks and officers to their newly appointed positions; but there were constant complaints and discontent amongst them, few of them liking the places or positions to which Fadl el Mulla had appointed them.

Constant rumours were floating about on all kinds of subjects, but they were so conflicting that it is no use speaking about them here.

Vita Hassan, the apothecary, had shared our imprisonment, and occupied one of the huts in our compound; we saw little of him except in the evening. He was very cast down and depressed, for the trial which was being held to investigate the accusations brought against him had lasted many days, and things were constantly coming out about him which no one had any idea of. In all these trials things constantly came out which showed the fearfully corrupt state of the Province—corruption of a kind which seems to be inseparable from Mahomedan, or perhaps I should say from Egyptian rule.

The rebels had again entered Vita's house, and possessed themselves of great numbers of his things; he was very low about it all, and seemed only to care for talking about Stanley's coming, and our chances of being able to get clear of the country on his arrival. In the evening we three would meet and sit out in the open, smoking our pipes, and talking over the events of the day. The subject of Stanley's coming, and of the best plan to pursue in order to reach him, was discussed again and again. We used to buy occasionally a jar of native-made whiskey, which we would drink at these meetings—anything to break the monotony of our imprisonment.

I record a conversation, one of the many I had with Vita on those occasions, for it gives an idea of the utter inability of these people to grasp the fact of what leaving the Province meant. He began by asking me, in case Stanley was able to get us out of the country, how many porters he would be able to give him to carry his goods. I answered probably not one. "And my women?" he remarked. "They must walk." "And my children?" "They must walk too, unless your women carry them." "And our food?" "Your food is on the road, and you and your people must forage for it as we do." "And our cooking pots, and all our boxes, chairs, angareps, bedding, &c."

"Well, you must throw most of them away," I replied.

At this he looked very blue, and, after thinking some time, said he thought it was a hard case.

"A hard case, man?" I said. "What are your cooking-pots, and angareps, your boxes, chairs, and tables, compared with your life and liberty?" I told him we used one box for a table, and another for a chair; we had no beds, but made our beds on the ground with grass or green boughs, and found it very comfortable; they would have to do the same. Here were these people, the scum of the earth, the off-scourings of Cairo and Alexandria, who in their own country lived a life of poverty, giving themselves airs as if they had been accustomed to be waited on all their lives by troops of servants. They had been petted and thoroughly spoilt in Emin's Province, where each person had been accustomed to have as many carriers as he pleased. They would carry about with them all sorts of rubbish; one man to carry a pipe and tobacco, another for a washing basin, and goodness only knows how many for other things. They now expected to travel to Zanzibar in the same manner, and carry all their worthless trumpery with them. They considered it a real hardship to be obliged to throw away anything. They also wanted all their women to be carried, which meant four men to each woman every day. These women, of whom each man had five or six on an average, most of whom were only savages a few years or even months before, and who all their lives had been accustomed to walk! There were altogether perhaps 8000 of Emin's people in Hatalastiva. How many porters would be required to carry the wives, women, children, and goods of these people to Zanzibar! The country could not support us, and we should be old men before we reached the coast.

It was maddening to see the inability of these people to understand that if they wanted us to help them, they must to a certain extent help themselves as well. Here were people to whom it was a matter of life and death to get out of the country (I am speaking more particularly of the Egyptians, Copts, Jews and Greeks, who would assuredly be massacred if Emin left the Province), and who, one would imagine, would do anything to get out of it, grumbling at having to throw away their few paltry beds, tables, pots, &c.

What a contrast to my companions; who had all more or less been accustomed to luxury; who had come out here to work, and had borne all sorts of trials and unpleasantnesses, merely for the sake of helping people whom they had never seen!

When I thought of all they had gone through, and of Nelson being abandoned in the forest; and, on the other hand, when I listened to these low-caste, worthless people complaining at being told that they must help themselves to a certain extent, one could only feel the greatest contempt for them.

This conversation was only one of the many I had heard when any of these people asked about the journey to Zanzibar.

Gratitude to us they had none. When they heard of the shifts we had been put to on the road; saw the tattered state in which we arrived; and had heard of the miserable way in which we lived, they despised us for it all, and could see nothing to admire in it.

If we had arrived in smart uniforms, covered with gold lace, and had given ourselves arrogant airs, they would have kissed our feet and thought us something like deliverers. It was useless to tell them that we officers had arrived at the lake with only two carriers each, they could not take it in. European truth and modes of expression had no meaning for them, one would have been obliged to adopt the Hatalastiva modes of thinking and speaking to enable them, ever so dimly, to understand what working meant.

The officers and clerks who had searched Emin's house had, we heard, seized all his cloth, beads and brass; his ammunition, guns, and papers, and had, in fact, committed a wholesale robbery. It was wonderful to notice how quickly the intense feeling against Hawashi Effendi evaporated when the rebels had once stripped him of all that he had. This, too, was to a certain extent the same in the case of Vita Hassan.

When once the chief offenders' houses had been looted, the excitement in the rebellion cooled, and a general spirit of discontent and do-nothingness pervaded the Province.

The rebel officers seemed chiefly occupied in stuffing themselves with the fat goats and sheep they had taken from Hawashi Effendi. The Council still sat for a short time every day, and the commission of inquiry into the accusations brought against the Mudir, Vita, and others, continued in a desultory way.

The afternoons were given up to sleep, and the evenings to drunkenness and debauchery, during which the officers seemed completely wrapped up in their private jealousies and quarrels.

CHAPTER X.

ARRIVAL OF THE MAHDI'S FORCES.

The Mahdists are upon us—General consternation—Intelligence department—Council called in haste—Soldiers are despatched to Rejaf—Defenceless state of the Province—Arrival of the Peacock dervishes—The Bible and the Sword—Letter from the Mahdist general—Emin commanded to surrender—Rebels ask Emin's advice—Abderrahim, son of Osman Latif—His courageous behaviour—The rebels' plans—The dervishes are examined—The Khartoum steamers—Royle's book on Egypt—Stores in the arsenal of Khartoum—Fugitives arrive in Dufilé—Robbery and violence among the soldiers—Emin's unselfishness—Letter from Osman Latif—The blow falls—Rejaf taken—General rising of the natives—Torturing of the dervishes—Brave fanatics—More news of the fall of Rejaf—A dangerous step to take—Superstition of the soldiers—Dufilé put into a defensive state—My advice to the rebels—Bravery of the dervishes—Their cruel death—Martyrdom.

Suddenly, on October 15th, in the midst of this in-action, the news came like a thunder-clap that the Mahdi's forces were once more upon them! A soldier had been dispatched in haste with a letter, and had travelled day and night to reach Dufilé. The news the letter contained was, that three steamers, with nine sandals and nuggars, had arrived at Lado from Khartoum; these steamers and boats were, the letter said, full of people. This news struck the rebels with consternation, trumpets were sounded, a council was hastily called, and the whole station was in an up-roar. There were a few who declared that these must be people from the Egyptian Government, and for a few hours this belief seemed to gain ground; but it was quickly dissipated, for soon another messenger arrived saying, that an officer and fifty soldiers had, on hearing the news, started from Rejaf instantly, and had returned, saying it was indeed the terrible Donagla.

These were without doubt the strangers of whom we had heard two months before as being in Latooka. Indeed, we since heard that they were the same people; they had landed at Boa, and had had a hard fight with the natives there, in which they lost many people. Had it not been for this, they would have been at Lado four months before.

Curiously enough, months after this, when I reached Cairo, Major Wingate, the head of the Intelligence Department, sent me an almost exact account of this repulse in Latooka, which he had picked up from native reports. One or two things were a little mixed, but it speaks wonderfully well for the Intelligence Department, that he should have been able to construct the story so faithfully from mere native reports.

A second council was called in the evening, and that same night Hamad Aga and two or three officers, with sixty soldiers and four boxes of ammunition, started hurriedly for Rejaf to relieve the station as rapidly as possible. The next day we heard that three dervishes, envoys of the Mahdi's people, were coming up to Dufilé with a letter to Emin. There were further particulars in the letter, from which we saw that the Donagla were very much on the alert. They had established themselves at Lado on the site of the old station, and had thrown out two stations

Arrival of the Dervishes.

to the west to stop the road from Makraka, and so cut off the soldiers and people there from joining the main body at Rejaf. The people at Dufilé were terrified at the news, and hardly a sound was heard in the station; a deep dejection had fallen upon every one. The people became paralyzed with fear, and knew not what to do.

Had the Donagla planned it, they could not have arrived at a more unfortunate time. Everything was at sixes-and-sevens in the Province; the northern stations had been drained of a good many of their officers and soldiers, who had come up to Dufilé to attend the Council; the stations were therefore all short of fighting men, and were only garrisoned by a soldiery justly incensed against their officers. There was no head to direct affairs, the officers gave a hundred conflicting orders, and no one obeyed; in fact the whole of the northern stations lay in an utterly defenceless position at the feet of the Donagla.

In the afternoon of October 17th, three Peacock Dervishes (so called by Emin's people from their many-coloured clothes) arrived with a letter addressed to Emin. This letter Fadl el Mulla at once confiscated and read to the officers.

The three dervishes were fine-looking fellows of the Arab type, with finely cut features, and with an exceedingly dignified bearing. They were all dressed and armed in exactly the same manner. White shirts of native-made cotton cloth reached nearly to their knees, these were patched all over with bits of red, blue, green, yellow, and spotted calico, the edges of these shirts being frayed, and left unhemmed, and ragged. Round their waists was a buff-coloured cotton cloth, reaching to their ankles; while an enormous parti-coloured turban was wound round their close-shaven heads, in many folds. Slung across their backs were thongs of leather, to which were attached numerous little round, oblong, and triangular leather cases, containing different verses from the Koran. Each man had a small volume of the Koran. For arms, each carried a large, straight, double-edged sword with a silver hilt, in a leather sheath, ornamented with pieces of iguana skin, and three immense spears, with bright iron heads, more than two feet long. These were eight inches broad, and were shaped like an elongated ace of spades. The shafts of these spears were made of bamboo, tipped with iron, and must have been from twelve to fifteen feet long.

They were almost literally armed with the "Bible and the sword."

They walked into the station without showing any fear whatever, and on being asked what they came for, they replied, "We have come to conduct you by the true path to Heaven, and to teach you to pray, as we the true believers, the true Mussulmen pray." There was a great controversy as to what should be done with them. Some were for putting them in chains, and sending them to Fabbo, or one of the southern stations; others were for killing them outright. They were, however, for the time being, put in chains, and shut up in one of the prisons. They appeared perfectly unmoved by their position. We heard the Donagla had with them a man called Osman Erbab, who was formerly one of Emin's clerks; he knew the country well, which would make him doubly dangerous. The soldiers were in an intensely excited state, and went in a body to the rebels' compound, and insisted on Fadl el Mulla's appealing to the Mudir to help them in their need. He, being thoroughly frightened by what had happened, consented, and an officer was sent over to Emin, to say the officers would all like to come and consult him about the news they had just received. Emin said he was willing to see them, and, chairs being placed ready, they all came in. Most of them looked very shamefaced as they entered, and all saluted him respectfully. They must have felt very ashamed after all they had done, that they were at last compelled to come to him for advice. The letter was as follows:—

"From the servant of God, Omar Saleh, officer of the Mahdi, to whom we give reverential greetings, appointed for conducting affairs in the Province of Hatalastiva.

"To the Honoured Mehmed Emin, Mudir of Hatalastiva.

"May God lead you in the path of His gifts. Amen.

"After greeting you, I would remind you that the world is a house of change and decay, and everything in it must one day perish; nothing in it is of value to a true servant of God except that which is for his good in his future life. If God wishes to be kind to His servant, He humbles him, and blesses all he does; and God is the blessing in everything, and no word or action proceeds from Him, which does not show His infinite compassion. God is the Master of all His creatures; in His hands are the keys of all things;

there is nothing beyond His power in the heavens or in the earth. He sees within and without, and all things good and evil are in His hands. The King gives His gifts to whomsoever He pleases, He says, 'Be,' and it is so.

"As you are intelligent and understand good advice, we think of you with all kindness, for we have heard of you from many of your friends, who have told us of your life and of your work. Amongst them our friend Osman Erbab, your messenger who has come with us, and from others. As we have heard you are kind to your people, and that you love justice, we have decided to tell you of our doings and of our position, because there are many people adverse to us, and they do not speak the truth about our affairs, and perhaps they deny the truth. We belong to God's army, and follow His word only; with our army is the victory, and we follow the Imam, Mahomed el Mahdi, the son of Abdullah—before whom we bow—the Khalifa and Prophet of God—to whom we offer our greetings, and of whom the Master of all has said, 'And in those days there shall be raised from my seat a man who shall fill the earth with justice and light as it was filled before with injustice and darkness.' We have now come by his order, and there is no possible result but what is good from his commands in this changeful world. We have given ourselves, our children, and possessions to him as an offering to God, and He has accepted them from us. He has bought His true believers, their souls and possessions with His Word, and Paradise belongs to them. If they are killed, they are killed as an offering to God, and if they kill, they kill in His cause, as it is written in the Old Testament, in the New Testament, and in the Koran. Whoever fulfils his duty towards God, is by His blessing bought by Him, as he also buys him, and He is Master of the world.

"In the month of Ramadan, 1298, God revealed the expected Mahdi, and made him sit on His footstool, and girded him with the sword of victory. He told him that whoever was his enemy was unfaithful to God and His Prophet, and should suffer in this world and in the next, and his children and goods should become the prey of the true Moslems, and he (the Mahdi) should be victorious over all his foes, though they were as numberless as the sand of the desert; and whosoever should disobey him should be punished by God. And God showed him His angels and saints, from the time of Adam till this day, and all the spirits and devils. He has before Him an army—its chief is Israel—to whom our greetings; and He ever goes before the victorious army, a distance of forty miles. Besides this, God revealed to him many miracles. It was impossible to count them, but they were as clear as the sun at midday, whose light is seen by all. And the people flocked to him by the orders of God and His Prophet.

"He commanded the people to collect and assist him against his foes from all parts of the country, and he wrote to the Governor-General at Khartoum, and to all the governors in the Soudan, and his orders were fulfilled. He wrote to every king, especially to the Sultan of Stamboul, Abdul Hamid, to Mahomed Tewfik, Vali of Egypt, and to Victoria,

Queen of Britannia, because she was in alliance with the Egyptian Government. Then the people came from every side and submitted to his rule, and told him they submitted to God and His Prophet, and to him, for there is only one God, and He is supreme, and they promised they would abstain from all evil, and that they would neither steal nor commit adultery, nor do anything which was forbidden by God. They would give up the world and strive only for God's Word, and make war for their Holy Belief for ever.

"And we have found him, the Mahdi, more compassionate to us than a pitying mother; he lives with the great, but has pity for the poor; he collects people of honour around him, and honours the generous; he speaks only the truth and brings people to God, and relieves them in this world, and shows them the path to the next. He reigns over us according to God's Word, and conforms to the words of the priests. And all religions and the Moslems have become brothers, and help one another for good, and have become slaves of the Prophet, who has said, 'All men are equal before God.' He was told by God that his time had come, and that his friends were God's friends, and the people believed in him, as did Abd el Kader el Geli, who believed in him and in his mission, and said, 'Who follows him goes to eternal blessing, and who denies him, denies God and His Prophet.' But the whole of the Turks in the Soudan, who saw the wonders and forewarnings which happened at this time, and did not believe, have been destroyed by God and have been killed one after another.

"The first army which fought against the Mahdi had for its chief Abu Soud Bey, who came with a steamer at the time when the Mahdi was at Abba, but though he was hard pressed, God killed all his enemies. Then the Prophet ordered him to go to Gedir, and he went, but he was followed by Raschid Imam, Mudir of Fashoda, and many people with him. Then followed Yuseph Pasha el Shilali, Mahomed Bey Suleiman el Shaiki, and Abdullah Wadi Defallah, one of the Kordofan merchants, and with them another army of great strength, and God killed them all. Then came the army of Hicks, a renowned man, and with him Al-ed-Din Pasha, Governor-General of the Soudan, and many officers, and with them a very large army, composed of the people of different countries—no one but God knows their number—and many Krupp guns, and they were all killed in less than an hour, and their strongholds were taken right up to Khartoum, the residence of the Governor-General, a very strong place between the two rivers.

"In Khartoum were killed Gordon Pasha, the Governor, and with him the Consuls, Hansal and Nicola Leontides, the Greek, and Azer the Copt, and many others of the Christians, and many of the rebellious Mahomedans, Farratch Pasha Ezzemi, Mahomet Pasha Hassan, Bachit Batraki, and Achmet Bey el Dgelab. And whoever was killed by the Mahdi's followers was at once consumed by fire, and this is one of the greatest wonders happening to confirm what is written, is to come to pass before the end of the world. There is yet another wonder. The spears carried by the Mahdi's followers had a flame burning at their points, and this we have seen with our eyes, and not heard only.

"And so event followed event, near Suakin and Dongola, until General Stewart Pasha, Gordon's second in command, died, and with him some Consuls, and this happened in Wady Kama. Then the other Stewart in Abu Teleah, he had come with an English army to relieve Gordon Pasha, but many were killed, and God drove them back ignominiously. And then the whole Soudan and its Dependencies accepted the Mahdi's rule, and submitted to the Imam, the Mahdi, and gave themselves to him with their children and possessions, and became his followers, and whoever opposed him was killed by God, and his children and property became the prey of the Moslems.

"The armies of the Mahdi under the command of our friend Wad en Nedjumi are beleaguering Egypt near Wady Halfa and Abu Hamed. Near Aksar Abu el Hudjadg is our friend Osman Digna. Abyssinia is in the hands of our friend Handan Abu Gandja. In an encounter with the Abyssinians God helped him, and he killed them, and amongst those killed was the chief of their army, who was called Ras Adrangi; some of his children were killed and some made slaves. Our people reached the great church in the town of Gondar, which is one of the most remarkable things among the Christians. In Darfour, Shakka, and Bahr el Ghazal is our friend Osman Adem, and with him Keremallah and Sebehr el Fahal. The whole country is in the hands of God's soldiers, who war against the foes of God, who deny the Imam, the Mahdi. They are always victorious by God's strength and might, as He promised by His word: 'Ye who believe, if ye fight, God will give you the victory.' And again, 'God is with us, and the victory is to the believers;' and yet again, 'God is well pleased by those who are slain in His service, they are like reared up strongholds.'

"So now we have come in three steamers, and in sandals and nuggars, filled with soldiers from God's army under our orders, sent to you from his Mightiness the great Chief of all the Moslems, the ever-victorious in his religion, who relies on God, the Lord of the world, the Khalifa, the Mahdi,—may God be gracious unto him!—with his sacred orders, which are the orders of God and His Prophet, and it is your duty to obey them by reason of their religious teaching, you and whoever may be with you, whether Moslems, Christians, or others, and we bring you such news as will insure your welfare in this world and in the next, and to tell you what God wishes, He and His Prophet, and to assure you of a free pardon, to you and to whomsoever is with you, and protection for your children and property, from God and His Prophet, on condition that you submit to God.

"There are with us some letters written, by permission of our Master, by some of your brethren who wish you well. They are from Abdul Kader Slatin, who was formerly Mudir of Darfour; Mahomed Said, who was formerly called Georgi Islamboulia; Ismail Abdullah, who was formerly called Bolos Salib, a Copt; and many others who sympathize with you, and who are now honoured by the Mahdi's grace. There are also letters from your companions,

Abdullah Lupton, who was Mudir of Bahr el Ghazal, Ibrahim Pasha Fauzi, Nur Bey-Ibrahim, Mudir of Sennaar, Seyd Bey Jumah, Mudir of Fasher, and Eskender Bey, commander of Kordofan. God has helped them all with His blessing, and they are now well-to-do and free from care, and God has given them more than they ever possessed in worldly goods and heavenly favour. When they became friends of the Mahdi, God rewarded them.

"Now the Khalifa, the Mahdi, out of compassion for your forlorn state, left alone in the hands of the negroes, for there has been no news of you for a long time, and you must have lost all hope, has sent us to you with an army, as I before told you, to take you out of the land of the infidels, to join your brethren, the Moslems. Submit, therefore, with gladness to God's wish, and come at once to see me wherever I may be, for I am now so near you, that I may honour you with the sacred orders. You will find them full of wonderful things, on which depend your salvation in this and in the next world, and you will find in them the contentment of God, the Ruler of the world. I have to add, I am ordered by His Highness, whom no one can deny, that I am to honour you, and take care of you, and when we meet you will have all your wishes fulfilled, and you will become one of the true believers, as our Master wishes.

"And now be of good cheer, and do not delay. I have said enough for one whose intelligence is bright, and now we pray God to lead you towards our Master, for we believe you are one of those who hear good advice and follow it, and in truth it is God's gift. Amongst the things in your favour in the hands of the Khalifa, the Mahdi, was the arrival of your letter brought by our friend, Osman Erbab, intimating your submission. He received this letter, and was well pleased with it, and because of this and the Khalifa, the Mahdi's compassion for you, we have come here as I told you before.

"May God bless you and assist you in all that you do. Salaam."

There was a second letter much shorter than this, addressed to the Christian clerks of the divan, in which Omar Saleh granted them free pardon provided they consented to embrace Mahomedanism, and assuring them they would be well received by the Mahdi.

When the letter had been read, the officers asked the Mudir if he would answer it. He refused, and told them as they had put him aside, and had brought the country to this pass, they must now manage the affair themselves. If they wanted his advice, however, he would give it, not for their sakes, but for the sake of the people whom they had misled, and in duty to the Government he served.

They asked him if he thought it was better for them to surrender. He replied such a thing was not to be thought of, for they would all be killed at once. It was not likely he said, that they had forgotten how they had been tricked, and repulsed by the soldiers three years before. The rebels agreed with him, and asked him what he advised. Emin told them to gain as much time as they could, and as quickly as possible move all the women and children from the northern stations up to Dufilé. The soldiers and ammunition would remain to the last, and then to evacuate and burn the stations north of Dufilé. He further advised the people to concentrate at Tunguru, which stood upon a peninsula, and a broad ditch could be easily cut which would make it an island and nearly impregnable, and it could be defended by a comparatively small garrison. The steamers would be able to supply the fort with food.

He warned them to look very carefully after the Irregulars, of whom there were a great number in the country; they were countrymen of the Donagla, and would be certain to go over to them if they got the chance. Above all, they must be careful of the steamers, for in them lay their only hope of safety.

They agreed that this advice was good, and said they would go and discuss it at once.

The chief speakers were Selim Aga, Fadl el Mulla, Osman Latif and Mustapha Effendi. Fadl el Mulla got very excited, and said there was nothing against the Mudir, except he had upheld Hawashi Effendi against the wish of all the others.

The Pasha said, "When you complained to me about him in Wadelai, more than a year ago, did I not tell you, if it was the wish of all the officers that Hawashi Effendi should be put aside, they should write an official letter, asking me to remove him, otherwise I could take no notice of it?"

Fadl el Mulla replied, "Yes, you did tell me so."

"Then," said the Pasha, "why did you not do as I told you? You can have nothing to complain of now."

The rebel officers then retired to consider the advice Emin had given.

The letter referred to in the last part of Omar Saleh's letter, was a letter which Emin wrote to

Keremallah, when he came up four years before, and had sent it by the hands of Osman Erbab, one of his clerks. Keremallah had commanded Emin to surrender, and in reply the Pasha wrote him a letter of submission, in order to gain time to enable him to bring his soldiers to the front. The ruse was successful, for Keremallah, on receiving his submission, and hearing trouble had broken out in Bahr el Ghazal, sent away the greater part of his army, so that Emin's soldiers attacked the remnant, and were able to drive them away. It can easily be understood that though the words of Omar Saleh's letter were friendly, the Donagla were burning to revenge their former defeat.

I may here remark that I was indebted to Abderrahim, a boy of seventeen, the son of Osman Latif, for the copy of Omar Saleh's letter. The rebels would not give the letter to Emin, but placed it with the government papers in their divan. I asked Osman Latif to try and get me a copy of it, and in accordance with my request, Abderrahim entered the divan at night, and copied a part of it each day. After eight days he handed me the full copy, which Emin translated for me. Great credit is due to Abderrahim for this, for he entered the divan at great risk to himself and his father, against whom the rebels would have been only too glad to have had a handle.

Almost immediately after the interview with Emin, Ali Aga Djabor, Farratch Aga Ajok, and Ali Aga Shamruk, started for Rejaf to try and bring in the soldiers and people from Makraka. They took sixty soldiers with them, and eighteen boxes of ammunition.

Osman Latif told me in the evening the result of the meeting of officers, after hearing Emin's advice. They had first decided not to surrender. They also intended to bring all the women and children into Dufilé, and draft them off to the southern stations, as Emin had advised. And further to do all they could to bring in the soldiers from Makraka to Rejaf, which they proposed holding as long as possible, till the intervening stations had been évacuated. For transacting business, a council of war was to be held at Dufilé, composed of officers and civil servants, which would sit every day from eight till eleven. The Irregulars were to be disarmed, and sent to the southern stations. The three dervishes, the bearers of Omar Saleh's letter, were to be kept prisoners until further orders. All people leaving the station to go to the north were to be carefully searched to see that no one held communication with the enemy. A letter was written to Omar Saleh, saying the Mudir was away in the southern part of the Province ; that he had been sent for, and would answer his letter when he returned to Dufilé. This was written as an attempt to gain time, but was an exceedingly transparent blind, for even if Omar Saleh had not already heard what had happened, he would easily see through it. Nearly all of these measures were what the Pasha had advised.

The rebel officers had the three dervishes up before them, and again questioned them concerning their people. They said that there were three steamers, the *Talahwin*, the *Safia*, and the *Mahomet Ali*, with nine sandals and nuggars. The dervishes added that there were two more steamers with some boats on their way up from Khartoum. More than this they would not tell, and did not answer when asked how many men the steamers and boats contained. Emin of course knew all Gordon's steamers, and was able to say approximately how many men each was capable of holding. The three steamers, he said, would carry about three hundred and fifty men each, and the boats perhaps forty. The whole force therefore, roughly speaking, might be estimated at one thousand four hundred and ten men. No doubt these men were armed with Remingtons, and Emin said they would probably bring mountain guns and rocket apparatus, as they had done four years before. We also heard that the two steamers spoken of by the dervishes as being on their way up from Khartoum were the *Bordein* and *Ismailia*. The *Bordein* would be capable of carrying three hundred and fifty men, and the *Ismailia* perhaps four hundred and fifty; these would probably bring three boats each, every boat containing forty men. This would make a further addition of one thousand and forty men, which, with the people who had already arrived, would swell the entire force up to two thousand four hundred and fifty soldiers. At the outside, eight hundred of Emin's soldiers could be mustered without leaving the southern stations in a dangerously weak state. Not more than two-thirds of these were probably armed with breech-loaders, moreover, they were discontented and insubordinate, and, if they fought at all, would only fight in a half-hearted way. There did not, therefore, seem to be much hope of their being able to repulse the Donagla. In reading Royle's book on Egypt, I saw that the four steamers sent down to meet the English force above Metemmeh were the *Safia*, *Bordein*, *Talahwin*, and another not named. The *Bordein* and *Talahwin* were the two steamers in which Sir Charles Wilson and Lieutenant Stuart Wortley went up to Khartoum. In coming down stream the *Talahwin* ran on a rock, and rapidly filled, while later on the *Bordein* ran on a sunken rock, and had to be beached, and abandoned by Sir Charles Wilson. The *Safia*, or as Royle spells it, *Safiyeh*, was the vessel in which Lord Charles Beresford came to Sir Charles Wilson's aid, and whose boiler being pierced by a shot off the enemy's battery at Wad-Habeshi, was obliged to be anchored and repaired under the enemy's fire. The *Safia* finally took Sir Charles Wilson's party on board, and returned to Gubat. Then there is the following passage: " Before leaving Gubat, Gordon's two remaining steamers were rendered useless by the removal of parts of the machinery." Considering the immense amount of machinery in the arsenal at Khartoum, and the tools, etc., for mending and building steamers, it seems a pity that they were not rendered useless more completely. It may have been that there were no means of doing so, or that the retreat had to be made too rapidly to admit of it; but it certainly was a great pity that it could not have been done more thoroughly, for here were two of those very steamers now brought by the Donagla against us, and the *Bordein* and *Ismailia* were on their way up to Lado. Emin told me there were so many artisans in Khartoum, that the getting up and mending of the steamers, unless they had been thoroughly destroyed, would be an easy matter.

Fugitives, chiefly women and children, were now daily arriving in Dufilé, from the northern stations. They all brought the same news of discontent among the soldiers, and disobedience of orders. News came in that the Donagla had attacked and taken Rejaf, that numbers of women and children had been captured, and that the soldiers were flying panic-stricken towards Dufilé.

Meantime nothing was being done in Dufilé. The station was not put into a state of defence, none of the decisions come to at the council of war, regarding the sending of the women and children to the southern stations, were being carried out; the officers were eating and drinking. Everything was being neglected just as if the country was safe. We could do nothing, for we were still prisoners. Osman Latif wrote to Emin, "Nothing is being done by Fadl el Mulla, and the other officers, they do nothing but drink and eat fat goats. Nothing I can say has any effect on them, everything devolves upon me, and I am unable to carry out the necessary precautions without help." Daily we heard of acts of robbery and violence going on among the soldiers, and the officers were too much afraid of them to try and check them.

It was incredible that the officers could leave things to go as they liked at such a time, whilst ruin and disaster were hanging over their heads.

Emin at this time begged me to go to Fadl el Mulla, and ask him to let me retire to M'swa, from which place, with Shukri Aga's aid, he hoped I might be able to reach Fort Bodo. This suggestion was naturally not thought of for a second, it savoured too strongly of what Gordon called "ratting out." I record it merely to show that Emin reproached himself for having brought me into this trouble, and would willingly have seen me leave him, and look out only for my own safety. This extreme unselfishness in his character must always draw people towards him. Unfortunately, this exceeding altruism was thrown away upon his people, and only had the effect of making them more selfish.

From Osman Latif, Emin received the following letter, which I give, as it gave a tolerably clear account of the fall of Rejaf :—

"My Benefactor,—I have been told that the Khartoum people, together with Chief Béfo's men, arrived near Rejaf at four o'clock in the afternoon of Oct. 19th, under the pretext of making a raid on Chief Loko's cattle, and that the soldiers left the station in order to prevent it. The Khartoum people took this opportunity of entering the station, and after having occupied it, they killed many soldiers, together with Abd el Aga and Hassan Bein Aga Barema, officers, and Achmet Zeinel, the clerk. The rest of the soldiers ran away, some towards Makraka, some to Laboré. Whatever was left in the station, of women, children, and servants belonging to soldiers and officers, has been lost. Amongst them are the families of Hamad Aga, Ali Aga Djabor, Ali Aga Shamruk, and Dgaden Aga.

"I have also heard that the garrisons of Bidden, Kirri, and Muggi have collected in Laboré. Of the Khartoum people no one has yet come to Bidden or

Kirri, but they are in Rejaf busy dividing the women, children, and servants.

"I kiss yours and Mr. Jephson's hands,

"OSMAN LATIF."

It was true. Before the officers and soldiers who left Dufilé could reach their comrades, the blow had fallen and Rejaf had been taken. We heard afterwards that the Donagla had, on arriving at Rejaf, marched round the station in order to cut off the people's retreat to the southern stations. They had then fallen on the station, and the slaughter had been terrible. Those who were able to escape fled towards Makraka. The women and children were divided among the Donagla, and were afterwards sent down to Khartoum.

Béfo was a Bari chief who at one time was friendly to Emin, but when the station of Lado was evacuated he turned against him. He was the most powerful of the Bari chiefs, and had his villages and country on the mountain of Bilinian, near Gondokoro. After the Dinka rebellion, between three and four years previous to this, he bought up, with cattle, etc., all the guns and ammunition which the Dinkas had captured from Emin's people when they took Boa. He was therefore a formidable ally to the Donagla; and eventually the rest of the Baris, eager to revenge themselves for the years of ill-treatment they had received at the hands of the "Turks," joined the movement against us. From the very beginning of the movement Emin had said he was sure Béfo would ally himself to the Donagla.

Stories frequently came in of desertions to the

Donagla on the part of those people who were of their country; Sheik Mooragan, the chief priest of the Province, being one of the first to go over to the rebels. Certain armed interpreters of the Madi tribe, in the service of the Government, also deserted and went over in a body to the Donagla, taking with them the Government guns. Letters from the Donagla, exhorting certain people in the Province to join them, were found, and the people in whose possession they were found were imprisoned. Letters to Tybe Effendi, a clerk of Wadelai, were also found, from a soldier who had deserted to the enemy, urging him to follow his example. The soldiers in a fury, looted Tybe Effendi's house.

Even now, if the people had only combined and placed the Mudir at their head and acted strictly under his orders, we might have done something, and many lives might have been saved. But they were resolved on following the headlong course they had adopted two months before, they had become utterly demoralized, and were unable to make up their minds to the right course. Some fresh disaster was needed to bring them to understand the danger they were in. It soon came.

The rebel officers again had the dervishes brought before them. They told the envoys that they had come with friendly words and letters from their general, and now he had attacked Rejaf, killed many of the people, and added, for this they should be put to death, unless they gave full information concerning the strength, etc., of the Donagla. The dervishes answered, "If you kill us it does not matter, it will not help you to escape the vengeance

TORTURING THE PEACOCK DERVISHES.

which will surely fall upon you. You officers will all be cut down. But the ignorant soldiers who are only acting under your orders will be spared."

The dervishes, who were heavily ironed, were then sent back to prison, and the officers, wishing to force them to give information about their own people, resorted to the slow torture of giving them plenty of salt food, but allowing them no water. For more than two days this went on, the poor fellows bore it without murmuring, and still they would not speak. The rebel officers, becoming impatient, resolved on some keener torture in order to wring the information from them.

Accordingly, a second time the dervishes were brought before them, and a cruel torture, common in the Soudan, was devised. A piece of split bamboo was tied round their heads, passing over the temples above the ears. This band was twisted so tightly by means of a piece of wood, used as a tourniquet, that it cut through the flesh to the very bone. With every fibre in their bodies quivering from the torture, and faint from loss of blood, not a word of information about their comrades, not even a groan, escaped the lips of these brave men, so strongly were they upheld by their fanatical trust and faith in God and their Prophet. They could only gasp out that God, through His Prophet, would bitterly avenge them. The Egyptian officers and clerks delighted in watching the torture, and laughed and exulted when the agony became too intense for flesh and blood to bear, and the poor dervishes sank fainting to the ground. The demeanour of the Soudanese, even, was not so disgusting as that of the cowardly Egyptians, for their low bestial faces showed no sign of pleasure in the sight, they merely gazed at the torture with a kind of stolid indifference. The people had pressed round in large numbers to see what was going on, and loud murmurs of sympathy arose from the women, who sobbed and wrung their hands in very pity for these brave men, who bore their sufferings with such indomitable courage. Surely the religion which could support them under such fearful torture could not be a low one! No one worthy to be called a man could help a feeling of respect and admiration rising in his heart for these poor fanatics. Some such feeling may have crossed Fadl el Mulla's mind, for he ordered the soldiers to unloose their bands and give them water, and they were carried back to prison in a semi-conscious state.

The officers, as I said before, hardly knew what to do, for orders were given and not carried out; the soldiers had become thoroughly sulky, and would do nothing. Achmet Aga Dinkaue went to Fabbo, with orders from Fadl el Mulla, to dig a ditch round the station and fortify it. This was, of course, only a useless order; it would take at least two months to dig a ditch round the station, with such a force of people as there was at Fabbo, meantime the Donagla would probably sweep down upon the station. The truth was, these people could not bring themselves to throw away one of the many little rubbishing things they possessed, and, instead of saving some, they would lose all.

Osman Effendi again wrote:—

"The officers intend to collect here and send the

women and children to the south, and with them some soldiers for opening a new station south of M'swa. The rest of the soldiers, with their arms and ammunition, will remain here, at least so I hear, but what are their true intentions no one knows but God, Whom I pray will assist us in our trouble."

We heard from different fugitives that the Donagla had now thoroughly established themselves at Rejaf, and had strengthened the station. The steamers were still at Lado, at which place they had made a small but strong camp. But Rejaf was now the stronghold and base of operations of the Donagla. A soldier arrived in Dufilé; he was one of the few who escaped from Rejaf, he was fearfully wounded about the head and shoulders from sword cuts. He had been left for dead by the Donagla, and had managed to creep away after dark; he was a horrible sight, it was a perfect marvel that he should be able to live, much less escape with such wounds upon him. He was allowed to come in to see the Pasha, who was always ready to help his people, whatever they did, and his wounds were carefully dressed by Emin.

He told us a slightly different story about the taking of Rejaf. He said that at about five in the afternoon the Donagla, accompanied by hundreds and hundreds of natives, were seen approaching the station. They had marched round with flags flying and drums beating; they then made a dash at the postern gate, and took it in the first rush. The soldiers had hardly made any resistance, they were so completely cowed and unnerved by the chaos existing in the country since the Mudir's deposition, and, having no head, had no heart to fight. The Donagla did not use their guns much, they were not good shots, but they committed fearful havoc with their broad-headed spears and long swords. They gave no quarter to any one excepting to women and small children. A good many soldiers broke out of the station on the opposite side and fled towards Makraka, but the number of deaths was great, for the natives pursued the fugitives, and cut a large number of them down in the flight.

The panic had been terrible, and there was a regular stampede from the stations of Bidden, Kirri, and Muggi, for Laboré, everything in these stations being left behind, even the ammunition. The Baris had entered the stations immediately the soldiers had left, and had looted everything.

Abdullah Aga Manzal, after the first panic was over, persuaded the officers and most of the soldiers, of whom there must have been over 300 in Laboré, to return to Muggi. This was done, as Muggi was a compact, well-built, and comparatively strong station. It was further decided by the officers to attempt to take Rejaf; a most dangerous step at any time, but in the state of discontent in which the soldiers were now it was certain to be fatal. Casati and I went to Fadl el Mulla, and begged him to urge the people to retire to Dufilé and concentrate there, where, having the river and steamers at their back, their retreat could not be cut off. We saw Selim Aga and several other officers, and they all agreed that it would be best to do so.

The chief clerk and Ibrahim Effendi Elham were therefore sent down to Muggi, to urge the rebel officers to relinquish their plan; but they utterly refused to do so, and clamoured for reinforcements of soldiers and ammunition. A rumour had come in that a certain number of the officers and soldiers who had escaped from Rejaf had been successful in joining the soldiers in Makraka. These were, we heard, now marching to join the people at Muggi, who intended to wait for them there. I feared they would indeed have to wait a long time.

The soldiers, curiously enough, had a strong superstition that these Donagla were under some charm, which made them impervious to ordinary bullets. They said that when they fired at the Donagla they could see the bullets dropping off them like rain. Numbers of Hawashi Effendi's dollars were therefore moulded into bullets, each dollar making a bullet. It was supposed that these silver bullets would be able to penetrate the charm. The ordinary bullets were also hollowed out, and a peg of ebony-wood or copper was fixed firmly in, these being supposed to be almost as efficacious as the silver bullets. For several days the artisans were at work on these, and finally when a great number had been finished, a further reinforcement of sixty soldiers was dispatched to Muggi armed with these bullets. They departed with renewed hope and courage, for they had immense faith in the virtue of these charm-piercing bullets, with which, they felt convinced, they could kill the devil himself.

It seems queer that such beliefs should hold among half-civilized people, at the end of the enlightened nineteenth century. And yet when one comes to think of it, it was not so very long ago that this belief held in Scotland; for Claverhouse was considered proof against bullets, and was finally supposed to have been killed by a silver button used as a bullet—and that was as late as William and Mary's reign. The belief in the efficacy of silver bullets holds, I was told, over the whole Orient, even to this day.

People are very apt to shrug their shoulders and express contempt for the ignorant superstitions of the negroes; but if they will only go back on history a little, they will find there is no African superstition, however ignorant, but has had its parallel comparatively recently in the annals of European history.

The officers now began to put the station into a defensive state, for hitherto nothing had been done to improve the defences, which were of their kind exceedingly good and strong. The ditch was deep and broad, and the earthworks strong, but in need of repair. Selim Aga and some of the other officers asked me to go round the station with them, and make such suggestions as I thought well for the further defence of the station, in case the soldiers at Muggi should be defeated, and the Donagla reach Dufilé. I went round accordingly, and pointed out to them where places should be strengthened and repaired, and told them the banks of the ditch and earthworks should be made smooth, so that no foothold should be offered to people endeavouring to climb them.

I further advised that the banana and sugar-cane plantations, of which there were numbers close to the station, should be levelled in order to afford no cover for the enemy; the interpreters' huts and the standing corn near the station should also be cleared away. The ditch, I advised, should be cut through the roads by which the station was entered, so as to have an uninterrupted ditch completely round the station; planks could be used as bridges across it meantime. Above all, I pointed out a place where the ditch had been left uncut close to the river. A narrow bridge of earth had been left which was used by people coming from work in the gardens outside, for entering at the corner of the station. Within ten yards of this was a thick grove of bananas and sugar-cane capable of sheltering several hundreds of men. It required no cleverness to see at a glance that this was a place exactly suited for carrying out the Donagla tactics. They could conceal themselves in the banana grove and enter the station on the first opportunity, falling upon the soldiers on the flank and rear, thus cutting them off from the steamers which lay at the wharves close to where the entry could be made.

Selim Aga and the officers all agreed that my suggestions were good, and promised to have them carried out; which I knew meant nothing. I may here add that eventually when Dufilé was taken by the Donagla it was precisely at this spot that they entered. My suggestion had never been followed, and the place had been left just as it was.

After going round the station, I went and sat with the officers in the gatehouse at the entrance of the station, and they told me what were their plans. They were not very extensive, nor did they appear to be in any hurry to carry them out. They saw no necessity for haste, it was not in them ever to hurry. While we were talking the dervishes passed, guarded by soldiers. They could only move slowly and painfully along, for their ankles were enclosed in heavy elephant irons with a link in the middle, to which was fastened a piece of rope, to enable them to hold the irons up when they wished to walk. Mustapha Effendi, an Egyptian, grinned, and pointed out to me the terrible marks of the torture, as they staggered painfully by, under the weight of their heavy chains. Though starved, beaten down and insulted, their bearing towards their captors was dignified and self-reliant as ever; but the sight of their poor lacerated heads, and the look of patient suffering upon their faces were too pathetic for any words to describe. I felt inclined to dash my fist into the grinning faces of those cowardly Egyptians who were pointing with such pleasure to the evidences of their cruel work. The dervishes looked full at me, seated among the Egyptians, as they passed. They probably thought I had some hand in the ordering of their torture. That look haunted me for days. It was as if I had been torturing some animal, and it had turned and looked at me with a human face.

The dervishes dragged out a miserable existence for several weeks, they were half-starved and constantly ill-used by the soldiers, but in spite of their long sufferings they could never be induced to give the smallest information against their comrades. Their Korans, the sole comfort they had, were taken from them, and I used often, in passing, to see them prostrate in prayer, with a rapt expression on their faces which showed that though their bodies were chained, lacerated, and starved, their faith in God and His Prophet enabled them to rise above

PEACOCK DERVISHES PASSING THROUGH GUARD-HOUSE.

Page 270.

their earthly sufferings. Finally, when the Mahdi's forces were before Dufilé, it was decided by the officers to kill them. They were taken down to the river and beaten to death with clubs, and their bodies were thrown to the crocodiles. Death must have come like a relief to them. In all our calendars of the men who have suffered for their religion, no one could have better deserved to be called martyrs than these three brave dervishes.

CHAPTER XI.

PRISONERS ON PAROLE.

Letter from Hassan Lutvi—Rumours of Stanley's arrival—Rising of the natives—Emin's house searched—Position of affairs at Muggi—Letter of warning written to Stanley—Osman Latif is sent to Wadelai—Mustapha flogs his wife to death—Children drowned in the river—Extraordinary weather—Epidemic among the cattle—Insubordination of soldiers at Wadelai—Shuli Sorcerer—Abdullah is the thief—Arrogance of Emin's soldiers—Negro troops—Emin's treatment of his soldiers—Second disaster at Rejaf—Officers killed in the flight—Stories told of the soldiers—Rebels decide to send us to Wadelai—Emin's farewell at Dufilé—Our arrival at Wadelai—Enthusiastic reception to Emin—Cowed attitude of people at the outbreak of the rebellion—Emin free from all responsibility—Joy of people at Emin's return—Our position at Wadelai—Europeanizing the negro—Possible improvement of negroes—Ropes of sand—Spread of Mahdism—Reported outbreak of Irregulars—Rumour of approach of Mahdists—Inactivity of the people—Egyptian effrontery—The soldiers make a demonstration—Emin unable to speak out—Emin declares he knows his people—A contemptible Egyptian.

HERE was a letter we received, which will show how readily the people were to believe the wildest conjectures and rumours, anything rather than face their trouble, and admit they were in a dangerous position :—

"Yesterday evening a private letter arrived from Hassan Effendi Lutvi, telling us the officers were preparing to start for Rejaf to crush the rebels, for the reason that they had ascertained that the soldiers from Makraka, with a great number of the tribe of Bombé, had arrived in Rejaf. After having attacked the Donagla, they had driven them out, and had retaken the station. The Donagla have come into this country flying from Khartoum, before the government soldiers and the Abyssinians, for the Egyptian government had retaken the Soudan. With the Donagla there are a great many regular soldiers, formerly in Egyptian employ. These, during the attack of the Makraka soldiers at Rejaf, had fired their guns in the air, and had sent two or three soldiers to encourage them, saying they would never fire at their former companions. The Donagla have brought with them many women and children belonging to the notables of Khartoum. Osman Effendi Erbab has not come of his own free will, but as a prisoner. This is what Hassan Lutvi writes, but God knows what is true."

It was always like this, any reverse soon plunged them into the deepest dejection, but they quickly recovered from this, and were ready again to believe any wild tale they heard, so that it enabled them to avoid facing the gravity of the situation.

The account Selim Aga gave me, that food was very scarce in Khartoum, and that there were hardly any clothes, and that this, and their revenge, had brought them to the country a second time, seemed likely.

Hawashi Effendi several times sent to ask me to go and see him, for I was now allowed to go about the station more freely, and could visit whom I pleased. I would not go to see him after what he had done, so he wrote me a little note, begging me not to think badly of him for what he had written against the Mudir; he said some of the rebel officers had come in, and threatened to torture him if he did not write as they dictated. He had done it under pressure, but what he had written was not true.

From the south we constantly heard rumours of Stanley's arrival, but we gave no credence to them, for they were never more than wild native reports. Rajab Effendi, Emin's secretary, who was now at liberty again, sent a note to me one day, saying he had heard from some men who had just come in from Wadelai, that Stanley had certainly arrived at N'sabe. He apologized for not having come himself to tell me, but naïvely added, "I was so drunk this morning, that I am not fit to come before you yet." I concluded, therefore, that the story of Stanley's arrival was only the outcome of his drunken fit. Meanwhile the officers and soldiers at Muggi were still waiting for the soldiers to arrive from Makraka, and were constantly writing to Dufilé for reinforcements. Twenty more soldiers were taken from Fabbo station, and as many as could be safely spared from the southern stations were also brought to Dufilé, and dispatched to Muggi. Still, however, the cry was for more reinforcements before the officers could decide to attack Rejaf, until Fadl el Mulla wished himself well out of his position as President, and regretted ever having accepted the post.

Hamad Aga, the Major, wrote from Muggi still asking for reinforcements and carriers. He said the Madi tribe had refused to act as porters, or bring in corn or food. He added, "The Madi tribe are all of them in rebellion against our authority, and only await the coming of the Donagla to break out and attack us." It was precisely the same at Dufilé, the native interpreters about the station had also refused to bring in corn, and defied all orders; the Shulis, too, on the other side of the river between Dufilé and Fabbo, were also rising. The natives all round were ready to join any one so that he was against the Turks. We heard of dissensions among the officers at Muggi, and a state of almost active mutiny on the part of the soldiers, who openly reproached their officers for not having listened to the Mudir's words four years before, when he wanted them to evacuate the northern stations, and move to the south. And now three months ago, when the Mudir and Mr. Jephson had come among them in order to help them, their officers had again deceived them.

They continued, that had it not been for their officers they would now have been out of harm's way, and would not have lost their women and children. Ali Aga Djabor tried to stop the murmuring, and threatened flogging and imprisonment; they openly defied him to lay a finger on any of them, and said they would only obey their Mudir.

A strong feeling on all sides among the soldiers and officers, a feeling impelled by fear and discomfort of the confusion reigning, was really rising now in favour of Emin's being reinstated as Mudir of the Province. Several non-commissioned officers came into our compound secretly at night, and told Emin that the soldiers were determined to have him back again in his place. A corporal remarked, " You see, isn't it ridiculous ? The officers have deposed you, and have called each other names. Who cares about their Beys, their Majors and their Captains, none of us look at such things." Emin told the soldiers to wait. Alas, that was his advice to every one, upon every subject!

Early on the morning of October 30th, the big steamer came in from Wadelai, bringing Casati. The steamer people had heard that the Donagla had arrived, but had heard nothing of the fall of Rejaf. They were very much downcast at the news. Casati reported the utmost discontent and confusion reigning in the southern stations. There, as here, the soldiers disobeyed orders, and would do no work.

The clerks and officers who had acted on the commission to search the Pasha's houses, had stripped them of nearly everything, they had gone down to Tunguru, had again entered Vita Hassan's house, and had almost completely looted it. From Tunguru they had gone on to M'swa, but Shukri Aga, hearing of their coming, had again gone away from the station, this time under the pretence of going out to hear if he could get any news to confirm the report of Stanley's arrival. They had waited several days but as he did not return they had gone away, leaving him still in command of his station. It was astonishing that at such a time as this, when disaster for the whole Province was hanging over their heads the clerks and rebel officers should still be thinking of robbing and looting.

Casati and I went to see Ibrahim Effendi Elhan on his return from Muggi; he told us that the soldier had declared that after their comrades from Makraka had arrived they would march down to Dufilé in a body and reinstate their Mudir. Fadl el Mulla and the other rebel officers were becoming very much afraid of the position they were in, and would gladly now have seen the Pasha in his place once more, but they feared that if he were reinstated he would use his position to take vengeance upon them.

Ali Aga Djabor, seeing how things were going in the Mudir's favour, proposed to the officers and soldiers that they should go over to the Donagla, but this they flatly refused to do—they would have received short shrift if they had.

The steamers had begun to carry loads of the refugees, who were now daily flocking in from the northern stations. I went and saw the first steamer load start,—such a nondescript lot of people with the most extraordinary collection of baggage imaginable!

Now that the steamers were running we were able to get a good deal of news from the few faithfuls at Wadelai and from Shukri Aga. They frequently smuggled letters to us by the pilot of the steamer, and we were tolerably *au courant* with affairs in the southern stations. We heard from the clerk of M'swa station, who was at Wadelai, that he was about to return to M'swa, and he asked me to write a letter to Stanley, and he would forward it through Shukri Aga to him. I wrote a long letter to Stanley, telling him as nearly as I could the position of affairs in the country, and of the coming of the Donagla, and I further warned him to be careful how he approached the country. At that time we felt certain that if he did not come soon we should be taken by the Donagla. Some horrible catastrophe seemed to be impending, for it could not be long before the Mahdi's forces were before Dufilé, and we felt nothing could save us. It seemed to me, in writing that letter, as if I were saying good-bye to Stanley and my fellow-officers, to my home and people. I had quite made up my mind that I should probably have to wander as a bare-footed dervish about the streets of Khartoum.

Amongst other people who were sent with their families to Wadelai was Osman Latif, so that now we had no one really to depend on for news of what was going on in the station. He, having been chief of the detective department in Khartoum, had a most wonderful way of rooting out news, without apparently looking after anything. He was up to all sorts of tricks and dodges, and although one did not like him any the better for them, we found him most useful. He was a man who was greatly disliked and distrusted by every one.

The Egyptian officer, Mustapha Effendi, whose compound was close to ours, and who I said before was constantly beating his women, at last beat one of his women so cruelly that she died. We could hear her shrieks and the sound of the heavy whip until there was a dull thud as of a person falling, and then all was silent. We heard that her back was most terribly cut, he had beaten her in a frantic manner. I think it was a case of some jealousy about another man. This Mustapha Effendi was the same man who had pointed so delightedly to the wounds on the dervishes' heads. He was a true Egyptian in his cruelty.

A very sad scene happened one day; three boys and a couple of girls were crossing the river in a canoe. They had been over to the other side to fetch wood

UPSETTING OF A CANOE IN THE NILE.

Page 278

The current was strong and there was a high wind blowing down stream, the consequence was, when the canoe was in mid-river, it upset, and all five were instantly overwhelmed by the current. Great efforts were made to rescue them, but they were all drowned. Probably the crocodiles took them before they were dead. I pitied the poor mother who was on the bank, and rushed frantically into the water when she saw what had happened. The women all came down, and took her back to her house. It was wonderful to see how sympathetic and tender these black slave women were to her, and how sincerely they seemed to share her grief. We heard them weeping and wailing all through the night. It reminded one of an Irish wake.

The weather for this time of the year was most extraordinary. Every day at about two o'clock the sky became black as ink, till it seemed as if it were twilight, the air was oppressively still and hot, and even the birds were silent. Then, with a howl and roar, the wind swooped down from the mountains upon the station. It was always accompanied by deluges of rain, not falling in drops, but seeming to come down in one solid sheet, whilst the wind lashed the trees furiously, and uprooted a great number. This generally lasted for about an hour, and then cleared away as suddenly as it came, while all round could be heard the torrents roaring down the mountain sides. Though this was the dry season, the river was at this time higher than I had ever seen it in the rainy season. During what should have been the rainy season there was a drought, and the river was very low. Everything was burnt up, most of the crops failed, and there was hardly any grass to be seen. In the southern stations the cattle died by hundreds, it was almost like an epidemic. In consequence of the prolonged drought, there was a perfect plague of flies, and all the savannas were infested with ticks and parasites of all kinds. The unfortunate cattle became covered with ticks, and were tormented by flies, which made them very restless and thin, and eventually killed them. In the stations of M'swa and Tunguru there were over 1200 cattle, and these were nearly all killed by the drought; and now, when it should be dry, the remainder were in a fair way to be killed by the constant rain. Wadelai was little better off, and great numbers of cattle died there. Emin said it was one of the most extraordinary seasons he had ever seen. The superstitious people put it all down to the coming of the Donagla, who they were convinced dealt largely in charms of all sorts.

Hawashi Effendi, having been stripped by the rebel officers, was allowed to proceed with his greatly diminished family and household goods to Wadelai, and Dufilé was gradually becoming emptied of its superfluous population. Suliman Effendi had been reinstated at Tunguru; he had a good deal of influence with his brother Fadl el Mulla, and used all that influence to get the rebel officers to release the Mudir. He declared he would not leave the station till he had seen Emin depart for Wadelai. Kodi Aga, the chief of Wadelai, also wrote at this time, urging Fadl el Mulla to release the Mudir, for the soldiers were deserting and getting perfectly unmanageable, and he declared nothing would quiet them but the return

of the Pasha. On hearing of all these reports, Fadl
el Mulla said he had no objection himself to release
the Mudir, but that he was unable to do so until he
had conferred with the officers at Muggi. There was
a very stormy scene, in which Suliman Effendi told his
brother the real reason was that he was afraid if the
Mudir got into power again, he, Fadl el Mulla, would
be one of the first to suffer punishment.

Some weeks before, when I was in Wadelai, a thief
had entered my boy's house at night, and had stolen
all his clothes and eighteen dollars. A soldier named
Farajala was convicted of the theft; he returned
the clothes, but insisted that he had not taken the
money. However, Kodi Aga put him in chains,
and said he should not be released until the money
was returned. After some time he sold nearly all
he had, and repaid the money to my boy, but he
came down to Dufilé after some days, bringing with
him a sorcerer of the Shuli tribe. He went before
Fadl el Mulla, and said the money was stolen by
one of my three orderlies, but he did not know
which, he had therefore brought the sorcerer with
him, and he would be able to discover who was the
thief. I told them to come over, and had my orderlies
up before them. The sorcerer first of all heated a
piece of iron to a white heat, and made each of my
orderlies touch it with his tongue. He declared that
the thief was Moorajan. Again he went through
some mysterious movements with three bits of straw
and some wood. Each time the lot fell upon Moorajan, and he was declared to be the culprit. I said
I could not allow him to be punished on such evidence,
but I had up my orderlies and examined them, and

had their things searched. A certain number of dollars were found in Abdullah's bag, which he could not account satisfactorily for, and after calling up many witnesses, and sifting the whole case, it was found that Abdullah was the thief, and after a good deal of persuasion he owned to it. Only ten dollars were found, so I had to make up the rest, and handed the eighteen dollars over to Farajala. I ordered Abdullah to be flogged, and he received 150 lashes without uttering a sound; when he got up, he gravely saluted me, and said, "Thank God, master," and went off to his house as if nothing had happened. However severely negroes are punished, they never bear any malice if they know they deserve it. Abdullah was a man who was of the greatest possible use to both Emin and me during our imprisonment; he was always clean, ready, and well mannered, and knew his duties as a soldier far better than most of our Soudanese. When Emin's orderlies were taken away, and he was short of servants, Abdullah always waited at table, and even did some of the house work. Stanley afterwards, hearing how well he had behaved, made him a sergeant, with a large increase of pay, on my recommendation.

We heard very little of what was going on at Muggi, except that it was the intention of the officers to attack Rejaf on November 12th.

The soldiers after having worked a few days on the defences of the station, refused to do any more; saying they were soldiers and not labourers.

If they were told to do anything, such as getting wood for steamers, making houses, or even at last digging the ditch to fortify the station, they answered, "No! we are soldiers, our only duties are to fight and do sentry work." Again, they would not carry their own food or clothes on a march, but insisted upon carriers; I have even seen soldiers with a boy each to carry their guns. They did not understand the duties of soldiers in the least. They never had drill, nor did they even understand that the first duty of a soldier is, obedience to orders; they knew nothing about fatigue parties, or such duty as the European soldiers have to do. One might be inclined to look over a good deal if they were good fighters, but they were not; for, if confronted by a tolerably determined enemy, they always ran. Emin at one time said to me, "If at the first volley the enemy do not retire, my people will never attack them hand-to-hand." In the last Mahdi war they had run every time from the Mahdists, and it was only when at last they were hemmed in by the enemy that they fought at all. I could not see one redeeming quality about them; they, who were only natives themselves, looked down on the other natives who were not "soldiers," and they treated them with the utmost arrogance. They were ill-mannered and insubordinate, and, in spite of their ignorance, gave themselves the greatest possible airs, and talked about being soldiers when they did not know even how to obey. I have no hesitation in saying that, as a body, I have never seen a more useless set of men. It was not altogether Emin's fault, for he had a miserable lot of corrupt officers under him, most of them being criminals. Officered by Europeans, they might have been made, by teaching them their duties, drill, and above all, obedience, a very good lot of soldiers, but commanded by such corrupt officers, they were both cowardly and useless. There was in them at times a sort of stupid indifference to danger, I will not call it courage, but with European officers this might have been fostered and educated, and would have been nearly as good. People in Europe think that all negro troops are good, because they have heard how well they fought in the Egyptian campaigns, and how much Gordon praised them, and they class them all under the generic name of Soudanese. They do not seem to understand that the so-called Soudan is a vast continent, and is practically unlimited. In it there are a hundred different tribes, who differ from each other in character, physique, and ways of living, just as much as the nations of Europe differ from each other.

For instance, take even a small body like Emin's soldiers. There were Dinkas, Madis, Baris, Niam-niams, Makrakas, Shulis, Wanyoro, Shiluks, and half-a-dozen others of various tribes; all of them more or less different. For example, the Dinkas and Niam-niams were exceedingly brave people; whereas the Baris and Makrakas were cowardly, and made very bad soldiers. Turkish or Egyptian rule increases and fosters their arrogance, but seldom brings out the good qualities in them, and there are many.

The truth was, Emin spoilt his people; he was too easy and good to them, and such goodness was not, I think, real kindness, for it only made them more and more absurd in their pretensions.

I remember when we were at Kirri, Emin's coming to me and telling me that we must leave the station, for his orderlies had nothing to eat. "But," I asked, "is there no corn in the station?" "Corn! There's plenty of corn, but they have got no women to grind it." "And do you mean to say, Pasha, that your orderlies, who have nothing to do all day long, cannot grind their own corn for a few days?" He answered, "You don't understand the customs of the country; such a thing is not done." I shrugged my shoulders, and said, "Very well, Pasha, but I should like to see any of our Zanzibaris coming up to Stanley with such a complaint, even after they had been carrying ammunition to help your soldiers all the day." Such spoiling was not kindness; it ruined the soldiers, and made them useless for anything.

On November 14th we heard rumours of a second defeat at Rejaf, and this was confirmed later on by Selim Aga, who told us he had just received a letter from Muggi. The soldiers had four days before left Muggi, and had marched against Rejaf. As soon as they entered the station, the Donagla had sallied out and attacked them furiously. The soldiers fired one volley, and then, without attempting to make any stand, turned and fled. And these, forsooth! were the men who said, "We are soldiers, our duties are only fighting and doing sentry work!" Some of the fugitives made for Makraka, and a good many reached Muggi that same night. Great numbers were killed, for hundreds of Baris joined in the pursuit, and cut down all those who could not get along.

Among the officers killed were Hamad Aga, the Major; Abdullah Vaab Effendi, an Egyptian; Ali Aga Djabor; Sheik Bachit; Salim Aga; Hassan Effendi Lutvi, a clerk, and several others whose names I do not know. The letter giving this information came from Abdullah Aga Manzal, the chief of Muggi, and he entreated the officers at Dufilé to send carriers at once to help them to retire.

We had foreseen this disaster, and both Emin, Casati, and myself had told the officers it would be madness to attempt to retake Rejaf; but they were not to be persuaded to give up their plan.

I was very sorry for Hamad Aga's death, he was the best by far of all Emin's Soudanese officers. He was a thoroughly good, honest, straightforward old fellow, and was, moreover, a firm friend of Emin in fair and foul weather. He was greatly beloved by the soldiers, particularly by those of Wadelai, of which station he was formerly chief. His death created a profound impression among the soldiers, and made them more than ever discontented with the rebel officers. At the taking of Rejaf some weeks before, all his wives and children were captured by the Donagla, and he seemed, from all accounts, to have become reckless in consequence. He was one of those fatherly-looking old negroes, with white hair, and I felt really grieved that I should not again see his kind old face.

We heard afterwards, that some of the officers were captured alive, but that they were eventually killed by the Donagla, who cut off their heads and stuck them on poles over the gate of the station.

Here we were cooped up indeed like rats in a trap;

we were neither allowed to act or to retire, and daily we expected the Donagla to be upon us. The panic among the people was terrible, and long strings of fugitives, who had thrown everything they possessed away, came flying hour by hour into the station, until it was full to overflowing.

The people then, with one accord, made Selim Aga chief of the Province. Shortly after the last of the fugitives had come in, the officers and soldiers arrived. They were all in great fear, for there was now nothing between us and the Donagla but abandoned and empty stations.

I was told a story by one of the soldiers, who had escaped in the flight from Rejaf, about the death of Abdul Vaab Effendi. According to his story, the greatest terror had reigned when the Donagla had sallied out of the station, and, joined by all the Baris, had fallen upon the attacking column. Abdul Vaab Effendi, it appeared, had a bad leg, and was not able to keep up very well with the rest of the soldiers in the flight. At last he fell from exhaustion, and called out to one of his soldiers to help him to reach his donkey, which was tied to a tree hard by. In answer to his appeal the soldier wrenched his Snider rifle from his hand, and threw him his old muzzle-loader, saying that that was a good enough weapon for one of the cowardly Egyptians, who had brought all this trouble on them by their intrigues. Abdul Vaab Effendi, being unable to reach his donkey, was eventually overtaken by the infuriated Baris, and fell pierced by the thrusts of a hundred spears.

Several stories like these made this disgraceful

flight all the more terrorizing to Emin's cowardly soldiers.

A council was called, and a long discussion took place concerning the Mudir. Some were for reinstating him at once, some were for sending him to Wadelai, and another party were still against him. Fortunately for us, Ali Aga Djabor, and four of Emin's worst enemies, were killed in the flight from Rejaf, therefore the party against the Mudir was in the minority.

Moreover, the soldiers came in a body and said nothing should be done unless the Mudir was instantly released; they said they dated the beginning of all their troubles from the time when he had been deposed.

The following day the officers came in, and after talking for a few minutes on indifferent subjects, as their custom was, they began to speak about the real reason of their visit.

They said, owing to the wish of the people, they had decided to allow the Mudir to go to Wadelai, where he would be a prisoner on parole, and would be permitted to go about the station and to his garden. Fadl el Mulla, however, stipulated that Emin should give him his word to make no attempt to regain his position as Mudir, and that he would take no part in the affairs of Government; it was on this understanding only that he was allowed to go. Emin said he had no wish to be at the head of affairs after the way in which his people had treated him.

We owed this step to the influence of Suliman Aga and Selim Aga chiefly, but we owed much also to the Donagla, for had they not suddenly appeared on the scene and so terrified the people, God only knows what would have become of us. I do not think we should have ever got out.

Certain it is, that had the rebel officers been able to prove a single instance of injustice and irregularity against Emin, he would most assuredly have lost his life during those first excited weeks of the rebellion. But they could prove nothing, for Emin was found to be perfectly innocent of any of the many accusations brought against him.

Even at the last the clerks would not give up mischief-making, but went in a body to Fadl el Mulla to beg of him not to allow the Mudir to depart, but luckily Suliman Aga was there, and, seizing a club and calling to the soldiers, he chased the clerks through the station.

On the morning of November 17th, Emin was released from prison, and was formally escorted down to the steamer by most of the officers. He had been in prison just three months, during which time he had never been outside the high walls of the compound.

The farewell which Emin received was a triumph over his enemies. The soldiers were marched down to the landing-place, and the Khedivial Hymn was played. They were all drawn up in two lines on each side of the road, and saluted as the Pasha passed between them. Salutes were fired from the mountain guns, and the whole station, with the exception of a comparatively small party of officers and clerks, turned out *en masse* to greet him and wish him God speed.

Every one seemed to breathe more freely now that

he was at liberty again. Nearly all came and kissed his hands and conducted him in triumph to the steamer. His own flag with the crescent and three stars, which he was allowed to fly as Governor, was flying at the fore, and two flags aft, as before the rebellion.

At 7.30. a.m. we steamed away from Dufilé, amid loud spoken expressions of good-will from everyone. As for Emin, he was in tremendous spirits. He seemed never tired of looking at the trees, the water, the mountains; the feeling of being at liberty again made him restless and excited. We talked of the probability of the Donagla taking Dufilé, and the unlooked-for turn of fortune's wheel, which had given us our liberty. We looked back at Dufilé, now growing indistinct in the distance, the station in which we had such extraordinary experiences, until a bend in the river hid it from our view. Thank the good God, that was the last we saw of it!

We did not arrive at Wadelai till the next afternoon, for we had to stop at Bora, a small station, in which there were one officer and twenty-five soldiers.

Emin had established it there in order to have a supply of wood always ready for steamers plying between Wadelai and Dufilé, for it was a fifteen hours' journey by steamer.

I will here quote a passage from my journal, which gives my impressions at the time.

"A third time we had to stop for wood this morning, so we did not sight the station of Wadelai till 2.30.

"On seeing the Mudir's flag flying at the fore, everyone flocked down to the water's edge, and when at three o'clock we steamed up to the landing-place, the whole station was assembled, the soldiers being all dressed in white, and drawn up for saluting the Governor. Directly the steamer was made fast, all the officers, clerks, civil-servants, and artizans, flocked on board to greet the Pasha, and escorted

HADJI FATMA'S JOY.

him with joyful acclamations up to his house, in front of which a sheep was killed, and we were made to step over the blood; some of the blood was also dashed against the lintels of the doors of our houses for luck. As we entered the compound, the old negress, Hadji Fatma, who looked after the Pasha's house, came running forward with the tears pouring down her cheeks, and having kissed the Pasha's hands, danced before him into the house, snapping her fingers like castanets, holding up her hands above her head, and crying, "Allah be praised!" The soldiers all marched up in front of the Pasha's house and saluted; he said a few words to them, and they filed off before him. All the officers, clerks, civil-servants, and employés came in and had coffee, and after talking some time to the Pasha, and congratulating him on his return, left. In his private compound there must have been fifty or sixty women at a time, who all came to kiss his hand and weep for joy.

"Every one seems glad to have him back, and the utmost contentment apparently prevails. The few faithfuls who have stuck to him, in spite of threats of imprisonment or death from the rebels, go about with grinning faces, showing the height of their delight that the bad days are over. The Pasha's return here is decidedly triumphant. I do not think the people actually against him were in the majority, but the rebels acted so promptly and quickly, that the people were cowed and astonished, and for a few weeks were completely taken in by the lies the rebels circulated about the Mudir. They therefore passively allowed the rebels to do as they pleased, as all negroes will in the face of determined energy, and acquiesced in all that was done. Then they heard the news of the coming of the Donagla, and the people were greatly startled and astonished to find that Khartoum had actually fallen, and that there was no road that way. They then saw that the policy which the Pasha had for the last three years been alternately commanding and entreating them to pursue was right, and they understood how completely they had been befooled by their officers, and how foolish they had been in throwing over the Mudir when such a crisis was at hand.

"They heard with dismay of the fall of Rejaf, of the death of the officers and clerks, and of the capture of all the women and children. They saw with disgust the utter inability of the rebel officers, who had usurped the authority, to deal with affairs in such an emergency. The feeling of discontent and insubordination grew and increased, until the news of this last disaster swept away all control, and with one accord they declared vehemently for the Mudir.

"He is now free, but refuses again to accept authority, moreover he has given his promise not to do so; I can only hope he may not be forced into it. It is better that he should not accept authority again, for, if he was not obeyed before his deposition, he certainly will not be obeyed now. Besides, he would be accepting the responsibility of the whole situation which has been brought about by the rebellion, and once disorder and robbery have taken hold of the soldiers, it will be difficult to eradicate it. As things have turned out, he is now in no way responsible for anything which happens in the country, and if Stanley comes to-morrow, he can, without the slightest blame being attached to him, leave as a private individual, leaving those who have thrown him over, and taking with him only such people as have been faithful to him throughout. When once the people said they deposed him, his duty towards them entirely ceased.

"It is true that these people are rejoiced at his return, but it is only the coming of the Donagla which has brought them to their senses. They think that their only hope of safety lies with him. Three-quarters of their rejoicing at his return is for themselves, they think he will save them the trouble of thinking.

"For thirteen years he has been with them, and there is not a single accusation of any real injustice or injury done to any one, which has been proved. Yet his people, while admitting he has been a just and beneficent ruler, have, on the word of their officers, believed the lies told against him, and thrown him over.

"They allowed him to be imprisoned, and would, I believe, have stood by and allowed him to be killed; they would never have wakened up to the fact that he was right and they were wrong, if they had not been suddenly startled by the coming of the Donagla. Though the process has been exceedingly unpleasant, it is not entirely a bad thing that this rebellion has happened, for it has freed him from the responsibility of dealing with a 'foolish and stiff-necked people.'

"All he has now to do is to get out of the country with the few faithfuls, and not trouble his head about the rest. If they want to follow, let them do so by all means, but they must take all the trouble on their own shoulders. I repeat it—he has now no more responsibility.

"The delight of once more being free after three months imprisonment in the middle of a noisy station, is very great. It is all so quiet here. At Dufilé there was nothing to be seen, it was so low-lying and depressing. Here the station is built on the top of a hill, and from my hut I get a splendid view through the open door, of the river winding below, with a great rolling grassy plain, dotted over with trees, between it and the distant Shuli mountains.

"When one has been long in a low-lying place, it is wonderful what an effect getting to the top of a high hill has on one's spirits and thoughts. I love to go alone on some mountain, and look down from a great height; one seems more or less to leave all the littleness of one's nature in the valley below. With the wide view, and the pure, fresh breeze, one's thoughts and ideas seem to expand and become elevated—to be freer and better. The Jews always built their altars on 'high places.'

"The long and miserable time we spent in the forest, with no view whatever, was still fresh in my memory, and no doubt strengthened the feeling of pleasure I always felt at being able to climb a hill and look round the country."

For several days after his arrival great numbers of people came in to see Emin, and to congratulate him on his release from prison. Officers, interpreters, and native chiefs all flocked in to assure him of their loyalty, and express their pleasure at once more seeing him among them. Old chief Wadelai came in and brought a present of a huge tusk of ivory; he was made quite happy by a present of a green glass tumbler in return. He looked as fat and jolly as ever.

Emin had plenty to do, for there was a good deal of sickness from some unknown cause, and a kind of pneumonia was raging like an epidemic in the station. Kodi Aga was suddenly struck down with it, and sent for Emin to come and doctor him. I went with Emin, who was much touched by the way Kodi Aga repeatedly kissed his hands, and kept telling him how glad he was to have him back again.

This feeling was perfectly genuine, and Kodi Aga really meant what he said from the bottom of his heart, but this with all the people never led to anything; it never made them come forward and help him when he really needed them. We heard many stories of what the rebels had done when they first came to Wadelai.

Dozens of people came to see Emin every day, and made all sorts of protestations to him of their devotion and loyalty; they all said how miserable they had been at what went on at Dufilé, but that they had not dared to do anything, as they were afraid of having their houses looted, and being imprisoned. These protestations were, of course, quite valueless, at least to me, coming as they did when everything was over; had these people behaved as they said they wished to have done, and acted tolerably firmly at first, the rebellion might have been crushed at its outset,—it could not have lasted a week.

The Khedive steamer returned the day after we reached Wadelai, in order to bring fresh refugees to the southern stations. We were all anxiously looking for her return to hear what was the news, for we knew the Donagla would in all probability follow up their victory at Rejaf without much delay.

For six or seven days we heard nothing, things at

Wadelai were going on comfortably and quietly. Emin was busy with the sick, and ineffably happy in his liberty, and in the feeling that he could again be at work among his people. The forced inaction of his trying imprisonment had been one of the hardest things to bear, and he was never so happy as when going about at Wadelai and tending the sick. Nothing seemed to tire him, and nothing concerning the welfare of his people was too much trouble. He seemed quite to have forgotten and forgiven all that they had done to him, and thoroughly believed in their renewed protestations of loyalty. I was more sceptical about it all; but I was different, for I did not love his people. To this day I am certain they were really glad to have him back, only it meant nothing, for I knew that if anything happened, we could never rely on them to help us in the smallest degree.

However, those few days following his release were very happy ones to Emin; the station was quiet, and the soldiers well behaved.

Our position was in many ways more dangerous than before, for although we were at liberty, and could retire if anything happened, still there was now nothing between Rejaf and Dufilé to check the coming of the Donagla, and if Dufilé fell the whole country was lost. No one, however would look at this contingency, and studiously avoided even thinking of it, and seemed only to rest content that things were quiet in the station after the long interval of confusion and lawlessness.

Here is another extract from my journal written at that time.

"It is most surprising that neither steamer has yet returned here, and we are all beginning to get anxious about their non-arrival. All things are possible just now, for we do not know what may have happened. Suliman Aga promised to be at Wadelai in a few days, with the Khedive steamer, to take the Pasha, Casati, and myself up to Tunguru with him. He is now several days over-due. It is quite possible, while we are quietly resting here in fancied security, that we may wake up one fine morning to find the Donagla are at our very gates, and that they have come accompanied by another party in the steamers."

Emin had given his word that we would not move from Wadelai, but would wait for Suliman Aga's coming. We could only therefore wait for him patiently, though somewhat anxiously.

I went out shooting teal and duck, of which there used to be a good many in the swamps near the station; but the ticks which infested the grass used to cover one's legs, and I had to give up going out. After coming in one day from shooting, my boy took fifty-eight off my legs and feet. They were very small, and buried their heads in the flesh, and it was quite impossible to take them off with the hands, it was necessary to use tweezers. They lived in the grasses, which were at that time very high and dry, and until the grass was burnt off it was impossible to go out. The bites of these little ticks always produced great swelling, for often in pulling them off with the tweezers the heads were left in, and the irritation caused by them was sometimes sufficient to bring on a strong fever for several days.

Emin was turning over his boxes, carefully packing up his collections of birds, and discarding all the useless things, preparatory to making a start immediately on Stanley's arrival at the lake. Such a collection of rubbish as had accumulated during all the years that he had been in the Province!

In turning out his boxes of letters he came upon one from Dr. Junker, which he showed me. In it he said, that after all the years he had been in Africa he had come to the conclusion that the natives were incapable of ever rising to any extent. That the only thing for Europeans to do was to try to improve their condition, and that a mild treatment would never answer with them. He concluded, " They must be ruled by fear." This was pretty strong, and I think not true, though perhaps it was partly so.

There was at the time he wrote a strong feeling in Germany against the negroes, which was as unjust in its low estimate of them, as the feeling in England was exaggerated in its admiration of their supposed virtues and capabilities. It seems to me the just estimation of their character lies between the two opinions. I do not think the negroes would ever become a great nation capable of governing themselves as Europeans understand government. But I do not see why people should expect or even want to Europeanize negroes. That they could, by education, become immensely higher and better than they are, is a fact which must be patent to any one who knows anything about Africa and the negroes. The negro has traits in his character quite apart, and often finer in their way than those of Europeans; it is better to educate and foster those traits, and leave him a negro still with all his own peculiar individuality, but educated and enlightened. Improve and train him, but never try to Europeanize him,—the trial has always proved a failure. Most of the mission boys I have seen are a servile worthless lot, talking a good deal about Jesus Christ, but not liking work. I would put forward my idea with all humility, and as a mere suggestion, that missionaries should not allow their mission children to copy the manners and customs of Europeans, nor even to allow them to dress in European clothes. Anything more painfully ludicrous than a negro dressed in European clothes, and aping European manners and phrases, it is difficult to imagine. They look so much nicer in their own clothes, or even in manufactured European cloth worn in the loose fashion of the country, which is far more suited to them and the country than European clothes. I remember talking to a negro in Usongo. He was a good fellow, and tolerably well educated, and I should say thoroughly trustworthy. He was, however, dressed in European clothes, and looked most uncomfortable and out of place in them, as well as exceedingly awkward. I was talking to him about railways, and he quite agreed with me in thinking what a good thing it would be when the arid and the fever-stricken band which closes in Central Africa was once bridged over, and a quick road opened to the healthy and fertile lands of the interior. He said, " I trust that when the railway is made that Jesus Christ will come up with it." He meant nothing irreverent, nor did he mean it, I am sure, in a canting way. It was only that he had, to a certain degree, become Europeanized, and he did not understand the fitness of things connected with European ways and phrases.

Trade, it seems to me, will be one of the best and strongest civilizing influences in Africa, for it must develop the resources of the country. As soon as the natives once find there is a ready market for their produce, they will cultivate and open up the country. At present each native only grows just enough to support his family, and all his spare time is taken up in idling or quarrelling with his neighbours. When he has more worldly possessions, and a greater stake in the country, he will think twice before he makes war upon his neighbours on every little paltry disagreement. He will have something to lose, and will therefore be more careful.

At the same time, I would like to see a better class of goods brought into Africa, than the cheap, tawdry Manchester cotton cloths, which are now introduced in exchange for native produce. I shall never forget the feeling of shame I felt when I saw for the first time the miserable flimsy cloth we brought with us on the Expedition to give to the natives. It was no fault of ours, for we were obliged to bring what was in demand in the country as money. But it is not much to the credit of the Manchester merchants that they should manufacture such rubbish.

Even without contact with civilization, certain peoples and tribes have become very much better than their neighbours.

For instance, the people of Uganda are, in their way, nearer civilization than the people of Unyoro, who are, in their turn, much higher than the surrounding tribes. Whilst the natives on the plains around Kavallis are certainly higher than the people near Fort Bodo in Ibwiri. The lowest people we have seen are, I should say, the bush natives of the Upper Aruwimi, about the village of Aveysheba, who were, judging from the appearance of the men we killed, a small, stunted, and degenerate race.

Emin told me one of the things a traveller notices when he enters Uganda is the cleanness of the people and of their dwellings, as well as the goodness of their roads and the improved cultivation. Their household utensils, jars, baskets, etc., are all beautifully made, and their bark cloth is fine, and made in considerable quantities. Unyoro is the same in a lesser degree. The natives round Kavallis make good huts, and wear skins particularly well cured, and the women are well behaved and modest. From Kavallis the natives seem to descend in the social scale until Aveysheba, where the lowest point is reached.

Certain it is that if the negroes ever become a great nation they will have a glorious country to develop.

Emin told me he always had an idea of importing Chinese into the country as labourers, and had had a very interesting correspondence with Gordon on the subject, when he was Governor-General at Khartoum. Gordon, however, whilst admitting the justice of his ideas, objected on the plea that the Chinese were the most immoral people under the sun, and therefore refused to further such a plan.

I had had such hopes about bringing Emin's people out with us, and settling them in a country near the Victoria lake. Emin had written of it to Nubar Pasha, and many of his people desired it; it seemed that it would have been the best thing for Emin's people, and the best for Egypt as well, for had all the Khedive's subjects in government employ come out with us to Egypt, there would have been arrears in their wages for many years to pay, which would amount to no less a sum than £350,000, and how could such a sum be raised in Egypt?

This rebellion had, however, put a stop to all thoughts of carrying out Emin's scheme, nor would I now, knowing what a lot of brigands Emin's people were, ever help to turn them into a new country among a lot of helpless natives. Every place they went to with their thin veneer of civilization, and all the vices and idleness of the Turks, they ruined. They would soon have turned any beautiful country into a hell upon earth. What a pity it was that Baker, Gordon, and Emin should have had such material as this to deal with! and what a glorious country might have been made if only the Turkish and Egyptian influence could have been kept out! The great work these three men did with so much labour and loss of life was lost entirely on account of the worthless tools they were obliged to use, and by the corruptness of the Egyptian Government. It was like trying to make ropes with sand, for the whole machinery by which the Province was worked was rotten, and had corruption for the main spring. I know Gordon and Emin many a time deplored the quality of the miserable material they were obliged to work with, and doubtless Baker did the same; the old adage held true, that silk purses have nothing in common with hog's hair. The coming of the Donagla, too, would for a long time close the road to some of the richest countries,—the countries of Makraka, Monbuttu, Latooka, and I may add, Niam-Niam, for doubtless the Mahdi's people would overrun all that country, and will depopulate it by slave-raiding, drain it of ivory, and ruin it by insufficient cultivation. Unless something is done there seems no knowing where Mahdism will stop. It is quite possible the movement may extend south till it reaches the Zanzibar Arabs of Manyema, who are gradually working up to the north.

We were still waiting anxiously for a steamer to arrive, and in consequence of a report we heard from Tunguru and M'swa, Kodi Aga sent a letter to Suliman Aga, at Dufilé, by the hands of some native interpreters, urging him to come as soon as possible and take charge of Tunguru, to which station he had been re-appointed.

The report was that the Irregulars at Tunguru and M'swa were conspiring to burn the stations, and make their way across country to join their countrymen, the Donagla, in Rejaf. The Irregulars in these two stations were in the majority, and, to add to the danger, a clerk named Tybe Effendi, himself from Dongola, and known to be friendly to the Mahdi's people, was at Tunguru. He was one of those who had been most active against Emin, and had been sent by Selim Aga to Tunguru from Dufilé, to get him out of reach of the Donagla, when they defeated the soldiers at Rejaf. He was a born intriguer, and it was quite possible he might do incalculable mischief. The Irregulars in the beginning of the rebellion had been very much cowed and frightened by the attitude of the Regular soldiers towards them, but on the coming of the Donagla and their frequent defeat of the Regulars, they had been getting more and more self-asserting. A party of soldiers was sent to Tunguru to bring back Tybe Effendi to Wadelai. There seemed to be no end to the complications in this country; troubles of all descriptions were constantly rising on all sides, troubles nearly always connected with treachery and rebellion.

Meantime no news had arrived from Dufilé, and we were beginning to think of moving on overland to Tunguru, and not waiting any longer for Suliman Aga, for we felt that the Donagla could not fail soon to follow up their victory. The only thing was to get Emin to move.

On December 1st we heard a rumour of the approach of the Donagla, and on that date I find the following entry in my journal :—

"To-day we heard news from the natives that a large party of the Donagla had come from Bahr el Ghazal, and had attacked and defeated the people in Makraka. They fled to a mountain called Gebel Wati, on the road between Makraka and here. They were followed by the Donagla, who again defeated them and established themselves on the mountain, which is only two and a half days' march from this station. We know from Omar Saleh's letter that Osman Adem commands the Mahdi's forces in Bahr el Ghazal, and that with him is Keremallah, the general whom the Pasha defeated in Amadi four years ago; so it is likely he is burning to avenge the trick played upon him then, and his subsequent defeat. If the news is true, the situation is indeed grave, for of course, it must be a preconcerted arrangement with the people of Rejaf. One believes this rumour more readily because it has always been a source of surprise to us that the Donagla at Rejaf have not followed up either of their two victories. It seems evident, therefore, that they were waiting for their people in Bahr el Ghazal to join them, and intend to act in concert with them. It is possible, too, that an attack has been made on Dufilé, and the steamers have been taken, and they have decided to march down on us from Gebel Wati, and at the same time send up the steamers from Dufilé to attack us by water simultaneously.

"We can never hold out against them here unless the soldiers were very courageous and steady, which they are not. Moreover, Wadelai is not well defended; there is, it is true, a ditch all round the station, but owing to the nature of the soil, which is all rocks and gravel, it has been impossible to cut very deep and make the ditch an effective defence. Besides, the station is far too large to hold. If Wadelai is lost Tunguru also goes, and M'swa will quickly follow, and then the whole country will be in the hands of the Donagla. How fearfully time has been frittered away! Had the retiring policy been carried out energetically, both Wadelai and Dufilé might by this time have been evacuated, and we might all now have been safely massed at Tunguru and M'swa, where we might have held out against the Donagla.

"It is maddening to see how these people work, or rather how they do not work,—they stand when they ought to run, and run like hares when they ought to stand and face the enemy. They are truly what my boy Binza calls them, 'watu m'bovu,' a 'rotten people,' it describes them exactly. I have spoken strongly to Emin of the expediency of at once retiring by land, and Captain Casati is also of my opinion. I would, I hope, be one of the last people to advocate a retreat if it were possible to do any good by remaining here. But it is agreed on all sides that defence is impossible, therefore what can be the good of staying here to be taken prisoners? It can benefit nobody. Men have been sent out to find if the Gebel Wati report is true, and if we find it is so, my advice to Emin is to start at once, and make for Imandi, a place on the edge of the forest, just on the other side of the Ituri. We should therefore have a large tract of land and the Ituri River between us and the Donagla, and should be only six days from Fort Bodo. There we can wait for Stanley's arrival, and when he joins us, strike south east, so avoiding going near this country. With fifty guns we could easily do this."

"On hearing the rumour of the Donagla being at Gebel Wati, an Egyptian officer came in to see Emin, and told him the people were greatly frightened by the news, and by the non-arrival of the steamers. He added, 'Of course you are responsible for us all, and cannot abandon us, we came from Egypt by the orders of the Government to serve under you, and you must look after us.'

"The Pasha answered, 'Indeed! You seem to forget that I have a paper in which it is written that the officers have deposed me, and no longer desire me to interfere with the affairs of Government, or to be their Governor; this paper was written at Dufilé, and was signed by you all.'

"'Oh!' said the Egyptian, 'that was all nonsense.'

"'Nonsense or not,' answered the Pasha, 'I was kept in prison for three months, and had I been free, and allowed to act, we should never have been in this predicament, so I have absolutely no responsibility now.'"

There is no measuring Egyptian effrontery! The position the country was in, was entirely due to them, and yet these people wished to shift the responsibility on to the Mudir's shoulders when they found themselves in a fix. It was far better that they should be swallowed up in the Soudan, than that we should take such a worthless lot of scoundrels to Egypt.

I here quote again from my journal :—

"In the afternoon all the soldiers marched up to Emin's compound, and drew up in line in front of his house, and he went out to see what they wanted. There were no officers, only soldiers and non-commissioned officers. On the Pasha's coming out, the non-commissioned officers stepped forward, and told him what they wanted, the soldiers keeping up a running chorus to all that was said. They wished the Pasha to take up his position as Mudir once more, saying, 'A ship without a pilot was lost.' They went on to say that since he had been deposed everything had gone wrong, nothing was done, and discipline was not kept up. The people from Dufilé had come here and made mischief, and if they came again they would meet with a hot reception, for now the people of Wadelai knew what mischief they had done, and how incapable they were of taking over the Government of the country. They ended by saying that the Pasha was their father and Governor, and he must look after them and get them out of this scrape. Emin answered them with a long oration. He told them he was unable to take command as before, he had given his word to the people of Dufilé that he would not do so, and he was unable to break his word. He, however, as they knew, went every day to Kodi Aga to hear what was going on and to give him advice. They knew, had he chosen to desert them when Dr. Junker left the country, that he could have done so, but that he had no wish to do such a thing. Where they were he was with them. But, he added, if I tell you some evening that we must retire, you must not contradict me, but must be ready to start the very next morning. Of course all the soldiers declared vehemently they would be ready to start when he told them; and equally of course I knew they never would do it, but would dawdle and dawdle until everything was lost. The soldiers then retired, happy in the feeling that they might leave everything in Emin's hands; that he had made himself responsible for their safety, and that they had nothing to do now but to eat and sleep. Emin did not say a single word of his real intentions, which are to leave here as soon as ever he can, taking with him such people as have been faithful to him throughout the rebellion, leaving the rest to follow or stay as they pleased. They will be able to get out just as easily as we shall, if they really wish it, but he does not intend to make himself responsible for their safety, and if they lag behind and dawdle on the road they will be lost. Such treatment is much more considerate than these people deserve. He has, however, told them he gives advice to Kodi Aga, and of course, if he does that he makes himself responsible in their eyes for the advice given, and by doing this makes it much harder for himself to get out. Besides, his speech has raised hopes in the minds of the soldiers, hopes which he does not intend to carry out. It would have been so much better if he had told them plainly that the present state of things has been brought on by the rebellion and by his imprisonment, in which the soldiers tacitly acquiesced, and that now he could not be responsible for anything. He might have said he would do what he could for them, but was not able to be responsible for their safety.

"This movement has evidently been got up by the officers entirely, they wish to entrap him into consenting to get them out of the predicament into which they have put everybody.

"Captain Casati and I groaned together over his speech to the soldiers; Casati said, 'He has been a good Governor, but he is not, and has not been good for the present crisis;' to use Casati's words, 'Il n'a pas de courage.' He will not speak out plainly and firmly, and say that the people must not look to him for anything now, as everything has been taken out of his hands. All through the rebellion, and even before it, has been the same.

"He has without doubt been an excellent Governor, and would be yet, if things were going on steadily and smoothly, but he is not firm enough to act in any emergency. Captain Casati and myself, when the soldiers fell in before him, implored him not to commit himself in any way to them. He said he had no intention of doing so, but was going to speak very firmly to them. But when he began to speak his words were by no means firm, and he certainly raised hopes which, as I have said before, he had no intention of carrying out. He saw afterwards that Casati and I did not like what he said, and told us he was afraid of offending the soldiers by speaking out too plainly. No doubt in treating with these people it is necessary sometimes to make a compromise. But these are no times now for making compromises; now is the time for plain speaking, and very soon, if I'm not mistaken, it will be a case of *Sauve qui peut*. If Stanley were here, he would very soon bring them to their true bearings. The Pasha perfectly agrees when I say he has nothing to thank his soldiers for, and yet he says he does not blame them for what has happened in this rebellion. He admits that the soldiers are the only real power in the country, and had they acted for him, no rebellion could have taken place. Yet he does not blame them for standing by and seeing him imprisoned, because he says that they themselves have never done any violent act! Why, the very sentries in front of his door at Dufilé were not only acquiescing, but were taking an active part in the rebellion! I cannot understand such reasoning; it seems to me in such a case the words of Scripture might be applied with great justice: 'He that is not with Me is against Me, and he that gathereth not, scattereth.' There can be no half-measures in a rebellion, people cannot remain neutral, they must be on one side or the other. All these things are perfectly maddening. Emin would in reality do his people a much greater kindness if he spoke to them more firmly and stiffly, they would then wake up to the fact that they must help themselves and not dawdle about till all is lost."

In the evening, Emin, Casati, and I talked the affair over, and all agreed it was a pity that the soldiers had come up. It was plain that both officers and men wished to force the Mudir again into a position of responsibility, not particularly because they wanted him for a Mudir, but because they were afraid of what was likely to happen, and thought if he were again at the head of affairs, he might be able to get them out of the scrape, and save them the trouble of thinking or doing anything.

Emin again said that he did not like to speak too plainly to the soldiers for fear of estranging them from him, and he might yet want their help. I told him, when the soldiers had assured him they would obey him promptly when he gave the order to move, that it was all nonsense, they would never stand by him when he needed them. He answered, "Mr. Jephson, I have known my people for thirteen years, you have only known them for seven months, allow me to know them best." "Very well, Pasha," I replied, shrugging my shoulders, "*Nous verrons*." It was quite hopeless to try to make Emin understand that his people were not to be trusted, for if anything bad was done by them, and they afterwards came up to express their sorrow for having done so, and assure him of their devoted attachment to him, and

Achmet Effendi Raif.

promised implicit obedience for the future, he was always ready to forgive and believe in them again. Certainly, for so clever a man, he learnt wonderfully little from experience.

The morning following the deputation of soldiers, Emin went to Kodi Aga and told him that he wished for no more such demonstrations. People were at this time being sent in in small bands overland to Tunguru by Emin's advice, and the refugees from the northern stations, who had been sent down to Wadelai, were gradually being drafted to the southern stations. But Kodi Aga complained that even now they did not wish to retire to Tunguru, and many of them had refused to go when ordered to start, though native carriers were in readiness to carry their goods. Emin told him that those who refused to obey his orders should be put in prison. Accordingly, Achmet Effendi Raif, a scoundrelly clerk, was put in prison for refusing to leave the station. He was a most contemptible little creature, and had been one of Emin's most bitter enemies in the Council at Dufilé. Now, neither the rebel officers nor any of the people liked him, he had sold all his things for drink, and was now "hounded about like a stray tyke," and no one cared to help him. He was an Egyptian, and almost a dwarf, and was always in the most tattered dirty state. He had a low cunning face, his legs were much bowed and his feet were turned in. The pictures of Quilp always recurred to my mind whenever I saw him. He would have made a good subject for some artist who wished to paint an ideal of all that was low, vicious, vindictive, and contemptible, clothed in rags and dirt. He was one of the valuable people we eventually brought out to Egypt! Osman Latif came in during the day and insisted that Emin was still responsible for all the people, and could not shirk his responsibility, but Casati and I utterly derided the idea, and he was somewhat abashed.

CHAPTER XII.

FLIGHT FROM WADELAI.

News of the fall of the northern stations—Council of War held—Soldiers implore Emin to take charge of them—Flight decided on—We prepare for the flight—We throw away our treasures—I disable the *Advance*—Binza, a regular character—Our flight from Wadelai—Desertion of the soldiers—Strange baggage of the fugitives—Heart-rending scene at the river—Curious ideas about evacuation—We camp—Arrival of the steamer—Letter from Selim Aga Matara—Description of the siege of Dufilé—Emin decides to go on—Further particulars of the siege of Dufilé—Cowardice shown by the soldiers—Our narrow escape—Conduct of soldiers in former Mahdi war—Rumours accounted for—We reach Okello's—Arrival at Tunguru.

On the morning of December 4th, at about midday, a small party of soldiers, accompanied by some women and children, were seen hurrying along as fast as they could go on the other side of the river. As soon as they arrived opposite the station one of them began to make signals by frantically waving a white flag. A boat was instantly sent to bring them over. They turned out to be the garrison of a small station called Bora, half way between Dufilé and Wadelai. They had come in haste to bring us the news which had been brought to them by some friendly natives near Dufilé, of the Lur tribe. Hamad Aga, who was the chief of Bora, told us that Muggi Laboré, Chor Aiu and Dufilé had all fallen before the Donagla, who had also taken Fabbo. A native chief near Bora had come to Hamad Aga, and told him that the interpreters whom we had sent down to Dufilé with letters had been killed on the road by the Shulis, who had all risen against the Turks. He said he told him this, and the news also of the fall of the northern stations, as he had always been Emin's friend, and he warned Hamad Aga to go for his life and bring us the news at Wadelai.

When the news was told to Kodi Aga he summoned all the officers, and they went in a body to Emin's house. Here a long council of war was held, at which all the officers spoke, and after a good deal of talking it was decided to evacuate the station at once; the non-commissioned officers were also sent for, and agreed to go. The soldiers were then drawn up in companies, and were told the news, and spoken to by their officers. Some few of them were for going, but the greater part were for waiting for a few days to see if the news was confirmed. They said if Dufilé had fallen refugees would have reached Wadelai. We accounted for there being none because all the natives between Wadelai and Dufilé had risen, and any fugitives would probably have been cut off. After talking with their officers for some time, and being unable to decide what to do, it was agreed that the soldiers should come down and see the Pasha. They came down, and Emin reminded them of their promise to him only two days before; after a good deal of quarrelling among themselves, it was decided to start for Tunguru early the next morning, and abandon the station. We were to go to M'swa, and then take to the mountains, and I was to show them the way to Fort Bodo.

The officers and soldiers all implored the Pasha to again act as their Governor, and to take command of them, and lead them in the flight. He was greatly averse to doing this, but at the earnest request of the people he complied with their wish on the sole condition of implicit obedience on their part, otherwise he told them he could do nothing. They all promised to obey his orders promptly, whatever they were. The rest of the afternoon was spent in the utmost confusion, selecting such things as we could manage to carry; there were hardly any porters to be got, for the natives had heard that we were going to retire, and would not obey the orders from the station. We threw away great numbers of things we were unable to take.

I had been for some months collecting useful things, such as boots, clothes, cotton cloth, tobacco, skin bags, etc., for my fellow-officers. I had got together quite a nice little lot of things, and was looking forward to the pleasure of giving them to them on Stanley's arrival. I had, however, to throw them all away, so as to cut down my loads to the smallest possible dimensions for the flight. I had a particularly good collection of curiosities of all sorts that I had collected from the different countries in Emin's Province. There were ivory hair-pins of strange shapes, bows, arrows, spears, shields, bracelets and necklaces, Bari girdles, made of little round discs of pink and white shells, and aprons,—altogether an immense variety of things. There was a very fine collection of huge iron and copper knives from Monbuttu and Niam-Niam, together with dwarf spears, light cane stools, and large queer-shaped iron bells. All had to be abandoned, and I even had to throw away the greater part of the scanty supply of clothes and boots which I had obtained after so much trouble and expense in the Province.

For the Pasha, it was really most heart-rending to have to throw away all his instruments, sextant, boiling thermometers, aneroids, apparatus for anthropological measurements, and several other valuable instruments. His books, clothes, papers, beads, brass bracelets, and all the useful things he had saved and collected for our people with so much care and forethought, all had to be cast away, and only the most necessary things taken so as not to impede our flight. There were four boxes of stuffed birds which Emin had collected; these were destined for the British Museum, but they had to be all thrown away. They are a great loss to science, for there were many new and interesting species amongst them; it went to Emin's heart to throw them away. I extemporized a hammock for little Farida out of two blankets, and slung it on a large light bamboo. In an ordinary way in Emin's Province women were carried on an angarep, but this was considered too heavy and unwieldy for rapid movement, besides, it would have required four men to carry it. The hammock was light and convenient, and did remarkably well. It was in this very hammock, made out of two blankets, that Farida was eventually carried all the way to the coast.

Everyone was busy all the afternoon packing up a few necessary things and discarding the rest,

I Destroy the Advance. 319

and though it had only been decided at three o'clock that afternoon to evacuate the station, all was ready by the evening to start at daybreak the following day. If we could once gain the mountains above M'swa, we felt we should be comparatively safe. But we

BREAKING UP OF THE *ADVANCE*.

knew that if the Donagla followed up their victories and came up in the steamers we should be lost; for in the steamers they could travel in one day a distance we could not do on foot in four. At the council of war which was held in the afternoon, I was asked to destroy our boat, the *Advance* which Stanley had left in my care, so that it might not fall into the hands of the Donagla. We had no oars with her, and no men to pull them if we had, so I reluctantly consented—I could not do otherwise. It was with a sore heart that I went down in the evening and unscrewed two of the sections, and threw the bolts far out into the river.

The poor old boat had been so useful to us, and was still as good as new. I had always looked after her, and she had been carried by my company of Zanzibaris. It had been part of my work in the Expedition to look after her, and to put her together or take her to pieces when necessary. I had done this numbers of times, and knew almost every bolt and screw in her. She had saved us walking many a weary mile when we were ill, and had, some time or other, carried all of us, when we had fever on the Aruwimi. She had been a sort of pilot to our flotilla, and with her Stanley had always protected our canoes from being cut off or attacked by the natives; he had constantly got goats and food which we should not have been able to procure without her, and one felt quite sad at being obliged to destroy her.

There she lay now, the poor old *Advance*, broken in three pieces on the sandy shore of Wadelai. Even my three Soudanese orderlies, whom I had taken down with me to help me to take her in pieces, were sad at seeing her broken up, and said, "Ah, she's been a good friend to us all." As for my boy Binza he made a long lamentation over her, quite a second "By the waters of Babylon we sat down and wept!"

He praised her shape and powers of going, and dilated upon the use she had been, and all she had done for us. He touched pathetically upon what I must be feeling at being obliged to destroy her, I who had looked after her so long, and had—so he was pleased to say—managed her so well. He described the Zanzibaris' sorrow at not seeing her again, and ended with a neatly rounded moral upon the whole thing, a kind of "Sic transit gloria mundi!"

Binza was a regular character, and often made me laugh by his quaint remarks upon people and things. He was formerly a Niam-Niam cannibal, but gave himself great airs of civilization, and looked down with the greatest contempt upon people whom he considered inferior to himself in cultivation and manners.

He was a good boy, however, and was ready and willing. He was a liar, yes! Most untaught negroes are. But all the time I had him, I am sure he never stole a thing from me, and in Emin's Province I constantly used to leave my money about. At times he was possessed of the devil, and had fits of idling and general cussedness, but I liked him exceedingly, and he was never impertinent. He was a general favourite with all Emin's people, who gave him a good many presents of clothes, etc., he was also well liked by all our Zanzibaris; but if any one molested or interfered with him, he poured out such a torrent of abuse at them, and used low expressions in Arabic or Ki-Swahili which made one's hair stand on end to listen to. He was of the regular flat-nosed, thick-lipped type of the negroes near the Niam-Niam country, his face, too, was generally flat; he had a sort of profile like a currant bun. He had—however ugly,—a very nice and good-natured face, the expression of which showed plainly that he possessed largely that most humanizing of all influences, the capacity for laughter.

We were up at daybreak on December 5th, and got our things all out ready for the start. We could only procure a few native carriers, and were by no means certain that these would not run away. I tied up my journals in an old towel, and carried them myself determined, whatever else I might lose, I would stick at least to those.

The first thing in the morning the soldiers were all marched down to the store-houses, and all the ammunition in the powder magazine was given out to them. There were about 120 soldiers, and each received 60 rounds of ammunition. Each soldier had before that from 40 to 50 cartridges in his belt, so that roughly speaking each man had about 100 rounds of ammunition.

No sooner had the ammunition been served out than the soldiers all refused to start, saying they did not care about going with the Mudir, but intended going back to their own countries, and no persuasion on the part of their officers could get them to move.

Emin's speech, only two days before, about his knowing his soldiers after twelve years' residence with them, recurred to my mind. However, it was no time for waiting, and we started off without them. Out of the 120 soldiers only five accompanied us, I had my three orderlies armed with Remingtons, and my own Winchester repeating rifle, Emin had a Remington, and Marco and some of the clerks had shot guns. We may have mustered twenty guns amongst us.

Women and children flocked up to Emin's compound, begging to be carried, for they declared they could not walk. Donkeys were given to the old women and sick people, but there were not very many in the station. We feared many women and children would fall by the way.

I here quote from my journal:—

"We got off by seven o'clock, and as we left the station we could see a confused straggling line of women and children, goats, cattle and sheep, donkeys, and baggage stretching ahead for three miles. All was utter confusion and noise. Some women might be seen hurrying along with their goods, and dragging little children or goats after them. Others were seated mournfully in small groups with their loads before them, trying to soothe the crying of their children, while they waited for their fathers or husbands to join them. There were sick people who implored us to help them to get along, and wept and wrung their hands in an agony of despair at being left. The shouting of the people and crying of the children, the lowing and bleating of cattle and goats, rose in a deafening uproar.

"Here and there a woman might be seen toiling bravely along with a huge load on her head, a baby slung across her back, and dragging a small child along. It was a pitiful sight. The whole road was strewn with things of all sorts, which they had started with and found too heavy to carry. We passed several small children, too, abandoned by the road-side.

"Some of the people took the queerest things with them. I saw one man carrying in his load four immensely heavy carved legs of a bedstead, while another had a great bunch of ostrich feathers, which he told me he had heard were valuable in Europe. Another was carrying a sledge hammer, a basin, and a heavy cross-cut saw, whilst others were carrying great round irons for baking bread on, and even grinding stones. Several people took their parrots, one woman had three, and I saw one man carrying a cat in a basket. Two soldiers had the tubes of Emin's thermometers hanging to their belts, they were under the impression that they were a sort of clock by which they could tell the time. I could have laughed, only that I felt so much more inclined to do the other thing. It was so awfully pathetic to see these poor half-savage people with their loads stuffed full of all sorts of useless rubbish, under the weight of which they were staggering along, carrying or dragging their poor unfortunate little children after them. There was even something pathetic in their very stupidity.

"At one place we had to cross a broad shallow river, with steep sloping banks on either side. Here a scene of the utmost confusion prevailed. The high bank was soon churned into a black slippery mud, in which the women and children sank up to their knees, and were continually falling. The press on the further bank was terrible, and when some unfortunate child or women fell, the dense mass of donkeys and people behind swept over them and trampled them under foot. It was perfectly heart-rending to see them and hear their cries for help. I stood for nearly an hour on one side, and helped such women and children as I could, to climb the

THE FLIGHT FROM WADELAI.   Page 324.

bank. Several times I made a plunge into the crowd to save some woman or little child from being trampled to death, until, sick with the sight of it, I had to hurry on to join the Pasha at the head of the column. Nothing makes people so cruel as fear, and the terror that the Donagla were following us made these people merciless.

"Folks at home have a queer idea of what evacuation in these countries means. They give a man an order to 'evacuate' much in the same way as they would tell him to eat his dinner, and apparently they do not seem to think that one is much harder than the other. They do not know the time it takes, the work it involves, and the general despair of ever moving the people that such an order produces. And then, when they are at last induced to move, what heart-rending and sickening sights are to be seen every day, and what distress and misery a wholesale and hurried evacuation makes!

"After the river was passed we got on a little better, but had to make frequent halts to allow the last of the women and children to come up. After one of the most trying and painful marches I have ever made, we camped at three o'clock, having done only ten miles. The last of the column did not come in till 5.30. The disorder during the march had been great, one lot of people wished to camp in one place, and another lot in some other spot. But at last they all came in weary and footsore.

"From the last stragglers who reached camp we heard that great numbers of people, being tired on the march, had returned to Wadelai, so that our caravan was reduced to one fourth of its original number. We were now in all about 400 souls. There was a rumour that as the last of the column left the station the smoke of the steamers coming up river was seen in the distance. We have no means of knowing the truth to-night, but shall probably hear all about it to-morrow. If it is the Donagla, they will probably come on us in the night. We at all events shall hear some time to-morrow. In any case we go on now we have once started. We made our camp in the grass and slept in the open air, small rough huts and shelters being made for the women and children. Fortunately it is now the dry season."

We were up early and got off by 6 o'clock the next morning; the people went somewhat better than the day before, but being unaccustomed to walk, their feet became very much blistered, and numbers of them sat down by the way-side. We afterwards heard that some of them were killed by the natives, who, seeing we were retiring, and hearing the reason why, took the opportunity of paying off a few old scores, and killed some of the stragglers.

At 9 o'clock from a hill we saw a steamer coming up river after us, and thought it was all up with us. The steamer kept up a constant whistling, and some of the people with us prepared to fire on her; two guns actually were fired, but she made friendly signals, and it turned out to be some of Emin's own men. The two steamers had arrived at Wadelai a few hours after we had started, bringing in refugees and officers from Dufilé. We halted in a village about half a mile from the river and waited for them to come up. The captain of the steamer soon arrived, and after kissing Emin's hands with every show of devotion, handed him a letter from Selim Aga Matara, of which the following is a translation :—

"From Selim Aga Matara,
    "To the Governor of Hatalastiva,
        "His Excellency Mehmed Emin Pasha.

"MY MASTER,—On November 18th the soldiers arrived here from Muggi and Laboré stations, and with them 120 soldiers belonging to the 1st Battalion, who had escaped from Rejaf. I ordered Bachit Aga Mahmoud to take a small party of soldiers to Laboré to find where the Donagla were encamped. At 11 a.m. some of the soldiers returned, and told us they had encountered some of them near Chor Itteen, and towards evening the rest returned and brought a letter from the chief of the Donagla, Omar Saleh, commanding us to surrender. The letter told us of the deaths of Hamad Aga, the Major, Abdullah Vaab Effendi, Ali Aga Djabor, Salem Effendi, and Hassan Effendi Lutvi, and threatened to destroy us if we did not obey. To this demand we made no answer, but burned the letter.

"On November 25th the Donagla surrounded the station and shouted out on all sides, 'We are the Mahdi's people.' At 4 p.m. they sent us another letter, repeating their commands to us to surrender, but the soldiers threw the letter out of the station back at them. The bearer of the letter, when asked why the people had come, gave no answer except that the Donagla wished to have the station in their hands. On the 26th they approached, and firing went on between us from 9 a.m. to 3 p.m., when a body of soldiers sallied out and drove away the attacking party, and killed twelve of them, besides wounding many; among our soldiers there were no losses. On the 27th the Donagla again approached, and a good deal of firing went on from both sides. On the 28th a night attack was made, and we had to beat the soldiers up to their posts at 4 a.m., and firing went on until dawn. On this day were wounded Achmet Aga el Assinti, Bachit Aga Ali, and Suliman Aga Soudan; some were shot, and others were wounded by sword thrusts in their hands and feet. Some few soldiers and non-commissioned officers were also wounded in the same way. In the midst of the affray some of the Donagla actually entered the station and killed Mahomet Effendi el N'djar, the captain of the Nyanza steamer, and Ali Achmet, the engineer, Mooragan Derar, the pilot, Khamis Salim, the chief fireman, and Farajala Moru, second fireman, all belonging to the Khedive steamer. After these accidents we mustered up all our energy to try to kill the Donagla who had entered the station. Towards 8 o'clock, a.m., the battle was won by our soldiers, and the enemy dispersed. They left behind them 210 killed, besides those we were unable to count, and such wounded people as reached their camp. We captured eleven flags, and among them that of the Emir, some Remington rifles, percussion guns, and a lot of swords and spears; we also took one prisoner.

"After the soldiers had celebrated this victory with a little ceremony, they returned to their quarters.

"On the 29th nothing happened, but there was a little firing from both sides. On the 30th the people of Fabbo came in at 7 a.m., and at 8 a.m. a Bari came in who had been a prisoner with the Donagla, and told us they had had great losses, and intended to start for Rejaf. Some little time afterwards on the same day, a boy belonging to Abdul Bain Aga came in, and told us the Donagla had started; a soldier from Laboré station also came in in the evening and confirmed these reports.

"A body of soldiers then started for the Donagla camp, and found there many killed and wounded; these latter they at once killed. They brought back with them some boxes of empty Remington cartridges. On December 1st, at noon, a soldier, who had formerly been a servant of the deceased Major of the 1st Battalion, Rehan Aga, came in and told us he had come with the Donagla from Khartoum; he confirmed what we had heard of their flight, and told us that their numbers now were greatly weakened. We then sent some interpreters to Chor Abdul Aziz, and they found the road strewn with leathern bags, containing clothes, they also found a Remington bayonet; these they brought into the station. To-day a soldier called Fadl el Mulla, belonging to Muggi station, came in; he had been captured in the Rejaf affray, and reported that the Donagla had started in a great hurry for Rejaf. They had with them 150 wounded, and many died on the road. They burnt the stations of Chor Aiu and Laboré and every station they passed through. And this is what I have to report to your Excellency about the Government soldiers.

"P.S.—Some of the chief men and the Kadi of the Donagla were killed in this fight.

"(Signed)   SELIM AGA MATARA,
"Bimbashi."

This letter had no number, and might therefore be considered as unofficial. From this it may be understood that though Selim Aga recognized and addressed the Pasha as Governor of Hatalastiva, he admitted that he was out of office.

The letter, like most Arabic letters, was somewhat hazy and disconnected, and one could not make very much out of it. No doubt the estimate of killed and wounded was exaggerated, it always is with Easterns, still the Donagla must have met with a severe repulse to drive them to return and burn the stations behind them, as if they expected to be pursued.

There was another letter from Kodi Aga telling Emin that the steamers had arrived a few hours after our departure from Wadelai. A messenger had come after him telling him of the arrival of the steamers; he had at once returned to the station, taking with him all the people who were behind him. As Emin was too far ahead to communicate with, he now dispatched the steamer to bring him back again to Wadelai.

There was also a letter from the officers who had come up from Dufilé in the steamer, in which they joined Kodi Aga in his entreaties to the Pasha to return to Wadelai. They were all anxious to make a triumphant demonstration in honour of the victory over the Donagla. They said they wished to offer him their congratulations. But after the conduct of the soldiers the day before, and the promises they had made and broken, I thought he had had enough of demonstrations. Casati and I used every argument we could to get him to go on, and not to return. We told him if he returned he would only have all the trouble of getting out again when Stanley arrived. Besides, too, we were told that directly after we had left the station the soldiers had entered the compounds and plundered all our houses. There was nothing to go back to but vexation and worry for Emin, he would be nearer the Donagla and further from Stanley. Emin held a council in a little village at the top of a hill overlooking the river, and after much talk it was decided that we should embark in the steamer, and go on to Tunguru, and then send the steamer back with letters for Wadelai. There were some who were for returning, for they wanted to go back and look after the things they had left behind them in the station; but Emin told these people they could go back in the steamer when she returned. When Emin told the officer in charge of the steamer that it was his intention to go in the steamer to Tunguru, and not to return to Wadelai, he said he had orders to return at once and bring the Pasha back with him. However, we seized the steamer and began to embark the people on board. We waited in the village about two hours to give the people who were behind a chance of coming up. As the women and children came straggling in, they were delighted at the idea of getting into the steamer, and indeed it was high time for them to have a lift, for their feet were terribly sore.

At 11.45 we started off in the steamer, which was densely packed with the refugees.

As we were steaming along the pilot of the steamer gave me the following short account of the entry of the Donagla into Dufilé. I quote it from my journal, for from what he said it shows the soldiers in their true light :—

"On November 27th the officers, fearing the station might be taken by the Donagla, who had arrived before the station on November 25th, decided to transport all the people as fast as possible on to the other side of the river. The steamers had been working all day and right through the night, transporting all those who had taken refuge in the station to the east side of the river. The steam was still up, but the steamers were lying against the wharves while the men were taking a rest, when at 4 a.m. on the 28th, forty Donagla who had been lying hidden in a small banana-grove on the river bank close to the station, made a rush for a small bridge of earth, by which the station could easily be entered, close to the steamers. The soldiers fled before them, and the Donagla entered the steamers and killed every one who could not escape, and tried to disable the steamers. They then made a rush through the station, driving the soldiers before them; they actually drove them right out of the station. Some 500 soldiers fled in confusion before only forty men ! So sure were the Donagla of the success of their stratagem, that they had a body of men on the other side of the station, ready to kill the soldiers when they fled. The soldiers, however, finding themselves between two fires, struggled back into the station. The Donagla, on driving the soldiers away, had collected in the large square, and from it had entered Emin's compound, crying out, 'Where is Mahomed Emin, where is the white Christian?' Not finding Emin there, they had scattered about the station, looting, and taking the women prisoners. It was then that the soldiers re-entered the station, and finding the Donagla scattered, they fell on them and killed them all one after another. Flushed by their success and encouraged by their officers, they sallied out, and drove the rest of the Donagla away from the walls of the station. It was most extraordinary that the Donagla, having the steamers and station actually in their hands, should not have opened the gates to let their comrades in. The only way I can account for it was either that it was dark, and they were waiting for daylight, or that they had such a contempt for the soldiers that they never imagined they would return and attack them. At any rate they must have managed very badly, having the station once in their hands, not to keep it. The place where the Donagla had entered the station was exactly the place I had warned Selim Aga would be the most likely place for them to attack.

Emin and I evidently had a very narrow escape, for we only got out of Dufilé three days before the Donagla arrived and commenced their attack on the station, and as the Donagla had, on driving out the soldiers, immediately entered Emin's compound in search of him, and the "White Christian," we should probably have been among the first to be killed.

I was told that most of the clerks had concealed themselves in the reeds, and even in the mud on the banks of the river, during the fight.

This affair with the Donagla was exceedingly like what happened when the Mahdi's people attacked the Province four years before, descriptions of which I had many times heard from different officers. It appeared that when the Mahdi's people came, four years before, under Keremallah, against Emin, the soldiers ran right and left, and retired, just as in this case, before them. At last a number of soldiers were surrounded at Rimo, and when a great number had been killed, women and children captured, and the people nearly starved, the soldiers, driven to desperation, had cut their way out. The Mahdi's people being so astonished at finding there was some fight in them after all, were defeated and fled before the soldiers. Emin's soldiers were great cowards, and always ran before a determined enemy; it was only when they had lost women and children, and were fairly caught in a trap that they fought; this was also the case at Dufilé. Had the Donagla opened the gates of the station and let their comrades in, there would not have been one soldier left to tell the tale; they would never have rallied.

We heard that the Donagla had sent another steamer down to Khartoum full of the women and children they had taken in the Province. They had, so a soldier said who had deserted from them, also sent for reinforcements. We knew that when the Khartoum people heard the news, and saw all the slaves that had been captured, they would come up in swarms and overrun the country. We expected reinforcements would come up in six weeks from the time the steamer left Rejaf.

The news we had heard of the fall of Dufilé was therefore to a certain extent true; for a short time the station and steamers had been in the hands of the Donagla. The news of the fall of all the northern stations between Rejaf and Dufilé was also true, for the people had fled from them in terror before the advance of the Donagla, leaving everything behind them. The rumour of the fall of Fabbo was easily accounted for.

On the arrival of the Donagla before Dufilé, Selim Aga had sent a messenger in haste to Achmet Aga Dinkaue at Fabbo, begging him to transport the soldiers and people of the station as quickly as possible to Dufilé. He told him to carry as many flags as possible, and get the refugees into good order on nearing the station, so that the Donagla should think that large reinforcements were coming to Dufilé from the other side of the river.

Achmet Aga Dinkaue, on getting the letter, had at once evacuated the station and marched to Dufilé, the people beating drums and hanging out all their bravery in the way of flags and cloths, in order to deceive the Donagla with regard to their numbers. The Shulis, who had risen soon after the first arrival of the Donagla, fell upon the retreating column and captured numbers of women, cattle, and goats. The frightened people were afraid to retaliate, and I believe a good many were lost in this retreat.

This would have been quite sufficient to cause a

rumour to reach the distant Lurs, near Bora, that Fabbo had fallen.

As to the report we heard of a large party of the Mahdi's people having reached the mountain of Gebel Wati, two days and a half from Wadelai, with the intention of falling on the station, we never heard if it was true.

Possibly it was true; for we heard that the Donagla, on making an attack on Dufilé, had sent a party towards Wadelai to act in concert should Dufilé fall before them, and they may have retired on hearing that their party at Dufilé had been repulsed and had gone back to Rejaf.

We reached Okello's village, at which Emin and I had camped five months before on our way down to Wadelai, at 4.30. As we were short of wood, Emin decided to camp there for the night. The steamer was awfully crowded and stuffy, and we were glad to land in this lovely bit of country. Smooth grass sloped down to the lake, and dotted about were groups of great wide-spreading trees; the villages all round were closed in by a hedge of trees, which gave them a particularly cosy and shaded appearance. The refugees, still tired with the long march of that day and the day before, tumbled delightedly out of the steamer and swam and splashed about, shouting and laughing in the clear blue water of the lake.

We camped under a clump of huge trees near Okello's village, and slept in the open with only our mosquito curtains for shelter. We had great fires made, by the light of which we had our dinner, Emin, Marco, Vita, and myself all eating Arab fashion out of the same dish with our fingers. We sat up by the camp-fires smoking our pipes and talking over the news we had heard that day. Though we were all pretty tired, we went to bed somewhat late, to sleep soundly all night, as one always does in the open, and to thank God that the Donagla had not caught us this time.

Okello's people brought in wood for the steamer early next morning, and he himself came to make his salutations and have a gossip with the Pasha. We got away by eight o'clock, but at eleven had to stop at Boki's village to take in more wood. We did not leave the steamer, but Boki, who had some time before the rebellion been released from prison by Emin's orders, came on board to greet us. The people *en masse* went over the side again for a swim in the lake, they seemed to have no fear of the crocodiles which were present in swarms.

At 3.30 we steamed up to the station of Tunguru, and every one turned out to greet the Pasha and express their contentment at once more seeing him amongst them.

CHAPTER XIII.

SUSPENSE AT TUNGURU.

Rumoured meeting of Irregulars untrue—Emin decides to stay where he is—More letters from Dufilé—Wrong impressions given by Dr. Felkin—Strange silence as to the real position of affairs—Letters of rebel officers to Selim Aga—Accusations brought against Emin—Mischief made by the chief clerk—Soudanese tricked by the Egyptians—Suliman Aga arrives, wounded, at Tunguru—Indifference of Soudanese to pain—Beating the Dervishes to death—Walks near Tunguru—Visit from Mogo—Christmas Day—Death of Suliman Aga—An Arab funeral—The last chronicles of Lupton Bey—The taking of Bahr el Ghazal—Negroes cut off the refugees—Dufilé is abandoned and burnt—Birds of the Equatorial Province—A day's shooting—Sketch of the dwarfish tribes of Central Africa.

THE officer from Wadelai in charge of the steamer decided to go back at once in order to lose no time, so Emin wrote letters on board and sent them to Kodi Aga and Selim Aga, and dispatched one of his boys also to see if anything could be saved from the wreck caused by the soldiers looting our houses; I told him to look after my things too, and save what he could.

The people who had come with us from Wadelai were Casati, Osman Latif, Hawashi Effendi, Award Effendi, Signor Marco, Vita Hassan, Basilli Effendi, with all their wives, children, and servants, and also seven or eight clerks, and a whole host of minor people. They had scarcely anything with them, and they were hurrying about the station arranging houses, and borrowing from their friends till a late hour. I found, to my disgust, that while I had been away, Casati's people had put his goats in my house, the consequence was there was a perfect plague of fleas, and I had to have my bed taken out into the courtyard.

There was no sign of the Irregulars mutineering, as we had heard when were at Wadelai, they seemed very glad to see Emin. I always hoped, if we were able to get out, that these people would come with us, for they were useful on the road, ready, and exceedingly handy in making things. They were much more courageous and obedient than the Regular soldiers. There was not much food in the station, but we hoped to start for M'swa in four days, at least Emin said that was his intention.

A couple of days after our arrival, a letter came in from Shukri Aga at M'swa, saying he was delighted to hear we were at Tunguru, and begged Emin to come on as soon as possible to M'swa, for he was sure Stanley would soon arrive. I too was very anxious to get there, for we should then be five days from Wadelai, and only four days in canoes from N'sabe, our former camp on the lake. In my journal at that time, December 7th, I find the following entry :—

"I shall not feel really safe until we are at M'swa, and then if things go badly we can take to the mountains at once, go to Kavallis, and on to Fort Bodo. It is possible of course that the Donagla may come up from Rejaf, and again attack Dufilé, but I do not think this is likely to happen just yet, as they have burnt the stations behind them. Still, in another month or so, reinforcements will probably come up from Khartoum in great numbers, and if Stanley does not arrive before that time, we shall most likely have to go for our lives."

Emin, however, decided to stay on at Tunguru, he feared that if we went on to M'swa it would create distrust among the people, who would, he said, at once think he was trying to escape. So here we rested many days with nothing particular to do. From time to time Emin got letters from people in Wadelai and Dufilé, telling about different incidents which happened during the four days' fighting at Dufilé. From one man we heard that certain clerks, at the time the Donagla had entered the station, rushed down to the river and sat up to their necks in the water. It was still evident that the people were not quite convinced that Stanley had come from Egypt, and what was the object of his coming, for these very clerks who had hid in the water, tried to persuade the officers to surrender to the Donagla when they appeared before the station. They said it was better to surrender to Mahomedans than to infidels like the English.

Letters kept coming in from time to time telling us that the people were evacuating Dufilé as fast as possible. Amongst others was another from Kodi Aga, telling Emin it was the wish of the officers to make great rejoicings at Wadelai in honour of their victory, and begging him to come down and superintend them. Emin's boy wrote and said he had been able to save a few things from the wreck, but the list was a very small one, for the soldiers had been quick in their looting, and had left hardly anything. He had, however, been able to save a few of Emin's instruments and his medicine chest. The soldiers, he said, had broken open all the boxes, and strewed the things they did not want, about the huts.

Amongst the different accounts of the soldiers' conduct at Dufilé, we heard some few examples of real bravery. The men who had behaved best seemed to be Suliman Aga who was badly wounded; Selim Aga, Bachit Aga, Burgoot, and a few others, these were chiefly instrumental, by their determined bearing, in rallying the soldiers, and it was under their leadership that the final sortie was made in which the Donagla had been repulsed.

Captain Casati and I had several long talks about the affairs of the Mudireh, and I was glad to find that he agreed with me generally on the view I took of events which had occurred. One of the things was that Dr. Felkin, Dr. Junker, and even Emin himself, had given people in Europe a very wrong idea of things in the Province. Dr. Felkin had given an excited, glowing account of everything; things were, I know, different during that short time he had been there, but even at that time they were never as he described them. Dr. Junker knew that the 1st Battalion had rebelled against the Governor, yet for some reason or other had not spoken of it, or of the many things he must have seen which showed that Emin's people were not very trustworthy or loyal. All that Emin himself wrote to Europe was perfectly true, except that he only told one half of the story.

The consequence was that we started from Europe

believing that Emin ruled over a loyal, faithful, and obedient people, who were devoted to him, and into whom, to use Dr. Felkin's words, Emin had been able to instil some of his own great enthusiasm. All Europe thought that Emin's soldiers were loyal and united—had he not himself in his letters called them heroes! and said that all his troubles were from the outside, in keeping the slave-raiders in check, or fighting against hostile tribes.

Our astonishment then may be imagined when we found a worthless people, whose one idea was conspiracy and rebellion; moreover, we found it had, more or less, been going on for years.

It used, therefore, always to anger me when Emin would remark, whilst we were discussing things concerning the Expedition, Mr. Stanley seems to think this, that, and the other, and people in Europe have a queer idea of affairs in these countries. From whom did they take those ideas, but from his friend Felkin, and Emin himself?

Therefore, it was natural for us to believe that either he and his people would follow us out of the country, or that they would receive us with a certain amount of gratitude, accept what we had brought them in the way of ammunition, and wish us God speed.

But we did not expect, nor had any one given us the slightest reason to expect, that after getting over dangers and difficulties on the road, the greatest danger of all awaited us when we reached Emin's country, a danger from plots to attack and rob us of our guns and ammunition, made by the very people we came to help.

To this day I do not understand why Dr. Junker did not warn us to be careful in dealing with Emin's people. Forewarned would have been forearmed. As it was, had our leader been one atom less wise and capable than he was, Emin would never have been rescued, and the Expedition would have been lost on the shores of Lake Albert Nyanza.

On December 17th the first steamer from Dufilé came in. It contained Suliman Effendi, who had his leg broken in the fight at Dufilé, and two other officers who had been wounded at the same time; they had brought with them all their wives and children. These people had come to put themselves under Emin's care, and he who was always kindness itself, was only too glad to look after them.

Rajab Effendi, one of the faithfuls, and Emin's clerk, wrote from Wadelai, saying that now the fear from the Donagla had decreased since their defeat, the party against the Mudir was again growing in strength. The chief clerk, who had arrived in the steamers at Wadelai the day we retreated, had written a glorious account of Emin's misdoings at Wadelai, to Fadl el Mulla, and his confederate in Dufilé, and Rajab Effendi sent Emin a copy of a letter which had been sent to Selim Aga, as head of the soldiers.

The letter was as follows :—

"To Selim Aga Matara, Major, 2nd Battalion.

"EFFENDI,—You are aware that Mehmed Pasha Emin, Hawashi Effendi, the Major, and Vita Effendi, the apothecary, have been suspended from service for having committed oppressions, for having killed employés and natives, and for having appropriated Government property, openly and secretly. These acts have been proved by a series of documents now in our hands, written by many people of this country against the above. To remedy these evils, Hamid Bey Mahomet, now deceased, was appointed Kaimakam (*locum tenens*) of the Province, and you Major of the 2nd Battalion. An assembly of officers and employés decided for the future that no one should be wronged, as is the wish of our Government, which is built on justice and humanity. By reason of the Donagla's coming, and of the war beginning, and of the deaths of some of our chiefs and brother officers, things changed; and some people whose names we can tell you, if needed, tried to reverse our former decisions, as we all know.

"Amongst others you have sent Ibrahim Effendi Elham to Wadelai, as chief of transports, and afterwards, when the Pasha and his companions arrived in Wadelai, he entered into their intrigues. They accused some people of being in communication with the Donagla, had them put in prison, and decided to kill them. Ibrahim Effendi Elham assisted them also to get back their property, confiscated formerly by order of Hamid Bey and the wish of many people. He helped them to run away from Wadelai in a shameless manner, to wreck the property of the Government and the people, to throw the mountain guns into the river, and to destroy the store-house registers of Wadelai, without thinking of being any assistance to the soldiers here. It was the intention of the aforesaid people to cut us off here in Dufilé, and to hand us over to the negroes or to the Donagla.

They therefore told the soldiers in Wadelai that Fabbo and Dufilé had been destroyed, and we, all the soldiers and officers, had been killed by the Donagla, whereas the soldiers vanquished their enemies, and you wrote officially about it. It would be too long to enumerate all the lies told by Ibrahim Effendi Elham, Suliman Effendi, Abderrahim, the Pasha, the apothecary, and the Major.

"Now, as it is our duty to defend the honour of our Government, to assure the people there is no risk and peril for their lives, their families, and property, and as it is also our duty to chastise such people as incline towards the Donagla, after a thorough investigation: we have decided to write this to you and to ask you to write on this our letter an order to Kodi Aga, ordering him to suspend Ibrahim Effendi from service, and not to allow him to go to Tunguru, but to leave him in Wadelai until we all come in, and are able to make an enquiry into his behaviour and that of those accused by him of being in communication with the rebels.

"We may also assure you that we absolutely do not wish the Pasha to be reinstated in his place, and that on meeting the envoy of our Government (Mr. Stanley) or His Highness our Sovereign, we shall tell him explicitly about the Pasha's deeds; even if we perish, there will always be one or two to do so. As, however, it is at present necessary to look after our southern frontiers, and as Suliman Aga was formerly there, you may send him in the *Khedive* steamer to Tunguru, and order Kodi Aga to be under his orders, and to give him the lieutenant Ali Aga el Kourdi to be his assistant until he recovers. Tell also the two captains in Wadelai that, by the goodness of God, we are all well, and not one of us has been killed. Order the officers of Tunguru and M'swa not to permit the Pasha and his companions to leave Tunguru. As soon as we get to Wadelai, and after we have sent people to ascertain what has become of our brethren in Makraka, we shall begin to put everything in order, and to give to every one his right, and to look after our own business as is our duty towards our Government which has honoured and preferred us.

"Please give us a receipt of this letter.

"December 10th, 1888.

"(Signed)

"*Captains* { Mustapha el Adjemi. Surore Aga. Fadl el Mulla Aga. Achmet Aga Dinkaue. Billal Aga Dinkaue.

"*Lieutenants* { Nur Aga Abdul Bain. Mustapha Effendi Achmet. Abdul Aga el Apt. Dowel Beyt Aga. Bachit Aga Mahmoud.

"P.S.—Order Kodi Aga to send copies of this letter to Tunguru and M'swa for tranquilizing the people, and tell them of the victory of the Government soldiers. Tell them likewise that none of us have died, and that the people of Fabbo, Bidden, Kirri, Muggi, and Laboré, have got in safely.

"(Signed) Fadl el Mulla Aga.
"Achmet Aga Dinkaue."

On the back of this letter, which Selim Aga sent to Kodi Aga, he had written,—
" Please to carry out the orders concerning Ibrahim Effendi Elham and Ali Aga el Kourdi."
About the other orders contained in the letter he had said nothing, so we did not know if they had been carried out.

The absurd and outrageous accusations in this letter will give some idea what sort of people Emin's officers were, and how easily they were led by the clerks to believe anything against him. First there were the accusations against the Pasha, Vita Hassan, and Hawashi Effendi, of poisoning people who were troublesome to them; then the accusations of having appropriated Government property openly and secretly; and afterwards the accusation of intriguing against the peace of the country immediately we got out of prison and went to Wadelai; finally of the Pasha and his companions having invented the story of the fall of Dufilé and Fabbo, in order to hand over the officers and soldiers to the Donagla or natives. There was also the accusation of having wrecked the Government property at Wadelai, the destruction of the Government books, and the throwing of the mountain guns into the river.

Hamid Aga, the chief of Bora station, who had brought us the news of the fall of Dufilé and Fabbo, was one of the men who had always been against the Mudir in the rebellion, and had been sent to Bora by the rebel officers to take the place of an officer who was thought by them to be friendly to Emin. The destruction of the Government books at Wadelai, and the throwing of the mountain guns into the river had been done by the soldiers themselves, in the the general loot which took place after we had left the station.

The high moral tone in which the letter was written was most amusing, especially the part referring to the determination on the part of the rebel officers to see that no one was wronged, as was their duty to the Egyptian Government, " which was founded upon justice and humanity." I should think that was the first time the Egyptian Government had ever been accused of such a thing. They spoke too of " tranquilizing the people," in an anxious and fatherly manner, which was diverting, seeing that they themselves had caused the excitement and confusion which reigned in the country. Their reign had been a time of pillage and oppression. However, this high moral tone no doubt went down with the people, and cast a kind of halo of patriotism over the rebel officers.

It was curious, too, to notice that after addressing Selim Aga as their Major and superior officer, whom they had themselves elected, they proceeded to give him distinct and decisive orders. It only shows what a farce the whole thing was.

It appeared when the chief clerk's letter arrived at Dufilé, giving his version of what had been done at Wadelai, and telling the rebel officers that the Pasha had taken the steamer and gone to Tunguru, it caused the greatest excitement in the station. The clerks, and others of that clique, went excitedly to Fadl el Mulla and the rebel officers, and declared that the Pasha had seized the steamer, and intended to escape from the country and go up to N'sabe, where he intended to destroy the steamer, and they concluded by saying that they would never see her any more. This they told also to the soldiers, and a burst of indignation against Emin was the result, and even Selim Aga for a short time faltered in his loyalty to the Mudir.

The excitement was so intense that Suliman Aga, wounded and weak as he was, ordered his servants to carry him out on his angarep before the soldiers. He was held up in his bed, and told the people that he would with his life guarantee that the Pasha had not done what he was accused of, and they were fools to be again led away by the clerks, who had led them by the nose so often before, and whom they had seen were always wrong.

While Suliman Aga was speaking the steamer was seen in the distance coming down the river. Of course there was immediately an outbreak of rage against the clerks, and certain of the officers swore when they reached the Mudir, they would kiss his feet.

These soldiers were so foolish; again and again they found themselves tricked by the clerks, and again and again they were ready to believe them. They never learned wisdom from experience. Such things might have gone on for twenty years, and still they would go on believing what they were told, always provided that it was something against the Mudir and his Government. Then when they found themselves deceived, they broke out into a sort of brutish rage, and threatened to do all kinds of things, none of which they did; and on the morrow again believed what the clerks told them as readily as ever. The Egyptian clerks held the whole of these ignorant Soudanese officers and men in their hands, they wrote all sorts of things, to which the Soudanese, who could neither read nor write, put their seals, and so the mischief went on. Gordon experienced precisely the same thing when he was Governor of the Equatorial Province, and afterwards when he was Governor-general of the Soudan. His secretaries brought him letters written in Arabic, and read what they said was in them. He put his seal to them, and constantly afterwards found that they contained something quite different to what he imagined. Emin got over this difficulty by learning to read and write Arabic immediately he became Governor, and, with his marvellous facility for learning languages, found no great difficulty in it. But of course the ignorant Soudanese were easily tricked, and during the rebellion constantly put their seals to things they never intended to do.

On such occasions, when they found they had been tricked by the clerks, they puffed and fumed, and threatened all kinds of things, and to a person who did not know them, it appeared as if they were going to do something terrible. A few flattering words from the clerks, and a present of some fat goats or sheep, always brought the soldiers in a very short time into a good temper, and they went away quite satisfied with themselves; they had made a great noise about sticking up for their rights, and had, so to speak, kicked up a bit of a dust.

In seeing them in these rages, threatening to do wonderful things, and doing nothing, Horace's line,

"Parturiunt montes, et nascitur ridiculus mus!" always recurred to my mind.

The party against Emin had again become so powerful that we daily expected some of the rebel officers would come down to Tunguru, and take the affairs of the station into their hands, in which case we should probably again be close prisoners. Another council was to sit at Wadelai immediately the evacuation of Dufilé was finished, to consider what next was to be done in the Province. We heard that most of the people wished to settle themselves in a country near the south end of the lake, but we knew they would talk, and would never settle anything. As I said before, therein lay our safety.

I went over with Emin to see Suliman Aga the day after he arrived. He was very bad, the bone of his leg being literally shattered, and all the flesh torn away. For three weeks it had not been properly dressed or washed, and was just tied up in green leaves smeared over with rancid native butter.

When these leaves were taken off it was seen that the leg was in a frightful state. Emin feared that mortification would set in. His case of surgical instruments had been lost when the soldiers looted his house, so he was unable to perform an operation. The shattered remains of the bones therefore had to remain in for some time, until they could be taken out with a pair of scissors and some pincers, which were the only instruments Emin had. It is wonderful to see with what indifference these Soudanese bear pain. When Emin was poking and probing to extract the shattered pieces of bone, or cutting away unhealthy flesh, Suliman Aga never once winced or groaned; he bore it all with a sort of phlegmatic indifference. Had he been a European he would probably have fainted. I have often noticed clouds of mosquitoes settling on a Soudanese, and he would not move, or even take the trouble to brush them off; had it been a European, or even a Zanzibari, he would have been driven almost mad. Zanzibaris seem to feel pain more than the Soudanese of the Nile, and Europeans in their turn much more acutely than the Zanzibaris.

Suliman Aga told us that the wound he had received was not from the Donagla, but from his own soldiers, who had fired blindly behind him, and one of their bullets had struck him. I should not be at all surprised if this had been done on purpose, for Suliman Aga was hated by his soldiers, and had been wounded in the leg once before by one of his own men, whom he had punished somewhat brutally. He gave a poor account of the soldiers' conduct during the siege of Dufilé. He told us that he saw *sixty* soldiers armed with Remington rifles flying before *one* of the Donagla armed with a sword and spear only. It was not until three or four of them had been cut down by the sword that it suddenly seemed to strike them that they had guns. They then halted, and fired a volley at their pursuer, which riddled him with bullets. He gave me a ghastly description of the way in which the three poor dervishes whom Omar Saleh had sent as envoys had been beaten to death with clubs. He spoke in admiration of the conduct of Selim Aga, Abdul Aga Manzal, Bachit Aga, and three or four other officers, who, during

More News of the Siege of Dufilé. 353

the panic, had fought splendidly, and at length induced the soldiers to rally. He said it was entirely owing to these officers that the station had been saved.

Before the steamer returned to Wadelai I went and had a look at her. She had been tremendously peppered by the bullets of the Donagla, but except in one case none of the shots had penetrated, though the plates were considerably dinted.

He told us many more tales of what different people did when the Donagla entered the station. One of his stories was that a certain clerk, called Achmet Effendi Mahmoud, an Egyptian, had buried himself in the river mud, and had put mud and grass on his head in order to avoid discovery! Near him one of his women was hiding with her child. On the child's beginning to cry he threatened to cut her throat if she did not go away, for he was afraid that owing to the cries of the child, his hiding-place would be discovered.

Suliman Aga confirmed the report we had heard that one of the first things the Donagla had done on entering the station was to search the Pasha's compound. He said he thought that had he and I been caught, we should have been taken down to Khartoum, for it would have been a great triumph to the Mahdi to have the last of the Governors of the Soudan Provinces in their hands. Suliman Aga's wound did not progress favourably, but Emin hoped, owing to his strong constitution, to be able to pull him through.

During the time we were at Tunguru, I constantly went out shooting, and was able to help Emin to get a few birds, which formed the nucleus of a new collection he was making to take out with him, and in the evening I always went for a walk along the shore of the lake, usually alone. There was always, at the time we were at Tunguru, a very strong wind blowing in the evening, and it was one of the greatest pleasures I had to start off for a walk along the hard sand at 5.30, seldom returning till 7.30. It was splendid to stand on the point of the peninsula in the bright moonlight facing south-west down the lake. There was nothing to be seen but water all round, bounded by a high, bold headland ten miles off, coming down precipitously in a great purple mass into the lake. A strong south-west wind, warm and yet cool, blew with a force almost amounting to a gale, and brought the great waves tumbling in upon the flat sandy beach, throwing up masses of weeds exactly like the sea. A long narrow spit of sand separated the lake from a chain of broad shallow lagoons inland, in which there were flocks of duck, geese, storks, ibis, and herons, all fishing and bobbing about in the water, while numbers of snipe and plovers were to be seen in the more sheltered bays among the mud and rushes. It was along this narrow spit, which extended some miles, that I always took my evening walk, with nothing round me but water and wild fowl; there was a great charm in it.

Mogo, who had returned to M'swa, came over to Tunguru to see us. He promised to start with my letters to Stanley as soon as possible. I added a second postscript to the one I had formerly added at

Wadelai, to the letter I had originally written from Dufilé. I told Stanley that we were at Tunguru, but were in some ways in a worse position than we were at Wadelai. Then we were free, and could come and go as we liked, but that since the repulse of the Donagla, the party against Emin had again become powerful, and the officers of the station were under orders from the rebel officers to prevent our leaving Tunguru. I told Stanley I would do my best to come down, but I doubted if Emin would be able to do so. I added this as a postscript, as Emin wished me to send the entire letter. We hoped Mogo would be able to place the letters in Kavalli's hands by January 5th.

The day before Christmas Day, Emin asked me to go out and try to get a bird for the Christmas dinner. I went out and was fortunate enough to get several, and among them a fat Nile goose, which was to be the *pièce de resistance* for dinner. According to the German custom the dinner was eaten on Christmas Eve, and Casati and Marco were invited in to partake of it. For Central Africa it was quite a smart dinner. I give the menu:—

Soup.
Fish.
Entrées.—Cutlets á la Hatalastiva—Hotch Potch.
Rotis.—Goose stuffed with Ground Nuts—Sirloin.
Légumes.—Kolokasias—Balmias—Beans.
Entremets.—Rice Pudding—Banana Fritters.
Fruits.—Bananas—Papaws.

After dinner I made a brew of hot punch out of some spirits of wine (which Emin had for pickling his frogs, lizards and bats), some honey, a couple of limes, and hot water. It tasted rather like furniture polish, but it was hot and cheering, and was a great treat. Altogether it was an exceedingly creditable entertainment to get out in the wilds.

On Christmas Day I find the following entry in my journal:—

"A most dreary Christmas Day, laid up with fever on my angarep. All sorts of evil rumours coming in about the rebel officers at Dufilé and Wadelai. The Pasha is still very seedy, bad chest, bad temper, no appetite, no sleep. Last Christmas Day I spent in a shirt and pair of trousers only, ferrying the Expedition across the Ituri river, after having swum across early in the morning to make a raft of banana stems, as we had no boat or canoes. That Christmas Day was, however, a more cheery one than this. Stairs and I were quite gay over our frugal dinner, especially when Stairs produced proudly from the depths of his box a medicine bottle wrapped in a bundle of old rags, and containing about a gill of whisky, which he had secretly saved through all the starvation days for that festive occasion."

Rumours kept coming in about the growing power of the party against Emin. Dufilé was slowly being evacuated, and the time when a fresh reinforcement of the Donagla might be expected to arrive was growing near, and we were anxiously looking for Stanley. As the party against Emin again grew in strength, we noticed that the restless and insubordinate spirit of the soldiers, which since Emin's arrival at the station had been lulled, was again increasing. The natives round the station were also uneasy, and gave considerable trouble; so much so, that Emin begged me to shorten my wanderings near the station, and always take at least two of my orderlies with me.

Suliman Aga, who had daily been growing worse, at length died on the night of December 29th. The Pasha and I were with him in the evening, and when Emin saw him, he told me he could not last many hours. Painful fits of hiccoughing came on, and in one of these fits he died.

At 10.30 we heard the crying and wailing of his women, of whom he had some fifty, and we knew that he was dead. He was buried the next morning, and Emin, Casati, and I, attended the funeral.

He had been so much hated by everyone in the station that there was but a scanty attendance at his funeral. The Regulars refused to attend, and the priest declined to read the burial-service over his body. Everything therefore had to be done by the Irregulars, who dug the grave, carried the body, and buried it; the service being read by one of the Irregulars who had made the pilgrimage to Mecca, and had the affix of Hadji to his name. Had it not been for the Irregulars the funeral would have been a scandal; these were the men whom Suliman Aga had ground down and ill-treated even more than his own men, but they, being a braver lot than the Regulars, were naturally more generous, so they buried him, and had everything done decently. A Mahomedan funeral is an extremely impressive sight; the women kept up a continued wailing throughout the ceremony, and, when the earth was filled in, threw themselves madly upon the grave. We heard afterwards that on the night Suliman Aga died, he had sent for his chief wife, and, before the people assembled in his house, spoke to her strongly against the soldiers, and told her that the funeral meat was not to be sent to them. It was the custom when a man died to have quantities of the meat from a bullock, which was slaughtered on the grave, cooked by the deceased's wives, and sent round to the friends, together with large plates of bread soaked in the gravy. This was a most unnecessary thing for the dying man to do, for he was sufficiently hated before, and this fresh expression of his dislike for them only increased the feeling against him.

Suliman Aga's death was, we feared, a bad thing for Emin; for he was friendly to him, and on account of his violent temper the rebel officers did not much care to interfere with him. We feared that now the rebels would send some officer strongly opposed to Emin to be chief of Tunguru, and things would become more difficult again. Besides, too, the clerks were almost certain to set it about that the Pasha had poisoned him, and so make capital out of his death. With these people anything bad was possible! In the meantime, Saleh Aga, who before Suliman Aga's return had been acting as chief of the station, resumed his place. He was strongly in favour of the rebel officers, but had not, I think, much influence.

One day Emin and I were speaking about Lupton Bey, and he said what a pity it was, when Lupton's soldiers deserted him, that he had not retired to the

Equatorial Province. He showed me the last three letters he received from Lupton, which he kindly allowed me to copy. They had been sent to him by the hands of refugees who were coming from Bahr el Ghazal for protection in his Province, so that Lupton, had he liked, could have retired also.

"April 12th, 1884.

"DEAR EMIN,—The Mahdi's army is now camped six hours' march from here; two dervishes have arrived here, and want me to hand over the Mudireh to them. I will fight to the last. I have put my guns in a strong fort, and if they succeed in capturing the Mudireh, will, I hope, from my fort be able to turn them out again. They come to you at once if I lose the day, so look out. Perhaps this is my last letter to you. My position is desperate, as my own men have gone over to them in numbers. I am known now by the name of Abdullah. I win the day or die, so good-bye. Kind regards to Dr. Junker. If steamers come to you, write to my friends and let them know I die game,

"Yours truly,
"F. LUPTON."

"April 20th, 1884.

"DEAR EMIN BEY,—Most of my people have joined the Mahdi's force, Nazir Bucho and Nazir Liffe with all their men have gone over; also the people from Gudju have gone over with the government grain. I don't know how it will end. I have sent Wazy Uller Effendi to the Mahdi's camp. I hardly know if I am Lupton Bey or the Emir Abdullah. I will write to you as soon as Wazy Uller returns. The enemy are armed with Remingtons, and have four or five companies of Regular troops with them, and some 8000 or 10,000 Orban and Jillaban (i.e. Desert Arabs and traders), but I will give you their correct strength as soon as I am sure about the matter; I don't think it is under the above number. Slatin wrote me two lines, he only said, ' I send this man Hadji Mustapha Kismullah to you,' he is now the Emir Abd el Kader,

"Yours truly,
"F. LUPTON."

"April 26th, 1884.

"DEAR EMIN,—It is all up with me here, every one has joined the Mahdi, and his army takes charge of the Mudireh the day after to-morrow. What I have passed through these last few days no one knows; I am perfectly alone. The man who brings you this will give you all particulars. I hear that an army was never so totally defeated as was that of General Hicks, out of 16,000 only 52 men are alive, and they are nearly all wounded. Look out you; some 8000 to 10,000 men are coming to you well armed. Hoping that we shall meet,

"Yours truly,
"F. LUPTON."

These are the last chronicles of poor Lupton! He had been with Emin some months at Lado, and had commanded the district of Latooka under him. He did his work so well as Governor of Latooka that Gordon made him Governor of the Bahr el Ghazal Province. Emin always spoke of him with great admiration and affection. He had only been Governor of Bahr el Ghazal some sixteen months, and on his succession to authority in the Province, after Gessi's retirement, he found himself landed in a nest of difficulties. Nearly the whole time he was Governor he was busily engaged in putting down revolts among the negroes, and Emin told me that he behaved most gallantly. On first coming into the Bahr el Ghazal as Governor he had been ordered to send nearly all his Regular soldiers down river to strengthen Khartoum. With the 900 Remington rifles he had brought into the country from Khartoum, he armed a lot of Irregulars, who were countrymen and friends of the Mahdi's people, instead of arming the people of the country and Niam-Niams, who made capital soldiers. Emin said, in consequence of this, on the approach of the Mahdi's forces the Irregulars deserted Lupton to a man, and went over to the Mahdi. He was left with only a few hundred Regulars, whose fidelity was questionable, and he decided on building a strong fort in which he put all his mountain guns and entrenched himself in it. It was a most reckless thing to do, for he could not expect to do anything against 8000 or 10,000 with only a few hundreds, and the natives against him as well. He even spoke of turning out the Mahdi's forces from his fort when they had once entered the country. Had he retired with the few faithfuls when he saw his people deserting him all round, he might have saved himself and them, by retiring to Emin's Province, where he might have helped him greatly in assisting him to repel the attacks of Keremallah.

A refugee from Bahr el Ghazal said that when the Mahdi's forces appeared before the fort the few hundreds of Regulars whom Lupton had with him went over in a body to the Mahdi. Hardly a gun was fired. Emin further heard that after poor Lupton was taken he was treated with the greatest ignominy by the Mahdi. It was said that just after his fort had been taken he was standing outside the door of his hut, smoking a cigarette, when an Arab coming by struck him in the face, and calling him a dog of an infidel, ordered him to give over smoking as it was against the commands of the Prophet.

What numbers of good men have been lost in the Soudan, and all for the worthless Egyptian Government!

On December 30th letters came in from Wadelai with news from Dufilé. We heard that in order to make the evacuation of Dufilé more rapid, great numbers were daily ferried across to the east side of the river, and, escorted by small parties of soldiers, they marched overland to Wadelai, the women and children being sent up by steamer. They said Dufilé would be completely evacuated by the middle of January. There was then to be a council held at Wadelai, and two of the officers of Tunguru were summoned to attend it.

We heard that Mustapha Effendi Achmet was

to be sent down to Tunguru with a party of soldiers to be a guard over the Pasha, and sentries were again to be put over his door as formerly in Dufilé.

This Mustapha Effendi was the chief military clerk, he was a Khartoumer or half breed, and was always fanatical in his enmity against the Pasha. We heard that all the other officers who were wounded in Dufilé during the siege, died. This made eighteen officers killed by the Donagla between the middle of October and the end of November. A good deal of quarrelling was reported to be still going on between the officers and clerks of Dufilé and Wadelai. This was not surprising, for it was the only thing they showed any energy over, and never tired of.

On the first day of the new year a good many friends came in to greet Emin, and were regaled with coffee. Numbers of them asked me anxiously when Stanley was likely to arrive; I told them I only wished I knew myself. We heard that the negroes of the Shuli and Madi tribe were giving the people marching up from Dufilé to Wadelai, on the east bank of the river, a great deal of trouble, and were constantly harassing them and cutting off stragglers. Emin had no doubt that Kabaregga's scouts were amongst them, for he had emissaries everywhere in Emin's Province, and knew almost as well what happened there as in his own country.

Some of the soldiers, when passing Boki's villages, had heard guns being fired on the east side of the lake, which was very narrow at that point, and Boki had told them that it was Kaba-rega's soldiers, who were out sweeping the country. Emin said probably Okello and Boki, and all the chiefs round, who had been friendly to him, would be killed by Kaba-regga if the Province was evacuated. It was very hard on them, for they had been forced to be friends with the Turks, sometimes against their wishes, and if the Province was evacuated Kaba-regga would take vengeance on them for having been so.

By January the 5th, Dufilé was entirely evacuated, and was then burnt. The evacuation had been got on with more quickly than was expected, owing to the increasing hostility of the natives, who had been forming in considerable numbers on the east bank of the Nile, and got daily more and more bold. As soon as the last steamer-load of refugees had left Dufilé the station was burnt, and Selim Aga, with a large number of soldiers, crossed over to the east side of the river, intending to march overland to Wadelai, and attack the natives on the way and punish them for attacking the refugees.

Having burnt numbers of villages, and taken many cattle and goats, he marched on to Wadelai; while Fadl el Mulla with another party went towards Fabbo in order to punish the Shulis for attacking and killing the stragglers of the retreating column when Fabbo had been evacuated. On his return the Council began to sit at Wadelai, but for several days we got no news of the result of the sitting. Emin decided to stay where he was at Tunguru, but said directly he heard Stanley had arrived at the lake he would move to M'swa. I went out shooting nearly every day, and brought in a fair number of birds, for Emin's collection. Among others I shot a hammer-head or oven-bird. It is a peculiar looking bird, of a dull blackish brown colour, about two feet high, and has a crest on the top of its head which it raises or depresses at will. Its nest is made in the shape of an oven, and is composed of sticks plastered over with mud, and is built usually on rocks or on the forks of very large trees. The nest is sometimes six feet in diameter and three feet in height, and is strong enough to bear the weight of a man. It is divided into two chambers, and has one outer entrance only, the two chambers being connected by an entrance inside. The inner chamber is for the female, and in it are deposited the eggs; the outer is a storehouse and sentry-house for the male. This bird is fond of collecting bits of shining stone or broken pieces of pottery and all sorts of queer objects in its store-house. It is, I think, described by Schweinfurth as living in large colonies in the jungle, but in Emin's Province it always lives in the open and builds its nest alone. The nest lasts two or even three years, and several broods of young are reared in it.

There were also numbers of goat-suckers, or nightjars, of a very peculiar form. They are nearly as big as hawks, with very long wings. From each wing grow two long feathers, a small distance apart; their stems are quite bare except at the tips, which are shaped like the round tip of a peacock's feather. They are very long, and when the bird is flying are waved so quickly that it looks as if four small birds were flying close round it, above and below. For this reason the Arabs call it Abu Arba, or the Father of the Four.

During the months of December and January there were great numbers of European birds about Tunguru, which had migrated for the winter, but, curiously enough, none of them sang, and the few notes they uttered were unlike their notes in Europe. There were nightingales, swallows, plover, quails, night-jars, redstarts, and snipe, and many other birds known in England, but they were all silent or nearly so. Emin had great difficulty in finding lead for making shot, and for some time I used beads, but these had no penetrating power, and I had to get a very close shot. I even tried round pebbles, but they scattered too much and spoilt the gun as well.

There were great numbers of birds of all sorts in the lagoons, which had come in consequence of the swarms of insects abounding on the lake-shore at that time of the year, and nearly every morning I went out shooting.

Here is a quotation from my journal which gives a description of the kind of sport I had :—

"I went out shooting to-day, and was fairly successful. I got stilts, bee-eaters, European plover, and others whose names I do not know, for the Pasha's collection; and for the pot I shot a large spur-winged goose and a black ibis; the latter is a

EVENING ON LAKE ALBERT AT TUNGURU.

queer-looking bird with a bright crimson beak; it is good eating.

"The Pasha was pleased to get a good number of birds, for since the days of the rebellion he had been obliged to give up collecting. The shot, which I had made yesterday, turned out to be capital, and did very good work. Unfortunately I only took eighteen percussion caps, and just after I had used the last cap to bring down the ibis, I came upon a great lagoon in which there were hundreds of birds of different kinds, swimming about or paddling on the mud banks in search of snails and insects. There were ibis, black and white, standing in a row, and from time to time giving out a shrill mournful note; storks and divers, ducks and geese were swimming about amongst the weeds and tilting up their tails in the most tempting manner for a shot. There were plover of many kinds, and painted snipe, and a great golden-crested crane was standing in the middle of the lagoon like a king amongst them all."

While I was in Emin's Province I had picked up stray pieces of information about the dwarfs. They were a very interesting people, and there were a good many in the Province. Casati and Emin both told me a good many things about them, and I had constantly gossiped with soldiers and natives from Monbuttu and Makraka, where these dwarfs exist in large numbers. Far away in the forest we had constantly come upon their traces, and had from time to time captured some of them, chiefly women and boys. During my stay in Hata-astiva I had seen a good many of them living in perfect good will with the soldiers. These had been captured in raids, and were also mostly women and children. I got what information I could from them, but they were somewhat reticent and shy; a great contrast to the natives around, who spoke about themselves with the greatest volubility.

Known from the earliest times and spoken of by Herodotus and others of the ancient Greek writers, the dwarfish tribes of Central Africa are ordinarily believed to represent the scattered remnants of an aboriginal population spread over almost the whole of Equatorial Africa, and dispersed afterwards by the movements and migrations of the surrounding peoples and tribes. Schweinfurth has written about them in Monbuttu, and Dr. Lentz has found dwarfish people as far west as the Upper Ogoweh river. Forming only rarely fixed settlements, they now roam over the forest regions in small bands, composed almost always of members of one family, and are never known of their own free will to leave them for the open country.

It is evident, therefore, that agriculture is not practised by them, except to a very small extent where they have fixed settlements. They are hunters, and live solely on the produce of the chase and what they are able to pick up in the forests.

The dwarfs go by the following names in different countries:—

Akka, in Monbuttu.

A-ticky-ticky, in the A-Sandai or Niam-Niam country.

Vorchow, in Momvu.

A-fi-fi, in Mabordai.

Batwa or Wattua, in Unyoro.

Obongo or A-bongo, on the Upper Ogoweh river.

Our Zanzibaris called them Wambutti in the forest through which we passed between the Congo and the Albert Lake. We found continual traces of them from 27° 30' longitude, a few miles above the Equator, up to the edge of the forest five days' march from Lake Albert. They are a hardy, daring race, always ready for war, and are much feared by their neighbours. Beginning from Monbuttu, eastwards, to within five days' march from Lake Albert Nyanza, they are found everywhere. As soon as a party of dwarfs makes its appearance near a village, the chief hastens to propitiate them by presents of corn and such vegetables as he possesses.

The dwarfs then generally settle down near some brook in the midst of the forest, and erect small huts for the married people, boys and girls merely making themselves small shelters by bending down branches of saplings and covering them with leaves. The huts are very small, being about four feet in height and three feet in diameter, they are roughly built and of a beehive shape; long thin sticks are made into a rough framework, and covered with green leaves. Their temporary settlements are always distant from villages, and are sometimes concealed under trees and bushes; I am speaking now of the settlements in Monbuttu and the adjoining countries, for the dwarfs' camps which we saw on our road were nearly always built in a cleared space where several paths met, usually about a mile from a village. The huts, too, which we saw in their camps were much larger than those in

Monbuttu and the adjacent countries, being usually from five to six feet high, and sometimes as much

DWARF WITH BOW AND ARROW.

as seven feet in diameter. I was told that in Monbuttu the dwarfs always sleep with their bodies inside and their legs sticking out of the door, owing to the small size of the huts. Every native of Monbuttu and every dwarf I have questioned held to this story.

After settling in some place where game abounds, they begin hunting, and, out of the produce, exchange feathers, skins, meat, ivory, etc., with the villagers, who, in return, give them such food as they require. As long as this system of exchange is fairly observed, they are on good terms with the villagers, but if they consider themselves slighted in the smallest degree—and they are very ready to take offence—they do not hesitate to retaliate on the villagers, laying ambuscades for them, shooting at them from behind trees, killing them, and pillaging their fields and banana plantations. They are excellent shots, and are very revengeful, their tiny bows and arrows being most deadly weapons; so it may be easily understood that the natives are always anxious to be on good terms with them, and seldom willingly molest them. They often stay for some time in one place, if game is plentiful, and the villagers friendly, and only leave it when game becomes scarce.

The dwarfs do not carry any household goods, cooking-pots, etc., on their peregrinations, and usually cook their food wrapped in leaves and placed on the red-hot embers. They occasionally, however, get cooking-pots from the village near which they are camping. They are, in fact, as primitive as it is possible for people to be. Their huts are probably larger and better made in their fixed settlements. I heard from Captain Casati, who was four years in Monbuttu, and from several natives of that country, that there is a settlement of dwarfs, consisting of two large and several smaller villages under a king called M'Galima. Schweinfurth also speaks of him. It is situated on the river Nava, to the south of Monbuttu, which has its source in the mountain of Abambola, in the country of Migo, whose chief is Nagiza. I have not come across anyone who has actually seen this settlement, though all the Monbuttu natives I questioned were unanimous in saying that it exists on the Nava.

From an anthropological point of view the dwarfs are by no means a degenerate race, as some writers have pretended. They are, as a rule, well built, and well proportioned, and have a fair muscular development; they have, however, for their size rather large bones.

Like nearly all negroes they have in their youth distended stomachs, caused I should say by irregular feeding, and their legs seem weak in proportion to the weight of their bodies, but as soon as they attain full growth their bodies assume a fair proportion. Schweinfurth speaks of their having "pendulous bellies," but though I have seen great numbers of them I have never observed it, except amongst the children, neither has Emin nor Casati ever noticed this peculiarity.

They are of a light brown reddish colour, and are sometimes of a yellowish hue. Most of them are from 4 feet to 4 feet 1 inch in height, and have well proportioned limbs and plenty of wool on their heads. The measurements of their height I have taken from Emin Pasha's anthropological notes; he has measured a good number of them, mostly women, but men or women have never exceeded 4 feet 1 inch in height.

They frequently intermarry with the natives in whose country they are staying, which would account for the difference in height given by Schweinfurth; he found that the men he measured, I think, were 4 feet 6 inches to 4 feet 7 inches in height; I believe he never saw any dwarf women.

Over the whole body is a thick felt of stiff greyish hair, which gives them a peculiarly elfish appearance. Their skins are in no way different from the ordinary negro tribes, at least in those dwarfs I have examined. Schweinfurth describes a thick network of wrinkles being round all the articulations.

Their eyes are bright and lustrous, and their teeth good and complete, ears rather large, lips small, and not very protruding; their hands and feet are small and well proportioned. The men have often very long beards, which is most unusual in the negro races. Both men and women have a peculiarly strong and very unpleasant smell.

Ornaments and tribal marks are not usually seen among them, nor do they mutilate themselves in any way. In their forests the men and children are always absolutely naked, the women wear fringes of green leaves round their waists, and occasionally small strips of skin or bark cloth.

For warfare they use bows and poisoned arrows and small spears; both spears and arrows are tipped with iron, and are heavily barbed. These weapons are made for them by the villagers with whom they traffic. They are very reticent and reserved, but it seems they have a language of their own in their permanent settlements, though in an ordinary way, they speak the language of the country in which they are staying.

Cannibalism seems to be practised amongst them. Many of the women are good-looking and well formed, and the neighbouring tribes willingly take them for wives when they can. The men are not as a rule as good-looking as the women, and they are on the whole an ugly people, many of them being extremely grotesque-looking, especially the men with long beards.

If brought in their youth to Emin's stations or settlements the women become good servants, and are indefatigable workers. Emin had a dwarf woman in his house who used to sweep out my hut every morning and bring me water for my bath; she was most industrious, and never seemed to be idle, and she was always cheery and good-natured. Emin brought her down to our camp at N'sabe, but when confronted by a dwarf woman we had brought with us some eighty miles west of the lake, the two could not at first understand each other, though after a while they seemed able to communicate with each other pretty freely. This dwarf woman who was in Emin's house came from Monbuttu. The men make fair servants, but will not do hard work like the women, and are always restless. Both men and women, however young they were brought to the station, always preserved some independence of spirit, which made them at times rather obstinate.

The Lur people told a story that the dwarfs once extended to the shores of Lake Albert, but were driven back to the west by an influx of people from Unyoro;

who were in their turn driven out by the Lurs, who now inhabit all the north-western shore of the lake, and extend some distance down both sides of the river. The dwarfs we had with us never did well in the open country, they did not seem able to stand the sun and the cold nights, and were constantly sick with fever.

CHAPTER XIV.

NEWS OF STANLEY AT LAST.

The Council sits at Wadelai—Emin will not move—Saleh Aga surrounded by natives—Method of declaring war—The grain tax—Natives on the verge of rebellion—Death of Boki—Quarrels among the officers—Drunkenness and debauchery at Wadelai—Grass fires—Their effect on trees—Biblical scenes—Stanley at last!—His letters to me—Official letter to Emin—A tale of death and disaster—Wreck of the rear column—Deaths of Barttelot and Jameson—Saleh Aga's perverseness—Saleh Aga cowed—Emin writes to Stanley—Preparations for a start—Arrival of the steamer—Rumours of Stanley's strength—Proceedings of the Council confirmed—Emin a man of compromises.

AT length we got news from Wadelai. The sittings of the Council had been most stormy, but the party against Emin had got the best of it, and a letter was written and signed by most of the officers and clerks condemning Emin to be hung; Casati and I were also condemned to suffer the same death for aiding and abetting Emin in his flight from Wadelai, in his destroying the Government books, and throwing the mountain guns of Wadelai into the river. We never saw the document which condemned us to death, but we were told it contained an indictment against us for conspiracy against the safety of the people in Dufilé, and in the Province generally, and for cowardice in flying from Wadelai. We heard that as soon as a few pressing questions concerning the defence of the

Province,—should the Donagla return,—had been settled, some of the rebel officers and a company of soldiers were coming down to Tunguru to see the decisions of the Council carried out.

As soon as Shukri Aga heard this news, he at once sent over a special messenger from M'swa with a letter to Emin. In this he urged him in the strongest terms to come to M'swa. He said Emin had only to give the word, and he would be down in two days with 200 carriers, and a party of soldiers to bring us and all our things to M'swa.

Here is an extract from my journal :—

"The Pasha decided to sleep on Shukri Aga's proposal before deciding what answer he should give. We had a long discussion about it, but I can see he will decide on remaining where he is. 'Ospa! ospa! ospa!' 'Bokra, bokra, bokra!' ('Wait, wait, wait!' 'To-morrow, to-morrow, to-morrow!') always seems to be the cry in Emin's Province of both Europeans, Soudanese, and Egyptians. There is something of course to be said against our going at once to M'swa. No doubt the rebel officers would in such a case be very incensed against us for doing so, and would probably at once dispatch a party of soldiers and officers to bring us back to Wadelai, and take M'swa out of Shukri Aga's hands.

"On the other hand, if we went to M'swa we should be four days from Kavallis by the lake, and further removed from Wadelai; moreover there is nothing to prevent our leaving M'swa the day we arrive there, taking Shukri Aga and such soldiers as are willing to accompany us, and starting right off for Kavallis. He would, I am sure, receive us in a friendly manner, and we could wait there for Stanley, who I am convinced must soon be here.

"I feel sure that in a very short time some of the worst of the rebel officers and soldiers will be sent to take over the station now Suliman Aga is dead. We shall then again be prisoners, six days from Stanley and only two from that nest of rebels at Wadelai. I have tried to persuade Emin to move, for naturally I look a good deal to what will most help Stanley when he arrives; whereas I do not think that this thought enters into Emin's calculations; he seems to think that as Stanley has had orders to relieve him, he must do it. I suggested to Emin that he had a certain amount of obligations to the Expedition which had come to help him, but this caused an outburst against me for being so ungenerous as to remind him of what we had done for him. I therefore said no more.

"January 11th. As I expected, the Pasha has decided to remain here, yet awhile, to see what happens, but when he hears of Stanley's arrival at the lake he intends, so he says, to start at once. The question is, shall we be able to do so then? Emin may be right, I only hope he will prove to be so, but I have my fears. It is getting on now for the middle of January, and Stanley has been gone nearly eight months. Of course, if we heard he had arrived, nothing would be simpler—away we would go for Kavallis. There is yet another thing against our stopping here. The Donagla will probably be up again at Rejaf shortly, with reinforcements from Khartoum."

It seemed quite impossible for Emin, so to speak, to

tear himself up by the roots and start off from M'swa. There was at that time absolutely nothing to prevent it; with a little energy we could have got out and gone down the lake with the few faithful people with us, and might have reached Kavallis. Emin would have deserted no one, for nearly all who were faithful to Emin were with us, and those others who were behind at Wadelai could just as easily have got out without us, for we were unable to help them in the slightest degree. As it proved it did not signify; but had things turned out as it was natural to suppose they would, Emin would have had no one to blame but himself if he had been trapped by the rebels. He would never have been able to get out, and he would, moreover, by his inability to make up his mind to move, have sacrificed those whom he made such a point of saying he would never sacrifice. We again noticed that as the rumours and reports of the proceedings against us of the Council in Wadelai reached the station, the soldiers got more and more turbulent and insubordinate. As a rule, rations of corn were given out for fifteen days, but the soldiers went to their officers and demanded a full month's rations to be given them at one time. Having so much corn they took to making merrisa or native beer, and consequently there was a great deal of drinking and brawling, which at length culminated in a fight amongst them, in which one man was nearly killed and several soldiers deserted to Wadelai.

Saleh Aga was obliged to take a party of soldiers and go up to the table-lands above the station to collect the grain tax. After he had been out three days, we heard that he had been attacked by the natives, and a fight had taken place in which some soldiers and several natives were killed. As there were very few soldiers in the station, more could not be spared to go to Saleh Aga's relief, so the officers asked different people to help by sending their armed servants out. The Pasha sent two of his servants, I sent two of my orderlies, and Casati sent two of his people. Altogether we made up a party of twenty-eight, armed with guns, and about the same number armed with spears; quite a respectable reinforcement to Saleh Aga and his twenty soldiers. The next day we heard that our relief party had also been surrounded by natives, and were unable to join Saleh Aga, and that some of them had been killed. In great excitement, at eight that same evening, thirty more soldiers were despatched to relieve them. That night scarcely anyone slept, for the station was almost defenceless. The negroes were all ripe for rebellion, and might have risen at any moment. Our anxiety was further increased by the news that the day before some of Kaba-regga's scouts had crossed the lake and had slaughtered a young girl and a black bullock which they brought over with them. These they buried only a few miles from the station in Boki's country.

This is the recognized method of declaring war against a country, and obtains in Unycro and Uganda. There was no doubt that Kaba-regga's emissaries had been very busy ever since the rebellion had broken out against the Pasha, and it now appeared that he intended to make war upon the country. We knew that all the natives would be ready at once to join Kaba-regga as soon as he gave the word to attack. Emin told me that in Unyoro and Uganda, when it was desired to declare war against a country, they send people over the border and slaughter a black cow and bury a boy up to his neck in the ground, but do not kill him. Sometimes he is taken out alive, sometimes he is left to starve. Large human sacrifices are also made to propitiate the spirits in the hostile country. In this case, however, the cow and the girl, who was a virgin, were both killed and buried. Fresh reports of insubordination and discontent among the natives kept coming in every day, till it seemed that a general rising round the station was imminent. Two days of intense anxiety passed before we heard that Saleh Aga and the soldiers were safe.

Two of my orderlies came in, and told me that the second relief party had reached them, and that they had gone together to the rescue of Saleh Aga, whom they found in a small village, round which they had rapidly run up a rough boma. He was completely hemmed in by large numbers of natives, and had been in that position two days. Of Saleh Aga's party of twenty soldiers, a non-commissioned officer and five men had been killed. Saleh Aga and the relief party arrived soon after, bringing with them as much corn as they could carry. This collecting of the grain tax had always been the signal for wholesale robbery of the natives by Emin's people, and, from what my orderlies said, the soldiers, thinking to do the same as usual, had begun to loot. The natives, however, being on the verge of rebellion, had attacked them, and would have exterminated

Saleh Aga and his party if we had not received timely warning of his position, and dispatched a relief party without delay. This little affair had a bad effect on the natives; beyond burning a few villages and taking some corn, Saleh Aga, even with the relief party, had judged it expedient to retire before them, for they were collecting against him from all sides. This method of collecting the grain tax had always been, even in Gordon's time, almost, an atrocious system. For, however stringent the Governor's orders were against the soldiers looting from the natives, with these semi-barbaric soldiers it was perfectly impossible to prevent it. Shortly after this we heard that chief Boki had suddenly died. He was taken ill in the morning with pains in his stomach, and before evening he was dead. Without doubt some agent of Kaba-regga had poisoned him. Before dying, he sent his greetings to Emin, and asked him to look after his son, who would now be chief of the country. Emin told me the son was a very good fellow, and had always been friendly to the Egyptian Government; Boki he had always distrusted, and thought he was in league with Kaba-regga, which now seemed unjust. He had a very hard position to fill, as most of the chiefs in the Province had. If these chiefs were not friendly to the Government, their villages and fields were destroyed, and their women, cattle, and goats taken. If, on the other hand, they were friendly, they had to pay a grain tax twice a year, and to lend a certain amount of men to work at the station so many days in a week. In return for this they were allowed the privilege of labouring on their own land,

Enforced Inaction.

but got little or no protection. It cannot therefore be wondered at that they were neither altogether friendly to the Egyptian Government nor to Kabaregga. They tried to conciliate both, and so got the character for double-dealing, which was unjust.

Owing to the immense number of ticks and insects which infested the savannas, my legs at last got so bad that I had to give up going out shooting. My legs were one mass of bites, and these quickly developed into large open sores, which were most painful, and kept me in a constant feverish state, and for several days I was obliged to remain on my angarep. Emin bathed me with a solution of opium and zinc, but, as it did no good, my legs were plastered over with a sort of ointment made of butter and the ash of burnt cotton pods; they got better, but the pain was so great I was unable to bear anything on them. I was eating my heart out with this miserable inaction, and was worn and worried by it all; the consequence was I got several bad attacks of fever, which made me very weak and irritable.

Owing to the hostility of the natives there was hardly any corn to be obtained, and we had to get nearly all our supplies of corn and vegetables from M'swa; the faithful Shukri Aga sending us stores in canoes twice a week. I heard from an Egyptian soldier who came in to see me, that much the same thing was going on round Wadelai. He told me all the natives were talking of rising, and from him I further learned that the soldiers and greater part of the people at Wadelai declared they would not leave, but were still in hope that they would be able to entice Stanley into the country and rob him of his guns and ammunition. However, I had given Stanley warning of their plot, and as we had heard that Mogo with my letters had reached N'sabe safely, I was easy in my mind about it. A party of soldiers came in later from Wadelai, but they gave a somewhat unintelligible story about what had been happening there since the evacuation of Dufilé. They told me that when they started from Wadelai the Council had already been sitting for ten days. The party against the Mudir had at first been very strong, and it had been agreed that their decision to hang us should be summarily carried out. But soon the officers began to quarrel a great deal amongst themselves on different subjects, and again our safety was assured by their being unable to agree. Some wanted to go out, others refused to leave the country. Some wanted to build stations on the east side of the river, and some on the west. Altogether no general agreement could be come to by them on any subject. We were told that the usual scenes of drunkenness and debauchery were going on until Wadelai had become a perfect hell. The soldiers at Wadelai disobeyed orders, and, as at Dufilé, again clamoured for the Mudir; not, as I said before, because they had any real affection for him, but because they had tried what the country was like under the rebels, and found it infinitely less comfortable than it was under Emin. They saw that every officer grabbed all he could, and did not really care for any one but himself, and then the soldiers completely lost faith in their officers once more. These were the people who had adopted such a high moral tone when they had written from Dufilé to Selim

Aga, concerning the "behaviour of Emin Pasha and his companions."

Fadl el Mulla was for very strong measures against us, and had tried to carry things with a high hand, but, owing to the jealousy between all the officers, he had not carried his point. Selim Aga, their self-elected chief, was completely put on one side, and Fadl el Mulla acted as chief throughout. The officers during the stormy sittings of the Council had even come to blows, and the utmost confusion had reigned in the station. We heard that the steamer *Khedive* was on her way up to Tunguru, but had stuck on the sand bar near Wadelai, and owing to the lowness of the river, she had had to be unloaded, and a good deal of time was being wasted by the sailors, who would only work in a desultory way.

This being the middle of the dry season, the natives were burning off the grass, and every night enormous tracts could be seen on fire on the mountain sides; the crackling and roaring of the flames could be heard a couple of miles off. The fires on the Unyoro mountains, on the other side of the lake, though twenty miles distant, looked very fine.

These annual fires must make a great difference in the vegetation, and would, I should say, account for the smallness and scarcity of the trees in the open country where the grass is high. On the tablelands about Kavalli's, there were scarcely any trees to be seen, except in the ravines. The few trees there were in the open were scarcely more than shrubs, usually from twelve to fifteen feet high, and these had a twisted and ill-tempered appearance, as if the annual fires were a great trial to their vitality and tempers. It is most extraordinary that these fires do not destroy the ticks more than they do. For the ground is perfectly baked on the surface after a fire has passed over it, and yet Emin told me that in a couple of months, when the grass had grown up a little, they were almost as plentiful as ever. The grass on the plain about Tunguru was eaten down short by the cattle, and presented a dreary, parched-up appearance, and the yellow glare of the dry grass was very trying to the eyes. There was one large, spreading fig-tree in the middle of the plain, and after a long tramp out shooting, across the plain, I always made for this, and rested under its shade. In those glaring countries any piece of shade, by reason of the contrast, was doubly grateful.

I shall never forget a certain country in Unyamwezi, through which we marched on our way from the Victoria Lake to the coast. After leaving Usongo we came to a wilderness called M'gunda Makali; there were no villages in it, and scarcely any water. It was a dreary place, so burnt up and parched, with only a few leafless bushes, and glaring, baked, yellow sand all round. There were great plains quivering with heat, the very sight of which made one gasp for breath. We had been toiling through a long march, and were parched and dried up, when in the distance we saw a huge pile of rock, rising like an island from the plain, in the shade of which we camped. Never did I so well understand what is said in Isaiah, "The shadow of a great rock in a weary land," as an ideal of rest and relief. The words came into my mind directly we sighted it, and I felt pleasure in repeating them as I actually sat in the shadow of the great rock with the burning "weary land" around. The sayings and similes in the Bible are so much more vividly understood when a person has been in these countries. I remember, once, when I had nothing to read, Stanley lent me his Bible; and, after being in the country on the plain about Kavalli's with people who lived amongst their flocks and herds, I could exactly see the lives of Abraham, Isaac, and Jacob, as described in the Bible; scenes I had remarked on those mountain plains rose before me on reading Genesis. There seemed to be a fresh beauty in descriptions which before I had passed by without notice.

After being confined nearly a week to my angarep, I was able to get about again, though my legs were still in a bad state. I went round the station, and paid visits to Casati, Vita, Marco, and others, to try and get them to add their persuasions to mine, to induce Emin to move to M'swa, for though the rebels had not as yet sent any of their men down to be a guard over us, we did not know if they might not appear any day. They all agreed it was much better to start at once, and, if necessary, go down the lake, without waiting at M'swa, and try to get to Kavalli's. Marco, who was a capital old fellow, was strongly in favour of going at once, and said he was quite ready to throw away most of his things if necessary, and start without delay. While I was talking with him, he showed me a little Colobus monkey, not more than a week old. A soldier had killed the mother, and had captured the little one. It was such a queer-looking little thing, exactly like a baby.

It had a red face, and was covered all over with white silky fluff. It sucked milk from a rag, and seemed to be doing very well.

Emin said he would start for M'swa directly he heard Stanley had arrived at the lake, but not before; it was no good urging him, it only made him more obstinate, so I gave it up, and could only trust that things would turn out all right.

The next day, January 26th, as I was having a bath after coming in from shooting, Emin came hurriedly into my hut, and in great excitement handed me two letters from Stanley; there was one also for him.

The faithful Mogo had returned to M'swa with the letters the evening before, and Shukri Aga had at once sent off a messenger in the middle of the night to hand them to Emin, at Tunguru. Mogo had arrived at Kavalli's the day before Stanley's arrival there, and had returned at once with them.

I leaped out of my bath, and eagerly tore them open. The news contained in them was startling. They were as follows :—

"Camp at Gavira's, one day from the Nyanza, and one day's march from Mazamboni's, west.

"*January* 17*th*, 1889.

"MY DEAR JEPHSON,—Your letter of Nov. 7th, 1888, with two postscripts, one dated Nov. 24, the other dated Dec. 18th, is to hand, and its contents noted.

"I will not criticize your letter, nor discuss any of its contents. I wish to be brief and promptly act. With that view I present you with a précis of events connected with our journey.

"We separated from the Pasha on the 23rd May last, with the understanding that in about two months you, with or without the Pasha, would start for Fort Bodo with sufficient porters to take the goods at the Fort, and convey them to the Nyanza. The Pasha expressed himself anxious to see Mount Pisgah, and if words may be relied on, he was anxious to assist us in his own relief. We somewhat doubted if his affairs would permit the Pasha's absence, but we were assured you would not remain inactive. It was also understood that the Pasha would erect a small station on Nyamsassie Island as a provision depôt, in order that our Expedition might find means of subsistence on our arrival at the lake.

"Eight months have elapsed, and not one single promise has been performed.

"On the other hand, we, faithful to our promises, departed from the Nyanza plain, May 25th, arrived at Fort Bodo June 8th, fifteen days from the Nyanza. Conveying to Lieutenant Stairs and Captain Nelson your comforting assurances that you would be there in two months, and giving Stairs and Nelson orders to evacuate the Fort, and accompany you to the Nyanza with the garrison, which with the Pasha's soldiers would have made a strong depôt of Nyamsassie Island; I set out from Fort Bodo on the 16th June, to hunt up the Major and his column, alone, unaccompanied by any officers. On the 10th August we overtook our couriers who had left Fort Bodo on the 15th February with Stairs. Of the twenty couriers, three had been killed, two were so debilitated by the effects of arrow poison, that they eventually died, fifteen were left, but only one has carried. On the morning of August 17th, at 10 a.m., we sighted the rear column at Banalya, ninety English miles from Yambuya, 592 miles from the Nyanza, on the 63rd day from Fort Bodo, and the 85th day from the Nyanza Plain. The rear Column, which on our departure from Yambuya numbered 271, all told, was a mere wreck. Major Barttelot was dead, had been shot with a gun, by one of Tippu Tib's Manyema, on the morning of the 21st of July. Mr. Jameson had departed on the 23rd July for Stanley Falls, and a letter dated August 12th, five days before my arrival at Banalya, states that he was about descending the Congo River for Bangala ; but the couriers who brought his letter to us stoutly asserted his last intentions were to go down to Banana Point. Mr. Herbert Ward had been sent to Bangala, and finally to St. Paul de Loanda. He had returned, and reached Bangala with letters, and instructions from the committee, but was detained there by order of Major Barttelot ! Mr. John Rose Troup had been invalided home in June, 1888. So no one was left with the wreck of the rear column except William Bonny, who is now with me in this camp. One hundred Soudanese, Zanzibaris, and Somalis had been buried at Yambuya ; thirty-three men were left at Yambuya helpless and dying, and fourteen of these died later on ; twenty-six deserted. So that when I saw Bonny and his people, the rear column, Zanzibaris, Somalis, and Soudanese, numbered 102 all told, out of 271, and only one officer out of five ! Besides this deplorable record, the condition of the stores was just as bad. Out of 660 loads—65 lbs. each—there remained only 230 loads, of 65 lbs. weight. All my personal clothing, except hats, boots, one flannel jacket, a cap, and three pairs of drawers, had been sent down to Bangala, because rumour had stated I was dead, and the advance party gone to the dogs; a remnant of thirty, however, had managed to escape to Ujiji ! ! !

"I sent my despatches to Stanley Falls, and thence to Europe, and on the 31st August commenced my return towards the Nyanza. Two days before the date stated I was at Fort Bodo, December 20th. On December 24th we moved from Fort Bodo towards the Ituri Ferry. But as your non-arrival at Fort Bodo had left us with a larger number of goods than our force could carry at one time, we had to make double journeys to Fort Bodo, and back to the Ituri Ferry, but by the 10th January all that remained of the Expedition, with all its effects, were on the east side of the Ituri River, encamped half a mile from the Ferry, with abundance of food assured for months. On the 12th January, I left Stairs, Nelson, Parke, and my servant, at the Ituri Ferry camp, with 150 people, and started for the lake with 210 people all told, to obtain news of the Pasha and yourself. Your absence from the Fort, and the absolute silence respecting you, all made us suspect that serious trouble had broken out. Yesterday your letter, as above stated, came to hand, and its contents explained the trouble.

"The difficulties I met at Banalya are repeated to-day near the Albert Lake, and nothing can save us now from being overwhelmed by them but a calm and clear decision. If I had hesitated at Banalya, very likely I should still be there waiting for Jameson and Ward, with my own men dying by dozens from sheer inanition. I should have found my strength, stores, and men exhausted.

"Are the Pasha, Casati, and yourself to share the same fate? If you are still the victims of indecision, then a long good night to you all, but while I retain my senses, I must save my Expedition. You may be saved also if you are wise.

"In the 'High Order' of the Khedive, dated February 1st, 1887, No. 3, to Emin Pasha, a translation of which was handed to me, I find the following words:—

"'And since it is our sincerest desire to relieve you with your officers and soldiers from the difficult position you are in, our Government have made up their mind about the manner by which relief from these troubles may be obtained.

"'A mission for the relief has been formed, and the command of it given to Mr. Stanley, the famous, etc., etc., and as he intends to set out on it, with all necessary provisions for you, so that he may bring you with your officers and men to Cairo by the route he may think proper to take.

"'Consequently we have issued this 'High Order,' to you, and it is sent to you by the hand of Mr. Stanley, to let you know what has been done. As soon as it reaches you, convey my best wishes to the officers and men. And you are at full liberty with regard to your leaving for Cairo or your stay there with officers and men.

"'Our Government has given a decision for paying your salaries with that of the officers and men.

"'Those who wish to stay there of the officers and men do so on their own responsibility, and they may not expect any assistance from the Government.

"'Try to understand the contents well, and make them well known to all the officers and men, that they may be fully aware of what they are going to do.'

"It is precisely what the Khedive says, that I wish to say to you. Try and understand all this thoroughly, that you may be saved from the effects of indiscretion, which will be fatal to you all if unheeded.

"The first instalment of relief was handed to Emin Pasha on or about May 1st, 1888. The second final instalment of relief is at this camp with us, ready for delivery at any place the Pasha designates, or to any person charged by the Pasha to receive it. If the Pasha fails to receive it, or to decide what shall be done with it, I must then decide briefly what I must do.

"Our second object in coming here was to receive such at our camp as were disposed to leave Africa; our Expedition has no further business in these regions, and will at once retire.

"Try and understand what all this means. Try and see the utter, and final abandonment of all further relief, and the bitter end and fate of those obstinate and misguided people, who decline assistance when tendered to them. From May 1st, 1888, to January 1889, are nine months, so long a time to consider a simple proposition of leaving Africa or staying here!

"Therefore, in the official and formal letter accompanying this explanatory note to you, I designate Kavalli's village as the rendezvous, where I am willing to receive those desirous of leaving Africa, subject, of course, to any new light thrown upon the complication by a personal interview, or a second letter from you.

"And now I address myself to you personally. If you consider yourself still a member of the Expedition, subject to my orders, then, upon receipt of this letter, you will at once leave for Kavalli's with such of my men, Binza, and the three Soudanese, as are willing to obey you, and bring me the final decision of Emin Pasha, and Signor Casati, respecting their personal intentions. If I am not at Kavalli's then stay there, and send word by letter by Kavalli's messengers, to M'pinga, chief of Gavira's, who will transmit the same to Mazamboni, where probably I shall receive it.

"You will understand that it will be a severe strain on Kavalli's resources to maintain us with provisions for longer than six days, and if you are longer than this period we must retire to Mazamboni's, and finally to our camp on the Ituri Ferry, otherwise we must seize provisions by force, and any act of violence would cut off and close native communication, this difficulty might have been avoided had the Pasha followed my suggestion of making a depôt at Nyamsassie. The fact that there are provisions at M'swa does not help us at all. There are provisions in Europe also, but unfortunately they are as inaccessible as those of M'swa. We have no boat now to communicate by lake, and you do not mention what has become of the steamers, the *Khedive* and *Nyanza*.

"I understand that the Pasha has been deposed, and is a prisoner. Who then is to communicate with me respecting what has to be done? I have no authority to receive communications from officers, mutineers. It was Emin Pasha and people I was supposed to relieve. If Emin Pasha were dead, then to his lawful successor in authority. Emin Pasha being alive, I can receive no communications from any other person unless he be designated by the Pasha. Therefore, the Pasha, if he be unable to come in person to meet me at Kavalli's, with a sufficient escort of faithful men, or be able to appoint some person authorized to receive this relief, it will remain for me to destroy the ammunition, so laboriously brought here, and return home.

"You must understand that my people are only porters. They have performed their contract with me with a fidelity unexampled, and having brought the boat and goods here, their duty is ended. You have been pleased to destroy the boat and have injured us irreparably by doing so. I presume the two cases of Winchester ammunition left with the Pasha are lost also.

"I ought to mention also that the people at the Ituri ferry camp are almost all sick, and will be unable to move for at least a month.

"And also I have brought with me about 100 Manyema, with forty-two of whom I have contracted to pay a tusk of ivory to each, for forty-two loads they have brought here for Emin Pasha.

"Therefore, to satisfy them, I require forty-two

tusks of ivory to pay them. Please consider how this can be done to their satisfaction.

"Also consider how we are to be supplied with food, pending the termination of this eventful part of our journey, if we have to return to the neighbourhood of Kavallis or the Lake, to await this long deferred decision on the part of the Pasha and his men.

"Finally, if the Pasha's people are desirous of leaving this part of Africa, and settle in some country not far remote from here, or anywhere bordering the Nyanza (Victoria), or along the route to Zanzibar, I am perfectly ready to assist, besides escorting those who wish to go home to Cairo safely. But I must have clear and definite assertions, followed by promptitude, according to such orders as I shall give for effecting this purpose; or a clear and definite refusal, as we cannot stay here all our lives awaiting people who seem to be not very clear as to what they wish.

"Give my best wishes to the Pasha and Signor Casati, and I hope and pray wisdom may guide them both before it is too late. I long to see you, my dear fellow, and hear from your own lips your story.

"Yours very sincerely,
"HENRY M. STANLEY.

"To A. J. Mounteney Jephson, Esq."

"*Strictly personal.* Kavalli's.
"*Jan.* 18*th*, 1889, 3 p.m.

"MY DEAR JEPHSON,—I sent a brief note of news from Mazamboni's the same day I arrived there with a view to confirm a rumour of our being in the neighbourhood, if any such was afloat. I hear that on arriving here, that the note was put into the hands of Mogo, who stopped at Kyan Kondo's, who seems to have built his new village on the very spot where we met the Pasha and yourself the day of our arrival at the Lake.

"I now send thirty rifles, and three of Kavalli's men down to the Lake with these letters with urgent instructions that a canoe should set off and the bearers be rewarded.

"I may be able to stay longer than six days here, perhaps ten days. I will do my best to prolong my stay here, until you arrive, without rupture. Our people have a good store of beads, cowries and cloth, and I notice that the natives trade very readily, which will assist Kavalli's resources in case he gets weary at our prolonged stay.

"If you can bring any thing in the way of food, such as a store of grain or a few head of cattle, then, of course, matters will be smoothed for a stay of many days. Some of the Pasha's whiskey would be desirable also, as well as a little oil for the whites for cooking.

"Be wise, be quick, and waste no hour of time, and bring Binza and the three Soudanese with you. I have read your letters half a dozen times over, but I fail to grasp the situation thoroughly, because in some important details one letter contradicts the other. In one you say the Pasha is a close prisoner —while you are allowed a certain amount of liberty —in the other you say you will come to me as soon as you hear of our arrival here, and 'I trust' you say, 'the Pasha will be able to come with me to see you.' All this is not very clear to us who are fresh from the bush. How, being a prisoner, you could leave Tunguru at all, I fail to see.

"If the Pasha can come, send, on your arrival at Kyan Kondo's, a native courier to announce the fact, and I will dispatch a strong detachment to escort him up here, even to carry him if he needs it. I feel too exhausted after my 1300 miles march, to go down to the Lake again. I hope the Pasha will have a little pity for me. Don't be alarmed or uneasy on our account. Nothing hostile can approach us within twelve miles without my knowing it. I am in the midst of a friendly population, and if I sound the war note, within four hours I can have 2000 warriors to assist to repel any force disposed for violence. And if it is to be a war of wits, why then, I am ready for the cunningest Arab alive. I said above that I read your letters half a dozen times, and my opinion of you varies with each reading. Sometimes I think you are half a Mahdist, or Arabist, then Eminist, I shall be wiser when I see you. Jameson paid a thousand pounds to accompany us. Well, you see, he disobeyed orders and we left him to ponder on the things he had done. Ward, you know, was very eager to accompany us, but he disobeyed orders and he was left at Bangala, a victim to his craving for novel adventures. Barttelot, poor fellow, was mad for Kudos, but he has lost his life, and all—a victim to perverseness. Now, don't you be perverse, but obey, and set my order to you as a frontlet between the eyes, and all, with God's gracious help, will end well.

"I want to help the Pasha somehow, but he must help me and credit me. If he wishes to get out of this trouble, I am his devoted servant and friend, but if he hesitates, something rises within me which causes me excessive wonder and perplexity. I could save a dozen Pashas if they were willing to be saved. I could go on my knees and implore the Pasha to be sensible in his own case. He is wise enough in all conscience, in all things else, save in his own interest. Be kind and good to him for many virtues, but do not you be drawn into that fatal fascination, which Soudan territory seems to have for all Europeans, of late years, for as soon as they touch its ground, they seem to be drawn into a whirlpool which sucks them in and covers them with its waves. The only way to avoid it, is to obey blindly, and devotedly, and unquestioningly all orders from the outside.

"The committee said 'relieve Emin Pasha with this ammunition. If he wants to come out, the ammunition will enable him to do so.' The Khedive said the same thing, and added, 'but if the Pasha and the officers elect to stay, they do so on their own responsibility.' Baring said the same thing, clearly and decidedly, and here I am, after 4100 miles of travel, with the last instalment of relief. Let him who is authorized to take it, take it. Let him who wants to come out of this devouring circle, come. I am ready to lend all my strength and wit to assist him. But this time there must be no hesitation, but positive yea or nay, and home we go.

"Yours very sincerely,
"H. M. STANLEY.

"*To A. J. M. Jephson, Esq.*

"P.S.—Yesterday, your letters were brought to me

in the midst of a bad attack of fever. To-day, I am all right and have marched nearer to you by eight miles, and it is bright sunshine.

" H. M. S."

These were Stanley's letters to me. His letter to Emin was as follows:—

" Camp at M'pinga's. One long march from the Nyanza, and ten miles east of Mazamboni's.

" To his Excellency, Emin Pasha,
" *Governor of the Equatorial Province.*

" SIR,—I have the honour to inform you that the second instalment of relief, which this Expedition was ordered to convey to you, is now in this camp, ready for delivery to any person charged to receive it by you. If you should prefer that we should deposit it at Kavalli's or at Kyan Kondo's on the Lake, we shall be ready to do so on the receipt of your instructions. The second instalment of relief consists of 63 cases of Remington cartridges, 26 cases of gunpowder—each 45 lbs. weight, 4 cases of percussion caps, 4 bales of goods, 1 bale of goods for Signor Casati—a present from myself—two pieces of blue serge, writing paper, envelopes, blank books, &c. Having, after great difficulty, greater than was anticipated, brought relief to you, I am constrained to officially demand from you receipts for the above goods and relief brought to you, and also a definite answer to the question if you propose to accept our escort and assistance to reach Zanzibar, or if Signor Casati proposes to do so, or whether there are any officers or men disposed to accept of our safe conduct to the sea. In the latter event I would be obliged to you if you would kindly state how those persons, desirous of leaving Africa, can be communicated with.

"I would respectfully suggest that all persons desirous of leaving with me, should proceed to, and form camp either at N'sabe or at Kyan Kondo's, on the Lake, with sufficient stores of grain, &c., to support them one month, and that a note should be sent to me, to inform me of the same, *viâ* Kavalli's, whence I soon may receive it.

"The person in charge of the people at this camp will inform me definitely whether the people are ready to accept of our safe conduct, and upon being thus informed, I shall be pleased to assume all further charge of them. Here below I beg to present you with an approximate statement of our movements, pending the receipt of your answer, which is compulsory on us, owing to the fact that, in the vicinity of the lake, the supply of food is very precarious and uncertain, unless seized by force, which, considering the state of affairs in your Province, would be very impolitic. If at the end of twenty days no news has been heard from you or Mr. Jephson, I cannot hold myself responsible for what may happen. We should be glad to stay at Kavalli's if we were assured of food, but a large following cannot be maintained there except by exacting contributions by force, which would entirely close our intercourse with the natives, and prevent us from being able to communicate with you. If grain could be landed at Kyan Kondo's by steamer, left in charge of six or seven of your men, I could, on being informed of the fact, send a detachment of my men to convey it to the plateau. It is only the question of food which creates anxiety.

Hence you will perceive I am under the necessity of requesting you to be very definite and prompt, if you have the power.

"If within this period of twenty days you will be able to communicate with me, and inform or suggest to me, any way how I can make myself useful, or lend effective aid to you, I promise to strain every effort to perform service to you. Meanwhile, awaiting your answer with great anxiety,

"I am, your obedient servant,
"HENRY M. STANLEY,

"*Commanding Relief Expedition.*"

These were the two letters. Stanley's letter to Emin was, of course, only an official letter, and quite impersonal. After reading his letters to me, I sat on my bed with a feeling of numbness at the terrible news about the rear column. We had all thought that there would be great troubles at Yambuya, but we had never conjectured anything so bad as this. Knowing the Manyema as I did, I could, in my mind, fill up the gaps in Stanley's short account of what he found on his arrival at Banalya. Poor Barttelot, what a fate was his! The tears came into my eyes when I thought of him, as I knew him at home, full of life and go, and spirits, with all his gaiety and brightness, and deserved popularity. And this was the end of it all! It was too sad to think of, his short and brilliant career cut off suddenly, without warning, by the cowardly shot of a Manyema slave-raider. The hardest part of the experiences a man travelling in Africa has to go through, is not the physical hardships, starvation, or disappointments, but the sufferings and deaths of his comrades, European or negro. The hardships and starvation may be forgotten; but the deaths of such men as Barttelot and Jameson, and of our faithful Zanzibaris, must ever remain fresh in my memory as the saddest of the many sad memories which rise in my mind whenever I think of these past three years.

That Barttelot had done his duty bravely and honestly, I never for a moment doubted. He may have been injudicious, he may have been hasty. The story of that terrible time will never, I fear, be correctly known; but whatever may have happened, any one who really knew him must intuitively recognize that he was honourable and upright and brave, and that, like Lawrence, he tried to do his duty.

Of poor Jameson's death we did not hear till long afterwards, when we reached Usambiro, on the Victoria Nyanza. We had been looking forward to seeing him again, and hearing the story of those dark days with the rear column from his own lips. Europeans and Zanzibaris alike were cast down when we heard of his death. We had only known him for five months, but during that short time he had endeared himself to us by a hundred acts of kindness. The Zanzibaris of the rear column all spoke in praise of him, for all of us, Europeans or negroes, had been strongly attracted to him by his kindly ways, cheeriness, and unselfishness.

We had been looking for Stanley's arrival, and were hoping, if the worst came to the worst, he would, with his augmented strength, be able to extricate Emin by force if necessary. But instead of his being strengthened, he had a tale to tell of death and disaster only.

However, it was no good sitting still and thinking. I went to Emin and handed him Stanley's letters to me to read. He seemed dreadfully hurt that Stanley had not sent him a private letter apart from the official one he had received. I pointed out to him that I had told Stanley to write chiefly to me, as I feared letters addressed to him might be seized by the rebels. I said that now was his chance to start; Stanley was at Kavalli's, and was ready to receive him at his camp; I reminded him that he had twice said that when Stanley arrived at the lake he would have no hesitation in leaving. But he still said he would wait and see what happened. It was hopeless to urge him. I then told him that Stanley had given me a distinct order, that on the receipt of his letter I was to start without delay, and that order I intended to carry out implicitly by starting the next morning to join him. To this he perfectly agreed, and did all he could to help me in every way. Saleh Aga, the chief of station, was sent for and was told that Stanley had arrived. Emin said I had had an order from my chief to join him without delay, and that he must give me the canoes to take me up to M'swa. The canoes, he said, were away. "Well, then," said Emin, "you must give Mr. Jephson fifteen carriers and an escort to take him to M'swa. Saleh Aga did not seem quite to know what to do, for he had received strict orders from the rebel officers that none of us were to leave the station. But Emin urged him, and he at last, reluctantly, I thought, agreed that he would do his best to get the carriers, but represented how difficult it was to collect them, owing to the disturbed state of the country. I then began my preparations for a start overland to M'swa, which I hoped to reach in two days. In the afternoon I sent my boy Binza into the station, with orders to walk casually about and try and learn what effect the news of Stanley's arrival had upon the people in general. After a couple of hours he returned and told me that every one was talking excitedly about the news, and that he had heard that Saleh Aga was going to send a letter down to the rebel officers at Wadelai, telling them of Stanley's arrival, and that it was my wish to join him, and that before allowing me to start he wished to have their permission to do so. This was just what I feared. I immediately despatched my boy with a message to Saleh Aga that I wished to speak privately to him in my house. In half an hour he appeared. The torrent of invectives I hurled at him must have astonished him, he stood looking at the ground and shifting uneasily from leg to leg. He assured me that he had no such intention as I supposed. But I told him that I did not trust the word of one of Emin's people who had gone against him in the rebellion. I continued that I intended to start early the next day, carriers or no carriers, I would go with my boy Binza and my three orderlies only, and if any one dared to stop me I should order my men to fire on them; my Winchester contained fifteen cartridges and my orderlies had three Remingtons. Saleh Aga was a little bit of a man, and seemed cowed by my very vociferous tirade; he left my hut protesting that the report I had heard was not true, and that I was labouring under a complete misapprehension. Be that as it might, I told him I was determined on starting. I told Casati I had been speaking to Saleh Aga, and asked him to look out for any reports he might hear in the station, as he always heard everything that was going on.

Emin wrote a letter to Stanley, which I was to take with me, and, with his usual kindness, busied himself all the afternoon by seeing that his servants provided for my journey with the very best his house could afford. Emin was one of those men who would deny himself things in order that he might have the pleasure of giving them to others, and nothing hurt him more than for a person to refuse his gifts. Gifts of no great value in themselves,— poor fellow! he had little enough to give; but they were tokens of an unselfish thoughtfulness which always made them doubly valuable. It was only when one came to large and important things that one found it impossible to do anything with him.

In the evening the steamer *Khedive* came in, bringing a number of refugees in her from Wadelai, among them Hawashi Effendi and a great many clerks. Emin sent for the captain and told him that Stanley had arrived, and that as I was going to M'swa he should take me down in the steamer. To this he agreed, and it was decided that wood should be collected on the next day, and I should start at mid-day in the steamer. The captain was one of those who had been wounded by the Donagla when they had captured the steamers at Dufilé. He had a frightful sword-cut from his forehead to his chin, which had laid his cheek completely open, but it was healing in the most remarkable manner. I have often noticed amongst negroes that either their wounds heal immensely quicker than those of Europeans, or become far more rapidly worse. Everything about negroes seems to be in extremes. It was decided also that the refugees which the steamer had brought from Wadelai should proceed with me also to M'swa, but the sailors refused to go further than M'swa, as they were under strict orders to return as soon as possible to Wadelai. Owing to the idleness of the soldiers very little wood was collected during the next day; it was evident they were doing all they could to delay my start until the rebel officers in Wadelai heard of Stanley's arrival. The sailors, we heard during the day, had left the steamer in a body, refusing to work. Casati came and told us about it, and we went to see what was the matter. The sailors first of all said they did not wish to go to M'swa, but after I had spoken to them for a long time they agreed to go on condition they were allowed to go with some other man as captain, as the proper captain of the steamer was obnoxious to them. It was agreed, therefore, that a man whom they chose themselves should act as captain, and that the former captain should remain at Tunguru.

Numbers of people came into my house during the day to ask me to take them to M'swa with me if possible.

Very little wood had been brought for the steamers, hardly enough to enable us to reach a certain place near some hot springs, where Chief Ouma usually had some wood stacked ready. However, I determined to start next morning, and trust to the chance of getting a further supply on the road.

In the afternoon I wrote a letter to Selim Aga, telling him of Stanley's arrival, and urging him, if the party for the Pasha was sufficiently strong, to come in the steamer if possible to Tunguru, and take the Pasha on with him to N'sabe to see Stanley. I further told him to bring down forty-two tusks of ivory to enable Stanley to pay Tippu Tib's men for carrying the ammunition to the lake. This letter was to be sent by special couriers to Wadelai after I had left Tunguru.

The rumours set about the station, concerning Stanley's coming, by the soldier who brought the letters from M'swa, had a very good effect, and though I felt certain they could not be true, I did not contradict them. The news he told was that Stanley had arrived with a marvellous machine gun, which mowed people down by hundreds, and that he had also brought with him an immense horde of Tippu Tib's Manyema, who were the terror of the country. Exaggerated stories had been told by the natives what terrible people these Arab slave-raiders were, and the soldier had added to the story, so that Stanley was supposed to be immensely strong. It had the good effect, however, of making the people somewhat nervous of putting the difficulties they probably would have otherwise made, to prevent my starting.

The rumours we had heard a few days before, concerning the Council, and the general condition of things at Wadelai, were confirmed by the people who came in the steamer, who said that there were now half-a-dozen different parties, each contending to get its own way. The two strongest parties were, however, headed by Fadl el Mulla, and Selim Aga, respectively, though I do not think either knew very well what he really wanted.

In the evening Emin read me the letter he had written to Stanley, and I see the following remark upon it in my journal :—

" The Pasha wrote a letter to Stanley in answer to his, but from what he read out to me I do not think he has written very definitely, and I hardly think, however easy and simple the circumstances might be, that it is in the Pasha to give a straight answer. Poor Pasha! long residence in the Orient has made him eminently a man of compromises."

CHAPTER XV.

START TO JOIN STANLEY.

I leave Tunguru for M'swa—Hot sulphur springs—Arrival at M'swa—Shukri Aga's helpfulness—Arrangements for refugees—Woman's gratitude—Left in the lurch—Consultation with Lur chiefs—Letter to Emin—Choosing a body-guard—Friendly tribes sacrificed—Final start in canoes—" Taking fire from a stone "—Native salutations—Magunga—Magala's complaint—Melindwa's country—Thievish Lurs—Dignified bearing of Wahuma—Contrast between soldiers and Wahuma—I reach Katonza's village—Enforced delay—My looking-glass creates a sensation—Fatiguing palaver with Katonza—We ascend the mountains—Met by Stanley's couriers—Boisterous welcome by Zanzibaris—I rejoin my leader—Letters from home.

On January 28th I started off in the steamer for M'swa, and even at starting more difficulties were put in the way of leaving, by Saleh Aga. Casati and I made a tremendous stir, and by dint of storming got him to arrange things.

Emin and Casati came down to the steamer to see me off. He and I stood talking long together of what was likely to happen after I had gone, and at the last I felt a kind of remorse for leaving him alone. Yet I knew I was doing the best thing I could by going to join Stanley, and concerting measures with him how best to save Emin. Good-bye is such a sad word sometimes to say, and I felt it doubly sad that day, when Emin clasped my hand, and looked down. He stood watching the steamer as

GOOD-BYE TO EMIN.

she moved away,—a lonely figure with all his treacherous people around him, he waved his hand for the last time as the steamer rounded the point.

The steamer was crowded with men, women, and children, and as the lake was very rough, everyone nearly was ill. It is not a pleasant position to be on a small crowded steamer, with everyone being sea-sick. At about two in the afternoon we reached the hot springs, where there was a large supply of wood ready collected by the natives. These sulphur springs were extremely hot, and at the place where the water gushed from the rock it was impossible to bear your hand in it. There was a strong smell of sulphur rising from the water, and the whole of the sides of the basin into which it ran was a bright yellow colour from the deposit of sulphur.

Here we found a large number of Egyptians and Soudanese, who had been camping there for the water, which was supposed to be very good for skin diseases. Many of these were a horrible sight from syphilitic sores, which were very frequently seen in Emin's province.

We took these people on board, and started off, but did not reach M'swa till after dark, and it was nearly nine o'clock before I was able to land. I found Shukri Aga waiting for me on the shore, and he conducted me up to my hut. I had a long talk with him that night about things in the Province and of Stanley's arrival. I asked him if he thought it would be possible to persuade the captain and sailors of the steamer to take me down to N'sabe, in which case I would take all the refugees who were willing to go with me, and establish them at

Katonza's village. He promised to do his best, and left me to go and see the captain of the steamer that very night.

Next morning Shukri Aga came in to see me, and told me he had spoken to the captain. He had given the sailors plenty of meat and corn, told them that I was going down to see Stanley solely in order to help them, that the lake at that time was very rough and dangerous for canoes, and further, that it would be risky for me to pass Melindwa's country with so small an escort as I could take in canoes. They agreed to go if plenty of wood was put on board, sufficient to carry them straight down to N'sabe. I sent for the captain, and gave him fifteen dollars, which was all I had, to land me at the south end of the lake. Shukri Aga also agreed to accompany me in order to help me to get native carriers when I arrived at Katonza's village, or, as Stanley called him, Kyan Kondo. I told Shukri Aga to bring all those willing to go with me up before me, and to explain to them what I wanted. He promised to send sufficient corn, etc., in the steamer to enable them to subsist until Stanley brought them up to the plateau. There were some fifteen officers and clerks who wished to go with me, and after I had explained to them what I wished, they all agreed to obey. I requested them to elect someone to act as their chief, and they all chose Abdul Wahad Effendi, an Egyptian captain. Shukri Aga, I heard, had left forty cattle with Katonza, which were to be kept for Stanley's arrival. He put a large amount of grain on board the steamer so that there would be an ample store of food for the new camp.

All the afternoon I was arranging with Shukri Aga and the clerks, settling things for the camp at Katonza's; and I had the greater part of the people's goods, as well as my own, put on board the steamer before night, so that there should be as little delay as possible in starting the next morning. I ordered Shukri Aga to place soldiers as sentries on the steamer, to see that nothing went wrong, but this order for some reason was not carried out, it afterwards transpired, and trouble was the result.

It was difficult to do anything with these people and clerks, they never would believe one knew best, and never obeyed orders implicitly as our Zanzibaris did. The whole afternoon I was worried by them, and every insignificant nobody came to me with some different plan; I had no right to order them, and had to argue away each plan till I brought them all round to my way of thinking: it was very wearying. As to being grateful for the trouble taken for them—they were not, but took it all as a matter of course.

I was sitting out in the evening after dinner, thinking of the helplessness and ingratitude of these people. I was utterly tired out trying to arrange things for them, and make them understand what was for their own interest, when suddenly in the darkness there was a flutter of a white garment, and before I knew where I was a negro woman had prostrated herself on the ground before me and kissed my feet. She spoke rapidly and excitedly, saying she had come to thank me for wishing and trying to help the people, and, as she heard I was starting the next morning, she had come to thank me, and prayed that Allah would bless me for coming to help them. She had brought me a small offering of food for the journey. Before I could prevent it she had again kissed my feet and disappeared, leaving me in astonishment with two clean straw trays on the ground before me. I called my boy and asked who she was, but he did not

A WOMAN'S GRATITUDE.

know, nobody had seen her. One of the trays contained some dry kuskussu and six fresh eggs, and the other a chicken, nicely cooked and clean, but in a common wooden plate, which she had tried to hide by piling bread round it. Poor thing! I was very much touched at her bringing me this little offering, no doubt she was some poor woman, and she had given me of her best, and woman-like she thought of one's creature comforts. So, after all, the people were not as wholly ungrateful as I supposed, but it remained for a woman to show it, probably some poor creature who was accustomed to be beaten by her master, and looked on as a mere beast of burden or an inferior animal.

I was up at dawn the next morning, and went out of my hut to see if the steamer was all right and had not drifted on the sand, as there had been a heavy gale during the night. To my despair, I saw her three miles off steaming round the point on her way to Wadelai, the people had got up steam during the night, and had slipped off at dawn! Let any one imagine in my place what his feelings would be after coming all this way and going through the greatest trials to offer help, and, at the last minute, when help was near, he should be treated as if he were an intriguing enemy. And yet Emin used to be angry when I was sceptical of the supposed virtues of his people, and did not look at them with his lenient eyes. I was too far gone to do more than shrug my shoulders and think this was a fitting climax to all their actions for the last six months. Since I had been in Emin's country I had been told we of the Expedition were impostors and wished to make the people slaves. I had been told we had forged the letters we had brought and that we were liars. I had had ninety loaded guns pointed at me, and narrowly escaped being massacred at Laboré. I had been made a prisoner for several months, and was at that moment under sentence of death by hanging, for standing by the Pasha, and now, finally, I had been tricked and abandoned by a handful of Egyptian and Soudanese sailors, and all because I wished to help them!

I sent at once for Shukri Aga, and told him what had happened, and he then admitted he had not carried out my order to put soldiers as sentries on the steamer. He said he had not thought it necessary, as he had felt so certain that the captain intended to act honestly. I ordered him immediately to send for Mogo and the Lur chiefs of the villages near the station, and soon they were before me. I explained to them my position, and told them they must give me men to take me in canoes to Katonza's village at the south end of the lake, and that I would see that they were well rewarded for their trouble. Mogo was sick and was unable to go, but Masa, his brother, stood up and said, " I will go with the Pasha's brother." N'juju, an experienced canoe man, who knew the lake well, said he would also go, and eight lithe active young fellows, fired by their example, promised to help me and conduct me in safety to " my father, Bula Matari." Fortunately Shukri Aga had two good-sized canoes, each capable of holding thirteen people and a few loads, provided the water was smooth. We immediately went down to the lake to see whether it had become calm enough to permit of a start, but it was far too rough, no canoe could have lived a minute in such weather, and I was unable to embark that day. We found, on arriving at the shore, that the sailors had thrown my three boxes, which I had had placed on board over night, out on the sand, but they had gone off with all the sheep, goats, and corn I was to have taken down to help Stanley to feed our people.

The steamer had an enormous supply of wood on board, so that there was no occasion to stop for more on the way at Tunguru; the captain had evidently made up his mind to go straight down to Wadelai and warn the rebel officers that Stanley had arrived, and that I was escaping from the country against their orders. There was no time to be lost, for my passage in the canoes, particularly as the lake was nearly always rough at that time of the year, and I thought the rebels might send the steamer after me and stop me before I could reach Stanley. I had, moreover, lost a day by waiting for the steamer, and had only seven days in which to reach Stanley, as he had told Emin if he did not hear from me by February 6th he would have to retire. I wrote at once to Emin to warn him of what had happened, and to beg him to come to M'swa, where Stanley could reach him by marching over the mountains. The letter was as follows :—

"M'swa, January 30th, 1889.

"MY DEAR PASHA,—You see I am still here, but start to-morrow morning, I trust. The day after my arrival, Shukri Aga and I spoke to the captain and crew of the steamer, and after giving them plenty of meat and corn, asked them if they would land me at N'sabe; I also gave the captain fifteen dollars, which was all I had; after a while they agreed, and promised to go if plenty of wood was put on board the steamer. I had arranged to take some officers and a number of clerks and employés with me, and form a camp at Katonza's, as Stanley suggested. Wood was put on board, and a great number of loads and boxes belonging to the people; I put three of mine also in the steamer, ready for an early start this morning. I was up very early, and was the first person to discover that the steamer had departed; I saw her just rounding the point in the distance. They had given us the slip in the night, and had thrown my things out on the sand. Thus you see Soudanese and Egyptian guile is once more too much for European honesty, and so it will be so long as people are foolish enough to put any trust in your men.

"By this I have lost a day, and I have now only seven days till February 6th, the day when Stanley will leave Kavalli's. Can you wonder at me and think me unjust when I am sceptical of your people? My only fear is that having so much wood on board they will slip by Tunguru without calling there. If such proves to be the case, let me implore of you, Pasha, let me beg and entreat you to come with your people here. If you have the slightest regard for those few faithfuls with you, come to this station, and I will do all in my power to induce Stanley to march to a point on the mountains near here, where you will be able to communicate with him; there will not be much difficulty or danger in our doing so, if you will only come here so that our efforts to help you may not be stultified. Help us this much to save your people and yourself; surely it is a little thing to ask, when the Expedition has been through such terrible trials to save you.

"Do not wait and trust any longer to the steamer, believe me, you will be depending on a broken reed. Shukri Aga, who is a capital fellow and has behaved very well, is most anxious for you to come here, and says his people to a man are ready to march over the mountains to Kavalli's. When we fled from Wadelai that was our intention, so why not follow the same plan to-day, when we have Stanley for a certainty ahead of us?

"You will think perhaps now that I am a 'Stanleyist,' so I am, but believe me I am also—what Stanley accuses me of being—an 'Eminist,' and it is for that reason that I cannot bear to think of you, waiting, waiting, waiting, for ever waiting, to see what will happen to-morrow. And after all, what good will you do your people by waiting? You would do them a far greater service by starting at once for this place, at any rate you would be able to save some of them.

"Shukri Aga has just come in from getting things ready for me to start, and I have told him what I am writing, and of my trying to get Stanley to move near here. He has said it is the best thing by far to be done, and that if you say the word, he is ready to bring carriers, the number of whom will be able to take you, Casati, Marco, Vita Hassan, and some of the others with their families. If you have no regard for yourself, at least have some regard for them, for I believe this to be the only way you will ever be able to get out; at any rate, nothing can be gained now by a 'masterly inactivity.' I send you this letter at once, to warn you of what has happened, and though I am writing it quietly, you must be aware of the suppressed state of indignation I am naturally in at this fresh example of faithlessness and deceit on the part of your people to me, whose only wish is to help them.

"Good-bye, my dear old man, keep up your courage and try to act. When one thinks of you left there with those fiends, one feels awfully sad and regretful.

"Yours ever,
"A. M. J."

This letter I sent off by a specially swift courier, and it reached Emin that same night.

I heard afterwards that on receiving it he had still decided to wait. When I wrote it I had not much faith in its power of persuading him to move. He had already thrown away two chances of going to M'swa and making his way to Kavalli's, and I was afraid no words would ever get him to make one step towards us. He was so fatally imbued with that sentiment which existed so strongly in his Province, " Let us wait till to-morrow."

In going down to the south end of the lake, I should have to pass the country of a powerful chief called Melindwa, he was a great friend of Kaba-regga, king of Unyoro, and had ever been one of Emin's most bitter enemies. We should, I knew, be obliged to camp two nights in his country, as it stretched for a great distance along the west shore of the lake. I therefore asked the M'swa soldiers whether any of them were willing to come with me in the canoes, as I had only three orderlies with Remingtons, and my own Winchester. Several of them volunteered to go, and I picked out seven of the best men to act as a body guard; I should therefore have ten rifles with me. I was in an agony of anxiety all day to start, but though the wind had dropped, there was such a heavy swell breaking on the shore that it was impossible for a canoe to live. At my earnest request Masa launched the biggest of the two canoes, but the waves at once toppled it over.

Several of the Lur chiefs came in to see me during the day and asked me if it was really true that the Mudir was going to leave the country. I answered that he was going to do so. They all seemed very dejected at the news, for after the Mudir had gone, Kaba-regga and Melindwa would fall upon them and punish them for having been friendly to him. They all spoke very highly of Emin, and said that his heart was good towards them, and that, though sometimes his soldiers treated them badly, they knew it was not by the Mudir's wish, for he was always—if they complained to him—ready to punish the soldiers and to see that restitution was made to them for what had been stolen. They said it was a hard case; that the news of the Mudir's intended retirement was a great blow, and that their hearts were dead within them. I quite agreed with them, it was a hard case, it was only the same story over again of what happened when the English retired from the Soudan; the friendly tribes were all sacrificed. I had been greatly struck, too, in reading Royle's book on Egypt when we were prisoners in Dufilé, to find many points in this rebellion so like those in the rebellion of Arabi. All the protestations of Fadl el Mulla and the people that Emin was "their father and mother," were so like what Arabi had said to the Khedive during his rebellion, and there were a hundred other small points which struck one as being similar.

Mogo and Chief Ouma came in to see me in the

evening; I found them both very amusing, and both equally expressed their wonder at the eccentricities of the white men. Ouma was just the same rollicking fellow as ever, and had become strong friends with Shukri Aga, who was one of the few of Emin's people who got on well with the natives and was really liked by them.

I had the Lur natives, and the seven soldiers who were to accompany me, sleeping in a hut near mine in order that I could call them at once to start if the lake became smooth enough to launch the canoes. I was up half a dozen times in the night to look at the weather, but the breakers were thundering in on the beach all night, though there was absolutely no wind. The lake took a long time to calm down after the strong winds which had been prevailing for so many days.

At eight o'clock on January 31st the lake had calmed down sufficiently to enable the canoes to be launched. There was a tremendous gathering to see me off, and every one turned out to wish me God speed; nearly all implored me not to desert them, but to try to bring Stanley to help them. My party consisted of myself, and my boy Binza, my three Soudanese orderlies, seven of Shukri Aga's soldiers, and fourteen Lur natives for paddling, with Masa, Mogo's brother, as chief, and N'juju as steersman.

The lake was rough; we got very wet at starting, and I had to keep my boy and orderlies continually baling. I was obliged to send the seven soldiers along the beach, in order to lighten the canoes, stopping now and then to give them a lift

ESCAPE FROM TUNGURU TO JOIN STANLEY.

round the places where the lake came right up to the cliffs. After two or three hours the lake went down sufficiently to admit of our landing, and I had luncheon of hard-boiled eggs in a shady thicket on the lake shore, and waited for the soldiers to come up. At about 11.30 we started off again, but had to land and send the canoe back to the place where I had lunched for four of the soldiers whom I had been unable to take in the canoes, as the lake was still running rather high.

I waited for them under a tree in the middle of a village, the chief of which was a very nice fellow called Vunja; the people all came and sat round me in a circle, and we had a long talk. While I was talking, I took out my pipe, and striking a match on a stone, lit it. I shall never forget the impression it made on the natives. They gravely watched me as I took a match from my match-box and struck it against a stone, and when there was a sputter, and they saw fire, their jaws dropped, and they gazed at me perfectly dumbfounded. But when they saw me light my pipe with it they all went off into roars of laughter, and slapped each other on the back. They exclaimed, "Oh, but these white men are bad people; look at the Inkama, he has taken fire out of that stone!" They took up the stone, and examined it gingerly to see if there was anything unusual in it, and it was passed round the circle for each to look at. They were not contented till I had let several matches off for their edification, the sputter of each match being the signal for fresh roars of laughter, and slappings on each other's backs, and even the women came to see the performance. However, matches were precious in Central Africa, so I refused to light any more, but made Vunja happy by a present of two wax matches, which he proceeded to wrap up in several small pieces of bark cloth and lash tightly to his body.

So much were they impressed by my cleverness in being able to take fire from a stone, that these friendly, hospitable negroes killed a cow, and loaded the canoes with meat for my men.

I always liked sitting down and talking to these natives, and their boisterous, hospitable, and joyous natures had a great charm for me.

The peculiar way in which the natives greeted each other in this part of the world amused me greatly. When two natives met they each put their two hands on the other's shoulders, and each began to spit alternately on his friend's right and left shoulders. Masa seemed to know every one, and if it was a particular friend of his he spat with a will, and made streams run down his friend's shoulders. The depth of his friendship for any one he met might be gauged by the size and volume of the streams. To those for whom he did not greatly care he merely slightly bedewed each shoulder. Whenever I saw two really big streams coming down some of his friends' bodies, I asked him, "Masa, is that man a great friend of yours?" and he answered, "Yes, master, he is just like my brother; I have known him since I was so high," indicating a height about two feet from the ground. The different shades in the cordiality of his greeting being thus so clearly marked, I could always tell which were his friends, and which people he did not care much about.

At three o'clock we reached Magunga, the chief of which, Magala, was an old friend of mine. I had slept twice in his village, once on my way up to M'swa for the first time in the boat, and again when I was with Emin in the steamer. The lake shore is beautiful here, quite Swiss in its scenery. We found on arriving that for some reason or other the natives had cleared out, so we had the place all to ourselves. Magunga was a small village, with some nine or ten huts, it was only Magala's fishing village, his main village being situated behind the mountains on the plateau, 1700 ft. above the lake. It was built on a flat delta, five acres in extent, formed by a fine large stream which came down from the mountain above in a huge cascade. The village itself was quite hidden from the lake by a magnificent grove of bananas, some of the finest I have ever seen. To my mind there is no shade so pleasant as that afforded by a thick grove of bananas, it is so cool and refreshing. For while there is a thick yet chequered shade, the air and breeze circulates freely among the banana stems, and there is no feeling of closeness or suffocation. Close to the lake shore, which was here a mass of tumbled rocks, was a narrow fringe of graceful mimosa bushes. At that time of the year they were covered with clusters of yellow flowers, which smelt like jasmine, and made the air heavy with their perfume. The mountains behind sloped down abruptly to the little flat below, and were covered with fine trees. Here and there, on the mountain sides among the trees, were small natural ledges, and on each of these might be seen a native hut, with its patch of pink-flowered tobacco ; they looked like little hanging gardens high up on the mountains. It was a beautiful spot to stay in, and seemed so peaceful and retired with its sheltering screen of banana trees and mimosa.

As it was still early, I went and had a swim in a great deep pool at the foot of the cascade. It was one of the most enjoyable baths I have ever had; it was delightfully refreshing to feel the cool water swirling round one's body. I went to bed early, having put everything ready for an early start the next day. Owing to Vunja's present, there was heaps of meat and food in camp, and the soldiers and Lurs sat eating and laughing and talking to a late hour. I was so accustomed to camp sounds by this time, that none of the ordinary noises in camp ever disturbed me, and I liked to hear the people laughing and talking all round me. The wind rose pretty strongly during the night, but dropped again towards morning, but on getting up at dawn I found the lake still running very high. These unavoidable delays were most annoying, but one could not expect at that time of the year to get along without a good deal of wind. Curbing my impatience as well as I could, I sat down and had an excellent breakfast of roasted plantains and hard-boiled eggs.

At about ten in the morning Magala came down to see me. He had heard from his people, who I suppose had seen me from the mountains, that I had arrived, and now brought me presents of ripe bananas and flour. He had a long complaint to make against one of the M'swa soldiers, who it appears had enticed away two of his favourite wives, and asked me to help him to get them back. I told him I would write to the Pasha about it, and I had no doubt that the Mudir would see that they were returned to him. He said, that as there was not good fishing just then, his men had left the village to look after the harvesting of their crops on the plateau above. Though there was no wind we were not able to get the canoes launched till three in the afternoon, but I was determined to go on as long as I could during the night. I was struck afresh by the great beauty of the shores of the lake at this part. The mountains, over two thousand feet high, were jagged and precipitous, but their outlines were softened and shaded by a mantle of delicate green grass and graceful trees. The gliding motion of a canoe, so silent and smooth, is much pleasanter than that of a boat, there is no jerking or sound of oars. The sun was just setting over the mountains, and everything was quiet and peaceful, the complete stillness being only broken by the gentle rhythmical plash of the paddles, to which the Lurs kept time in a low, crooning, and not untuneful song. One wished it could have lasted for hours; but alas! tropical evenings are short, and night soon closed in.

At 8.30 we reached Maboko's village; it was situated on the border of Melindwa's country, from which it was separated by a fine mountain stream. It was considered advisable by the Lurs to stop here, and to try, by starting early the next day, to get past Melindwa's, if possible, in one day.

The chief was an old friend of Masa's, with whom he went through the usual moist salutations. He received me with great hospitality and kindness, and brought me a quantity of bananas and eggs. It was pitch dark, and the wind came down from the mountains in gusts which made me shiver, but great camp fires were lighted by my people, around which they and the natives seated themselves, and large piles of meat were soon smoking on the red-hot embers. The chief came, and talked to me after I had had my dinner; he spoke about his friendship for Emin, and showed me two large copper bracelets, which he told me were a present from him. He also expressed his sorrow that Emin was going to retire from the country. It would be dangerous, he said, for me to sleep in Melindwa's country, as he was very bitter against Emin, and he warned me to keep a good look out, if I found I was obliged to do so. Melindwa's people, he told me, were a treacherous lot, and had lately cut off a small party of his men who were camping for the night at the foot of the mountains.

It was late before I retired for the night to a hut which the chief lent me. I got little sleep, however, for the hut was swarming with rats. Owing to the wind, which always seemed to rise in the night, I was unable to get off till nine o'clock the next morning. One of the canoes was upset by the waves in getting off, but fortunately for me it was the one which carried the soldiers. Their guns went to the bottom, but, by good luck, the water was shallow, and they were able to recover them all. The lake shore was still a continuation of the M'swa Mountain range, and though fine, was less interesting than the part we had passed the day before. The mountains were nearly as high, but not so abrupt, and there was a gradually broadening plain between them and the lake. We stopped at mid-day for a rest at a small village on one of the flat deltas formed by the streams from the mountains. I sat and had my luncheon under the shade of a large tree near the shore, where a clear impetuous stream rushed into the lake. As I was smoking my pipe after lunch, a body of natives approached through the bushes, with unfriendly gestures, and fired two arrows at some of my Lurs, who were bathing in the stream.

I had my Winchester at hand, and at once fired a couple of shots over their heads. The echo and reverberation among the mountain gorges was something startling, and the natives took to their heels, and climbed up the mountain side, followed by the jeers and shouts of my Lurs. It was amusing to watch their delight, for they were not particularly brave themselves. They entered the huts, which by my orders they had abstained from doing before, and brought out numbers of baskets of imperfectly cured fish, with which they proceeded to load one of the canoes. We paddled along, passing many prettily situated villages, until it was nearly dark. Finding we could not reach the limit of Melindwa's country that night, I camped in a large settlement, the people of which ran away to the mountains on our approach. There were quantities of bananas, and my men, as usual, thieved right and left, chickens, fishing lines, or dried fish—these Lurs were incorrigible thieves, and it was impossible to stop them. They belonged to the same tribe as Melindwa's people, but because they were unfriendly with them, and the natives cleared out before them, they considered themselves justified in appropriating whatever took their fancy.

I had three sentries put round the camp, which I made as small and compact as possible, throwing up a light boma made of the wicker doors of the huts. This was sufficient to turn arrows, and I had the canoes ready to be launched, should the natives come upon us in any numbers during the night.

I hardly slept, and continually got up to see that the sentries were awake and at their posts. A strong wind blew steadily all night, and it was bitterly cold, but fortunately the wind was off the shore, and the lake in the morning was as calm as a mill pond. I found it somewhat difficult to get Emin's soldiers and the Lurs off next morning, for the evening before I had given them a fat sheep and a large goat, with which Shukri Aga had presented me as a provision for the road, and they were busy eating before starting.

At nine o'clock we reached Kanama, the large village at which I had stopped the first night on my way to M'swa in the boat. Vaju's son, and all the people of the village, came down to a point on the shore, and asked me to land and have a talk with them. I sat and talked with them for half an hour, and they told me Stanley was still at Kavalli's, and had never left it since his arrival nearly three weeks before. Native reports are so unreliable that I did not place much faith in this news.

The people were all full of tales about Stanley's having fought and beaten the Wa-regga, who were Kavalli's enemies. These people told me the Wa-regga had long been the scourge of the country, and everyone was glad to hear of their defeat.

In the afternoon we passed Stanley's and Emin's former camp at N'sabe, the huts were still all standing, though they were in a somewhat ruined state, but the grass had grown over everything, and the place looked most dreary and woebegone. At five o'clock we reached Nyamsassie Island, which was inhabited by some of Nampigua's people, their sole occupation being making salt from the earth. This salt supplied Nampigua's people on the plateau, and was also sold to the surrounding tribes. I never saw a finer-looking lot of men; each man had the bearing of a Sultan. They were tall, beautifully made, and strong. Each man was dressed in a long, finely cured skin, with a narrow border of white hair left round the edge as an ornament. This skin was worn depending from one shoulder, and was fastened by a bright iron ornament; it completely covered the figure, and reached to below the knees. They were armed with large strong spears, bows, and unpoisoned arrows. They were beautifully clean, and extremely nice-looking, and their features fine; they were evidently Wa-huma. As we were now near Katonza's village, I camped on the island, and the chief promised to give me men the next morning to carry my loads to Katonza's village, which was about three-quarters of a mile inland from the lake. I felt almost ashamed at asking such splendid-looking men to take the loads out of the canoes, but my Soudanese had no such compunction, and hurried the natives about with little ceremony. These Wa-huma took the loads with a dignity of mien which was most unusual, and smiled at each other as if unaccustomed to such work. I had never before been so much struck by any negroes. There were not more than thirty men with their wives and children on the island; the women had nice gentle faces, with a particularly kind, modest expression.

The treatment of these people by my soldiers made me very angry. They ordered them about, and jostled them in their usual arrogant way, which was most exasperating. Their treatment of ordinary natives and their domineering ways towards them always annoyed me, but with these people such bearing seemed a positive insult. There certainly was a great difference between these natives and the soldiers; but to the advantage of the natives. As far as I could see, the difference between them was this: the soldiers carried a gun which they did not know how to use, they were dressed in ragged clothes, were dirty, and were slaves; the natives, on the other hand, carried spears and bows which they knew how to use right well, they were fine-looking and clean, were gracefully dressed in beautifully cured skins, and were free. The reason the soldiers considered themselves so vastly superior to the natives was solely because they carried guns. The natives had killed a hippopotamus, and they were drying the flesh in strips, and the whole place was surrounded by strings of meat hanging up. I slept in a small, clean hut, given me by the chief, it was made of strong scented grass which had a pleasant smell.

I got so angry the next morning at the way the soldiers dawdled that I took a stick and drove them into the canoe; there was always a difficulty in getting them off in good time in the morning. Some of the Wa-huma came with us to carry the loads. We had to paddle about three miles down the lake, which was very shallow here, and full of banks of mud and sand. On these banks crowds of crocodiles were lying, and there were great numbers of snipe, plover, geese, and ducks, I longed to have a shot gun with me. At 8.30 we landed, and the natives went to a small village near to get more people to carry my things, for owing to my soldiers' rough treatment of the people on Nyamsassie island, only five Wa-huma had turned up. The people soon returned, saying the village was deserted, but they had seen one native who had told them that all the people in the villages round had fled to the mountains for fear of Kaba-regga's scouts, who were making raids in the neighbourhood.

Taking six soldiers and some Lurs with me, and leaving the rest of the people to guard the canoe and loads, I started off for Katonza's village. We passed through the place where Stanley was camped, when he first met Emin. When we reached Katonza's village we found it deserted, except by two natives, who told me that Katonza, with his goats, cattle, etc., had retired to the mountains, taking the greater part of his people with him. He had left his village under the care of his brother N'guaba, and a few people, all of whom were dispersed among the clumps of forest in the vicinity. I at once dispatched one of the natives to tell N'guaba, I was in his village, and to bring some carriers in as quickly as possible. In about half an hour he came in, and his men also dropped in by twos and threes, bringing some of their women and household goods with them, until perhaps there were some twenty men and ten women assembled in the village.

Whilst waiting for the people to come in, N'guaba told me that the Wa-ganda were invading Unyoro; a very common occurrence, and that Kaba-regga had sent his women, flocks, and treasure to a place at the south end of the lake. There was a guard of Warrasura left to look after them, whilst his General Babadongo went to fight the Wa-ganda, Kaba-regga himself always retiring on such occasions. It was this guard of whom the natives were afraid, for fearing the natives might attack them, the Warrasura had determined to act on the defensive, and had made several raids. After sitting talking for some time, N'guaba and his men started off for the lake and brought my loads and people back with them, and established me in a hut.

In the evening I sent for N'guaba, and had a long talk with him. I told him I wished to start for Kavalli's village to join Stanley, and asked him to give me fifteen or even ten men to carry my loads. He said he had so few people that he could not give me any men, but that on my arrival that morning, he had sent a messenger to Katonza, saying I was here, and had told him to come at once, and bring people with him. He would without doubt arrive the next day, when he would be able to give me plenty of men for the start the day after. He therefore asked me to remain where I was, and await Katonza's arrival. I tried every argument I could think of to get him to give me men, and even thought of leaving some of my loads in his charge, while I went on with my own men, and sent down some of Kavalli's people to bring the rest up to the plateau. However, as Kabaregga's scouts were in the neighbourhood, I was loath to leave any of my loads where they might be captured, so I reluctantly consented to await Katonza's coming the next day. If by that time he did not arrive, I told N'guaba I should be obliged to start and get on as best I could.

N'guaba seemed a very good fellow; ready, and even anxious to help me; his plea that having so few people with him—he was, owing to the disturbed state of the country—afraid to send any away, was, I think, a just one. It was very annoying, but it could not be helped, people need a great store of patience in Africa. I had already been eight days on the road, and nine from the day I had got Stanley's letter, and it was possible I should yet be three days, by which calculation I did not think I could arrive till Feb. 7th, and Stanley had positively said, that one of us, the Pasha or I, must be there by the 6th, or he would be obliged to retire. My impatience therefore at the delay may be imagined.

In the evening several women came in to see me, and I showed them my looking-glass with which they were greatly delighted. At first they were frightened at the clear reflection of their own faces, but after a while they got used to it, and it was handed round from one to the other. They all pushed their heads together to get a sight of their faces, and smirked and bridled in front of it, turning and twisting their faces round to get a view of them in every position. I noticed that it was the oldest and ugliest that kept the glass longest, I could hardly get it away from an old woman who sat admiring her wrinkles with a pleased smile on her face. Soon I had the whole village, including the chief, round my hut to look at themselves in the glass, the men were just as pleased with it as the women.

There was nothing to do the next morning but to wait the coming of Katonza. N'guaba and his people came in in the morning to squeeze my hand—the natives never shake the hand—and to look at me as soon as I was up. Most natives are fond of sitting smoking in perfect silence, gazing at the white man. In the afternoon Katonza came in, bringing a cow with him as a present for my people. He brought a good many of his men with him.

He was somewhat difficult to deal with at first, for he had a long list of complaints to make against Kavalli, and seemed very jealous that Stanley should have settled in his village. He was most anxious for Stanley to come down to stay in his village to defend him against the raids of Kaba-regga's people. He wanted me to leave my loads in his charge, so that they would be ready when Stanley came down to camp on the plain.

I was afraid of offending him by telling him that Stanley had no intention of doing this, in which case he would probably have refused to help me, so I told him I would lay his story before Stanley, and he would decide what to do. I impressed it upon him that it was of the greatest importance that I should reach Kavalli's the next day, and if he wished to please Stanley he must give me carriers to take my loads, in order to show Stanley he was really anxious for his friendship. Upon this he promised to give me carriers the next morning. He was greatly pleased to hear that perhaps Emin and some of his people would come in the steamers and establish themselves near his village, and he said he would treat them well and give them plenty of food. He had numbers of stories to tell me of the different chiefs, and about Kaba-regga's doings. This shauri, or palaver, took me more than four hours and a half to arrange. I had to say what I wanted to my boy Binza in Ki-Swahili, who spoke to a soldier in Arabic, he in his turn interpreted it in the Lur language to Masa, who finally handed over my meaning to Katonza in the Kinyoro language. There was almost time to smoke a pipe between the time when I put my question until I got it answered. However, in spite of it Katonza and I made ourselves quite understood. I presented him and his brother N'guaba each with a large piece of white cotton cloth, which was all I could give them as a present, but they seemed more than satisfied with it.

In the evening I had another crowd of natives round my hut to see my glass lantern, which was hanging up inside, lighted with one of Emin's wax candles. They all expressed much astonishment at it, and were evidently so inquisitive to know what it was made of, that I told them to go in and examine it. They went in in a body and tapped the glass, after which they shook their heads and said that the white men were wonderful people.

I was up early on February 6th to get off in good time, so that we should have finished the ascent of the mountains before the sun got very hot. I knew the path up the mountains of old; it was steep and rocky and full of small sharp quartzy stones, which caused one to slip often in the steeper parts. Over two thousand feet of this sort of climbing had to be done before the high table-lands above could be reached; at about two and a half hours marching from the edge of the plateau was Kavalli's village. I wished, therefore, to get over the worst part of the climb before midday. But he who trusts to prompt action from negroes is generally doomed to disappointment, and requires an inexhaustible stock of patience. Katonza, in spite of his emphatic promises that everything should be ready early, came and told me that his people had not yet come in in sufficient numbers to admit of his sending carriers with me. I talked with him for a long time with a sort of impatient patience, and explained to him that it was absolutely necessary for me to reach Kavallis that day. I told him that if he did not help me, Stanley was not very likely to arrange things for him with Kavalli, and so, after much talk, and many arguments, he gave me eight men. I gave some of my loads to the Lurs, who were splendid fellows, and who, for the time they had been with me, had been devoted to me, and had looked after me with the greatest care. Three loads I left with Katonza, who promised to take charge of them until Kavalli's men should arrive to take them up to the plateau. He was better than his word in this, for two days afterwards he sent them up by his own men. I was able to get off at last at 8 o'clock, Katonza and N'guaba accompanying me for a couple of miles, and we parted at the foot of the mountains with mutual expressions of good will.

SIGHTING THE ZANZIBARIS.

I noticed that one of my carriers was a little bit of a woman, she had picked out the heaviest box of all, and yet she kept up with the men and carried her load right up the mountains with apparently no great effort. We went gaily along through the lovely park-like plain in which great herds of hartebeest, kudu, and springbok were feeding. Groups of buffaloes stood under the spreading trees whisking their tails, and here and there flocks of guinea fowl might be seen picking up a living on the fresh green grass. It all looked lovely, and my spirits rose as I ascended the mountains and got into the clear breezy atmosphere of the table-lands. It was so beautifully fresh after the steaminess and heat of Emin's Province. When we were three-quarters of the way up the mountains, I ordered a halt for a rest, under the shade of some trees close to a cool rushing mountain stream. The people threw down their loads and jumped into the water, and everyone had a good bathe while I ate my lunch. Just as we were thinking of starting, Masa, who was on the bank above, called out that he saw people in gay-coloured clothes descending the mountains. I climbed the bank, and could see a line of people in the distance descending the winding path. When they got nearer I waved my hat over my head and cheered. They turned out to be a party of our faithful Zanzibaris. As they caught sight of me, they came bounding down the mountain side, shouting and firing off their guns. They seemed delighted to see me again, and rushed up in their boisterous way, shouting out congratulations and words of welcome, while the faithful Uledi took me in his arms and embraced me.

They told me that Stanley had been very uneasy by my non-appearance and the absence of news; that each day he had become more and more anxious, until he had at last decided to send for Stairs and the rest of the Expedition to join him. He had found there was plenty of food coming in from the natives, and had remained at Kavalli's ever since January 18th.

The night before, natives had come in bringing Stanley the news that a white man had arrived in canoes at Nyamsassie. He had at once concluded it was I, and had sent down a party of Zanzibaris to meet me, and conduct me to Kavalli's. After a halt of half an hour to rest the Zanzibaris, during which time a stream of questions and answers was passing between us, we started on. At a large clear stream about a mile from Kavalli's I stopped, and had a delightful bathe, and put on a clean suit of clothes, so that I might arrive in camp decently dressed. The whole camp had turned out to see us arrive, and in the distance I could see the Manyema moving about in their white clothes. Stanley had the men fallen in, but as soon as I approached they all broke from the ranks, and surrounded me, shouting congratulations and shaking my hands nearly off. It was delightful to be so boisterously welcomed, after I had been smarting for so many months under the treatment of the Soudanese and Egyptians.

Stanley received me in his usual calm manner, tempered, however, by a smile; I think he was pleased to see me again, I know I was glad to see him.

The Manyema chiefs and different people came up to greet me cordially, and Stanley conducted me to his tent—amid a running fire of greetings from the men—to give me tea and hear my news. Two letters were put into my hand, dated June, 1887; this was February, 1889. However, it was news from home, and I tore them open and read them eagerly.

CHAPTER XVI.

EMIN'S RELIEF.

Our camp at Kavalli's—A difficult story to tell—Plans discussed—Stanley sends for Stairs—Letter despatched to Emin—Among friends again—Letter from Emin—Emin's arrival at Wéré—Zanzibaris welcome Emin—The Pasha's story—Unlooked-for turn of Fortune's wheel—Refugees require carriers—Start with Emin for Kavalli's—Patient Zanzibaris—Emin's and Stanley's second meeting—Stairs and his party arrive—The Expedition re-united—" Dead! Master! Dead!"—Reflections.

THE camp, which was close to Kavalli's village, was of a good size, and there was a camp for Tippu Tib's people a hundred yards distant below our camp. The Zanzibaris had built their grass huts in a circle, and Stanley's tent was pitched in the middle, near which a nice grass house was built ready for me. Bonny alone was with Stanley. The three officers, Stairs, Nelson, and Parke were still at the camp on the Ituri Ferry with the sick, and a good many loads.

I dined with Stanley, and we sat up till late that night exchanging news. I explained as well as I could Emin's position, and gave Stanley to understand—as was most emphatically the case—that hitherto Emin himself had been the principal obstacle to his own rescue, for he had thrown away two chances of making his way to Stanley. If I could get out with only ten rifles, he could have got out

I REJOIN MY LEADER.

Page 442.

with the thirty or more he probably would have had. I explained to Stanley it was utterly impossible for me to tell him briefly the position of affairs in the country. What the people intended doing, I, even after eight months' residence there, had never been wholly able to understand. I could only tell my story, quoting certain incidents which had happened, and relating certain conversations I had had with Emin, and then leave him to draw his own conclusions.

Stanley asked me what plan I, who knew the country, would suggest, in order to help Emin to get out. I told him I thought the best plan was to march to Magala's village, on the plateau above Magunga, which was some eight or ten miles from M'swa, and then if Stanley would let me go down, accompanied by my boy Binza, to M'swa station, I could signal to the party of Zanzibaris, who could remain on the plateau in sight of the station. If the Pasha was there, and all was well, the Zanzibaris could then descend into the station, and conduct Emin to Stanley's camp, when we could immediately return to Kavalli's, and wait for such people as were willing to join us afterwards. I think Stanley made up his mind, if the worst came to the worst, to adopt this plan, though he never actually said so. He merely said that he must get the rest of the Expedition to Kavalli's before he could do anything, as his numbers at present were too small to admit of his taking any decisive step towards helping Emin.

He declared that if he did decide to adopt this plan, he would not move until he had actually heard that Emin was at M'swa. Knowing Emin as I did, I thought Stanley's decision was exceedingly wise.

There was one thing about Stanley which made working under him interesting; he was always ready to listen patiently to what his officers said with regard to any step which it was proposed to make, and even if he did not agree with them he never merely said shortly that it was impossible, but carefully explained why he thought that the suggestion made was not good, or was impossible to follow. By this means we received a great deal of useful instruction, which we should not otherwise be in the way of getting. Stanley was also constantly sketching an imaginary situation, and then turning sharply on you, and asking you what you would do under those circumstances. It was a good school.

Stanley had already written to Stairs, ordering him to come at once, and had given him extracts from my letters to him, saying the Pasha and I had been made prisoners. He now added a postscript, telling him that I had arrived at his camp. This letter he despatched to Stairs with a party of thirty-five men on February 7th, the day after I had arrived.

On February 8th, the seven soldiers who had accompanied me from M'swa, with Masa and the Lurs, started off to return to M'swa. They took with them a letter from Stanley, begging Emin to come to M'swa, at which place he would probably be able to help him. I also sent a letter to Emin, telling him such news as I had heard, and adding my persuasions to those of Stanley's. Before starting, Stanley told me to give each of the Lurs a necklace of large blue beads, and a number of cowries; with these they were delighted. Stanley sent messages to Shukri Aga, and a present of a handsome silk sash.

During the next few days there was plenty to do. I had to build several huts to take in the rest of the officers of the Expedition when they arrived, and to make my own tent out of a large tarpaulin he had given me for the purpose. I had also my report to write for Stanley of my stay in Emin's Province. During these days when we were alone I had my meals with Stanley, and we constantly talked of my experiences. By relating the whole story, explaining different things in it, and recounting incidents which had happened, and conversations I had had with Emin, Stanley was at length able to grasp the situation.

During these evenings Stanley would sit outside smoking his pipe, and I would be with him talking. I shall never forget the pleasure that time was to me. To again be with a man who never hesitated, whose word was law, and whose every order was implicitly obeyed; to talk to this man, and to listen to his clear sensible remarks and judgment on events, —was like a tonic coming after the disorder and vacillating policy which I had been accustomed to for those preceding eight months. Things which had somewhat mystified me before, now became clear as I listened to Stanley's comments and remarks; while all around were the camp-fires lighting up the happy, contented faces of our Zanzibaris. With the shouting and laughter of our men about us, I lay back in my chair with utter satisfaction and content in the feeling that the days of treachery which had hemmed me in for so many months were over, and that at last I was again surrounded by faithful friends. It was like coming home.

Stanley and I were sitting together talking after dinner on the evening of the 13th, when a native came in and handed him a letter. Eagerly he tore it open and tossed an enclosure over to me. The letters were from Emin, who had arrived in the steamer the evening before, at a place called Weré, near Nyamsassie Island.

He had brought a number of officers and people with him, and now wrote to ask Stanley to send down a party of his men to escort him to Kavalli's. He said he had brought the boat *Advance* with him, which had been fitted up with fresh bolts and screws, and he had also brought sixty tusks of ivory to pay Tippu Tib's people.

Stanley was delighted with the news, and leaning across the table said, " Shake hands on it, old fellow ! we'll be successful after all." I told him if any one deserved success, he did, for he had toiled hard for it. Stanley went outside his tent and called out to the Zanzibaris, who immediately came rushing up. He told them that the Pasha had arrived at Nyamsassie, and that we should be able to save him after all. They cheered and shouted frantically, and were dancing and singing over the news half the night.

My letter from Emin was as follows:—

"Camp at Weré, near Katonza's,
"*February* 13*th*, 1889.

" DEAR MR. JEPHSON,—Yesterday, in the afternoon, I arrived here with the two steamers, accompanied by Casati, Marco, Vita, Selim Aga, Bilal Aga, Surore Aga (of Laboré fame !) and a lot of officers with forty soldiers as a guard. There are Rajab and Arif

Effendi and some more people, every one with me has his things and traps. I've brought the ivory and *Advance* ready for service. I wrote to Mr. Stanley asking him for carriers to fetch some sesame, duchan, etc., for your party, but as the officers are very anxious to see him, and hear from himself what he proposes, I shall probably, after two or three days, start with them for your camp—if I can. I am somewhat ill, and walk only with great difficulty and pain. If I am unable to come I shall write explicitly. We have things now in our hands and must make the best of it. They have made submission to me, and are quite willing to obey, but I do not think they will come in all from Wadelai.

" There are with me Bachit's and Binza's wives, two girls, the boy Sabuni and a woman and child you left with us, belonging, I think, to some of your people.

" I am greatly obliged for your kind remembrance of my girl; she is, of course here, and kisses your hands.

" How much I should like to be with you, you may well understand. There are so many things to be talked over, so many provisions to be made, that only an interview with Mr. Stanley can help us. I shall, therefore, come there as quickly as I can. The steamers go back to M'swa to fetch clerks and Irregulars; if you need anything from there write to me at once. I hope the news you received from home was pleasant and satisfactory to you; after your trials on the road, your imprisonment here, and your long afflictions with me, you merit, at least, a fair reward. For the political news you kindly gave me, my best thanks.

"I have been greatly rejoiced by a cutting from a paper I found in one of my letters sent to me by Mr. Stanley; the whole batch of boxes I have sent to the British Museum, has been received in a good state.

"Please give my greetings to your fellow-officers. Casati and the others desire me to make you their obeisance.

"Hoping to see you very soon,

"I am, yours very sincerely,

"Dr. Emin.

"P.S.—I have rewarded the people you recommended to me. The chief of Magunga shall have his women."

Stanley told me, that on the morrow I was to start off for the lake with some Zanzibaris and natives, and bring Emin and his people and loads up to Kavallis without delay.

On February 14th, I started off at seven o'clock with sixty-four Zanzibaris, and about the same number of native carriers, with orders to bring the Pasha, his loads, and such officers as wished to come and consult with him. These officers, after consulting with him, were to return to Wadelai, there to remain, or to bring out their families as the case might be. We all got off in the highest spirits, the caravan going well, led by Uledi carrying the Egyptian flag. We reached the foot of the mountains in good time, but the natives who were leading us to Emin's camp missed the path, and took us down a very bad mountain road, which was like the dry, rocky bed of a torrent. They led us in a semicircle through the plain, and we did not arrive at the lake shore till nearly five, after a hot and weary march of seventeen miles. We arrived foot-sore and worn out, and almost parched with thirst, for there was very little water on the way, and that only of the filthiest description. We passed herds of antelope of all kinds, and numbers of buffaloes and pigs feeding on the plain, but the people were too weary to care to leave the path to shoot them, and only thought of reaching Emin's camp as soon as possible. On arriving, however, in sight of the lake, the Zanzibaris, in spite of their weariness, rushed madly into the camp, shouting at the tops of their voices "Salaam! Basha! Salaam!"

They went through the usual mad antics of expressing their satisfaction at seeing the "Basha," as they called him, and they surrounded him shouting out all kinds of welcomes; he stood amongst them laughing, and looked very pleased at being so boisterously greeted.

The Soudanese soldiers looked on the antics of the Zanzibaris with astonishment depicted on their heavy, unsmiling faces, evidently wondering what kind of people these noisy, and apparently unruly Zanzibaris could be.

Emin greeted me warmly, he seemed very unwell, but cheered up wonderfully at the idea of getting out of the country. The little Farida came to see me, and all the officers, clerks, and people came up also and had a long talk. Emin told me he had decided to call all his officers together the next morning, and asked me to speak to them, and get them to decide upon what they wished to do.

The camp was in a splendid situation, some seven miles south of our camp at M'sabe. The plain there, as at Katonza's, was like a park, and sloped up gently from the lake from which a beautiful view through the trees could be got from the Pasha's hut. There were great clumps and rows of forest trees; the huts were dotted about amongst them, and looked very pretty and picturesque; but it was very hot, and there were swarms of mosquitoes. Emin, Casati, and I sat out in the moonlight after dinner smoking, and Emin told me what news there was from his Province.

General chaos and confusion still reigned there, and the usual impossible stories and rumours were floating about. No more news had been heard of the Donagla, who were still at Rejaf, waiting for reinforcements to arrive from Khartoum. Emin professed himself greatly astonished at being able to get out of the country after all; the Donagla had certainly turned out to be our best friends, for they had frightened the people into letting us leave Dufilé, and had we not been able to get away from there when we did, we should most certainly have been lost.

He had with him Selim Aga (now a Bey), Bilal Aga, who had fought so well in Dufilé; Surore Aga, who did his best to get Emin and me massacred in Laboré, and several other officers and clerks with their wives and children.

It appeared that Selim Bey, on receiving the letter I wrote before starting from Tunguru, read it out before all the rebel officers at Wadelai, and he at once announced his intention of going in the steamer to see Stanley. There were, as a matter of course,

Effect of the News of Stanley's Arrival. 451

great dissensions amongst the officers who wished to go out with us, and those who wished to remain, and the quarrel became violent.

But both officers and soldiers were very much alarmed to hear that I had actually got out of the country without their permission, and had probably reached Stanley by the time they got the letter.

Exaggerated reports of Stanley's strength and number had been bruited abroad, and they feared that as I had reached Stanley, and had told him the story of the rebellion, he would probably be down on them, and attack them from the south. To the north were the Donagla, so they would be between two fires. Selim Bey's party therefore prevailed, and a number of officers and people took the steamers, bringing with them the tusks of ivory I had asked for Tippu Tib's carriers, and they started for Tunguru to see Emin. Surore Aga and certain others, I am persuaded, had no idea of coming out, they had only come to see what Stanley's strength really was.

On arriving at Tunguru, they all came before Emin, and desired him to accompany them to M'swa, this he agreed to do, and went in the steamer, taking with him Casati, Vita, Marco, and as many people as he could.

After waiting a few days at M'swa, the officers again came before Emin, and asked him to accompany them to Stanley. He asked them in what capacity. They answered they wished him to go as their interpreter. Upon this, he told them such a thing was impossible, he could never go in that capacity. They then retired and there was a consultation held—they always were holding consultations—at which Shukri Aga came to the fore and spoke up in the Pasha's favour, drawing a dreary picture of what would happen to them if they did not gain Stanley's friendship; after much talking they decided to go to the Pasha again. By the advice of Shukri Aga and Selim Aga they went in a body to Emin, and said they had come to make their submission, and wished him to go with them before Stanley as their Mudir. On this understanding Emin consented to go. Shukri Aga was, of course, delighted at the turn affairs had taken, and made great rejoicings in the station. Quantities of meat were got ready, and a great feast was made, at which the officers ate and drank to their hearts' content, and were put into a good temper. Shukri Aga knew well how to deal with them!

Emin then made Selim Aga a Bey—a rank equal to a Lieut.-Colonel—and told him to send him in a list of the names of such men as had behaved well in the fight at Dufilé, and he would give them promotion.

He also promoted Shukri Aga, on his own account, to the rank of Captain—he was only a second lieutenant before—in consideration of his loyal service to him throughout the rebellion.

In two days they had started in the steamer, and had arrived at Weré on February 12th, just six days after I had reached Kavallis.

So after all, everything was well, there was no need for us to march to M'swa, and the ivory was there to pay the carriers.

On the next morning Emin called all the officers together and I spoke long with them. It was decided that Emin and eight officers should start the next day for Kavallis. The officers, after speaking to Stanley, would stay a few days at Kavallis, to settle things, and then return to Wadelai to make their preparations for starting. They asked me if I could give them twenty carriers to carry sufficient things for three days; I said certainly. Emin had a great many loads, but most of them contained corn and sesame, of which a good deal was for us. I afterwards asked Casati if he would come with us the next day, but he said he preferred to wait a bit, when he would bring all his loads up at the same time.

I asked him how many carriers he wanted, to which he replied, with a shrug of his shoulders, "Oh, I am very poor, I have not much baggage, all my things were, you know, taken from me by Kaba-regga, I will manage to do with eighty carriers!" Marco wanted sixty! and Vita Hassan, the Apothecary, fifty! One hundred and ninety carriers for three people! We had but 250 men in all, and those were principally taken up with carrying ammunition, cloth and beads for money, and such things. The time I knew could not be far distant when they would be brought to their bearings pretty smartly, and I was content to wait.

Emin told me that Casati had been strongly averse to his going to M'swa, and had urged him not to come down to us as it would be "impolitic" and would anger the rebel chiefs. This advice was given in the face of the miraculous opening which Emin had of getting out of the country, an opening equally unexpected by Emin or by us.

I went round to see most of the people and to have a

talk with them; they were just as selfish and helpless as ever, and I became quite disgusted at trying to arrange things for them, this sort of thing was doubly aggravating to me after coming fresh from our well-ordered camp. Selim Bey took me down to the lake shore to show me our boat, which he had got ready for us. He had found some bolts in the storehouses, which had just fitted her, so she was as good as ever. We were, however, unfortunately obliged to leave her on the lake when we came away, as we were quite unable with our small caravan to carry her.

During the day, Nampigua and Katonza came in to see the Pasha, they both complained of Kavalli. As there was no meat in the camp, I sent some of the men to try and get some antelope. In a very short time they returned, bringing in a hartebeest, two kudu, a springbok and a buffalo. The Zanzibaris were very bad shots, so this will give some idea of the abundance and tameness of the game on the Nyanza plain. I gave out a large packet of salt, which Emin had brought amongst others with him; it was very scarce in the country, and was a great treat to the men. Emin's people gave them plenty of flour, so with the animals they had shot they were quite happy.

Next morning, I was up early to get the loads off; such a confusion and waiting as there was for the loads of the officers and clerks who were coming with us! Some of the loads were enormously heavy, others were absurdly light, the officers were too lazy to take the trouble to equalize them. One saw a great load of pots, kettles and pans, heavy enough for two men to carry; and another basket containing only a lantern and a pipe. The two equally divided would have made two fair loads, but Emin's people never thought of that.

The officers looked at me with intense surprise when I fell my men in and gave each his load with my own hands—they made no attempt whatever to help me. I saw, with a feeling of amusement, that I had fallen fifty per cent. in their estimation, and that they found me only a low-caste person after all. Had I sat still and deputed someone else to do my work they would have respected me immensely.

I asked Emin to go ahead with my Zanzibari chiefs, who would lead the way, whilst I brought up the rear and looked after stray loads. Marco very kindly lent me his donkey, for my feet were sore from the long march down from Kavallis.

The Zanzibaris went along well, and after three hours, I came upon Emin and all the people, stopping for an hour's rest by a large stream at the foot of the mountains. After we had rested we began the ascent to our camping-place which was by a stream, about three-quarters of the way up the mountains.

It was now that I felt so indignant when I saw our hard-worked, faithful Zanzibaris, patiently toiling in the broiling sun up the mountain side, staggering under the weight of the heavy loads belonging to some of Emin's worthless people. They were mostly loads of rubbish which would have to be thrown away when we made our final start from Kavallis. Selim Bey, a huge fat Soudanese, a sort of mound of flesh, rode up the mountain side on a small donkey, and never got off even at the most precipitous places. I, who was below, occasionally got views of the profile of him and his donkey against the sky line, which were most ludicrous. This huge fat man, seated on his very small donkey, well over its tail, which hung down from directly beneath him, and looked as if it belonged to himself!

We got up to our camping-place in good time, and Emin and I had a bathe in the stream, and afterwards clambered about its rocky bed in search of botanical specimens. Emin saw some new treasure at almost every turn; getting up to the heights, and marking the changes in the flora, was to him an endless source of joy. I sat on a rock in the middle of the stream, and watched him with amusement, as he stumbled among the rocks, poking about everywhere with his stick, and peering inquisitively into every hole and corner with his short-sighted eyes.

We slept in the open, for we had no tents with us, and as it was a very exposed spot, the wind, which blew from the mountains, was bitterly cold.

There was considerable difficulty next morning in getting off, for some of the native carriers had run away in the night owing to the unconscionable weight of some of the officers' loads. Some of the officers even wanted to distribute the extra loads among those carried by the Zanzibaris, which were already too heavy. I heard a disturbance going on at the other end of the camp, and found some of my men loudly expostulating with some of the officers who wished to add to their loads. One of them had the impertinence to threaten a Zanzibari with a stick, but I very soon put a stop to that, and told Emin's officers these men were not our slaves but our friends; they smiled, as if I were chaffing them. By insisting on the servants of the officers carrying, and giving the rest of the loads to my Soudanese soldiers, I got them to the top of the mountain, where I was able to obtain some more native carriers from a neighbouring chief. For two months this was the sort of trouble we experienced in bringing the things of Emin's people from the lake to the plateau above.

At a river which ran about half an hour's distance from Kavalli's, we stopped, and every one bathed, and put on his best clothes. We were quite an imposing-looking caravan, with all the bright cloths, and snow-white clothes of Emin's people, as with flags flying, and trumpets playing the Khedivial hymn, we marched into our camp. So, for the second time, I had the pleasure of witnessing the meeting of Stanley and Emin.

During my absence, Stanley had had a large open shed built as a divan, and here a long palaver was held. Stanley, Emin and I, sat out after dinner talking, and we had the satisfaction of seeing Emin in our camp at last, and feeling that now we could see some chance of our prolonged stay in Africa coming to an end.

At about ten o'clock the next day, February 18th, the caravan, bringing all the loads, men and Europeans from Kandekori (the station at Ituri Ferry, which Stanley had left under the command of Stairs), was seen winding over the hills. In about an hour and a half the head of the long column entered the camp. Most of the faces of the Zanzibaris I knew, but a good many, chiefly those of the rear column, I had forgotten.

Many of them looked well, but some of them were perfect skeletons, they had never got over the starvation in the forest, and many of them still had bad ulcerated feet.

Stairs, Parke and Nelson were all looking well, I was indeed contented at seeing them again, and once more being with them.

The Expedition was now re-united for the first time since our leaving Stanley Pool. Re-united, but alas! with what sadly diminished numbers! It was sad when the men were all gathered at Kavallis, and I missed some of the well-known faces, to hear that I should never see their cheery, kindly faces again.

"Uledi," I would say, "I do not see Wadi Mabruki, where is he?" "Dead, master, dead," would be the answer. "He was drowned in the river." "And where is Markatubu?" "Dead, master, too, shot by Wa-shenzi" (natives). And so I heard, one by one, of the deaths of many of the men who had worked cheerfully with us so long, and had fed us during the days of starvation. In looking round on the faces of our men, there was scarcely one that had not done me a good turn some time or other.

Of the difficulties we afterwards experienced from the intrigues and ingratitude of Emin's people, and of our final start for Zanzibar, it is not my intention to write. Of the experiences we passed through on our way to the coast, and the discoveries made; of the patience and splendid qualities of our faithful Zanzibaris, and a hundred other events, Stanley has written, far better than I could. Throughout the months we have been together in Africa; through the darkness and misery of the forest; through starvation, uncertainty, and sickness ; and through the long march to the coast, there have been three things above all others which have kept us up, and which have enabled us to be steadfast and comparatively cheery. First, the love and interest we all had for our work. Second, the implicit trust and confidence we have ever had in our leader. And third, and I think not least, the strong friendship which has always existed between Stairs, Nelson, Parke, and myself. When starvation stared us in the face, when our faithful men fell around us, and when there seemed to be no break in the black cloud which enveloped us, these three influences cheered us on, and prevented our giving in. It was my intention only to relate my experiences in Emin's Province, as I alone of Stanley's staff could fill in this gap in the story of the Expedition.

During the time I passed in the Equatorial Province, it was my lot to see many things concerning the government and treatment of the natives which I could not too deeply deplore ; things which happened from no fault on the part of Emin, but which were owing to the miserable quality of the material with which he had to work.

The outcasts and worst characters in Egypt—men who had been transported for all kinds of horrible crimes, were the people who were sent to Emin to help him to govern a country—a vast country, containing many different tribes, which, even with good officers, would always have been difficult to rule. Its very vastness made it impossible for him to supervise such officers sufficiently, and so prevent the many iniquitous abuses, the robbery and ill-treatment of the natives from creeping in—abuses which no one hated and deplored more than did Emin himself. Yet, though I pitied him deeply for the disappointment he experienced at seeing his work of thirteen years tumbling in ruins, I could never regret the downfall of the last of the Soudan Provinces, with its corrupt Egyptian rule.

It is a beautiful country—a fertile land—and might, if properly governed, be made a magnificent and rich Province. It is lost now, but I trust it will not be lost for long. I would rather say, let us return to Central Africa, to the Equatorial Province, and build a Government there, founded on another footing than that of cruelty, robbery, and corruption. Let us raise a new Government, firmly built upon the foundation of humanity, justice, and fair trade. These are the three influences which will civilize Africa, and let in light for ever on the Dark Continent.

CONCLUSION.

Emin's unreasoning acerbity—Treatment of women on the march—Major Wissmann's letter—Emin's curious forgetfulness—Emin's attack upon Stanley—Accident to Emin—Treatment of refugees at Zanzibar—Farewell to Emin—A curious combination.

THE preceding chapters of this book were all written before the end of March, 1890; that is before Emin had taken up the unexpectedly hostile tone he has subsequently adopted towards the Expedition which was sent out to rescue him. I have endeavoured to write without mentioning several things in Emin's character which I did not think necessary to make the story intelligible. But the unexpected manner of my parting with Emin, with whom I had been intimate for many months as a guest and fellow-prisoner in his Province, and his recent utterances, call for a few parting words from me. And though many may perhaps think that these words should be uttered with their due weight of severity, yet I shall endeavour to strictly adhere to the sympathetic and friendly tone I have hitherto adopted when speaking of him.

My personal duty to the Pasha terminated when he himself had appeared at Kavalli. From thence to the East Coast of Africa I had little or nothing to do with him, except maintaining those social relations which were due to him from me as his former guest and fellow-traveller. Scarcely a day passed but we met and exchanged kindly greetings, and often when work was over I proceeded to his quarters in the camp to enjoy an afternoon chat. I was a silent witness of what transpired at the Kavalli camp, but all those incidents have been sufficiently described by Mr. Stanley, and I was grieved to find that the idol of my imagination was not quite equal to my cherished expectations. We had fancied that once free from the onerous responsibilities of his position he would show himself in a more favourable light, that while not forgetting his rank and dignity, he would avail himself of the opportunity to show the more amiable side of his character. He would have a chance to shine as a conversationalist, to devote himself to collecting bird and insect specimens, register his meteorological observations, dispense medicines to the refugees who were about to return with him, and act as a father to the many orphan children that accompanied him from the Province, besides proving an agreeable companion to those whose sole thought was how to be serviceable to him.

Could he have but remembered that he had also duties to perform to his people as their Governor and their protector; to his own reputation, as one who could still show—however critical some might be disposed to be—much that deserved becognition; to us of the Expedition, a little gratitude; I would not have added another word. But the Pasha, instead of doing the least of these, contented himself with collecting birds and insects, diligently noting his observations on the temperature, and writing his journals. His sick people were placed under the care of Dr. Parke, and I can remember no instance when he was otherwise than apparently indifferent to the fate of any of the women or children. He kept himself mostly indoors, as though he indulged in resentment against someone, or suffered from a settled melancholy. With his friend Casati he often affected to be strangely distant; and he was also frequently inclined to be reserved with members of the Expedition, though I never could understand the reason. He arrived at our camp loud in praise of Vita Hassan, the apothecary, but in a few weeks their relations were strained, and then broken off altogether. At first he could find no words to describe his high opinion of Shukri Aga, to whom he had given a Captain's commission, and of whom he often spoke in admiring terms; but in time Shukri Aga was left severely alone, and he never omitted to put in a word of disparagement if any of us happened to mention that he was exceptionally faithful. We were made aware also that this system of dispraise was pursued in each of our own cases. There was no person of any importance in the camp but had the misfortune to fall under his unreasonable displeasure.

However, we thought that when once we were on the move, this jealous temper would improve. And we were glad to see that it did in a day or two; but Mr. Stanley's dangerous illness at Mazamboni's, and the long stay caused by it, revived the unpleasantness in a worse form than ever. For a time it became so marked that he was altogether changed; nobody pleased him. The slightest thing provoked him to make remarks that were to say the least ungenerous. Lieutenant Stairs, who acted as the executive of the Camp during our chief's illness, came in for a fair share of the Pasha's unreasoning acerbity, and the next day it was somebody else, and so it went round.

During all the time that we were at Mazamboni's he never even spoke to Casati.

We started again, and in a few days things were better. As we drew nearer Usongora, it was proposed to the Pasha that all the young and able-bodied men of the refugees should be formed into a company, on reaching the grass land, to assist in the common defence. To this the Pasha readily consented, and he expressed his opinion frankly that it would be a wise and proper precaution.

On reaching the open country, the names of all men available for the service were taken, and they were enrolled into a company, and Shukri Aga, as the fittest officer, was appointed captain. Rifles and ammunition were then served out, and a new company, well armed and equipped, had been added to the Expedition for the common good. But without a word of warning that anything out of the way, or that any slight had been put on him, the Pasha came in an excited state to demand that his people should be restored to him. He had no orderlies, and insisted on having them, he had no guards, and he would have them; he resolved that he should have four guards in front, and four in rear, two to attend to his daughter, besides two orderlies and servants for his tent, and then cried out to Mr. Stanley, "I am sorry that I ever agreed to go with you." We could not help thinking that this was most intemperate language and utterly uncalled for, because the position of himself and family on the march was always in rear of No. 1 company, and three companies immediately followed his family; while another company acted as rear-guard of the column.

Besides this, two of the most respectable Zanzibari chiefs had the honour of conveying his daughter in a hammock, and several armed porters had been detailed to help his servants to carry his luggage. The country we were now about to enter we expected would prove hostile, as it swarmed with Kabba-regga's bandits, and any moment an attack might be made on us. In such an event it was natural to expect that the able-bodied of the refugees would assist in their own defence, since we had so many rifles and so much ammunition to serve out. We were glad to hear the Pasha apologize for the warmth of his manner the next day.

I grieve to say that we saw many things on the road between the Albert and the Victoria Lakes, that we should have preferred not to have seen. We were really distressed to see the laden porters belonging to the refugees so cruelly treated by the lazy Egyptians and Soudanese. We could not help being witnesses to many atrocious acts. Then the callousness with which the women of the party were treated, shocked and angered us greatly, so that frequently I and the other officers were compelled to interfere. Poor women, young girls from twelve or thirteen, with ulcered limbs, heated with fever, and footsore, would be seen miles away from the column, loaded down with sheer rubbish, that neither had value nor use for anyone. A word from the Pasha, backed sternly by our force, would have relieved these poor creatures of the agony they endured, and would have saved many lives. But the Pasha never could, or would, give such an order, and unless we desired a rupture with him, it was unwise for us to interfere openly; though scarcely a day passed but one of us attempted to hint to him that it would be advisable for him to exercise his authority. Many a time, however, we took it upon ourselves to toss the rubbish from the bearer's head, as we saw the poor thing about to yield under the weight. Had the Pasha, however, insisted at an early period that every superfluous article, however valuable or ornamental it was, should be discarded, I feel sure that our chief and my fellow-officers would have considered it as the most humane act possible, and I do not think I am exaggerating when I say that we should have arrived at the coast with a hundred more refugees.

Excepting these unsightly incidents, which happened too often for our peace of mind, I know of nothing unpleasant between the Pasha and any of our party, from the Equator to the coast. At the end of every day's march we exchanged visits, and frequently gifts of prepared food, and all was pleasant and amiable as between friends. He may have nourished many resentful thoughts, as I think his peculiar disposition was most prone to do, but at least I can say that they never found expression, otherwise we should have heard of them. I am now inclined to think from what I hear Pére Shyntz has written, that he must have confided some of these fanciful grievances to him, but what remedy could be applied to them, when all of us were ignorant of their existence? Speaking for myself, I am utterly unaware of any offence having been given, and at Mackay's table he publicly acknowledged that everything had been done for him that the best of friends could have suggested, or that he could have wished.

While we were in Ugogo, he received a letter from Major Wissmann which he showed to one of us. There was a sentence in it that was very significant. It said: "It is true that the English have sent you a relief Expedition to bring you out, but I hope you will believe that your countrymen would have been just as ready to do what the English have done. I hope that when you reach Bagamoyo you will allow us to offer you the hospitality which you deserve, and remember that whatever the English have done for you, we, the Germans, are your countrymen."

One of my fellow-officers, upon hearing the contents of the letter, ventured upon the following bold expression, which has since turned out to be a true prediction. "I can see what Wissman intends to do, he intends to get hold of the Pasha for the German company. All I can say is, that from what we have seen of Emin during the last few months, it is the best thing which could possibly happen for the English company, for the Pasha is bound to make a mess of any thing he puts his hand to."

I was inclined to be of the same opinion, and yet I was fain to believe from what I thought I knew of Emin's kind and considerate heart, that he never would be capable of taking up the position he has of late.

That Emin should have preferred to take service with his countrymen is not unnatural, even though he had frequently said that his one wish was to take service with the English, to whom he had appealed for assistance, and who (he was pleased to say) had answered his appeal so generously. It must be remembered, too, that before the Expedition for his relief had been thought of, Emin had written to his friends in England, saying that the Egyptian government he knew was too weak to rescue him; that his own countrymen were indifferent to him; but that he looked to England to be true to her humanitarian traditions and help him in his need.

We reached the coast, and among the many congratulatory telegrams Emin received on his arrival at Bagamoyo, was one from a well-known philanthropic English lady, who had subscribed largely to the relief fund, offering him a home for himself and his daughter for as long a period as was convenient to him. He answered briefly that he would write, but from that day to this she has heard no more of him.

It has often struck me that Emin suffered from a singular defect of memory. Most of us could furnish many instances of this curious malady. The book lately published, called " Emin Pasha in Central Africa," reminds me of several. It will be found that he has long been in the habit of writing, " I purpose to-morrow to do this, or I am going shortly to travel to such and such a place, or I am going next week to, or I hope to visit within a few days chief so and so;" but it is a certain fact that Emin almost invariably forgot to do what he thought of, or proposed doing. He proposed to visit the south end of the lake to search for our Expedition; he proposed to take service with the English; he proposed to furnish us with his meteorological observations at Kavallis, for which he obtained his instruments; he proposed, with great emotion, to present each officer of the Expedition, on parting, with a small souvenir;

he proposed to read a paper before the Royal Geographical Society, and to present himself before the Emin Committee of Relief to express his gratitude; and a hundred other things, but owing to his habit of forgetfulness he has failed to carry into effect any one proposition.

I was first made aware of this curious malady by the following grotesque instance, which at the time affected me uncomfortably.

On the morning after our first meeting at M'swa, I was admiring a chair on which I was seated, and said that I thought it was a most comfortable one, upon which Emin remarked, " Yes, it is a very good chair. I am indebted to Gordon Pasha for it. He gave it to me with many kind words at Khartoum, the last time I parted from him." But in the afternoon while he was talking to me about Gessi Pasha, he said, "And before he went down the Nile for home, he presented me with many things which he did not care to take with him, and among them was that very chair on which you are sitting." As the chair had become an object of considerable interest to me, since it had been associated with the name of Gordon, I was greatly taken aback at this, and wondered for some time what could be the meaning of this singular incorrectness. However, after a bit, I put it down to forgetfulness. This is only one small instance of the many examples we have had of this strange habit of Emin. I prefer to call it forgetfulness.

Here is another example in the shape of a paragraph which appeared in the *Pall Mall Gazette* of August 22nd, 1890 :—

"A Fresh Attack on Stanley by Emin Pasha.

"*Details of Negotiations with Wissmann.*

"Writing from Mpwapwa, in June last, to a friend in Germany, Emin Pasha, giving an account of the circumstances which accompanied his retirement from the Egyptian and his entrance into the German service in Africa, makes a fresh attack on Mr. Stanley. The Berlin correspondent of the *Standard* sends the following translation of Emin's letter:—

"'On the day after my unlucky fall, Stanley made my people embark under a threat that otherwise he would lay them in chains, and he caused them to be taken to Mombasa, *via* Zanzibar, without allowing them to communicate with me in any way. An Egyptian steamer I had asked for arrived, but got its orders from Stanley, and took my people to Suez without my being permitted to see one of them again. I myself received letters and messages which I can only call inappropriate. I lay suffering from a fracture of the skull, and could not write. During my stay in the hospital, Wissman showed himself my friend in the most magnanimous manner. You know that we were all penniless when we reached the coast. The Egyptian Government has never asked whether I needed anything, or troubled itself about me, except some amiable inquiries of the Khedive as to my health, for which I am, of course, bound to feel very grateful to him personally, the answers to which, however, cost much money, and I had none.

"'When I was staying with Mackay I had bought

a riding ass with saddle, a suit of livery, a shirt, and boots from the French missionaries at Bukumbi, and had given them a cheque on the English Consulate-General, trusting to the fact that Nubar Pasha and Sir John Kirk had written to me officially that I was to draw bills on the latter for all my wants. At the Consulate-General the payment, one hundred and fifty-seven dollars was declined. [Here the *Kölnische Zeitung*, which prints this letter, adds the insolent footnote, 'Emin overrates the durability of English agreements.'] You can imagine what a mood I was in—anxieties about my own future, anxieties for the preservation of my people, illness, the indifference of Egypt, Stanley's invectives while I was still lying ill in the hospital. In the course of conversation, Wissmann had asked me whether I would work in future for the English, and when I told him that I should, of course, prefer to work for my Fatherland, he asked my leave to report the fact to his Majesty. I willingly allowed him to do so.

"'In repeated subsequent conversations the theme of an expedition to be sent to the interior was discussed, and when Wissmann complained that he had nobody for it, I offered myself. His Majesty had done me honour, and here was an opportunity to show myself grateful. I had then left the hospital, and gone to live in a house at Bagamoyo. Wissmann telegraphed, and permission came for the expedition, and to Wissmann's new telegrams the answer was to the effect that there was no objection to my being entrusted with the conclusion of treaties with the chiefs between the Victoria and Tanganyika

Lakes, or to my being employed as a commissioner under the proviso of my future definitive appointment. In the month of April I left Bagamoyo. Whether I shall return safe and sound this time appears to me more than doubtful. Well, God's will be done.'"

Here also is another paragraph I read in the *Times* of August 26th, 1890 :—

"Herr von Hoffmann, ex-Minister, proposed 'The Emperor,' who, he said, had personally taken the keenest interest in Dr. Peters's expedition, and he elicited no slight cheering by referring to the 'forcible abduction' of Emin Pasha by Mr. Stanley."

I would fain believe that both these paragraphs are due to Emin's forgetfulness, still, I think that they call for some answer.

That answer, will, I think, be most satisfactorily given by my relating as simply as I can, how we reached Bagamoyo and the manner of our parting with Emin; for, strangely enough, I was the last of the Expedition to part with Emin at Bagamoyo, as well as having had the honour of being the first to meet him in the Equatorial Province.

I shall never forget our feelings of triumph and satisfaction when the Expedition marched into Bagamoyo. The faces of our weary Zanzibaris lighted up with joy and thankfulness as they saw the ocean lying at their feet, and once more heard the well-known sound of its waves.

The German military band played "God save the Queen," and to the glorious tune of our National Anthem we marched into the German settlement.

Here we saw Emin safe and happy among his

Accident to Emin. 473

countrymen; our long work was finished, and we felt with a sigh of relief that at last we might relax and rest.

Most of the Europeans of Zanzibar and the neighbourhood had assembled to do Emin honour, and to greet him with cordiality—I may almost say—with reverence.

At the dinner which Major Wissmann and the German officers gave in honour of Emin, the utmost cordiality existed between everyone. And when Emin made a speech in the kindest and most graceful manner, the enthusiasm of all was intense.

Emin came round and talked with each of us separately. He spoke of the long months he had been shut up in Central Africa, and thanked us all personally for such small help as we had each been able to give him.

He told us how he had never again expected to see such a scene as this, surrounded as he was by people each vieing with the other to do him honour. He seemed to have grown younger, and to be transformed by happiness and content.

Suddenly, in the midst of our gaiety, an ominous whisper reached us that Emin had fallen from the window, and was dead.

We hurried out, and found him senseless and bleeding on the pavement below. He was carried to the hospital, where our good surgeon, ever ready when needed, attended him; while we retired to the houses prepared for us, to brood dejectedly over the sad termination of our happy day.

The next day our surgeon gave a more favourable

report of Emin's condition, though he said the case was most serious.

Large bales of clothes, gay-coloured handkerchiefs and cloths, tabooshes, boots, and cooking utensils had been sent over from Zanzibar by the orders of the Relief Committee; sacks and baskets of bread, and food of all sorts, had also arrived.

These we distributed among the refugees who had arrived in a tattered and shabby condition. The camp was soon transformed into a gay and busy scene, and preparations for a feast were begun by the servants; while their mistresses and the heads of the families formed themselves into groups apart, and with fresh satisfaction they compared their new clothes and talked contentedly of their marching days over, or of their meeting with their friends in Egypt.

The German and English navies were lying anchored in the roads, all gaily dressed from stem to stern with flags and pendants. They had arrived to transport us in triumph to Zanzibar. It had been agreed that Emin should go in the English man-of-war *Turquoise*, which should lead the way, followed by the German man-of-war *Sperber*, with Mr. Stanley on board. The other vessels, German and English, were to follow with our officers and men, and to sail in a long triumphal procession to Zanzibar.

On the morning of the 6th, however, our surgeon informed Mr. Stanley that Emin could not be moved for many days.

It was impossible for the ships to wait for so long a time, especially as our refugees were anxious to be on their way to Egypt; so leaving with Emin all his servants and orderlies, we embarked, and reached Zanzibar the same afternoon. Here we found that General Mathews, the head of the Sultan's troops, and his right-hand man, had prepared the old British Consulate for the reception of the refugees. We had assigned to each family comfortable and roomy quarters, and then food, which the general's people had ready in huge cooking-pots, was served out to the entire force of refugees.

Here the refugees remained for six days, and became strong and well by reason of the good food and entire rest.

Soon, however, complaints of drunkenness and rioting on the part of the refugees came to the ears of the Consul-General, who deemed it advisable to transport them to Mombassa. Here they would be far removed from the temptations which existed in the town of Zanzibar, and might quietly await the arrival of the Egyptian steamer, for which Mr. Stanley had written to the Egyptian Government when we reached the Victoria Lake.

Whilst we were in Zanzibar several plans were formed by the Consul-General, Mr. Stanley, and ourselves for visiting Emin at Bagamoyo, and a vessel was actually got in readiness for our use. But for some unaccountable reason we were always prevented from doing so by some fresh report of a relapse in Emin's condition.

Our good surgeon, Dr. Parke, while nursing Emin, had himself been stricken down by a malignant fever, so that we were entirely dependent on the German doctors for news of Emin's condition.

On the arrival of the Khedive's steamer *Mansourah*

at Zanzibar, the captain, finding that Emin was still at Bagamoyo, reported himself to the Consul-General and to Mr. Stanley. The steamer was then sent over to Bagamoyo with Mr. Stairs on board, the captain having orders to report himself to Emin and take his orders. Mr. Stairs visited Emin in company with the captain of the *Mansourah*, and remained with him some hours. Emin expressed himself anxious to leave Bagamoyo, but said he was afraid yet awhile to attempt to move from the hospital. The steamer then proceeded to Mombassa, and the refugees were embarked by Mr. Stairs, and the steamer left the next day for Suez.

Before leaving Zanzibar, Dr. Parke, who was still in the hospital, urged me to go over to Bagamoyo and try to persuade Emin to accompany us to Egypt in the mail steamer *Katoria*, which had now arrived, and was to take us to Suez; for he said a sea voyage would be Emin's salvation.

On the morning of December 28th, I went over to Bagamoyo and remained with Emin till the next day. He seemed delighted to see me, and asked why we had not been over oftener to see him, for he said, "You know, though the Germans are my countrymen, I can never think of them in the same friendly way as I think of you, of the Expedition who have rescued me, and who have been through such dangers and difficulties with me."

I told him that several times we had proposed to come over to see him, but that we were either told by the doctors that he had had a relapse, and that it was inadvisable to see him, or that there were no German steamers available.

He seemed to be extremely angry when he heard this, and spoke most sharply to Captain Rieklemann, the commandant of Bagamoyo, who had accompanied me to the hospital.

I sat long with Emin that day and talked with him. I told him that Parke had said that if he could be carried on board the mail steamer, and accompany us, he would be well before we got to Suez.

Emin shook his head and sadly replied, "I know it, and I wish I could go with you, but I cannot."

It was no use urging him after that; but we sat and talked of the experiences we had passed through together, of his future, and that of the little Farida. Emin seemed overcome by a profound melancholy; he complained of the noisy position of the hospital, surrounded as it was by native shops, and several other things which annoyed him, he repeated how he wished he was going with us, but again said sadly that he could not.

He asked me to give him the addresses of each of my fellow-officers, for he said, "I have prepared for each some little souvenir which I trust you will all keep as a remembrance of the days we passed through together."

In parting he held my hand in both his, and told me how deeply grateful he was for what we had done for him. He said, "You I shall never forget, for you have been my companion and friend through those months of our imprisonment together, those months which were the worst months of my life."

It seemed as if he was taking a long good-bye, and profoundly touched by the inexpressible sadness of his tone, I once more urged him to come with us. Again he shook his head and said it was impossible, so I sadly bade him good-bye and returned to Zanzibar.

From Zanzibar, Aden, and Egypt I have written to him, but from that day to this I have had no word from him.

That Emin meant all that he said to me about the Expedition during those last few hours I was with him, I am absolutely certain. His simple words of friendship and touching manner were, I am convinced, sincere. But a will stronger than his own must have compelled him to act against his better nature, or he never could have taken up the attitude he has against us.

His natural kindliness, coupled with a weakness of character, were no match for the strong will which ever seemed urging him to act against his better nature, leading him to do things which he never would have done if left to himself. Insinuations must have been whispered in his ears; ungenerous motives must have been attributed to all that we did; his poor, quick sensibility must have been played upon by that master will, until Emin, stung to madness by the taunts and inuendos of his "friends," took that fatal step which has hurled him down from the pedestal of sympathy and admiration upon which he stood.

On reading these constant ebullitions of spite on Emin's part, I sometimes feel a certain amount of indignation, but it quickly develops into a feeling of pity.

For, from my long and close intercourse with Emin, I feel sure, when he thinks of the events of the last two and a half years, that he must burn with shame and regret for the ill-advised course he has of late pursued.

How much pain and unhappiness for himself might Emin have prevented had he acted with the same simple straightforwardness he invariably received from us. I ought perhaps to conclude this chapter with a finely rounded moral, but I am not much given to moralizing.

I have merely in this book told my story plainly, and have endeavoured to place before my readers a picture of Emin Pasha.

A man with a kindly and generous mind, physically courageous, but morally a coward.

A clever accomplished gentleman, enthusiastic for the science of natural history, but not of that firm temper required to lead men, or of that disposition to attract and sway them.

A man whose natural kindness of heart is being constantly spoilt by his delicate susceptibility and childlike vanity.

A man whose straightforward European directness and accuracy has been warped by a too long residence among Orientals.

And yet too, if you appeal to his generosity, he will always meet you more than half-way. Emin would always be to a certain extent subject to the influence of those by whom he was surrounded.

Here I leave him, with a feeling of sincere affection for him, by reason of his many kindnesses to me during those hard times when we lived intimately together, when there seemed no hope for us, and our only comfort was our mutual sympathy.

But I cannot do otherwise than express my great surprise and regret at Emin's extraordinary conduct ever since his unfortunate accident at Bagamoyo, conduct which has deeply offended many sincere friends. But the first feeling of indignation passed, I only feel a profound pity for a man who could sacrifice all feelings of gratitude and friendship to a causeless resentment.

Emin can dream noble things, but he cannot act them, because, unfortunately, he is nearly always below his best self.

> "Unless above himself he can
> Uplift himself, how poor a thing is Man."

THE END.

...بالاعیان ولیس بعد
...یں حکمداریہ وما معہ نہ
...س انگلیزیر فتلوہ و

MAH
...sha demar
...by was m
...ahim, son
... or se
...and of
...ce.———

INDEX.

ABAMBOLA Mountain, 372.
Abderrahim, Osman Latif's son, 255, 345.
Abdul Bain Aga, 329.
Abdullah (orderly), 173-4, 281-2.
Abdullah Aga el Apt, 154.
Abdullah Aga Manzal, chief of Muggi Station, 97-8. 110, 113, 118-9, 122-4, 266; death of, 286; 352.
Abdullah Vaab Effendi, 195-9, 220; death of, 286-7; 327.
Abdul Wahab Effendi (Lieut.), 41-2, 233, 412.
Abu Soud Bey & Mahdi, 249.
Achmet Aga Dinkaue, 154, 163, 165, 184, 202, 207, 208, 264, 335, 343-7.
Achmet Aga el Assinti, 328.
Achmet Effendi Mahmoud, 41-2, 103, 163, 353.
Achmet Effendi Raif, 234, 313-4.
Advance steel boat 2; 3-14, 185; broken up, 320-1; 446, 447, 454.
A-fi-fi, see *Dwarfs.*
Africa, trade and goods in, 301.
Agricultural implements of Bari tribe, 132.
Akka, see *Dwarfs.*
Albert Lake, arrival at, 2; and steel boat, 3; scenery about, 8-9; water of, 10; rapid falling of, 40-1; Sir S. Baker and, 116-7; at Tunguru, 354, 442; scenery of the shores, 425, 427; Zanzibar and, 449.
Al-ed-Din Pasha, Mahdi and, 249.
Ali Achmet (*Nyanza* S.S), 328.
Ali Aga Djabor, 43, 102-3, 153, 172, 175-6, 180, 183-4, 221, 235, 255, 260, 275, 277, 286, 288, 327.
Ali Aga el Kourdi, 345. 347.
Ali Aga Shamruk of Rejaf, 172, 174, 255, 260.
Amadi Station, 305.
Amadji, Chief, 58.

Anthropological specimens, Emin's, 62-3.
Antinori, Marquis, and bustards, 119.
Arab dinner, an, 86-7.
Arabi's rebellion, 43, 69, 421; and Abdullah Vaab Effendi, 195.
Arif Effendi, (clerk), 149, 159, 446-7.
Arms, etc., musket of Kaba-regga's, 36, Bari bows and arrows, 101-2, 120-1, 317; knives of Monbuttu, 70, 121; Dwarf spears, 121, bows and arrows, 373; spears of Dervishes, 244.
Aruwimi River, Emin and, 24-5; natives of upper, 302; and *Advance* boat, 320.
Aveysheba natives, 302.
Award Effendi, 338.
Ayu River, 90; the ford of, 93, 156.

BABADONGO, General, 434.
Bachit (Soudanese orderly), 173; (sheik), 286.
Bachit, Mahmoud, 327.
Bachit Aga, Chief of Kirri Station, 99, 100, 105; Emin and, 108-10; at Dufilé. 172, 328, 341, 343-7, 352; wife, 447.
Bagamoyo, Emin at, 468, 470, 471-6.
Bahr-el-Ghazal Province, Gessi and, 196, 305; and Lupton, 361-2.
Baker, Sir Samuel (or Mlidju), and S.S. *Khedive*, 28-9, and Lady Baker's work in the province, 65-6; and Faratch Aga, 65-6, 68-71; and Dufilé Station, 81-3; whale-boats, etc., brought by, 84; and Taha Mahomet, 116; and the Latooka rain-maker, 143; and northern stations, 235; 303.
Banalya, rear column at, 390, 402.
Bari tribe; and hunting of crocodiles, 73-4, 209; country of. 96; women, 96-9; villages of, 98, 120-1,

123; ornaments of women, 99-100; bows and arrows, 101-2; manners, customs, etc., 125-144; physique of, 125-6; ornaments of men and women, 126-7; tattooing, 127-8; fines for offences, 128; warfare and weapons, 129-30; hunting, 130; huts and villages, 130-2; polygamy, 132; dogs, cats, and cattle, 132-5; alimentation, 135-6; tobacco, etc., 136-7; cookery, 137-8; relations between married people, 238; ceremonies about child-birth, 138-9; marriage, 139-140; diseases, 140; funeral ceremonies, 140-1; superstitions, 140-2; office of rain-maker, 142-4; Chief Béfo, 261, 266; Emin and, 285, 287; girdles, 317; 329.

Baring, Sir E., and Emin's relief, 399.
Barttelot, Major, 18, 31, 169, 390, 398, 402-3.
Basilli Effendi, 338.
Batwa, or Wattua, see *Dwarfs.*
Béfo, Chief, 260-1.
Beilefonds, Linant de, 93.
Beresford, Lord, and the *Safia*, 258.
Bible, Jephson and the, 386-7.
Bidden Station, 102; rebel officers from, 165; garrison of, 260, 266, 346.
Bilinian mountain, 261.
Billal Aga Dinkaue, letter from, 343-7, 445, 450.
Binza, servant boy, 33, 50-1, 119, 121, 147, 150, and Emin's Soudanese, 152, 307; 168, 174-5, 186; and wife, 225-6; and *Advance* boat, 320-1; description of, 321-2; 394, 397, 405, 422, 437, 443; wife, 447.
Birth, an extraordinary, 187-8.
Boa, 242, 261.
Boat-building at Dufilé, 84.
Boganza, Chief, 11.
Boki, Chief, 55; and wife, 55-6; village of, 337, 363-4, 380; death of, 382.
Bombé tribe, 272.
Bongo tribe, 52.
Bonny, Mr., 390, 442.
Bora Station, 78, 290, 315-6, 336.
Bordein, steamer, 257-8.
Boru tribe, 52.
Botany, etc., Emin and, 456; fig-trees, 23, 81, 385; Palmyra palms, 78, 80; borassus palms, 216; corn, millet, etc., at M'swa, 22; near Tunguru, 55; at Wadelai, 64; at Dufilé, 84-5; cotton at M'swa, 22-3; at Laboré Station, 95; acacia, 30, 54, 55-6, 59, 61, 90; and tamarind trees, 30, 38; tobacco, 425-6; jasmine, 56-7; lime and orange trees, 61; red dhurra corn, etc., of Bari tribe, 135-6; sesame, 64; banana, 425-6.
British Museum, Emin and letter from, 34; skulls for, 62-3; birds for 318, 448.
Brown (Mrs.) on, "*Cleopatra's Needle*," 222-3.
"Bubarika," see *A. J. M. Jephson.*
"Bula Matari," see *Stanley.*
Bumbireh, Uledi and, 7.
Burgoot, 341.

CAMERON's travels, 222.
Cannibalism among Dwarfs, 374.
Canoe accident in Nile, 278-9.
Canoes of Bari tribe, 130.
Casati, Captn., and Kaba-regga, 18-19. 35; meeting with Jephson, 24, and Stanley, 29; and rebellion in Emin's Province, 44-5; 193-6, 201, 202, 207-9, 215-6, 223-5, 227-9; 266, 276, 286, 307, 310-3, 331, 338-9, 341, 355; and dwarfs, 367, 371-2; 387, 394, 396, 400, 406-7, 410, 446, 448, 451, 453; Emin and, 463-4.
Cascades, into Lake Albert, 9-10.
Cataracts of the White Nile, 77.
Cattle, 12, 54, 123, 280; of Bari tribe, 133-5.
Chinese, Emin and, in Africa, 302.
Chor Abdul Aziz, 329.
Chor-Ayu Station, 90, 93, 101, 151, 152-7; 315, 329.
Chor Itteen, 327.
Christmas Day at Tunguru, 355-6.
Circassian tinker at Dufilé, 162.
Claverhouse, superstition about bullets, 267-8.
Cloth-making at M'swa Station, 22-3.
Cock-crowing, elephants and, 92.
Colobus monkey, 387-8.
Congo River, Emin and, 25.

Index. 483

Cooking of the Bari tribe, 137–8.
Copyright Law, Stanley and, *Preface*, ix.
Council of rebel officers, 173–180, 210–222, 224, 240, 364–5, 376–7, 379, 384, 408–9.
Crocodiles, 41; in the Nile, 72–3, 78, 130, 192, 209, 279, 337, 433; and Bari tribe, 73–4, 209.
Customs; wedding, 74; grain tax, 123; to welcome with honour 79; greeting, 224, 427; see also *Bari tribe*.

Dance of the Lur tribe, a, 38–40, 106; of Makraka tribe, 106.
Darwin, and African dogs, 133.
Dervishes, the Peacock, 242–5; questioned, 256–9; torture of, 262–4, 269–71.
Dgaden Aga, 260.
Dinka tribe, 52, 96, 284; clubs of, 129; rebellion, 261.
Diseases, epidemics, etc., of Bari tribe, 140; pneumonia in Wadelai, 295–6.
Dogs of Bari tribe, 132–3.
Domestic animals of Bari tribe, 132–3.
Donagla, at Rejaf, 265; bullets of, 267; at Dufile, 269; 272, 276, 286–7, 296–7, 303–7, 319, 327–31; in Dufile, 332–6, 339–40, 353, 356, 378, 406, 450.
Dongola, 51; people of, 199.
Dowel Beyt Aga from Rejaf, 172, 343–7.
Dufilé Station, ivory at, 76; start for, 77–8, arrival at, 79–80; description of, 81–5; plan of, 82; departure from, 90; compared to Laboré, 95; stations north of, 100, 110; news from, 152; Emin in, 190; rebellion at, 154–7; entry into, 158–63, 205–8; people of, 243; defences of, 259, 261, 268–9, 261, 274–5, 290, 294, 305–6, 315–6, the Donagla in, 332–6, 340; fight at, 343, 347–8, 352–3, 356; evacuated, 362–4.
Dwarfs, bows and arrows of, 102, 373; in Monbuttu, 201, 367–74, names of, 368–9; settlements, 369; and game, 371; colour and measurement of, 374–5; weapons of, 373; cannibalism, 374–5.

Dwellings, between Tunguru and Wadelai, 54–5; houses at Dufilé, 80; of Bari tribe, 120, 130–1; in Uganda, 302.

Effendina, see the *Khedive*.
Egyptian officers and clerks, 44–5, 69, 85–6; letters to, 45–51; decision of. 51–3; 175, 199–200, 209, 210, 308; and dervishes, 263–4, 270–1; 377, 418, 441, 465.
Emin Pasha (or Mlidju), and Mr. Jephson, Preface, xi. to xiv.; and Mr. Stanley, vi. to ix.; first communication from, 2, 5; and Chief Vaju, 7–8; and Chief Mogo, 11–13; at Tunguru, 14; Mr. Holmwood and, 17–18, 27; and rescue of Captain Casati, 19; letter from, 20–1; meeting with Jephson, 23–7; note-book, 26; and the Relief Expedition, 26–7; steamers, 28–9; meeting with Stanley, 29–30; and entomology, 34; attack on Kibero, 35–7; and Chief Ouma, 37–8; and the smell of different tribes, 40; and Tunguru Station, 40–1; and two Egyptian clerks, 41–2; and the 1st Battalion at Rejaf, 43–5, 66; letters to, 45–51; and Nubar Pasha, 53; depart for Wadelai, 53–9; and Boki's wife, 55–6; headquarters, 60–1; daughter, 61; meteorological observations, 62; anthropological specimens, 62–3; and the Galla tribe, 63; and fever, 65; illness of, 67; European opinion of, 70; and deputation from Rejaf, 70–2, 74–6; 105–10; and crocodiles in the Nile, 73; ivory, 76; and Dufilé Station, 79–80; and Hawashi Effendi, 85–9, 222, 254; and elephants, 91–2; and geese, etc., 92; and Khamis Aga, 93; a, Kirri, 100; and Hamad Aga, 100–1· 106–7; and Ali Aga Dgabor, 102–3, and Bachit Aga, 108; and hrs story, 111–13; and Rejaf soldiesit 114–6, 118; and Taha Mahomet, 116–8; orderlies, 121; at Muggi Station, 122–4; and Bari tribe, 125; and the Latooka rain-maker, 143; at Laboré Station, 145–52; orderly, 154, 155–6; position at

I i 2

Index.

Dufilé, 160-3; imprisonment at, 162-90; letter to Stanley, 170-1; rebel council and. 180-3, 212-16; treachery of Emin's people, 189, 203; at Dufilé, 207; books, 222-3; orderlies, 226; and rebel officers, 227, 230-2; and Osman Latif, 233-4; Omar Saleh's letter to, 245-56; to be reinstated, 275-6; and his soldiers, 283-5, 303; released, 288-90; at Wadelai, 292-300; boxes, 299; soldiers and, 307-14, 334; flight from Wadelai, 318; letters to, 340; Drs. Felkin and Junker, 341-3; and birds, 353-4, 367; and Jephson on Christmas Day, 355-6; and Lupton Bey, 358-62; and dwarfs, 367, 372, 393-7; letter to Stanley, 406, 409; good-bye to, 410; Jephson's letter to, 417-20; Stanley's letter to, 388, 400-2, 404, 443; letter to, 444; from 446-8; and Jephson, 457, 459, 461-80; and botany, 456.
Entomology, Emin and, 34, 462; butterflies, 57; mosquitos, etc., 58, 78, 134, 192, 352, 366, 383, 450; plague of flies (ticks, etc.), 280, 298, 383; fleas, 339.
Equatorial Province, soldiers of, 14-15; letters to, 45-51; Dr. Felkin and, 25; intriguers at Tunguru, 41-3; 1st and 2nd Battalions at Rejaf, 43-5, 66-7, 100; unfriendly small tribes, 93; officers, &c., at Kirri, 103-5; and the Mahdi, 153; rebellion in, 199-200; books of, 212, 347; corrupt state of, 236-9, 240; soldiers of, 282-5, 349, 459-60.
Ethnology: Zanzibaris and African dialects, 7-8; dwarfs of Central Africa, 368, 372.
Europeanizing the negroes, 299-302.

Fabbo Station, 154; mutineers from, 161, 163-7; 264, 274, 315, 329, 335, 336, 346-7, 364.
Fadl el Mulla Aga, 154-5; and Selim Aga, 156, 163-7; letters to, 168; and Rejaf rebel officers, 172-3, 175-85; brother, 198-9, 207-8; and rebel council, 211-15, 218-21, 223-6, 229-34, 236, 243, 245, 254, 259, 264, 266, 274, 276, 280-1, 288-9, 343; letter from, 343-7, 364, 385, 409, 421.
Farajala (soldier), 280-1.
Faratch Aga, Lady Baker and, 65-6; sent to Emin, 66-72, 74-6, 172, 249, 255.
Farida, Emin's daughter, 61, 187, 204-5, 233, 318, 447, 449, 465, 477.
Fatiko Station, 235.
Felkin, Dr., Preface, xii.; description of Emin, 24; and province, 25, 341-2.
Fischer, Dr., and Emin's relief, 49.
Fishing, Bari tribe and, 130.
Forest near M'swa Station, 40.
Fort Bodo, 2, 18, 32-3, 67-8, 87-8, 97, 145, 259, 302, 316, 339, 389, 392.
Funeral ceremonies of Bari tribe, 140; of the Kirri clerk, 209.

Galla Tribes, 63.
Gebel Wati Mountain, 305-7, 336.
Geology: near Kirri Station, 98; near Dufilé Station, 158-9.
Germany, and the negroes, 299-302; Emin and, 476.
Gessi and Dufilé Station, 81-3; and Taha Mahomet, 117; and Casati, 196; Emin and, 469.
Gladstone, Mr., compared to Gordon, 99.
Gondar and Mahdi forces, 250.
Gordon, Gen., and stations at North end Lake Albert, 40, 93, 235; killed, 49; and Dufilé Station, 79, 81-3; favourite spot at Kirri Station, 99; and Taha Mahomet, 117; and the grain tax, 123; and treachery, 189-190; stations in Unyoro, 235, 249, 250; steamers, 257-8, 260; and his soldiers, 284; and Chinese in Africa, 302-3; and Soudanese, 350; and grain tax, 382; Emin and, 469.
Grain tax, the, 123, 379, 381-2.
Granaries of Bari tribe, 132.
Graphics at Dufilé, 223.
Grass fires, 385-6.
Greeting, mode of, 424, 427.
Grenfell, Gen., and Khedive's letter, 153.
Gubat, 258.

Hadji Fatma, 204, 291-2.
Hamad Aga, Major of 1st Battn., 66,

Index. 485

69-72, 74-6; and dinner by Hawashi Effendi, 86-9; Emin and, 100-2; letter from, 106-7; letter to, 153; at Dufilé, 172, 175, 198, 219-20, 223-5, 227-9, 242, 260, 274, 315-6, 347; death of, 286, 327.
Hamid Bey Mahomet, 344-5.
Hassan Aga, 149.
Hassan Effendi Lutvi, letter from, 272-3; death of 286, 327.
Hawashi Effendi (of Dufilé Station), 81-9; letters from, 116, 152, 154-5, 156; a prisoner, 164-7, 172-3, 177, 212; and rebel council, 216-22, 226, 229, 232-4, 240, 254, 267, 273-4, 280, 338, 343, 347, 406.
Herodotus and Dwarfs, 368.
Hicks Pasha and the Mahdi, 249.
Holmwood, Mr., Consul-General of Zanzibar, and Emin, 17, 27.
Huts of Bari tribe, 131-2.

Ibrahim Aga (chief of the irregulars), 51, 198, 233.
Ibrahim Effendi Elham, 266-7, 276, 344-7.
Id el Kebir, Mohammedan festival, 152, 160.
Imandé, 307.
Insects, &c.: black ants, 56; mosquitos, 58, 78, 134, 192, 353, 366, 383, 450; beetles, 62.
Islands in River Nile, floating, 77-8.
Ismail Aga, 111, 113.
Ismail Pasha and Sir Samuel Baker, 28-9.
Ismailia steamer, 257-8.
Ituri River, 194, 307, 356; Ferry camp, 391, 394, 396, 442, 451.
Ivory stores, Emin's, 75; stores at Wadelai, 203; 446, 447, 457.

Jameson, Mr., 18, 390, 398, 403.
Jephson, A. J. M., or "Bubarika," and steel boat, 3; at Kanama village, 6-8; and baboon, 11; at Magunga village, 11-13; at M'swa Station, 13-27; clothes, 16, 26; luggage, 17; letter to Mr. Stanley, 20; meeting with Emin and Casati, 23-7; and N'sabe Camp, 30; decision to accompany Emin to his Province, 30-3; and Chief Ouma, 37-8; and fever, 40-1, 53, 65, 93, 180, 186-7, 356, 383, 387; and intriguers at Tunguru, 41-3; and Stanley's letter, 50; departure for Wadelai, 53-9; and River Nile, 57; at Wadelai, 60-5, 75-6; and deputation from Rejaf Station, 66-72; and Hawashi Effendi, 85-9; and ornithology, 96; at Kirri and Muggi Stations, 98-111; chat with Emin, 111-3; address to Rejaf soldiers, 114-5; experiences at Muggi Station, 119-24; at Laboré Station, 145-52; imprisonment at Dufilé, 160-90; letter to Stanley, 170-1; before rebel council, 174, 176-80, 216; start from Wadelai, 182-6, 188; at Tunguru, 192-202; and Hawashi Effendi, 219, 273-4; at Dufilé, 223; and Osman Latif, 234; and Vita Hassan, 237-8; and Fadl el Mulla, 266; and defence of Dufilé, 268-9; letter to Stanley, 277-8; and Emin, 307-313, 341; flight from Wadelai, 317-9; and journals, 322; 323-6, 330; and Emin, 259, 377-9; and Stanley's letters, 388-400, 404; 415-6; letter to Emin, 417-20; and Chief Vunja, 423-4, 426, 431-3; natives and looking-glass, 435-6, 437; and Stanley, 443-6; letter from Emin, 446-8; meeting with, 449, 452-5; and Emin, 461-480.
Junker, Dr., and the Nepoko River, 24-5; Emin and ——'s cigars, 25-6; and servant-boy Binza, 33; and revolt of the 1st Battalion, 44, 341, 343; and Hawashi Effendi, 219; and Osman Latif, 229; and Emin, 299, 309.

Kaba-regga, King of Unyoro, and Captain Casati, 18-19, 35, 196, 453; and our letters, 27; attack on, 35-37; and Chief Ouma, 37; and natives, 55; Boki and letter for, 55-6; 168, 363-4, 380-1; and Boki, 382-3; 420-1, 433-7, 465.
Kabobs, dish of, 57.
Kajalf, Chief Mogo's son, 12-13.
Kanama village, 6-8, 430.
Kandekori, 457.
Katonza's, 412-3, 417, 431, 433-8, 450, 454.

Katoria, S.S., 476.
Katto, Kavalli's brother, 5-6, 9.
Kavalli, Chief and village, 2; brother, 5-6; and Emin's letter, 11; 194, 302, 339, 377-8, 387, 394, 397, 401, 418, 434, 436, 438, 453-4, 457, 462.
Kavirondo, Stanley, Emin, and, 53.
Keremallah, the Mahdi's General, defeated, 70, 250; Emin's letter to, 255; and Emin, 334; 305; Lupton and, 362.
Khamis Aga (chief of Chor Ayu station), 93.
Khartoum, the fall of, 40, 43, 49, 164, 235; and River Nile, 77; Government at, 107, 112; Hawashi Effendi and, 116; cats from, 133; 241; Governor-General of, 247, 249; steamers, 256-8, 265; artisans in, 258; food in, 273, 292, 334.
Khedive, Fadl el Mulla and, 176; and Arabi, 421; and Emin, 470.
——— 's letter, the, 31, 45-7, 51; Stanley and, 48-50; and Emin's soldiers, 52; the clerk of Tunguru and, 103; read at Kirri Station, 103-5; read at Muggi, 110; read to Rejaf soldiers, 114-5; copy sent to, 153; read at Laboré, 145-6, 177-8, 214, 220-1, 392-3, 399.
Khedive, S.S., 23, 28-9, 36, 170, 277, 296, 298, 328, 385, 395, 406.
Kibero, 18; attack on, 35-7; Casati and, 196.
Kilyia and the baboon, 10-11.
Kirk, Sir J., and Emin, 471.
Kirri Station, 88-90, 98-109, 113, 165; death of clerk of, 209; 260-1, 266, 285, 346.
Kismullah, Emin's collector, 159, 161, 230.
Knees of Bari tribe, enlarged, 96-7.
Kodi Aga (chief of Wadelai Station), 75; and Emin's ivory, 76; letter from, 169, 189, 191, 203, 280-1, 296, 304, 309-10, 313, 316, 330, 338, 340, 345.
Kölnische Zeitung, Emin's letter in, 470-2.
Kyan Kondo, or Katonza's village, 397-8, 401; see also *Katonza's*.

LABORÉ STATION, arrival at, 93-5, 101; mutiny at, 145-152; 156, 165, 260, 266, 315, 327, 329, 346.
Lado Station, 43, 235, 241-2, 261, 360.
Latooka, soldiers from, 65, 116-8, 122, 242, 304, 360.
Lenz, Dr., and Emin's relief, 49; and dwarfs, 368.
Leontides, Hansal and Nicola, 249.
Linant de Bellefonds killed, 93.
Lip ornaments, 58.
Loko, Chief, 260.
Looking-glass, natives and Jephson's, 435-7.
Lucas' expedition, Emin and, 83.
Lupton Bey, and blocks in River Nile, 77-8; and the Mahdi, 252; last letters of, 358—362.
Lur tribe, chiefs of, 11 (see also *Ouma*); settlements of, 21-2; a dance, 38-40; about Wadelai Station, 63-4; faces of, 126; interpreters, 191, 315; chiefs, 416, 421-2, 427, 429, 438; and dwarfs, 374-5; 444.

MABOKO'S VILLAGE, 427-8.
Mabruki, death of, 33.
Mackay, Mr., 466, 470.
Madi tribe, 52, 96, 100, 274-5, 284; villages of, at Dufilé, 85; faces of, 126; carriers, 159; chiefs, 219; interpreters, 262, 363.
Magala, Chief and village, 425-6, 443.
Magunga village, 11-13, 34, 425, 443, 448.
Magungu Station, 40, 55, 235.
Mahagi Station, 40.
Mahdi (son of Abdullah), the, 246-253.
Mahdi's forces, the, 43, 48; Emin and, 111, 118; at Boa, 152, 198, 241-3; battles of, 246-253, 257-8, 260-3; see also *Donagla*.
Mahmoud Effendi el Adeini, 102-3, 153.
Mahomet Achmet's forces; see *Donagla*.
Mahomet Ali steamer, 256.
Mahomet Effendi, 328.
Makraka Station, 43-4, 102, 153, 243, 255, 256, 261, 266-7, 274, 284, 285, 304, 305; dwarfs in, 367.

Makraka tribe, 52, 98; dance by, 106.
Mansourah steamer, 475–6.
Manyema, or Arabs, 304, 395, 408, 441–2.
Marco, Greek merchant, 61, 187–9, 191, 202–3, 322, 336, 338, 355, 387, 446, 451, 453, 455.
Masa, Mogo's brother, 416, 421–2, 424, 427, 440, 444.
Masai-land, cattle custom of, 134.
Mason Bey and Dufilé Station, 81–3.
Matches, Chief Vunja and, 423–4.
Mathews, General 475.
Mazamboni, 394, 464.
Melindwa, Chief Kajalf and, 12–13; country of, 412, 420–1, 427–9.
Metemmeh, battle of, 258.
Meteorology: Emin and, 62, 462; rain, in Central Africa, 158–9; 186, 192; wind, 192, 354, 430; extraordinary weather, 279–80.
M'Galima, King of the Dwarfs, 372.
M'Gunda Makali wilderness, 386–7.
Milan Geographical Society, Casati and, 196.
Milking custom of Bari tribe, 134.
Mlidju, see *Emin Pasha*, also *Sir Samuel Baker*.
Mogo, Chief, 11; son, 12, 13, 194, 354–5, 384, 388, 397, 416, 421.
Mohammedans, pious, 154; children, 228; funeral, 358-9.
Molotes, current coin of Africa, 227.
Mombassa, 475–6.
Mombuttu, land and tribe, 52; knives, etc., of, 70, 317, ivory in, 76, 98; Casati and, 196, 201, 304; dwarfs in, 367, 369–72, 374.
Moorajan, Sheik (Chief Priest), 66, 71, 74–6, 172, 175–6; (orderly), 173, 262, 281–2.
Moru tribe, 52.
M'pinga, chief of Gavira, 394.
M'ruli Station, 40, 235.
M'swa Station, 5; Kajalf and, 12; arrival at, 13–14; description of, 21–3, 63; start once more for, 34–5; departure from, 40, 197; clerk of, 201–2, 277; cattle of, 280; 304, 316, 339, 377, 383, 388, 405–7, 411, 443, 447, 451.
—— Mountains round Lake Albert, 425, 428.
M'tama beer, see *Pombé*.

Muggi Station, 95–7, 101, 108, 109, 113, 119–124, 165, 260, 266–7, 274–5, 281–2, 285, 315, 327, 346.
Murabo, 4; Emin and, 25.
Musical instruments of the Lur tribe, 39; of Makraka natives, 106.
Mustapha Effendi, 69, 183, 234, 254, 270, 278, 362–3.
Mustapha el Adjeini, letter from, 343–7.
Mwanga, King of Uganda, and our letters, 27.

NAMPIGUA, Chief, 11, 194; people, 431–2, 454.
Natural History, see *Botany*, *Entomology*, *Ornithology*, *Zoology*, etc.
Nava River, 372.
Necklaces, crocodile teeth, 73, 78; dogs' teeth, 127.
Negroes, chivalry in, 180; superstitions of, 268; and Germany, 299–302.
Nelson, Captain, 18, 33, 67, 239, 389, 391, 442, 458–9.
Nepoko River, Emin and, 24–5.
N'guaba, Katonza's brother, 433–9.
Niam-Niam tribe, 52, 98, 284, 304, 317, 361.
Nile, River, flowing from Lake Albert, 55; a low, 57–8; from Wadelai to Dufilé, 77, 191–2; rise and colour of, 77; at Dufilé, 83–4; boat-building on, 84; and Ayu River, 90; scenery on the banks of, 92–3, 95–6; at Muggi, 97; in 1879, 117; near Dufilé, 157–9; upsetting of canoe in, 278–9; near Wadelai, 385.
N'juju (canoe man), 416, 422.
N'sabe Camp, 30, 32–4, 67–8, 87–8, 95, 411, 431, 450.
Nubar Pasha's letter, 31, 47–8, 51; Stanley and, 48–50; Emin and, 53, 302–3, 471; rebel council and, 177–8, 214, 220–1.
Nyadué (or the Morning Star), see *Lady Baker*.
Nyamsassie Island, 5, 11, 29, 389–90, 395, 431, 433, 441, 446.
Nyanza, S.S., 29, 36, 192, 208, 277, 328, 395.

OBONGO, see *Dwarfs*.

Okello, Chief, 57-8; village of, 336-7, 364.
Omar Saleh's letter, 245-55; answered, 256, 305, 327.
Ornaments, etc.: iron and brass necklets and bracelets, 37, 100; lip, 58; of Bari women, etc., 99-101, 126-7; of dwarfs, 373.
Ornithology, Emin and, 92, 101, 112, 462; Jephson and, 96, 365-6; swallows, 101; bustards, 119; weaver birds, etc., 96, 135; fish eagle, 8-9; tame eagle, 62; hammerhead, or ovenbird, 365; kingfishers, 9; herons and water fowl, 77, 79, 80, 354, 366; guinea fowl, 54, 62, 96, 119, 440; ducks, geese, cranes, &c., 79; fowls of Bari tribe, 135; teal and duck, 298; goat suckers, or nightjars, 365-6; plovers, geese, &c., 266, 354, 433; Nile goose, 355.
Osman Adam, 250, 305.
Osman Digna and the Khedive's letter, 153, 250.
Osman Erbab, 244-5, 253, 255, 273.
Osman Latif Effendi, 220, 223, 228-9; letter to Emin, 233-4, 254, 256; son of, 255; letters from, 259-61, 264-5, 278, 314, 338.
Ostrich eggs in Dufilé mosque, 84.
Ouma, a Lur chief, 37-40, 407-8, 421-2.

Pall Mall Gazette, extract from, re Emin Pasha, 469-472.
Papyrus swamps, 78.
Parke, Surgeon, and the steel boat, 3-4, 18; meeting with Emin, 29; departure of, 33; 391, 442, 458-9, 462, and Emin, 475, 477.
Pisgah, Mount, 389.
Polygamy, Bari tribe and, 132.
Pombé, or native beer, 8, 11, 15.
Prout, and Dufilé Station, 81-3.

RAIN-MAKER, office of, to Bari tribe, 142-4.
Rajab Effendi, Emin's secretary, 149, 159, 274, 343, 446-7.
Raschid Imann and Mahdi, 249.
Rehan Aga (Major), 329.
Rejaf Station, First Battalion at, 43-5, 66-8, 88-9, 165, 168, 170-1; deputation from, 74-6, 100-2,, 105-9; rebels and Bachit Aga, 110-11; and Ismail Aga, 113; and Laboré soldiers, 150-1; Ali Aga, Djabor and, 235-6; start for, 255-6, 259; fall of, 260-1, 265-7, 274, 282, 285-7, 293; Donagla at, 450.
Religious belief among the Baris, 140-1.
Rickleman, Captain, 477.
Rimo, battle of, 334.
Royle's book on Egypt, 222, 421; and Khartoum steamers, 257-8.

Safia, steamer, 256-8.
Saleh Aga, 196, 358, 379-82, 404-6, 410.
Salim Effendi, 327.
Salt, manufacture of, at Kibero, 36-7; and Nampigua's people, 431.
Schweinfurth, and ovenbird, 365; and Monbuttu dwarfs, 368, 372-3.
Sebehr, Gessi Pasha and, 117.
Selim Aga, 94-5, 118, 145, 147, 149-52, 156, 163-6, 169-70, 175, 219-220, 225, 235, 254, 266, 268, 273, 285-8, 304, 333, 338, 341; letter from, 327-30; letter to, 343-7; 348-9, 352, 364, 384-5, 408-9, 446, 450-2, 454-6.
Shefalu tribe, 52.
Sherbet, made from palms, 78.
Shukri Aga, Chief of M'swa Station, 14, 17, 21, 167; and Kaba-regga, 18; letter from, 169-71, 194; message from, 201-2; 259, 276-7, 339; letter from 377; 383, 388, 411-13, 416-19, 422, 430, 440, 452; Emin and, 463-4.
Shuli tribe, country of the, 63, 116, 158; natives, 78, 275, 284, 295; sorcerer, 281-2, 316, 335, 363-4.
Shyntz, Père, 466.
Slatin Bey's note to Lupton Bey, 360.
Smell of different tribes, Emin and the, 40; and Baris, 128; of Dwarfs, 373.
Soudanese, Emin's, 50-3, wedding custom of, 74; address to, 75-6; officers, 97; Binza's opinion of, 152; 175, 199-200, 210, 215, 218; and dervishes, 263-4; 350-1, 377, 418, 441, 449, 456-7, 465.

Index. 489

Speke, Captain, and the Wahuma tribe, 63.
Sperber, German man-of-war, 474.
Springs, hot sulphur, 411.
Stairs, Lieut., 2, 356, 389, 391, 440, 442, 444, 457-9, 463, 476.
Stanley, H. M., or "Bula Matari," Prefatory Letter by, v. to x.; 2, 6; Chief Vaju and, 7; letter to, 20; Mr. Holmwood, Emin, and, 27; meeting with Emin, 29-30; arrangements to leave Jephson with Emin, 30-33; and Egyptian clerks from Tunguru, 40-1; address to Emin's soldiers, 48-51; propositions to Emin, 53; advice required, 88; and Linant Bey, 93; and Selim Aga, 95; proclamation at Kirri, 103-5; and giving out orders, 108; letter, 110, 168-170; Hawashi Effendi and, 116; plot against, 167, 170-1; false report of arrival, 169; rebel officers and, 174, 176; rumours of, 178-9, 189, 194, 198, 202, 274, 276; Fadl el Mulla and, 211; Jephson's letters to, 277-8; letters to, 354-5; plot against, 383-4; letters to Jephson and Emin, 388-452; Jephson and, 443-6; letters from Emin, 446, 447, 451; meeting with Emin, 457; at Mazamboni's, 463.
Stewart, General, and Mahdi's forces, 250.
Sudi, 4.
Suliman Aga or Effendi (Egyptian officer), 20-1; 41-2; and leaving the Province, 45, 51-3; letter from, 168-170, 181, 192; and Casati, 194; 196, 198-9, 202, 280-1, 288-9, 298, 304, 305, 328, 341, 343, 345, 349, 351-3; death of, 357-8.
Superstitions: of the Bari tribe, 141; of negroes, 268; about Donagla bullets, 267; in Scotland, 267-8; 280.
Surore Aga (Chief Laboré Station), 94-5, 150, 165, 172, 175, 343-7, 446, 450-1.

Taha Mahomet, 116-8.
"*Talahwin*,' steamer, 256-8.
Tewfik's letter, 31, 45-7, 51; Stanley and, 48-50; and Emin's soldiers, 52; read at Kirri Station, 103-5; read at Muggi Station, 110; read to Rejaf soldiers, 114-5; copy sent to, 153; read at Laboré, 145-6; and Mahdi, 247.
Times, extract from, 472.
Tobacco of Bari tribe, 136.
Torture of the Peacock Dervishes, 262-4, 269-271.
Trade in Africa, 301.
Trees, scarcity of, 385.
Troup, Mr. J. R., 390.
Tunguru, 2, 5; Emin at, 14; arrival at, 40, 75; description of, 40-1; intriguers at, 41-3; road, 54; Jephson at, 192-7, 202; Emin and, 254; 276-8; cattle of, 280; 304, 316, 331, 337, 340, 346; Jephson at, 353-5, 386, 451.
Turquoise, H.M.S., 474.
Tybe Effendi (clerk), 262, 304-5.

Uganda, stoppage of letters in, 27; and Kibero salt, 36; people and dwellings in, 301-2; mode of declaring war, 380-1.
Ugogo, 467.
Uledi, 3-4; at Kanama village, 6-7; at M'swa Station, 20; Emin and, 25; and Jephson, 440, 448, 458.
Unyamwezi, 386.
Unyoro, Mountains of, 5, 55; and Kibero salt, 36.
Unyoro, King of, see *Kaba-regga*.
———— Casati in, 196, 201; people and dwellings in, 301-2; mode of declaring war, 380-1; grass fires on mountains of, 385-6.
Usongo, negro in, 300; rock near, 386.
Usongora, 464.

Vaju, Chief, 6-8; son, 430.
Vakeel, Casati's boy, 195.
Vita Hassan, apothecary, 25; mule, 53; and dinner by Hawashi Effendi, 86; at Laboré, 149; at Dufilé, 159, 164, 194, 197, 207-8, 212, 222, 235-7; 240, 276, 336-8, 343, 345, 347, 387, 446, 451, 453; Emin and, 463.
Vorchow, see *Dwarfs*.
Vunja, Chief, 423-4, 426.

Wadelai Station, 41, 43; journey to, 53-9; arrival at, 60; description of, 63-5; curious wedding custom at,

74; address to men of, 75–6 ; Jephson at, 186–191, 202 ; fire at 203 ; 204–5 ; 277–8 ; cattle at, 280 ; theft in, 281–2 ; 290, 304, 306, 308, 316 ; flight from, 322–6 ; 343, 347–8, 353, 364, 376, 383–4, 417, 419.
Wadelai. Chief, 59, 295.
Wadi Mabruki, 458.
Waganda and Unyoro, 434.
Wahuma tribe or shepherd kings, 63–4, 431–3.
Wambutti, *see Dwarfs*.
Ward, Mr., 390, 398.
Waregga tribe, 7 ; Stanley and, 430.
War. mode of declaring, 380–1 ; Bari tribe, 129–30.
Warrasura, 434.
Watusi or Wahuma tribe, 63–4, 431–3.
Wedding custom at Wadelai, 74.
Weré, 446, 452.
Wilson, Sir E., and Khartoum, 258.
Wingate, Major, 242.
Wissmann, Major, and Emin, 467, 470–3.
Woman's gratitude, a, 413–5.
Woods, etc., forests of Ambatch, 79.
Wortley, Lieut. Stuart, 258.

YAMBUYA, 390–1, 402.
Yankumbu, Chief Vagu's son, 6–7, 430.

ZANZIBAR, Emin at, 473–5.
Zanzibaris : crews, 4 ; and African dialects, 7–8 ; at Mogunga, 11–13, at M'swa Station, 15, 19–20 ; clothes of, 15 ; Emin and, 25 ; and Emin's arrival, 29–30 ; and the smell of forest cannibals, 40 ; chivalry in, 180 ; and *Advance* boat, 320–1 ; 352 ; and dwarfs, 369, 403, 413, 440–1, 443–9, 454–8, 465.
Zebehr el Fahal, 250.
Zoology: antelopes, 3, 119, Baris and, 130 ; 449, 454 ; buffaloes, 3, 440, 449, 454 ; baboons, chimpanzees, monkeys, etc., 8, 10, 11, 40 ; Colobus monkey, 387–8 ; hippopotami, 5, 77, 78, 432, Bari tribe and, 130 ; springbok, hartebeest, kudu, &c., 54, 439–40, 454 ; pigs near Muggi, 119, 449 ; donkeys, 26 ; elephants, 54, herd of, 90–2, Baris and, 130 ; giraffes, 192 ; lions, 130, 142 ; leopards, 54, 58, 62, 130, 142 ; hyænas, 54, 58, 142.

PRINTED BY GILBERT AND RIVINGTON, LD., ST. JOHN'S HOUSE, CLERKENWELL ROAD, E.C.